The Ta~~

Elle Cuardaigh's life is a series ~~ and reunion, birth and death, she follows them until, in the most unexpected of ways, finally unravels even the most knotted to find they formed a tapestry.

A true story of love, loss, and reunion.

- Born into the social experiment of closed adoption
- Growing up with loving parents at the mercy of a sociopathic son
- Overcoming the violent loss of childhood and death of her mother
- Reuniting with her original mother while rejected by her father
- Seeing her husband and marriage destroyed by addiction
- Regaining her genetic identity
- Finding (again) her destined soul-mate
- Connecting with lost family through dreams and psychic events

Both moving and riveting. *The Tangled Red Thread* kept me on the edge of my seat. I highly recommend it to those in the adoption community and also the rest of the world.
~Sandy Musser, adoption reform activist and author, *To Prison With Love* and *I Would Have Searched Forever*

The Tangled Red Thread will resonate with any adoptee who has searched and survived the roller coaster years of reunion. As someone who was there during her search, I can vouch for the author's story.
~M. LeClair, WARM confidential intermediary

Right away you get the sense that Elle Cuardaigh is a no-nonsense storyteller: she sums up her adoption with the words, "I cost $400." And yet this economy of emotion in describing some of the most traumatic experiences of her life has the to power to draw you in, take hold of you, and compel you to fill in the missing anger or grief or sadness. The reader trusts Elle, wants to see her untangle the red thread; we struggle with her, root for her, and in the end admire her. If, as she says, Nordic people consider tragedy the ultimate form of literature, then Elle is the ultimate storyteller, in recalling and redeeming a life of remarkable consequence.
~Amy Hollingsworth, author and speaker, *Gifts of Passage* and *The Simple Faith of Mister Rogers*

The Tangled Red Thread

By

Elle Cuardaigh

An Dà Shealladh, United States of America

Dedicated with much love to:
My parents
and
My children

An Dà Shealladh,
United States of America.
2014

Cover Art: Rachel Stene
Formatting: Rachel Stene
Copy Editing: Amanda Beaty

elle cuardaigh: following a tangled thread
ellecuardaigh.com

ellecuardaigh@gmail.com

Contents

Epilogue

Acknowledgments

This never would have been written without the constant lament of friends, wailing, "Just write a book, will you, and leave us alone!" So remember, you have only yourselves to blame.

My name isn't really Elle. Or Noelle. When considering pseudonyms for this project I wanted my name to mean "girl" since my original birth certificate said only "Infant Girl Linden." And since I was born at Christmastime, I thought it would be funny to call myself Noël ("Christmas") for the book and Elle ("she") as a pen name. Elle/No-Elle. What can I say? I have a twisted sense of humor.

I should also mention my original surname is not Linden. In fact none of the names in this book are real. They have all been changed so I can avoid the unpleasantness of being sued or excluded from family gatherings.

Other identifying details have also been changed, such as locations. If I write, for example, "Spokane" chances are good the actual location is somewhere *in the vicinity* of Spokane. I tried to stick to cities large enough to be recognizable. The one exception for this is Tacoma since the city itself plays a large part in the story. So when I write "Tacoma" I mean Tacoma. But even then the neighborhoods are of my own invention, as is my hometown of Cedarlake.

If you really know me, you will see through all this. You may even recognize yourself as you read. If so, you may wonder why some characteristics of your person and/or life have been changed or merged with another person. Two reasons: simplicity and confidentiality. Simplicity in that I wrote only concerning certain themes. If I put everything and everyone in, this would be the first of a rambling ten-book series. I don't think anyone wants that. Confidentiality in that although I tried to focus on the best in people, I realize not everyone likes attention, even in a good way (see: Norwegians). So while some information has been "rearranged" to disguise the characters, the essential facts are true.

One disclaimer: I use the term "birth" family, including "birth mother" because this was the fashion in the 1980s when I searched. I prefer this over "natural" mother because the adoptive mother would then be "unnatural". I now understand many women prefer "original" or "first" mother. Please know I meant no disrespect with the wording I use.

I began writing my memoir so my daughters would finally know, "Why is Mom like that?" Early on I was drawing family trees – which resemble algebraic equations in my case – to leave as a sort of map. But after fielding certain questions, I knew that wouldn't be enough. The only way to explain my story is to tell it, and the only way I can tell it is to write it.

I tossed out a few sample passages to my book club friends and they encouraged me to get published – anything so I would stop bothering them. They did say though, that others might benefit from my experiences, but that I would need to put it *all* in – even what I have actively avoided thinking about most of my life – or it would not add up. I thought my life was too weird to be believed, much less something others could relate to, but my friends wearily pointed out that although few might be able to empathize completely, most could identify with *some* part of it. After deciding to use pseudonyms the process became much easier. It was even healing to finally get these memories out of my mind and on to paper.

Another reason was to make sure my history wasn't mangled in the passage of time. The kids understand I am afflicted with an overly-analytical nature; I notice mistakes, be they spelling errors or attacks on common sense in general. It's why they hate for me to watch TV with them. There must be a reason I was "blessed" with an unusually good memory. I remember things other people should remember but don't. So I write them here.

I also knew if I was going to write it needed to be while I was physically able and mentally lucid. I am keenly aware how suddenly everything can change.

Finally, I wanted to create a tribute to my parents and this was the only way I could think of doing it. Though their names are changed to protect their privacy from strangers, the stories are true.

I was only conflicted in regard to my daughters' feelings. I know it's difficult hearing about our parents' personal lives, but without that there would be no story. I did agree to mention the kids themselves as little as possible. My hope is to be so successful that they will be blinded by wealth and forget all about their embarrassment. Until then children, please know you are and always will be the most important part of my life.

To everyone else: If you don't like it, write your own damn book.

Elle Cuardaigh… *"She searches"*

Foreword

I sat with my back to the afternoon sun, enjoying a rare moment of quiet outside the bookstore. Iced coffee in one hand, magazine in the other, I had grabbed the one available chair on the sidewalk. The shops put them out in good weather, hoping people will linger. Knowing what was waiting for me I was in no hurry to leave.

So when I heard the voice, my heart sank.

"Act small."

Not looking up, I casually reached for my purse from between my feet and pulled it into my lap, under the magazine I was now pretending to read.

The sound of sprinting feet went around me, one on each side, very close. Two men – young – that much I could tell. In my peripheral vision I saw dirty jeans and old running shoes. The doors of the car just behind me on the street opened, then slammed shut. I could feel the eyes of the man on the passenger side burn into the back of my head. Still, I did not move. The car peeled away.

More running feet. This time a woman. Feeling released from the command, I looked up to see the owner of the little teriyaki restaurant two shops down, flushed and shaking.

"Did you see them?! Did you get the license number?!"

"No," I said. "Why?"

"They just robbed me!" she wailed, "At gunpoint! They had masks on. Didn't you see them *at all*? Didn't you *notice the car?*"

"No," I said dejectedly, wanting to explain, but at the same time - not. How do you explain a voice only you can hear? And even if I tried, what comfort would it be that I deliberately did not help because I always did what the voice told me?

Gathering my things I started for home – the place I was avoiding just minutes before.

Everyone has a recurring theme that runs through their life, if they look for it. I have two.

The first is the ancient Chinese belief of The Red Thread. An invisible thread that connects those who are destined to meet, regardless of time, place or circumstance. The thread may stretch or tangle, but will never break. This usually refers to soul mates but can also be people who will help one another in a critical moment. Their paths will cross once, twice, or as many times as necessary to complete their destiny.

The second is that of a personal paradigm shift. Where everything you believed about something or someone is radically changed in an instant. Like standing in a familiar room you have seen from just one vantage point. Suddenly, you are in another part of the room, dragged as if by unseen forces, and you are looking at the same things but from another angle, a side you have never seen. And it changes everything.

It reminds me of the line from Ursula Le Guin's *The Lathe of Heaven* where George Orr discovers his friend/wife/lover does not remember him as he does her, because their histories and memories were forever changed in what they called The Break:

"He stood and endured reality."

Chapter 1
~My Real Birthday~

I arrived just before Christmas, but I wasn't really born yet. That happened when my parents brought me home. I was kept a secret until Christmas Eve, when my mother Lillian walked into her mother's house with a baby daughter. Gramma would say often of that moment, "She was as proud as a peacock." This was the magic of adoption in post-WWII America. The law states the child will become "as if born to" the new parents. No matter that when I was supposedly being born to them they were miles away, drinking coffee, caring for their young sons, watching the evening news. No pregnancy or labor for them. I may as well have come via the proverbial stork.

So while documentation rightly says I was born at Tacoma's St. Joseph Hospital, reality was officially altered in the form of an amended birth certificate, replacing the names and circumstances of my actual parents with those of my adoptive ones. I was now legally born to Walter and Lillian Ardahl. The amended became "real" by law while the original became "false". The original was then sealed and locked away. This was supposed to protect all parties involved. From what, I'm not sure.

So I had new parents and presumably new genetics. I was a blank slate and all my parents had to do was love me and I would be theirs completely. That was the promise. They had received similar promises for their first two children - Keith and John - who could not have been more different from each other or our collective adoptive family. My parents were to discover nature cannot be trumped. It was a long and gut-wrenching process.

The doctor who delivered me was our family physician and had arranged the adoptions for all three of us. I cost $400. That was the fee in the early 1960s. I remember feeling very expensive when Daddy kidded me about it.

I became aware I was adopted around age five. We'd pile into the station wagon every Saturday night and go out for ice cream. Daddy would drive, and I would sit between him and Mommy in the front. Keith and John were relegated to the back seat, where they still found ways to annoy me. We were on our way home, ice cream cones in hand, when my parents said something about a baby being adopted. I asked what "adopted" meant. My mother said it meant someone else had the baby but new parents raised it. I'm sure the topic had come up before but this was the first time I took notice. Of course I had to ask: "Am I adopted?" and incredibly, they said yes. "Are Keith and John adopted too?" – "Yes." A casual answer to a huge question. My first reality shift. They were always very matter-of-fact about it and I knew from that young age that they could not have children themselves so they asked their doctor to find babies for them.

They were also casually matter-of-fact about all non-indentifying information about our birth parents. This was back during the zenith of adoption, where white, healthy newborns were plentiful. You could practically order what you wanted. My cousin and his wife wanted a red-haired, blue-eyed boy so he'd look like them, and they got one. My parents were not that choosey, but wanted children who were part Scandinavian, since Dad was 100% Norwegian and Mom was 100% Swedish. Both from farmer stock. Hard-working, honest as the day is long, very traditional. Their brothers and sisters had all married people of some Nordic background. It's what they knew. They didn't want or expect any surprises, so they asked for the familiar. But even if we had sprung from some dark race, legally we would have been white, born of white parents. That's what it said on the birth certificates and that made it so.

I grew up thinking I was half Swedish with a little bit of English, Irish and possibly German thrown in. The part that mattered to me was Swedish because my mother was Swedish and this was my tangible link to her. Although they never conveyed adoption as anything "less than", I needed to feel as if the magic law actually worked; because they loved me I was becoming theirs biologically. Real like the Velveteen Rabbit.

I did not look the part. Neither did my brothers. Dad had light brown hair, gray-blue eyes, and a sturdy build. Mom was tall with red hair and light green eyes. We kids had varying shades of brown eyes. In biology class they'd tell you that isn't possible, but my coloring doesn't look possible anyway. A strange shade of golden brown hair that never lost its baby-fine quality, extremely pale skin and eyes so dark they look as if they belong on a different person altogether. Dad said I got them from drinking too many chocolate milkshakes. Although they are my best feature I wanted them to be green. And I wanted red hair because my mother had red hair. I wanted to look like I really belonged to my parents and besides, brown hair/brown eyes are boring.

The other non-identifying information they knew via Dr. Clark was that my birth parents were or had been married (to other people, not each other) and were college-educated professionals. There was a vague mention of siblings. No physical characteristics given, just that she was Swedish and he was possibly German. I didn't care about the German part. Everyone (outside my family) seemed to be part German. It was almost as boring as having brown hair and brown eyes. Besides, Germany was known for things like sauerkraut, beer, cuckoo clocks and Nazis. Why would anyone want to be associated with that? So I decided I was Swedish. Keith and John weren't, but I was. I claimed my spot. That was the first time I chose my identity and my reality, but it wouldn't be the last.

This is the way I thought birth happened when I was little: The mother would say, "It's time!" and people would run around boiling water and forgetting the mother-to-be by the door while the hapless husband drove off without her. There was no sweat, no blood. The mother would be whisked away at the hospital and the father would pace with the other fathers. I knew from inside knowledge (TV) that the baby would be spanked into breathing. The doctor or nurse would come into the waiting room and tell the new father if it was a boy or a girl and they'd all light up cigars. Upon going home, there were endless diapers and sterilizing bottles and sleep deprivation and it was all very funny.

I asked my mother what it was like to have a baby. I thought she knew by virtue of the fact she was a woman. As if the knowledge was imparted upon adulthood, not that it had to be experienced. I was sure there was some club or class one took so they'd know. She looked ever-so-slightly hurt and said, "You'll have to ask your aunt Betty." I didn't want to ask Aunt Betty because 1) she wasn't my mother and 2) she had her last child at nearly forty, way past the age married people were supposed to make babies. I knew making babies started with kissing and one thing led to the other, but it was all very mysterious.

I would find out later I was forced into this world via modern medicine for the sake of convenience. I was actually due the week after Christmas, but the doctor had my birth mother come to the hospital and drink a "cocktail" – something to make her relax and go into labor. She was then knocked out cold with "Twilight Sleep," the standard of the day. They must have really hit her up with it because she didn't regain consciousness for two days. The idea of Twilight Sleep (a combination of morphine and scopolamine, given in a shot) was to provide "pain-free childbirth," when it actually only provided no memory of the birth. Women had to be strapped to the delivery table because of their wild thrashing. There was pain; there was just no memory of it later. There was no memory of the birth, period. They went unconscious pregnant and awoke not-pregnant, having no idea what happened between. Sometimes if not given enough of the drug there would be nightmarish holes in their memory, causing post-partum trauma.

When I was born in the early 1960s it was considered normal as a woman in labor to be taken into a hospital in a wheelchair, separated from your husband, put into a hospital gown, shaved and given an enema. When the doctor was available you'd be drugged. Until then you were expected to be quiet and "good". You were forced to birth lying flat on your back on a hard metal table with your feet in stirrups (if you weren't begging for pain killers before, you would be then). If you had been knocked out completely you were held down by restraints. If the baby was "stubborn", forceps would be employed. Afterwards, you were given extensive stitches which took weeks to heal.

Meanwhile, your baby was measured, jabbed, medicated and tested, then put in a glass bassinet under bright lights in a nursery, separated from you and your husband by a window and guarded by nurses who knew better. When you recovered (i.e. "could form words") the baby was brought to you for scheduled feedings from a bottle while you got a shot to dry up your milk. The nurses enforced the rules.

You were expected to be grateful for this.

In my earliest memories there were my parents, my brother John, our house, and our pets. They were the center of my universe. I expunged Keith from as much of it as possible. Even in my baby book, Mom wrote, "John and Noelle play well together. She and Keith fight!"

We had a nicer-than-average house in a rural area called Cedarlake. There was a lake nearby, surrounded by cedar trees, but it was privately owned so we never swam there. Cedarlake was on a hill where small farms held all sorts of fruit, vegetables, flowers, berries, hay, and also horses and cows. Most raised produce only for their own families by then, not to sell. We always had cattle for beef and a nice little orchard, but my parents had no desire to raise vegetables. I think they both had enough of that sort of farming in their youth and figured they could afford store-bought which was "just as good."

We had a beautiful yard. Dad somehow made time to keep it picture-perfect. Huge fir trees, rhododendrons, azaleas, a variety of flowering trees, ferns, irises, daffodils, tulips, lily-of-the-valley (which Dad considered weeds, much to Mom's frustration), Japanese maple, bamboo, pyracantha, and several prominent birch trees – obligatory for any Scandinavian home.

Children think however it is for them, it is that way for everyone. So I thought everyone had a nice house and nice parents and one nice brother and one rotten one. Of course I knew some had a sister or two and I wanted one of those as well. I asked for one for my birthday several years running. Other girls want a pony. I wanted a little sister.

I also did not find it the least bit unusual that I had a widowed grandmother who lived next door on either side of us. Swedish gramma on one side and Norwegian grammy on the other. Gramma Nelson had devised the perfect retirement plan: She gave each of her children ten acres of land when they married, so they never really left. Betty had one corner, Clarence had another and my mother Lillian got the last.

My parents' house was solid like their marriage. As if to illustrate their commitment, it was built before their wedding and they moved in immediately following their honeymoon. Friends and family did most of the work. Strong men building a strong house, meeting the Industrial Weight Requirement that Scandinavians seem to have for every object. Studs spaced twelve inches apart. Wood siding treated with linseed oil and paint before going up. Patios, stone steps and walkways connecting three beautifully kept yards. Inside were hardwood floors, huge picture windows and many, many stairs.

"This place is no good for babies or old people," predicted Grandpa Ardahl. Dad had a house built for his aging parents on small plot on the property, mercifully devoid of stairs. I don't remember Grandpa Ardahl. I wish I did.

One of the huge evergreen trees around the house came down in a windstorm. Upon hitting the roof of the living room, the tree split in half, while the only damage to the house was a tiny hairline crack in the paint on the wall. I firmly believe when "The Big One" finally hits, the only thing left standing will be that house.

Walt Ardahl grew up on a 1000 acre wheat farm in the Midwest, the biggest in the county. People really worked then, first on their own farms, and if a neighbor was injured or ill, on theirs also. It's just what people did. The women birthed at home, and breastfed while cooking five meals a day for up to thirty hungry men during harvest season. They had horses for plowing and going into town, cows for milk and beef, pigs for meat, chickens for eggs and (of course) chicken, dogs for protection and cats to catch mice. Children were expected to work from a young age. They socialized at church and school but family came first. Being Norwegian and Lutheran they were a stoic, solid bunch.

Dad wasn't home much when I was a baby. As a sought-after mechanic and child of the Great Depression he was driven to be the kind of provider his own father was. "He could lay up twice as much feed as any two other men," he reminisced quietly.

He had wanted to be a veterinarian and would have made a good one, but all the money he saved for school had to go to a brother who got into trouble with alcohol. That's just the way it was. He was a certified welder and had considered moving to Saudi Arabia to weld pipes in the new oil fields. His father convinced him to instead buy a service station located on the main road through town, if you could call it a town. I'm sure his father's true motive was to make sure this son – the one most like him – stayed put.

Even though he was a good welder and would have been a good veterinarian, his God-given talent was with cars. He understood mechanics and devised the most efficient methods for everything from blowing carbon off the valves to greasing the brakes. People knew him and trusted him. Soon they would bring their vehicles nowhere else. He worked twelve hours a day most of the time, eighteen or more if necessary. The trick? "Don't sit down," he said.

The endless demands drove him to build a shop on our property. That way he could continue to work but be at home. He was afraid we wouldn't even know him because he was home so rarely. Now I could sort fasteners and clean the sink for a nickel and get rides on the "hoist". When my legs were long enough to reach the pedals, I helped bleed brakes. I felt very important.

"Whose little girl are you today?" he would tease. To me, about three years old, it was a very serious question. I would try to remember what I had said the day before, Mommy's or Daddy's. I wanted to be fair. In reality, I was usually Mommy's girl since I was with her all the time. But once when I didn't get my way, I took my security blanket, sat by the front door facing the direction of his service station and bawled my eyes out at some injustice. Mom must have called him because he came home, scooped me up and said, "I could hear you crying all the way from the shop." I knew he would hear me. I knew he would understand.

I would climb into his lap to read the funnies to him, only I couldn't read yet so I would make it up then tell him he could read it to me if he wanted.

I also enjoyed helping him feed the cows in the evening. This meant walking down the path to the lower part of the property, past the cedar trees and rhododendrons, to the barn where the feed was kept. When I was very small he'd carry me on his shoulders. Later in his arms. Finally I'd just walk with him, doing my best to keep up with his determined stride. He loved packing little kids around; at any family gathering you could count on him carrying a child, usually a girl. There was a spot near the fence on the way to the barn, behind a cedar tree, where the grass would lie flat. He would say, "Do you think we'll catch the tiger this time?" and we'd sneak up, super-quiet, then…pounce! No tiger. "We must have just missed him," he'd say every time. "Look, you can see where he was sleeping." I don't know if he stamped the grass down to make the story more believable but I wouldn't put it past him.

Lillian Nelson was born in Tacoma of Swedish Baptist parents who had arrived a few years earlier. Her father worked for the railroad. They were not used to city life though, and when they had the chance they bought a farm in the country. He still worked for the railroad while she ran the farm. They had hundreds of chickens and an apple orchard and grew all sorts of vegetables in the fertile ground. There were cows and a dog and cats and much later there would be sheep. Dad would tell me his mother-in-law was the hardest-working woman he had ever known. Considering where he came from that's really saying something; there were no slackers in his family.

Dad never told me much about his childhood (or anything) except to say although it was the Depression, they never went hungry. But Mom would regale me with sad stories. Nordic people consider tragedy the ultimate form of literature. Even fairy tales are sad. Hans Christian Andersen, Danish literary giant of children's stories, being the worst. At least Grimm fairy tales had a cautionary value. These were sad just for the sake of being sad, as if a constant state of melancholy was some sort of nirvana. There was no happily ever after for *The Little Mermaid*. She was turned to foam, forever caught between the land and the sea. What brought her to this sad end? Love. My mother's favorite was *The Little Match Girl*, which was even worse. How she would sigh over the sadness. Stories of her own childhood were at least realistic. One "good" dress and one "play" dress was all she had. Her lunch pail invariably contained a baloney sandwich and an apple. She wouldn't look until it was time to eat just in case there was a rare piece of cake as a surprise. They were expected to work hard at home and at school. But they didn't think of themselves as poor since they were like any of their neighbors.

While church was more of a formality with Dad's family, it was central to Mom's life. They went to church at least three times a week: Wednesday night and twice on Sunday. She read the bible daily, plus a lot of study guides and inspirational books. She belonged to Ladies Aid and bible study groups and prayer circles. When they married, they agreed to raise their future children "non-denominationally" which, ironically, is its own denomination. Sometimes though, Mom took us to a Pentecostal or Baptist church nearby since she felt Dad was not keeping his part of the bargain by not coming along. When Dad found out, he was angry at the deception and even decades later still felt he was in the right. I think it was the only thing he ever held against her.

So while I went to Sunday school and church with Mom at the little non-denominational church, I went to vacation bible school in a variety of places and to her Baptist church on Wednesday and Sunday nights. I felt special wearing my hat and white gloves just like Mommy on Sunday mornings. But while I professed my Christian faith and "asked Jesus into my heart" when I was only five, it never really stirred me. It was part of me, but not like it was with my mother or the rest of her family. I just wanted to be like her and this was part of the deal.

She was a governess in her early twenties to a wealthy family with three boys. They loved her and she in turn decided she wanted six boys of her own, since these were so wonderful. She traveled with them all over the country, and when she married they sent a telegram and an expensive gift. By then her services were no longer needed and she settled instead on being a waitress in a neighborhood café. Except for when she was a governess she lived at home, never having a college dorm or apartment. She had no grand career plans. Besides, in the 1950s there *were* no grand careers for women.

They met when he walked across the street from his service station to grab some lunch where she waited tables. They were both past thirty, which was not considered "old" by their families' standards for marriage. He loved her flaming red hair. She loved his new Chrysler. It was a match made in heaven.

Over 400 people packed the small Lutheran church for the wedding. They settled into their new home and new roles and waited for the first of those six boys to arrive. Only they never came.

Not long after procuring two Nordic sons from Dr. Clark they were offered another. This time a full-blooded Norwegian with pale blond hair. "No more boys," they said. Then they got me. Three years later they were offered another girl: part Spanish, a beautiful mix of Viking and Moor. "No more babies," they said. This from the couple who originally wanted six. I'm sure the way I could scream like a banshee had nothing to do with it.

When I was eighteen months old, Mom wrote in my baby book that I did most everything well. Then, "She is very loving toward Walt and I, but very slow to make friends with others and very scotch with loves for anyone else." This would prove to be a very unfortunate characteristic.

The most traumatic thing to happen to me as a baby actually happened to her. She fell from a ladder while picking apples in her mother's orchard next door and broke her back. Gramma would tell me later, "Walt didn't just come running, he *jumped* over the fences to get to her."

This meant we had to be parceled out to family members while she recovered. Keith went to Gramma. John went to Aunt Betty. I went to Aunt Evelyn, Clarence's wife. I didn't like Evelyn, mostly because she wasn't my mother. Also, I suspect she didn't like me. At one and a half, I was unable to understand why my family and my home had been suddenly supplanted. I had only a primitive recollection of hearing sirens and then knowing my mother was gone. I lashed out at Evelyn, calling her a stinker and a bully – the only bad words I knew. I wanted to go home. I wanted my mother.

When things were back to normal, they really weren't. Being abruptly taken from my parents at the peak age for separation anxiety left its mark. They would tell me later that whenever I heard a siren I would cry, or even scream, and was inconsolable. One visitor who witnessed this display suggested I needed "help." They coolly declined. "She'll get over it," became their mantra. Professional help was something only weak people needed. It wasn't "normal".

My earliest clear memory happened one year later. I was riding my red tricycle on the patio. Sirens sounded from the fire station up the road. Panic instantly took over: *They're coming to take my mother.*

I had to get to her. I ran to the back door and pulled. It was locked. *They're going to take her away again and I can't stop them.* With total, primitive terror, I yanked the handle again and again, screaming. Only seconds had passed but by the time Mom got there I was completely hysterical. She knelt down and gathered me in her arms. I clung to her and sobbed. No one was taking her away from me ever again.

Wherever I went, I had my ba-ba with me. My baby blanket. It was a silky white blanket with a picture of the Three Little Kittens on it, only by the time I was done "loving" it there was nothing left but a tattered cloth with one piece of brown thread attached. I nearly had a heart attack when Gramma tried to dust with it, mistaking it for a rag. Mom had to sneak it away from me while I was sleeping in order to wash it. Since we did not use a dryer all the laundry had to be hung. One summer day I did not come when dinner was called. Dad looked out the kitchen window to see me hugging my dripping blanket as it hung on the line. I was waiting for it to dry.

One night I fell asleep on the couch. I woke enough to realize Daddy was carrying me upstairs. "Ba-ba?" I mumbled. "Here it is," I heard Mommy say gently, laying it over Daddy's strong shoulder as she followed. Even then I knew it was a perfect moment of security and was content.

I was one of those infuriating children who always asked, "Why?" My poor, long-suffering mother. "Why did the cat in the movie die? Why is the paint spilling in that picture? Why don't they clean the top of the train station so it's shiny? Why couldn't you have a baby?" No matter how many times she explained I would keep asking if I didn't understand the answer. Often I was really asking, "Why did God let that happen?" but did not have the words.

"Sometimes God is saving us from something worse," she would say.

I liked going places with her, just the two of us. The bank, the grocery store, the post office were all familiar. I felt everyone everywhere knew me. I also felt no place was off-limits. Mom once received a phone call from the neighbor who lived across the street on the far end of the property. She found me in her daughter's room playing with dolls. I had walked over without telling anyone, came in without knocking, and settled down playing with Toni's toys as if they were mine. At the age of three I did not have healthy sense of fear and obviously no respect for property rights.

I hated footwear of any kind (how is a person supposed to climb a tree?) but *really* hated – with a passion – my soap saddle shoes. I devised a plan to rid myself of them once and for all. While at the grocery store I wandered off (as I always did), pulled the hated things from my feet and buried them in the peanut bin. No one would find them there! Of course, someone did almost immediately and they were given to my mother, who sighed. Still, when we left I was given an 8¢ Hershey Bar and she held out her hand, saying "Come on, Sunshine." I liked it when she called me Sunshine.

I was very attached to our pets. We always had a big dog and several cats. The dogs were considered important as protection. The cats were supposed to keep away mice. Mom and Dad grew up on farms where cats earned their keep. No cat food, no vet care. We had cat food but wasting money on spay/neuter was not even considered. So we often had kittens. I once saw a pair of cats mating when I was very young and asked my mother what they were doing. "We'll have kittens soon," she sighed. I wasn't sure how this bizarre ritual led to kittens but I was happy. I would play with our pets for hours. They were my friends.

I performed a wedding for the cats when they finally stopped copulating. I thought it was against the law to have children if the parents were not married. Whenever my parents would say something, like "Don't pick the trilliums in the woods," I would ask, wide-eyed, "Is it against the law?" Not that they ever told me it was, but to a very young child "rules" and "law" are one in the same.

I figured that's why we were adopted, because our original parents were not married and would go to jail if we were not given to married people. I knew adoption had a judge involved and I knew from TV that judges rule on punishments for crimes; therefore having a baby while unmarried was illegal. I didn't want my cats to be lawless fugitives, so the wedding commenced.

Often a cat would disappear or die, and I would be left sobbing. I heard in church that animals had no souls and this left me distraught. I asked my mother if it was true, that I would never see my animal friends again.

"Everything you've ever loved will be in heaven. God is too big for us to understand."

If my mother said it was so, it was so.

Grammy Ardahl seemed incredibly old even though she was only one year older than Gramma Nelson who still chopped kindling, worked in her garden, kept her house tidy, and was very active in general. Grammy was delicate in her seventies, long past the years of being a farm wife, with a sign that said "Day Sleeper" on her front door so people would not knock. I didn't knock, but then again I never knocked anywhere, I would just go in. If she was sleeping I would quietly leave. Otherwise I knew she was always good for some Nilla Wafer cookies and milk.

One day my mother sent me to her house to dry a top I needed to wear. Grammy had a clothes dryer. We did not. With the all-important top in the dryer, we had what is the only private conversation I can remember. We sat at her dining room table. She had weak coffee. I had milk. We both had Nilla Wafer cookies. I felt I should "make friends," and when you're five years old you do that by asking a question.

"Which do you like better, dogs or cats?" I asked. This was the most profound question I could think of.

She seemed surprised by the query but said in her wobbly, old-lady voice, "Dogs, I guess."

"Oh," I said, trying to hide my disappointment. "I like cats." I decided I liked her anyway. She died the June before I started Kindergarten. I cried and cried when I saw the obituary photo in the paper and realized it was her.

I loved Kindergarten. I remember it vividly. It was in a big, sunny room. The arts and crafts, story time, recess, singing, making "pizza" by pressing Play-Doh on the radiator then insisting to the teacher we didn't do it – it was all fun. Girls wore skirts or dresses. Boys, slacks and shirts. No one wore jeans or t-shirts to school then. The most exciting day of my life was the spring field trip to the zoo because girls were allowed to wear pants. I went shopping with Mommy for just the right outfit: pants with a yellow daisy pattern and a yellow short-sleeved top. Yellow was my favorite color.

I was in the morning class. The bus would take me home at lunch where Dasher, our faithful collie, would greet me. Then the best part: Mommy would have lunch ready for me – a sandwich of Budding meat with lots of mustard and the crusts cut off, a little bowl of Campbell's soup, and a glass of milk, served on

the blue TV tray with fold-out legs. I would plant myself on the living room carpet in front of the TV, tuck my legs under the tray and watch a rerun of *Bewitched,*
my favorite show. Eating in the living room was against the rules, and Keith and
John would have been furious if they knew of the preferential treatment. I was
"spoiled," they said. I was "a baby," they said. I didn't care. I knew my mommy
loved me when she cut those bread crusts off my sandwiches, because wasting
food was a sin. Everyone knew that. It was preached at church, admonished at
dinner, and told again and again in the stories of our parents' childhoods during
the Great Depression. And here she was willfully sinning just to make me happy.

Even as a young child, Keith had anger issues. But it wasn't just that. He
was cruel. There was good reason we didn't get along. I was on guard whenever I
was around him. Instinctually, I kept my distance as much as possible. But how
do you do that when you live in the same house?

He was an ongoing lesson in nature vs. nurture. Keith should have been
the golden child. The much desired first-born. Intelligent. Handsome as a child,
even resembling our adoptive father.

But something had gone terribly wrong, at birth or in utero. He was the
legacy of a man who got a lot of young girls knocked up (told to me quietly by our
mother). Other than that, I didn't know anything about his background.

He was violent, showing no restraint or remorse. Crude. Without conscience. He would steal money whenever he could. From my secret hiding places
or Mom's purse; he didn't care. He lied with ease, but often wouldn't bother,
instead rudely admitting to whatever petty crime he committed. He told our honest and kind grandmother, "I don't need to show anybody respect. I don't respect
anybody."

Only Dad seemed to have any influence because he was bigger and stronger, but he was at work most of the time. Our parents had not grown up with
violence so this was completely beyond them. Mom read book after book looking
for the answer and prayed and prayed and prayed. She held onto the promise of
Proverbs 22:6, *Train up a child in the way he should go, and when he is old he will
not depart from it.*

They had no way of knowing his anger was inborn, that they had been handed a defective product. That there was no "training" that could fix this.

When he was no more than eight I found him peeling the shell off a robin's egg to see (and watch die) the undeveloped bird inside. It was "cool," he said.

He shot me with a BB gun. He often pinned me to the floor and hit me. Once he molested me in my bedroom. I can't remember a single time he ever said anything to me that wasn't rude. Furiously, I would fight back, but how much can a little girl fight against someone more than twice her size and weight?

Our parents would endlessly separate us and admonish or restrict Keith. Someone asked me once why they didn't employ corporal punishment. It wouldn't have helped. In fact it would have fueled his anger and given him justification to do more damage. Still, I fantasized about him being, in the words of a friend, "beaten within an inch of his life…and then about another foot."

Over forty years later an old neighbor asked about him. My mother confided in her when Keith was only a toddler, saying, "He has such *rage*."

The older he got, the worse he became. Before he even reached puberty, he was showing sexual aggression. He tried to spy on me when I took a bath. He found pornography amusing. He glorified violence. He was disgusting. He was the reason I didn't like boys. The only exception was our brother John.

If Keith was born to be a career criminal, John was born to be a pet whisperer. I have never met anyone who could so instantly charm an animal. Dogs and cats worshiped him. His calm and quiet demeanor helped, but it was beyond that. They instinctively trusted him. As much as I loved our pets, they loved him more.

Dad told me years later that when he and John were cleaning the shop they uncovered a field mouse. Before Dad could make a move to kill it, John scooped it up and put it in the woods.

"He wasn't hurting anything," John said simply.

Once we visited Dad's family back in the Midwest. Endless flat land, nearly no trees, no other kids, and nothing to do. We decided it would be fun to catch a prairie dog, considered a nuisance for farmers because of the holes they make in the ground. With the promise of a 25¢ bounty we made a snare over a hole and waited. The unfortunate animal popped up his head, the trap was pulled, and we suddenly had a very dead prairie dog. That's not what we expected. We thought we would catch it, collect the reward, and it would be released into the "wild" somewhere. We had watched enough *Mutual of Omaha's Wild Kingdom* to understand tag and release. What we didn't understand was this *was* the wilds of South Dakota.

John crouched and petted the little thing, apologizing again and again, "I didn't mean to kill you." I stood by, very sad in my support. Dad could not believe it. Here we had actually managed to catch one (he had had doubts) and now we were sorry? Instead of collecting our bounty we buried it and had a funeral. No blood money for this prairie dog. Dad shook his head. Where did these kids come from?

I liked playing with John. We had many adventures. I would pretend I was an Indian princess or a leopard, or an Indian princess with a leopard, and he would go along with it. Even when we would fight I knew I would not be mad the next day. Once we really got on Mom's nerves with our carrying on and she separated us. It was the best trick she had. Ordered us to go to our rooms and stay there. Quiet reigned. Eventually she came to check on us only to find us on our stomachs in the doorways of our respective rooms, which met at a corner in the hall. We were coloring and sharing a box of crayons between us.

John also hung out with Keith. Being close in age forced them to be companions despite their opposing personalities. Besides, they had been constant playmates since they were just babies. Keith was the dominant one. John was a "follower," Dad would lament. I don't recall John fighting back during Keith's attacks, but he just wasn't aggressive by nature. Keith did well in school, at least academically. John struggled. I hated it when our parents would tease him. I don't know if they were trying to inspire him to greatness or what, but it had the opposite effect. He never graduated from high school.

They were also opposite in appearance. Keith was huge with dark coloring and just got bigger and hairier as time went on. John was blond and slender. I "imprinted" on John the way most girls imprint on their fathers. I have always preferred slender, blond men and avoided large brunets. I hated Keith. I loved John. It was very simple. Only I had to live with both of them.

On Dad's side of the family, I was the youngest of all the grandchildren, but on Mom's side I was one of four girls close in age, and we all lived on the same acreage so we grew up like glorified sisters. I had other cousins (two boys and a girl) but they did not feature as prominently. I was very different from these sister-cousins in both personality and appearance. They were much more compliant. Britta (called Britt), the eldest, was like a quiet version of Mom. Linda and Laurie were more like their mother, my aunt. They loved the "cute" folksy things their parents liked. My mother's tastes were more sophisticated, but still, she was raised on the same farm. She'd use phrases like "okie-dokie" and could relate on a personal level to *The Waltons*. We were not allowed to watch *All in the Family* as it was considered crass. We would watch *Lawrence Welk* on Sunday nights after church although Mom did *not*, as a devout Baptist, like the dancing or the fact they called it "champagne music." There was no dancing, drinking, gambling (including playing cards for no stakes), smoking, or even spitting allowed. That was fine with Dad since he had no use for any of it anyway.

There was also no crass language. In fact we couldn't use the word "butt", instead saying "bottom." If someone was a certifiable nut case, Mom called them "troubled". Saying "God" unless it was followed by "bless you" was completely out of the question. I never even heard the word "fart" until I was nearly a teen, but we didn't have a substitute word as they never felt the need to comment on passing gas. To this day I do not understand people who do.

Once a friend of Dad's stopped by after having one (or five) too many drinks and proceeded to swear up a storm. Mom stood by quietly and said nothing. The next day he was back, with flowers and apologies for talking like that in front of a lady.

No one complained about her being uptight though, because she was a genuinely nice person. Everyone liked her. They knew they could count on her to visit if they were hospitalized or needed someone to host a party. I wanted to be just like her.

As much as Mom loved me, she couldn't help but compare me to her sister's two daughters. One a year older than me, one a year younger, me sandwiched in the middle and never able to measure up to their standards. They fit-in in a way I never could because they were born into their families. Not only did they resemble each other with their tastes and mannerisms, they were obviously related in appearance. They had blue or green eyes. They had the same ruddy Scandinavian complexions. They had the same luxurious hair. How I envied them their hair: long, wavy and thick. My hair was no more than silky baby down, barely reaching my shoulders by Kindergarten.

"I read about a girl with hair just like yours," Mom said more than once. "But her mother brushed it every day and it got thicker and thicker."

"Would that really happen?" I said hopefully.

"We'll see."

At least she didn't lie. It wasn't in her to give false promises. She stroked and stroked my wisps with a delicate baby brush for years, and then one barely stronger than that. But my hair remained fine and thin.

"If you cut it, that will make it strong," said Aunt Betty, as if I was a shrub in need of pruning. Lillian, to her credit, left it in a pageboy style. No one in the family had hair like mine, or dark eyes like mine, or pale skin like mine. But that was nothing compared to the difference in personality.

Sometimes she would say, "Linda and Laurie never..." or "Linda and Laurie always..." and it stung because I felt she was saying, "If I had been able to have my own children they would be like me, not these changelings I had to settle for." I wanted to be her "real" daughter, but at the same I detested the country charm they found so appealing.

Instead of trying to fit in, I shined where I could. I found I could draw well, even at age four. So I would draw and draw, honing my skills. "Noelle's an artist," they proclaimed. Gramma said with admiration, "You can't learn that, it has to be *in* you." They recognized genetic traits and yet I wondered if it had been possible to order the "right" personality like it was to order the "right" physical characteristics, if they would have asked for someone else.

Chapter 2
~Neither Normal nor Grateful~

First grade began with a card that came addressed to me by my new teacher, Mrs. Grayson. It made quite an impression on me that this stranger would send a nice card with a kitten on it, telling me how much she looked forward to having me in her class. A personal note was enough but with a *kitten*, well! I liked her before I even met her.

I arrived early on the first day and sat at my newly-assigned desk, very excited to begin the adventures of first grade. Mrs. Grayson was the quintessential teacher. Silver hair kept in a neat bun, old lady cat eye glasses, and dull colored suits - the kind with matching jacket and skirt. Since I felt we already had a rapport (because of the note) I thought I'd share something important with her.

"I'm adopted," I said. It was like how kids say, "I have a new puppy," or whatever they thought was conversation-worthy at the moment. Usually when I'd offer this bit of information people would say, "Oh, isn't that nice?" but she had a different response, and I never forgot it.

"Aren't you grateful?" she replied in rehearsed and dulcet tones, more of an expectation than a question. This was something I had never considered. What exactly was I supposed to be grateful for? Being alive? Not being with my original family? This was running through my head with a six-year-old's limited understanding. I was sure of one thing though: My cousins would not be expected to be grateful for *not* being adopted. I knew unfairness when I saw it. And for the first time, I felt singled out. Less-than. Different. "Special" in a way no one wants to be special.

My baby book and "School Days" scrapbook are filled with reports of what an exceptional student I was. I liked sitting in the little circle of chairs and reading aloud from *Fun with Dick and Jane*. ("See Jane. See Jane run. Run, Jane, run.") I did wonder why it was written so strangely, since no one I knew talked like that. I preferred the books my mother read to me, though they were often way over my head, because they seemed more real.

I made friends, some who also attended our non-denominational church. Our mothers were friends as well. We stay with what we know. None of my friends were adopted.

I was very attached to my best friend Kimberly, called Kimmie and later just Kim. We were only a few days apart in age. Every Sunday after church we cajoled our mothers into letting one of us spend the night at the other's house. Her home was so different than mine. She was a middle child. They lived in a barn until her father, a master carpenter, finished building their new house on the same property. I found it a wonderful adventure sleeping in a barn, one with electricity and running water but with blankets that served as door coverings and bits of plywood put together for walls.

On Sundays they would have chicken dinner. Mrs. Kelemen must have been afraid I'd eat them out of house and home. Because we raised beef it was nearly all we ever ate, with the exception of the huge salmon Dad would bring home from Westport. Besides, Mom was raised on a chicken farm. She must have been sick to death of the stuff. But I didn't make the connection at the time. I thought we couldn't afford chicken and the Kelemens were so rich they had it every Sunday.

Kimmie would stay at my house too. Once Dad came along as we played and I put my arms out to be picked up. Dad told me later that Kimmie looked so sad down there on the ground he picked her up as well. He found her hatred of all vegetables quietly amusing. Back then, you obeyed your friends' parents as well as your own. Dad told Kimmie she had to eat three green beans at dinner. Not looking at him, she dutifully took the smallest bean she could find and cut it into three tiny pieces. This was very serious to her. But if she had looked at Dad's face she would have seen the slightest glimmer of a smile.

When Kimmie came to my house, my mother gave us matching sack lunches to take to school, with "Noelle" written in fancy letters on mine and "Kimberly" written in fancy letters on hers. Mom always remembered the way Kimmie liked her sandwiches and spoiled us with extra treats. I figured this must be what it's like to have a sister, but Kimmie said it was good we weren't because, "Sisters fight." I decided if I ever had a sister I wouldn't fight with her.

Mr. Kelemen made my dad's reserved Norwegian behavior look jovial. If Norwegian men are a serious lot, Hungarians (or, "Magyarok" as they would say) are completely dispassionate. His face was as unchanging and unreadable as the Sphinx. Mrs. Kelemen, on the other hand, had a beautiful laugh like a tinkling bell. I loved listening to them speak in their native language.

Mrs. Kelemen had her final child when Kimmie and I were seven years old. It was my first up-close experience with pregnancy and childbirth. It was all strange to me; nothing like what I had seen on TV. And after the baby was born I was shocked to find Mrs. Kelemen breastfeeding.

Once I found an encyclopedia and in it a diagram of a woman's breast. At the center was something called (at least in this book) the milk sack. Very surprised, I took the book to my mother. I wondered why this place for milk existed since "no one" fed their babies that way anymore. She told me it was there but we didn't need it because babies drank from bottles now. I asked if there really was milk there, then? She said no. In my mind I took that to mean we had evolved so far that this was just a leftover of a more primitive time. She actually meant milk didn't come in unless stimulated but I didn't have the vocabulary to ask the right question. I really believed no one could breastfeed. Apparently Mrs. Kelemen didn't get the memo because here she was, doing it.

I decided it was because she was an immigrant. In one generation's time the milk would dry up. It was the only thing that made sense to me. We used bottles and formula now. That was normal. And it was very important to be normal.

Just after starting first grade, I had a shot (Mom called them inoculations) for rubella, more commonly called "hard measles". I didn't like getting shots of course, but never had a problem with the few that were called for then. We were told at school how important they were and how thankful we should be that no one got polio anymore. They were magic, these shots.

I was usually brave in the face of pain. I didn't even get anything to numb my mouth when given the numerous fillings I required at the dentist. I expected it to hurt and it did. Shots were nothing compared to that. Only this time was different. The shot was in the tush and it hurt like nothing ever hurt before. The doctor thought I was just bent out of shape, since I was known for being non-compliant. In truth it felt as if the needle was imbedded in my body. I screamed all the way home in the car, holding on to the back of the seat, not sitting down. I was terrified at the heat rising in me. After we were home, my distraught mother looked at my bottom and discovered a raised red lump the size of a quarter where the shot had been administered. She called the doctor. I don't know what he told her but she remained concerned long after.

A few weeks later I opened my eyes in the morning to see Mommy and John looking at me with a reserved sort of horror. I looked down at my stomach, which was exposed by Mom lifting my pajama top, and found I was covered with angry bright red spots, so many it made a lacy pattern, all connected. I felt betrayed. Shots were supposed to be good for you. It was supposed to keep me from getting the dreaded rubella. And now I had it.

Mom called the doctor. Even though it was obvious I had hard measles I needed to be brought in so it could be confirmed. Because nothing is real until the doctor says so. This was Dr. Clark, the same doctor who delivered me and arranged my adoption – the one who made me "real". Even though the virus is incredibly contagious and dangerous to pregnant women, I had to be brought in. Mom carried me wrapped in a blanket through the waiting room, directly from the car to an exam room. I was surprised she could still carry me like that. I didn't like the curious eyes of the other patients as we passed.

I was out of school for what seemed like months. The curtains were kept shut to avoid damaging my eyes. I drank grape juice through a glass straw. Mom bought me a toy dog that could bark and summersault backwards. I named him Flip. I had to stay in bed. It really wasn't much fun.

I would tell people I got measles from the shot but my parents would shush me. That's not what was supposed to happen. They were doing the right thing, being responsible parents. The doctor said, "You can't get the disease from the shot." Even though the stuff they shot into me *was* the disease. Even though I obviously had a bad reaction. Even though the vaccine was still new at the time.

Even though no one else at school had it. Even though I came down with the very disease I was inoculated against exactly fourteen days after getting the shot (classic incubation time period). There was no cause and effect. The experts said so. It unnerved Dad to think doctors could be wrong. The mark, meanwhile, stayed raised and hardened like scar tissue, finally smoothing out and turning white more than ten years later. My distrust of doctors began.

Every few summers, family came from Sweden. Mom's aunts or uncles or cousins and their children as well, almost invariably girls. My second cousins. It was very exciting. I still have a little plastic coin purse shaped like a cat, a charm bracelet, and a little book about (what else?) kittens in my possession. Gifts from afar. They'd stay next door at Gramma's but would come up to visit. This is when Mom would really shine. She was a terrific hostess. In my baby book she noted, *"Noelle's 1st birthday. Dinner for thirty-seven."* How many people could pull that off just a few days before Christmas? She made special cakes and wonderful dishes like shrimp cocktail served in long stemmed glasses. My brothers and I would fight over who "got" her as room mother in elementary school. She would make individual treats for each of the children, their names etched in frosting. She hosted Ladies Aid, wedding receptions, bridal showers and birthday parties, decorating for each to the hilt.

The house had to be spotless. The food plentiful. The yard perfect. "He keeps that place like a park," Gramma would say of her son-in-law with admiration. In the midst of these gatherings on long summer days I was so proud. They made it look effortless. I pitied anyone who didn't have parents like mine.

One birthday party Mom hosted was for my second cousin Inge-Marie, who turned eight while her family was here. We have pictures of her standing shyly by her cake, looking for all the world like our cousin Linda. Same blue eyes, same light brown hair, same perfect complexion. Soon after she came down with measles, which she brought with her from Sweden. Since I was the only child immune I became her personal playmate. In Sweden, children were expected to be fluent in three languages by the time they finished high school, starting with English at age seven. But since she was only now eight she knew about as many words in English as I did in Swedish. Amazingly, we still understood each another.

There was no language barrier as we played with my Barbies. "I know what she *meant*," I insisted when others would offer to translate. Even if I didn't understand the words, I understood her. And she, me.

I wanted my mother to teach me Swedish. I knew only a few words and phrases and a little song. Although she was fluent, as were her brother and sister, they flat-out refused to teach their children. They spoke a country dialect, a more colloquial version of "High Swedish" that was looked down on back home. They thought it would be a waste for us to learn that. Besides, Dad would point out, "they" (Europeans) all speak English. He only knew a Norwegian table prayer and I think he felt pressured with these expectations from the Old Country. When his father came over as a young child they essentially gave up being Norwegian. He knew very little about his background since – like all the males in his family – his father didn't talk about it.

I continued to pester Mom. It was part of my quest to be Swedish. And I wanted to be able to do something better than my cousins, who should have come by it naturally. She tried, but was unenthusiastic. I know only a handful of words and phrases, even if the culture has been ingrained in me.

The one phrase everyone knew though, even my dad, was: *Förstår du nej ingenting?* (Roughly, "Don't you understand *anything*?" said with much exasperation.) We all heard that from time to time. It was seared into our psyches like the bite of the homemade apple cider at Christmas.

Another carry-over was having a summer house on a lake. In Scandinavia, it's unusual *not* to have one, rather than considered a luxury. Some of our Swedish-American cousins had such a place but we did it differently. Our "summer house" was a nice travel trailer we would take to a lake or the ocean for six weeks every July-August. I loved to swim. It didn't matter to me that the pool was never heated at the place by the ocean, despite the annual promise that next year it would be fixed. I could swim for hours. We would go for long walks. Mom fried trout in butter for breakfast with Dad's early-morning catch. We developed friendships with the others who would stay at the same place every year. I would draw wherever we went. We made s'mores around a campfire at night. It was really wonderful. Often my best friend Kimmie came along. One night, after the customary campfire by the lake, we walked ahead of my parents back to the trailer. Suddenly we realized they weren't with us. Looking back we saw them in a passionate embrace in the shadows. "Look – they're kissing!" Kimmie whispered. Seeing them like that, with none of the decorum of their traditional morning peck on the cheek, made them more real to me. They were Mom and Dad but they were also Lillian and Walt.

When I was six, Mom made plans for the two of us to go to Sweden. I was so excited; I was sure to learn Swedish now. She knew Dad wouldn't go and the boys wouldn't want to go, so it was to be a special trip for the two of us. Dad wouldn't hear of it. We didn't need to go there when "they" came to visit here already, was his logic. Just like we didn't need to learn a foreign language because "they all speak English," we didn't need to go anywhere outside of the United States because "it's nicer here." I don't know what he was so afraid of or if he really felt that superior, but his mind was made up. Mom quietly promised me we would go one day, but we never did.

The only good thing I remember from third grade was having *Pippi Longstocking* books read to us. I loved how Pippi was Swedish and had red hair like my mother and how she outsmarted all the grown-ups even though she didn't go to school. I wonder if teachers ever considered that they were idealizing a smart-aleck kid who never went to school and did not seem to need to.

At dinner I would say, "Do you know what Pippi did today, Mommy?" Keith would sneer about how stupid it was. Keith sneered at everything. Although the part about Pippi being the strongest girl in the word was the most far-fetched thing in the stories, I would fantasize about being able to throw Keith over the house. I liked to imagine his shocked expression.

He mocked me every chance he got and would encourage John to do the same. I liked John when he was away from Keith and felt very alone when they would join forces.

I loved the fantasy of *Pippi Longstocking* stories for the same reason I loved *Bewitched* when I was small: They were magic. Good magic. We were warned against "real" magic in Sunday school, but this was pretend. I would walk in the woods with the cats and dogs and find magic in everything – the trees, the wild flowers, the rocks. They were alive. I felt I could talk with them, that I was connected to them. And I was sure I could communicate with my pets.

The most magical things to me were rocks. When we'd stay at the lake in the summers when I was really little, Daddy would carry me on his shoulders in the evening as we went for a walk. I would point out all the special "wocks" on the path I just *had* to keep. He'd pick them up and put them in a bucket by the door of the trailer, quietly disposing of about half of them when I was sleeping so we wouldn't take home fifty pounds of what was essentially gravel.

I pored over books on gemstones. Friends gave me cracked thunder eggs and other wondrous things such as rose quartz and agates. I would tie three favorites in a scarf along with some scented talc and carry it with me to school. They were my magic rocks that protected me from danger. I wanted a rock polishing machine so I could make all my rocks "magic". School was so dull at this point it would have taken magic to make it interesting.

Mom had a dim view of public schools also. She dropped in on my class one day to find us watching *The Electric Company* show on PBS. At home she read *Little Women* and *The Hiding Place* to me, and here I was supposed to be enthralled with "T-I-O-N, shun-shun-shun-shun?" Not long after that she came to pick me up for a forgotten appointment.

"Am I going to the dentist?" I asked, getting into the car. "No, we're going shopping. Don't mention it to your father." Mom never lied, but she didn't feel it necessary to share every little thing, either. This *was* an appointment: mother/daughter appointment. We went to lunch at a nice café, just the two of us. As usual we sat at a booth. We never sat at the counter, although I really wanted to, because "Truck drivers sit there." Mom had a low opinion of truck drivers. She never said why – maybe they weren't nice to her when she was a waitress. Then we went shopping for dresses and shoes. It was a wonderful afternoon. She knew what was important.

A few years later she told me we were going shopping with my cousin Britt, her brother's daughter. Britt spent a lot of time at our grandmother's. She felt more at home there than at her own house next door. She seemed surprised when Mom asked her to go with us (and I thought it was strange that Britt didn't know about it, since that seemed to be the purpose in going) but we were soon at the big department store in the valley. Mom told her we were there to get her a bra and no one needed to know about it. "No one" being Britta's mother. Aunt Evelyn had rather unusual views on what was appropriate, one being the age a girl needs to start wearing a brassiere. Britt was tall and athletic but she was developing a slouch from trying to hide her bust. Several bras were fitted and purchased. Mom advised her to keep them in her locker at school. There was no reason given. There was no need.

I doubt Mom consulted her brother in this first. It was known from whispers among cousins that Clarence wanted to give his kids nice things like a swimming pool or a horse and his wife would not allow it. At the same time he refused to own a TV, which he called an idiot box. But he watched the idiot box at his mother's every night. Although she loved him, Mom did not idolize Clarence like their younger sister did. I think she recognized he was a shyster. Not in real criminal ways, but he always had some small scam going; ways for him to get around the rules or get something for nothing. One day he came up to the house to talk with Mom about plans for their mother, who was about eighty at the time and in excellent health. He wanted something written up, a sort of contingency plan, so she would be "taken care of." Mom said shortly, "None of us will ever be so bad off that we can't take care of Mom." That was the end of the discussion.

Mom would go next door every Saturday night to put-up her mother's hair. I would go along to watch. I can still see her standing behind Gramma at the dining room table, putting her mother's graying hair into little curls held with Dippity-Do and bobby pins, listening to them chat and laugh. I thought it was funny that we "put-up" both hair and fruit. I helped Mom put-up dozens of quarts of peaches, cherries and pickles in the summer. It was my job to carry the jars two at a time down the flights of stairs to the "fruit room" in the basement. I liked these kind of projects. It felt good that she trusted me to help her with something that important.

I tried to be like her in every way I could. She would read in the evenings, either aloud to us or silently to herself. While she would read I would draw. If she was working on some elaborate needlepoint, I was doing a simplistic version on felt. While she easily made dresses for us on her Singer, I would make a tangled mess on my toy sewing machine. She and her sister could sing in harmony and Linda and Laurie were like duplicates of them. I could sing only passably and never in harmony. Mom would set her own lush hair with pink hair tape and water and it held as if it grew that way. She resolutely set mine with Dippity-do and plastic curlers, wrapping my head in a towel in an attempt to make it comfortable enough to sleep in. In the morning I would cry the entire time she unwound the curlers now caught in my baby-fine tangles. Within five minutes my hair would melt into the familiar unmanageable wisps. She sighed. She didn't understand my hair in the slightest.

I took piano lessons with Mrs. Bessette starting around age seven, as did all my girl cousins. The boys were given lessons briefly before the project was summarily abandoned. Mrs. Bessette was what my family would call a "glowing example of Christian witness" and she could really make a piano sing. She was a Pentecostal, and since Lillian's family definitely leaned that way even while being officially Baptist, they got along famously. Mom would sit in a chair next to the piano. Mrs. Bessette sat so she could see the student's hands and posture. They would chat the entire half-hour but if I played an eighth note instead of a sixteenth they'd both point it out.

Mrs. Bessette was much like my mother in religious conviction, but she was more gifted spiritually; she had visions and premonitions, as her mother did before her. I always wanted her to have a vision concerning me, but she only assured me I'd be a teacher.

I was told by everyone that I had "a nice touch," a vague compliment that means that while you do not excel technically people do not want to run away screaming when they hear you. I was much better at drawing but was never given lessons for that. My parents thought we got enough art instruction in school. Or, since art needs to be "in you," they thought extra lessons unnecessary. What they understood was music. So I got music lessons.

This is where I was exposed to white gospel music, heavy on Sacred Harp, but with piano accompaniment. I never grasped "shape note" singing, and it came so naturally to Mrs. Bessette and my mother that they had a hard time explaining it. It was like explaining poetry to someone who does not understand rhyme and cadence. I tried and tried to learn harmony and key changes, but just like drawing was something that was "in me", this definitely was not.

Early on I was frustrated and hated practicing. I wasn't good at it and wanted to quit. My mother promised me that if I kept trying that one day I would suddenly realize I liked it. Since she always told the truth I kept practicing, mainly to please her. I wanted to do well because it would mean belonging.

There was a recital every spring. Girls were expected to wear dresses and curtsey after performing for all the other students and parents. Boys wore their best church clothes and bowed. We all dreaded it. When I was around age nine, I was to play "Prince Rupert". It wasn't a difficult piece but for some reason (probably because I knew I had to perform it) the more I practiced the worse it sounded. The day before the recital I was in tears, trying and trying to get it right, knowing I was going to be a public disgrace. My parents, my piano teacher, my aunts and cousins and friends – they'd all laugh or feel sorry for me because I couldn't play this simple song. It was the end of the world.

While I dissolved there on the piano bench, I heard my mother go to the phone in the kitchen. I heard her call Mrs. Bessette. I heard her say I wouldn't be at the recital, that this song was just upsetting me the more I tried to play it. There were pleasant good-byes and the phone clicked back onto the hook. She came back to the living room and gave me a reassuring smile. I gazed up at her with my tear-stained face and thought she must be some sort of angel.

I never asked to get out of the recital. I didn't even know that was possible. I thought everything had some sort of law or rule connected to it, like how unmarried people can't keep their babies or how we had to go to school. I thought it was a rule to go to the spring recital, no matter how awful it was going to be. My mother saved me. Saved me from the horrible, aching panic in the pit of my stomach. And without so much as a word about wasting their time and money with these lessons.

Years later I was alone, playing the piano, and suddenly realized I liked it.

Around the same time as that doomed recital, Mrs. Bessette mentioned a locally famous pianist by the name of Frank-something. Asked my mother if she had heard of him.

"Heard of him?" she snorted. "I was engaged to him." My hands fell from the keyboard.

"You were going to marry someone besides Dad?" The idea was inconceivable.

"Yes, but I broke it off. I wanted a *real* man, like your father."

I tried to imagine this scenario, replacing my strong father with this wimpy pianist. I wondered how different life would have been if she had gone through with it. I wondered if I would still be her daughter. My world as I knew it wouldn't exist. I shuddered. It was unnerving to think I could have been somewhere else, some*one* else, with another family and another name.

Dad's brothers fought in the war while he was deemed unfit due to a withered hand. I was at least six years old before I noticed this condition. With the possible exception of being a pianist like the jilted Frank, there was nothing he couldn't do. He was athletic and played football in high school. Once John and I were trying to "play baseball" (i.e. connect the bat to the ball) and failing miserably. Dad happened to walk by and we asked him to hit the ball. Barely slowing his pace, with one smooth movement he tucked the bat under one arm, tossed the ball into the air with the other, moved the bat to his good hand and *crack!* the ball shot through the air out into the rhododendrons. He then continued on his way. We never found that ball. It was really the loss of our Armed Forces that he was not allowed to serve, but at the same time I was glad he didn't. The war did terrible things to people even if they survived physically unscathed.

Dad's younger brother George lived with us for years. A fun-loving farm boy from the Midwest, he broke down the moment he was to parachute over the Pacific. Never the same, in and out of homes for soldiers and mental hospitals and even subjected to electroshock therapy, he lived the rest of his life shattered. Seeing this man who Dad described as a playful jokester sit and chain smoke, never cracking a smile much less a joke, made me grateful my father was not put in the same danger.

Sometimes God is saving us from something worse.

George smoked and drank but those activities were confined to his room or outdoors as Mom would tolerate neither. She and Dad never spoke of it, but it was understood that while this was Walt's brother, it was also Lillian's house, and it was the women who set the standard for the home. If George had any ill-will about this, we never knew. He showed no emotion and expressed no thoughts the entire time he lived with us.

George had just one moment I know of where his youthful nature made a return. When Walt and Lillian married, George was put in charge of the "get-away car." Dad felt they were too mature for JUST MARRIED in soap on the windows and tin cans dragging behind. He asked his brother to keep the Chrysler hidden to make sure they looked like a regular couple taking a trip.

True to his word, there was nothing on the car when they left, no hint of a wedding. Halfway to Oregon they stopped at a service station and (being it was his honeymoon) Dad for once didn't pump his own gas. The attendant started the fill-up then came back to the window.

"So…just married, huh? Honeymooners, huh? Crazy romantic kids…" he kidded. They were dumbfounded. How could he possibly know? The smiling attendant handed them a small slip of paper he found tucked in the gas cap:

JUST MARRIED. PLEASE TEASE.

Mom had precarious health from the time she was twelve and contracted scarlet fever, which left her with an enlarged heart.

As a teen she had a mysterious illness that caused loss of muscle control. She was confined to bed, unable to even hold a book. Sometimes she was found on the floor or even under the bed where she had fallen. This went on for months. She couldn't finish high school.

At some point in her teens or twenties, while playing volleyball with friends, she had massive bleeding. The blood turned pink and finally white. The doctor told her mother, "She had a miscarriage." Gramma drew herself up to her full height of five-foot-nothing and said in no uncertain terms, "My daughter is *not* that kind of a girl!"

She broke her back mid-spine before the age of forty. After previously having a figure to die for, her torso was never the same and she never could shed herself of her now-flaccid stomach.

When I was about eight, she was badly burned by a hot canning jar exploding on the stove. I was only told Mom was in the hospital and was sent to live with Aunt Betty. I kept asking what happened but Linda and Laurie would resolutely turn away and say nothing, on their mother's orders. Finally, when I was allowed home, I asked Dad.

"They didn't tell you?! Oh for crying out loud…!" Apparently they were trying to "spare" me but my imagination was much worse than the reality. I thought she was dying. They could have spared me by telling me the truth.

Then, starting when I was about nine, Mom developed pneumonia every winter. It was decided that as the daughter I was to stay with her. I do not recall the schools making much of a fuss. It was different then. I was a good student and could easily make up the work.

I was happy for those times. It was like the afternoons in Kindergarten, just Mommy and me. I read to her. I washed dishes. I answered the phone. I made her lunch – half a canned peach or pear on cottage cheese nestled in a lettuce leaf was one of her favorites. I would bring it to her on the same blue TV tray she used to bring to me.

One day she had a craving and dictated to me the recipe for beef barley soup. I wrote it in a steno pad with my special pink pen while she lay in bed. "You can do it," she said, maybe wondering if I really could. I did. I was inordinately proud of myself.

This went on three years in a row. She even had a type of pneumonia the doctors had only heard of but never seen. One day while vacuuming the living room, I heard a terrible thud and looked to see her in a heap at the bottom of the stairs. She was so delirious with fever she turned the wrong way trying to find the bathroom. Fortunately Dad was in the next room reading the newspaper. I remember her flowing nightgown and how easily he seemed to carry her back to bed. He was so strong then.

We had a large extended family. Mom's side stuck together more than Dad's, especially after his parents died. Because only a handful of Mom's family immigrated, those who were here were very close, and they all came to Gramma's for every holiday or to just drop in for coffee.

I didn't know how we were related, I just knew everyone belonged there. They go back in my memory to where my memories begin. I can still conjure up their voices, their laughter, their traits, their habits. I knew if I went to Gramma's on Thursday afternoons I would see Martin and Alice and be offered cookies and milk to go with their coffee. When a guest was leaving Gramma would always say, *"Tack for titten,"* (Literally, "Thanks for the glance," i.e. "quick visit.")

If I would ask, I was told we were cousins. As it turns out, some were, and some were cousins *of* cousins. Some from Gramma's side and others from Grandpa's, but they were married so long ago that no one kept track of who was actually related to who; they were all just family. They were in each other's weddings and together for every special occasion.

One such relation was Eleanor. I was told she was the widow of Grandpa's cousin Matthew, who had died many years before, as did Grandpa. In fact, "Grandpa" never was a grandfather in life, dying several years prior to the birth of the eldest grandchild.

Eleanor was born in Colorado to Swedish immigrants. Her mother died when she was only ten. She had just one sibling, a brother. She married Matthew and moved to the Seattle area to be nearer to his family, the closest being us – his cousins. They never had children. Then her husband and brother died the same day, both suffering fatal heart attacks, one in Denver, one in Seattle. She remained in the same house with the same furniture, the same car, the same everything, for the next thirty years.

Though she was Swedish, Eleanor looked and sounded nothing like the others in the family. She had a proper, clipped manner of speaking you'd expect from a graduate of a girls finishing school. She almost invariably wore silk dresses and a strand of faux pearls. Her hair was kept in a proper, waved bob style from long ago. She reminded me of the Queen Mother. But she never acted as if she was too good for a visit to the country. She loved to visit, in fact.

Being childless, she was affectionate toward the cousins' children, one of her favorites being Lillian. Mom got to stay with her in the city when she was young. It was like another world compared to the farm. And when I was old enough, I got to stay with Eleanor as well. This is when I made a discovery about myself.

Staying in her house with all her nice old things so perfectly kept, eating in a "breakfast nook," riding the bus downtown, looking out the bedroom window and seeing hundreds of other neatly kept houses down the hill...I realized I liked the city. I felt at home. This from a girl who swore she'd always live in the country, feeling sorry for anyone who did not have acreage. And not only that, I felt connected to the era. Something about the bungalows with white painted brick, venetian blinds and sheer curtains, art nouveau decor, tiled bathrooms, old flowering plants and delicate dishes struck a chord with me. As a teen the one Christian "romance" novel I liked, and read again and again, was from this era. I wasn't interested in the love story – I just liked the background descriptions. I tucked it away in my mind that when I was grown I wanted a house like this, with a breakfast nook and a yellow tiled bathroom. Yellow was my favorite color.

I stayed with Eleanor twice, two summers in a row. Then she made the decision to move into a retirement home with a twist: You give them nearly everything you own and they in turn take care of you the rest of your life. That meant she had to sell the house and almost everything in it. We were invited to her "estate sale." Eleanor had a nice set of Spode china she started collecting in the 1930s and Mom wanted that for me. Some nominal amount of money was exchanged and we took it home where it sat in my bedroom closet for the next decade.

I don't know when I started making lists, but they were of the strangest things. Just lists of things I liked: trees, cat breeds, whatever. I also created a fantasy family where I was the mother and had four daughters. I don't know why it was always me (no husband) and four daughters. I didn't care much for boys, but *four* girls? My favorite number was three. It really made no sense.

I wrote the names *Faith, Hope, Grace, Joy* and tucked the list away in a box where it was gradually forgotten over time.

Chapter 3
~End of Childhood~

In fourth grade, I had the best teacher of my all my years in public school: Mrs. MacKenzie. She knew what was important and she knew how to make her students love her. She would deviate from the dull lesson plan to instead give us a quiz of her own making, with questions like, "How many days are in a year? From which direction does the sun rise? How many nickels are in a dollar?" Incredibly, most of these very practical facts were not taught. Instead, in second and third grades, we had to diagram sentences and show if one number was bigger than another number by using the < or > symbols. In fourth grade we had to memorize multiplication tables and learn long division. She even made that fun. Well, as fun as it could be.

What she was really known for was artist appreciation. We learned about a new artist or poet every week. And she kept it spicy with infamous details of their lives. We heard about Picasso's many lovers and illegitimate children, Van Gogh's insanity, Lautrec's deformities due to inbreeding. We learned about cubism, pointillism, impressionism.

She read aloud from Emily Dickinson, Robert Frost, *James and the Giant Peach*, *Charlotte's Web*, *Where the Red Fern Grows*, *Mrs. Piggle-Wiggle* and *Tar Baby*, the latter allowing her Southern roots to show with a perfect accent. We were a bunch of middle-class white kids from the Pacific Northwest. We knew nothing of the South. It was like a foreign country. We were entranced.

She made no secret of who she liked or disliked among the staff. She had no pretenses. She kept a glazed pottery piece made by a former student whose parents thought the work was ugly and wouldn't take it home. This made her so angry she kept in on display in her classroom thereafter. We listened to 45s, one of her favorites being "Smoking in the Boys Room" by Brownsville Station. She was divorced. She was scandalous. We adored her. I would have gladly remained in fourth grade the rest of my life if I could be with her.

I was one of her pets and she made no secret of that either. She allowed me to work alone while others had to work in groups because I did better that way. She offered me "bribery" in the form of a pack of gum if I would stay in from recess to draw a picture to be used as a header for...something...some school publication. I cannot remember what it was for, but I'll never forget the feeling of being cherished and appreciated. She knew what was real, what was important, and she didn't let school rules stand in her way.

She told my mother during a parent-teacher conference that one day she strode up and down the aisles, assailing us about some infraction. As she passed my desk she looked at my face and her resolve crumbled. I didn't know what that meant when Mom relayed this to me in amused tones; I supposed Mrs. MacKenzie saw how sorry I was for whatever we had done. It was "that look" that could alternately get my brothers in trouble or get me out of it and would disarm certain men later in life. All I know is I wasn't doing it deliberately.

I was at the top of my game at the age of nine. Straight A's. Lots of friends. In the best class I would ever have. Doing well in piano lessons. I was even athletic, being one of the best runners among the girls. I felt good about myself. Then it was over.

It was spring. That much I remember. I'm glad I don't remember the exact date. I came home from school on the bus to find Mom gone and Dad still at work. Keith was in the living room watching TV. I sat down and said, "Where's Mom?" Keith said, "I don't know."

Suddenly I was on the floor. My pants were ripped from my body. "*Mommy?*" I instinctively cried. "Mommy's not here," sneered Keith. At least twice my weight of seventy-five pounds, he easily pinned me to the carpet. His filthy fingers thrust into my previously-inviolate vagina. There was searing pain, my tender skin tearing. Everything went black then the blackness was also torn away, like stitches ripped from my psyche.

I heard screaming and realized it was me. "*Stop! You're killing me, you're killing me!*" He tried to silence me with his mouth. I gagged. He showed me his disgusting penis. "It won't hurt. It doesn't have a nail." – "NO!" I kept struggling, kept fighting, kept screaming.

I caught some movement in my peripheral vision and turned my head to see John in the kitchen doorway, looking at us with a stunned expression. *He's come to save me,* I thought and was about to cry out his name when he turned and went down the basement stairs. All hope drained from me at the sight of him walking away.

Finally Keith released me. I grabbed my pants and ran out the door, sobbing and gasping for breath, the pain still searing inside me. I had to escape. I ran. Keith yelled from the porch, *"I'm sorry! I said I'm sorry!"* I ran to Gramma's. I could still hear Keith yelling. Gramma was just stepping out onto the back porch but I realized I couldn't stay there – I had to get further away. I saw Aunt Betty's station wagon going slowly down their driveway on the other side of the field. I ran. They stopped. They were on their way to Linda and Laurie's piano lesson. I gasped out with rambling words, not having the vocabulary to fully describe my terror, my outrage. Aunt Betty said I would come with them and she'd explain it all to my mother later. I sat curled up in their car. I remember nothing else.

After dropping her daughters at their house Betty brought me home. She told me to stay put. Lillian came out the front door, smiled and said, "There you are," but I didn't get out of the car. Betty spoke to her sister in hushed tones. Mom started to cry. I was allowed out of the car. Mom went to hug me but I pulled back. She asked, as if hoping for the impossible, "Did he hurt you?" I could only nod. She cried more. Keith was brought out onto the porch as if facing a judge. Betty grilled him. "You know what you did was wrong!" Keith played the contrite criminal, crying and admitting his guilt.

I could not go back into that house. I could not be in the same room with him again, ever.

"Let's just leave," I begged.

"Where would we go?" Mom asked.

"I don't care. Please, just anywhere."

"There's nowhere to go," she said sadly. And I knew I was really trapped with this monster, this animal that would violate his own sister.

Mom told Dad but I think he couldn't take it in. I wasn't able to adequately describe what happened and it was so out of the realm of normalcy. There are no Bringing Up Baby books that prepare you for when your son rapes your daughter. They dealt with it the way they dealt with anything they couldn't handle: They acted as if nothing had happened and waited for me to get over it.

In the haven of Mrs. MacKenzie's class I sought refuge for the remainder of the school year. But in the mysterious way that children know when someone has been victimized, my classmates treated me differently. I was teased and shunned. In my mind I was ugly. I was dirty. The proof being the black-stained mucus I found on my underwear.

My cousins mentioned it in hushed euphemisms like "your experience," which made me feel dirtier. Keith, though, tried to use it to his advantage.

"I'll tell everyone what I did," he taunted.

"Go ahead!" I countered, which took him aback. I hated him more every time I looked at him.

He was put into therapy. It was the breaking point for my parents, who had little respect for "pop psychologists." I was not taken to the doctor nor was any authority informed. The word "rape" was never articulated. I was left to "get over it." The only thing I was given as a sort of acknowledgement was a lock for my bedroom door, one that could only be worked from the inside.

My childhood ripped from me, I no longer played with dolls. All the little girl things I previously enjoyed now made me feel empty. It was all fake. If friends asked to play Barbies I went through the motions, hoping the feelings would come back if I pretended everything was normal.

I stayed in my room as much as possible, door locked, drawing house plans that did not have a place for Keith. I hated my tender, changing body and denied as long as I could that I was developing a figure. Although I needed a bra by the time I was ten, had cramps soon after and a fully developed figure by thirteen, I did not start to menstruate until I was fourteen. Arrested development. Everything *but*.

I turned within myself. Where I had been easy to cry or laugh before, I became the very picture of Nordic restraint. After being used to climbing into Mom's lap and getting hugs from Dad, I now held back. They were not a demonstrative bunch in the first place, but I never wanted anyone to touch me ever again. They may have thought it was part of me entering puberty, if they thought about it at all.

Mom tried to shield me, act as my voice. Maybe she thought I was too young for The Talk beyond the basics she finally told me. I knew rape meant forced sex, but I did not understand what sex was supposed to be. It's possible she meant to explain more when I was older. But meanwhile I had a very distorted view. I didn't even know I had been raped; I only knew I had been attacked in a vile way. Once, as I wandered through a department store, I randomly picked up a book and opened it. There a rape scene (or reproduction scene, if you will) was described from the clinical point of view of an anthropologist. I started shaking. I felt sick. It was wrong. I knew it was wrong but I had no idea what was right.

A rare happy time after this was having an extended stay at Aunt Betty's during the summer. She was a great cook and made everyone feel welcome in her home. Even though I was "different" I felt they liked me anyway. Uncle Raymond was a gentle, quiet man. His milquetoast appearance belied his history as a war veteran. He was a teacher now and fiercely protective of his daughters when necessary. My parents must have arranged for me to stay there for that reason. I had a taste of what it would have been like to have sisters in Linda, Laurie, and baby Lisa.

We played Life, rode bikes around the driveway, made camps in the hay field even though we weren't supposed to, ate frozen blueberries, listened to the same records over and over, and slept on the big covered porch, just like they do in Sweden in the summers.

We read every *Nancy Drew* book ever written. I loved how competent she was, how everything worked out for her. That everyone respected her and treated her like an adult. I would have settled for being taken seriously. I hated being called a little girl. I wasn't a little girl anymore.

One night when Uncle Raymond gave Linda and Laurie their customary good-night kisses he glanced over at me and must have seen the wistfulness on my face because he bent down and kissed my forehead as well. He smelled clean like soap and cologne, completely unlike Dad's well-earned aroma of car grease.

"Good night, Noelle," he said. He never called me his niece, instead introducing me as "Betty's niece" or "the girls' cousin." I don't know why that bothered me except I wanted to be wanted. To belong.

I was envious of the cohesiveness of their family. They sang together. Uncle Raymond willingly went to church with them. No one hit. No one yelled. As natural as that was, it was strange to me. I had become so accustomed to walking on eggshells at home and all of us living as separately as possible in the same house because of Keith, that anything other than that wasn't "normal." I was still striving to be normal.

Keith became more volatile. Anything could set him off. Once at dinner I must have smirked at some stupid thing he said because he threw his milk in my face. I in turn smashed my entire dinner plate into his. He then screamed he would kill me as I ran to lock myself in the bathroom.

Another time he cut some clothes line, pressed it to our mother's throat as she sat reading and told her how easy it would be to kill her. Mom ran outside and he locked her out of the house. I spent two weeks with Aunt Betty after that incident. When I was finally allowed back, he sneered, "Where has *she* been?"

His mantra became *"Prove it!"* as if this would end all discussion. It was all about him, all the time. He was a disgusting, violent slob with no conscience and no moral compass. People he met were nothing more than potential victims to him. He respected no one.

The cause was not his upbringing. And he was adopted as a newborn. When I heard the term "sociopath" it was as if a light had been switched on.

From *Profile of a Sociopath:*

-Manipulative and conning

-Pathological lying

-Lack of remorse, shame or guilt

-Callousness/lack of empathy

-Early behavior problems/juvenile delinquency

-Promiscuous sexual behavior/infidelity

-Criminal or entrepreneurial versatility

-Contemptuous of those who seek to understand them

-Has an emotional need to justify their crimes

-Incapable of real human attachment to another

-Narcissism, grandiosity (self-importance not based on achievements)

It used to be called "moral insanity". Then "psychopathic inferiority". Hervey Cleckley's 1941 work, *The Mask of Sanity,* created a 16-point checklist of psychopathic traits, some of which are included above. The terms psychopath and sociopath are still used interchangeably although psychopaths are considered more smooth and calculating.

The experts will tell you psychopaths are born and sociopaths are created. I beg to differ.

I lost my one chance for vengeance. One day we both happened to be in the basement rec room by the pool table. Uncle George was casually lounging in a chair, dressed – as usual – as if it was still 1945. I don't remember what set me off – the way Keith looked at me, something he said – but I picked up a pool ball and threw it with all my strength at his ugly, sneering face. My aim was off and the ball sailed just past his head and hit the wall behind him, where it dented the paneling before cracking in half and falling to the floor.

For the only time in my memory, George showed emotion; leaping to his feet and yelling, "Hey!" All the color drained from Keith's face as I leveled my gaze at him, never looking away, and reached for another ball.

This time I wouldn't miss.

He bolted.

I had failed.

When relaying this to someone in adulthood, my shocked listener asked, "Weren't you sorry?"

"For missing?" I said. "Yes. If I had killed him, no one would have convicted me. I was only ten years old."

I have never hated anyone more than I hated Keith. Even now.

My parents bought me a rock polisher and set it up in one of the sheds. Now I could make all the special rocks I wanted. They looked at me expectantly, knowing how happy this would make me. I looked at the thing I had wanted for so long, the thing that would make rocks magic. And I felt absolutely nothing.

Rocks weren't magic anymore. Nothing was. I had truly believed magic or angels or *some* good thing would protect me from evil. But it was all pretend. The reality was, I didn't matter. Only the "right" people mattered, apparently. I was expendable.

I never used my rock polisher even once. Dad was dumbfounded and irritated. Mom didn't understand, but knew there must be an underlying explanation. The polisher sat in the shed, untouched, for the next thirty years.

I was baptized at the age of eleven in the little white church. My brothers were baptized as infants in the Lutheran tradition, but for me Mom put her Baptist foot down. I would be baptized when I asked to be baptized. Although I didn't feel any different, I was glad it was done. I still wanted to be like Mom but didn't idolize her the way I used to.

She was of the belief we were in the Last Days, the seven years of Tribulation. Dad would just shake his head, but it was very serious to her. Her family did not share her opinion but were still obsessed with the subject. We all saw *A Thief in the Night* (a truly awful movie), discussed the book of Revelation, and looked forward to the Rapture. We were ready for the end, when we had to refuse the Mark of the Beast, and we resolutely rubbed the 666 out of our school erasers.

"God has a plan for your life," I was told by Sunday school teachers, my piano teacher, family members. I wondered what it could be.

I was more interested in the beautiful songs they would sing and hearing verses that stirred my soul. I just wasn't a very good Baptist. So much didn't make sense to me.

I had a dream:

I was at a summer camp. There were many other kids but I didn't know them. Far away I could see my parents - they were talking to other children. I started to go to them but a camp counselor stopped me.

"You need to wait here to be adopted."

"I'm already adopted. Those are my parents over there," I said, pointing.

"They wanted new children, so you'll have to wait to see if someone takes you."

"You can't do that! It's forever! Adoption is forever!" But no one seemed to hear me. My parents continued to serenely shop for children. Panic swept over me. I was being abandoned.

Who would want me now? I thought.

After leaving Mrs. MacKenzie's class, school became fake and meaningless, junior high being the worst. The sight of the buildings made my stomach tighten. It reminded me of a prison and I felt trapped whenever I was there. Where before I looked forward to school, I now hated it with a passion. I hated the classes being broken into forty-five minute segments. I hated the classes we were forced to take. I hated nearly all of the other students for no good reason. I hated how we were expected to act like adults but treated like children. It became my mission to be there as little as possible.

"It's not normal," my parents agreed.

The little I do remember fondly about junior high had nothing to do with academics. Girls wore suede leather loafers, jeans, v-neck tops and puka shell necklaces. Everyone tried to copy Farah Fawcett's hair and everyone failed. All the girls who could play piano had to play "Nadia's Theme". There was "horse club" – for girls only, of course. Since I only liked horses but would not profess my undying love for them, I wasn't part of horse club. I also did not have the shoes, puka shell necklace and definitely not the hair. I *could* play "Nadia's Theme".

I didn't have a high opinion of boys in the first place and the advent of puberty didn't help matters. If they were just bothersome in elementary school they were completely disgusting now, because they all reminded me of Keith on some level.

I felt sick nearly all the time. Puberty came down on me like a brick wall. My periods were nothing like the reassuring 5th grade health film *Very Personally Yours*. I had not one but two cycles a month with debilitating bleeding and clots. Sometimes the cramps actually made me vomit.

After being an excellent student in elementary school, I nearly failed both seventh and eighth grades due to absences. They only passed me because I was too smart to hold back. Or because they didn't want me there any longer.

Then things got worse.

Actually it all overlapped. It could not be divided and labeled and explained away, although the doctors tried.

Keith was put into group homes and boys' homes and even "kid jail" when he was caught doing something – I don't remember what. While in juvenile detention he sold drugs to another kid, who overdosed and had to go to the hospital. This pattern would be repeated over and over. He would be incarcerated then make it worse. It tore my parents up, despite the equal pain of having him around. The first time he was sent away I asked Mom as she made dinner where he was.

"He's gone," she said and started to cry.

"When is he coming back?" I asked, cautiously.

"He's not coming back," she cried.

Good, I thought. I felt they were finally making him pay for what he did. But he did come back eventually and when he did I felt betrayed all over again. They had failed me, failed to protect me. The childish façade I created where they were perfect parents – natural for any child – was crumbling.

I noticed now how unfashionable my parents were, any "fault" magnified. They were weak and ineffective and even stupid. My parents, who before had been so wonderful. Now I found it ridiculous when Mom would fall asleep in a recliner after seeing Dad off to work, angry that she didn't wake me in time for school. Angry she wasn't strong. Since John was a child like me I didn't expect much from him, but now I expected nothing. I felt as though I was living alone with a group of strangers and we were just pretending to be a family, like on TV. The real became unreal.

My brother didn't rescue me.

My mother didn't escape with me.

My father didn't avenge me.

I was nothing.

Dad, Mom and John had been the center of my universe. I needed them to be my champions, and when they weren't it nearly destroyed me.

I hated having to go along to the therapy sessions, if I was in the room or not. How many hours did I waste in the cavernous lobby of Remann Hall? While I grudgingly admired my parents for never giving up and doing everything possible for their eldest child, I just wanted him to go to prison – permanently – or die.

The Princess Bride[1] has been described as a perfect movie, containing "fencing, fighting, torture, revenge, giants, monsters, chases, escapes, true love, miracles..." as the grandfather narrating would tell you. In a climactic scene, Inigo Montoya faces the man who murdered his father; the man who scarred Inigo's cheeks with his father's own sword, as a lesson and a warning to never come after him. Instead, Inigo dedicates his life to tracking down the killer:

Inigo Montoya [*enraged*]: Hello! My name is Inigo Montoya! You killed my father! Prepare to die!

Count Rugen: No! [*Inigo corners Count Rugen and slashes his cheek. The count is terrified.*]

Inigo Montoya: Offer me money! [*He slashes the count's other cheek.*]

Count Rugen: Yes!

Inigo Montoya: Power, too. Promise me that!

Count Rugen: All that I have and more. Please!

Inigo Montoya: Offer me anything I ask for!

Count Rugen: Anything you want...

Inigo Montoya: [*plunging his sword into the count's chest*] I want my father back, you son of a bitch.

In the same way nothing less than the death of his father's murderer would satisfy Inigo, nothing less than Keith's death, or at least social/spiritual death in the form of life in prison, would satisfy me. When Count Rugen offers "anything" to be spared, Inigo wants only one thing: He wants his father back, alive. To turn back time to when he was a child. He wants the impossible. And he knows it's impossible, but that doesn't stop him from wanting it.

---

1   Screenplay and original book of the same name by William Goldman. *The Princess Bride*, 1987, a Rob Reiner film, produced by Rob Reiner and Andrew Scheinman, distributed by Metro-Goldwyn-Mayer and Twentieth Century Fox Home Entertainment.

If being raped as an adult is living through your own murder, being raped as a child is surviving your soul being ripped out. I did not understand what happened to me. I only knew something in me died. Something that could never be resurrected. Something that I have always missed and longed for.

If I had such a moment, with Keith at my mercy and him offering me "anything," I would say:

"I want my innocence back, you son of a bitch."

I made a new friend in junior high – Renee Tanaka. Several elementary schools funneled into our junior high and high school. She lived in the valley. I lived on the hill. So we didn't meet until seventh grade. I told my mother about my new friend. She considered quietly. "Tanaka? Is her mother called Meg?" I said I would ask.

The next day, Renee asked me if my mother was Lil Nelson. I said Yes, and is her mother Meg? She said yes, that her actual name is Megumi but her childhood friends called her Meg.

Soon after I found myself at Renee's house in the valley, where our mothers caught up after more than thirty years apart. They knew each other just one year before Megumi and all those of Japanese blood were "evacuated" to internment camps. They were told it was their patriotic duty and for their own protection. I don't know if anyone believed this. The 1942 high school annual showed a thriving student body with the valedictorian being of Japanese descent. 1943 had only two-thirds the number of students, all white. Mom told me as the Japanese families were shipped off (actually bussed), everyone stood outside the school and sang "Auld Lang Syne". Many were not seen again, regardless. Lil and Meg saw one another's wedding announcements in the paper years later but their paths never crossed.

Mom asked Mrs. Tanaka about the camps. Mrs. Tanaka answered freely. Later, when Mom relayed this to Dad, he was upset. This was something to be left in the past, he said, not dredged up to cause bad feelings. Dad determinedly ignored anything that made him uncomfortable. He had Japanese friends. He admired Asian cultures while having little tolerance for "Mexicans" (anyone remotely Hispanic), Indians, or blacks. He didn't know any and didn't care to. I asked why the Japanese were okay when their traditions were so foreign while the others were more "American". He looked at me in disbelief.

"They're *farmers*," he said. The Japanese farmers were considered the best around.

"What about migrant workers?" I said. (Most being Mexican.) "They're farmers."

"They don't own anything."

"Then what about the Indians who owned the land first?"

"They didn't even know how to farm."

Farming apparently trumped all. To be a land owner and farmer was honorable. It was where he came from. He stayed with the familiar.

In a rare quiet moment after dinner one night, Dad and Mom sat at the kitchen table sipping coffee and talking. Suddenly Mom said, "I don't feel well," and fell to the floor. She would describe it again and again to visitors and friends on the phone. A sudden headache, then fainting. What she didn't mention – because she didn't see it – was that she had changed.

Where she used to be gentle and mild, she was now harsh and critical. "I'm not different. All of you are different!" she said to me sharply one day. Even I, who knew next-to-nothing about health, knew she had suffered a stroke. Nothing else could explain the sudden personality change. Her sister tried to reason with her. Mom agreed to a brain scan just to prove us wrong. Her doctor, Henry Olson, informed my aunt there was no stroke. "She's play-acting for attention," was his diagnosis. I decided Dr. Olson was a moron. Dad was conflicted. He didn't agree with Dr. Olson, but still, he was *a doctor* and that impressed him. Besides, he had a full practice; not taking any new patients because he was so popular. How could he be wrong?

We pretended everything was normal and went on.

One day I came home from school and informed Mom a classmate's mother had died unexpectedly. She instantly reached for a cookbook. "I'll make something and we will bring it over."

"Mom," I protested, "I hardly know her, I don't know where they live and I doubt they'll be hungry right now."

She looked at me disdainfully, closed the book, and said, "You're hard-hearted, Noelle."

"No, I'm just not like you," I said, flatly. *I never was.* We stood and stared, as if seeing each other clearly for the first time. An invisible chasm that could not be crossed split the ground between us.

Driving her beloved Chrysler one day, she drew in her breath. I had learned to brace myself whenever she did that because it meant she was about to say something I didn't want to hear. She drew in her breath and blurted out:

"Sometimes I wish I could just run away."

I asked you to take me and leave and you said there was nowhere to go, I thought bitterly. But I said nothing. Any remark only led to a hysterical argument where she would again tell me she wasn't sick – it was the rest of us.

I wondered what worse thing God was saving us from.

My new friend Renee and I made plans for a sleep-over. I was to come to her house the last day of school before Christmas break. That day, she chatted happily about the fun we were going to have. I felt strange. Things were moving slowly. I could barely swallow. It was my first bout of tonsillitis. I was given sulfa, which tasted like charcoal, and confined to bed for my birthday and Christmas. Renee and I promised to make up the sleep-over later. It never happened.

Mom collapsed in the living room. Paramedics were called. They knew us because Dad's service station had been directly across the street from the fire station for many years. They gave her oxygen and asked her a series of questions, which she answered. Finally one asked her to smile. She thought it was just to put her at ease and she cracked a very crooked grin. This time she went to the hospital.

St. Joe's, as it was informally called, had been rebuilt as a very modern hospital in the 1970s. I could look down from the oval window of Mom's room onto the old brick building where I was born and contemplate this was the last place I was with my biological mother and now here I sat with my adoptive mother. I did not know what happened to my birth mother then and I did not know what was going to happen to my adoptive mother now. They were both a mystery.

Dr. Olson changed his diagnosis to that of a stroke. But he didn't apologize. We came every day to see her. I can't remember if Keith was home at that time, but Dad and John and I would come. Many other visitors as well. She received so many flowers they moved her into the next room and left the first just to hold all the tokens of good wishes.

Not long after, we were there one night while Mom ate dinner. She remarked that the food wasn't so bad, even for a hospital. Suddenly her face went slack and her eyes were unfocused. She started to drool. Dad yelled for the nurse. They swarmed the room and advised me to leave. I went to sit in the hall. Time went by. Finally Dr. Olson came from her room and walked passed me, a perplexed expression on his face.

"Is she play-acting for attention now?" I said. He glanced at me briefly and slowed his pace but did not answer. The moron.

Dad told me later that Mom had suffered the worst possible stroke one can have without dying. And that she could last two years, tops. I didn't say it, but I hoped she would pass quickly. Watching her struggle was agonizing. One side of her body lay useless. She could not speak. She could not eat. She could not stand on her own or walk. Instead she moaned piteously, was fed hideous glop through a tube that was put down her throat for every meal, and had to use a bedpan in place of a toilet. She helplessly drooled, her face slack, emotionless, but her eyes were so sad. If she had been an animal there would have been mercy. She would have been "humanely euthanized". But being a civilized society, she was forced to suffer, to linger in this horrible existence that wasn't living or dying.

Dad went to the hospital every night after dinner and sat and talked with Mom. Every single night, without fail. I went along about half the time. Sometimes I just couldn't face the sight of it, or the smell, or the tubes and needles, or the moaning of the patients. I wasn't strong that way. It made me nauseated, and the more I was exposed to it, the worse I became. I wanted to be brave, not be a wimp about needles and such, but ever since getting that measles shot, I had a worsening phobia about anything medically invasive. And it was obvious these doctors could do nothing for my mother but watch her slowly die.

Chapter 4
~Raising Myself~

Mom languished for months. Finally it was decided she could go home, but to her mother's house next door, because of all the stairs in ours. This required a hospital bed and a lot of other medical equipment. And a private nurse. Nearly all of Dad's paycheck went to the nurse but there was no way he was going to put his wife in a nursing home.

So now we went to Gramma's every day. I was there often already, but now had even more reason. My cousin Britt was there nearly every day as well. We watched *The Three o'Clock Movie* on channel 5, seeing many classics our classmates were not the least bit interested in: *High Society, A Patch of Blue, Ben Hur, To Have and Have Not, A Streetcar Named Desire* and *The Lion in Winter*. My reading also matured. Besides bypassing Harlequin romance novels for *Gone With the Wind*, I also discovered Taylor Caldwell. I bought nearly every book she ever wrote, starting with *A Testimony of Two Men*, after seeing it in a TV miniseries. And I kept drawing house plans. I even bought several books of house plans and graph paper and designed to my heart's content.

I was twelve for at least three years. As long as Mom was trapped in this limbo, the rest of us were trapped also. I don't know how Dad kept his sanity. He went to work every morning, came home in the evening, visited Mom, and we'd either have a meal there or go out. Eating in restaurants was his one personal luxury. He never wanted anything fancy or expensive, but it had to be good. Everywhere we went, people knew him and asked about Mom. "About the same," he'd say. He and I talked when it was just the two of us. I think he missed being able to have real conversations with Mom so I became the substitute.

I took over care of the house. Before, I was expected to do chores on Saturday mornings, after enjoying an hour of Bugs Bunny cartoons. That used to mean vacuuming and dusting and pulling dandelions. Now it meant every day I washed dishes, did the laundry (with no dryer), kept a list of groceries we needed to buy (and then bought them), swept, scrubbed, cooked, and on and on. Honestly, I did not have to cook much, because Dad thought I didn't know how and I wasn't going to disillusion him. But if I was in the kitchen and he or Uncle George walked through and asked for a sandwich, I was on the spot to do it. I couldn't keep the house as nice as Mom did, because 1) I had to go to school and 2) I was learning as I went along.

Sometimes aunts or aunty neighbors or church ladies stopped by to help or bring food. I appreciated the food but felt I was being judged about the housework. It was next to impossible to match Mom's standards with her perfectly-organized drawers, the way the curtains were drawn "just so," and her daily cleaning schedule.

I started babysitting a cousin's son when I was only nine, which was not an uncommon age among our family and friends. I continued into my teens. This was a cousin on Dad's side. Jerome was the eldest, I was the youngest. Their house was so peaceful, clean, and modern, yet inviting. Being there was like being on vacation. They took me camping one otherwise-dull summer. Jerome took me for a ride on his snowmobile one snowy winter. They even stopped by unannounced one night to take me to see a new movie phenomenon called *Star Wars*. They were one of the few bright spots in my life.

Another oasis in the desert was my cousin Christina, called Christie. By "cousin", I mean one of the far-flung Swedish relations who were there for every special occasion. She patiently explained to Britt, Linda, Laurie and me that she was our third cousin, older by about ten years. She took it upon herself to impart feminine wisdom upon us. She was very much a lady, like Lillian. She loaned me *The Fascinating Girl,* a sort of how-to-catch-a-man book for Christians. I found it uproariously funny when the author referenced *The Picture of Dorian Gray* as proof that giving one's virginity away before marriage ruins a young woman's chance at happiness. I wondered if the author even read the book to know Dorian Gray was a monster. It would be like trying to have a happy marriage with Dracula.

Despite being warned again and again in church how any sex outside of marriage was a sin, I just couldn't see it. Sex was natural, not dirty, or bad, or wrong – unless it hurt someone. I still had no clue as to what "when two become one" meant, but I doubted *The Fascinating Girl* was going to explain. Sex was apparently not something girls were supposed to think about. We were supposed to be innocent and winsome and engaging, and everything would be fine because this would bring around the Right Sort of man. Maybe I should have asked if this still applied to me or if I was now "ruined," as they said in *Gone With The Wind*. I didn't even know if I was still considered a virgin.

Christie did introduce me to a wonderful set of books later. I was sick with tonsillitis once again on my birthday when she gave me *The Chronicles of Narnia*. Never having heard of it, I had no idea what to expect. Instead of another dismal birthday-holiday season trapped at home, I escaped to Narnia, completely engrossed in book after book. I finished the series just before winter break ended. School was a horrible reality.

I no longer went to the little white church since Mom couldn't go and there was no one else to take me. Instead I sometimes accompanied my cousins to their Baptist church in town. I knew a lot of people there and they were nice, but I felt like a poor orphan child. First adopted and now no parents in sight. I was a freak.

"God has great plans for you," I was told by the youth group leaders. *It sure has been working out so far,* I thought sarcastically.

I stayed home from school as much as possible. I felt sick at least half the time because of my mysterious pre-menstrual problems. But it was more than that. I hated school. I hated how I felt when I was there. School wasn't real.

When word got back to Dad about my absence record (which *was* a record, I think) he was concerned, but couldn't be bothered too much with everything he already had on his plate. Besides, he didn't understand it. He missed only two days of school in his entire life. And he never, ever missed a day of work. I was not going to get much empathy there.

Instead he delegated to his sister-in-law, my aunt Betty. She and her husband were teachers and their daughters were excellent students. She expected the same from me. And no nonsense about not feeling well, either. She knew it was all because my mother was sick. I tried to explain to her about the cramps and the pain but because I wasn't menstruating yet she didn't believe it. She made it her mission to make sure I got to school every day. I made it my mission to escape her grasp.

It was nothing against her, really. I just wanted to be left alone. I didn't even care if I flunked. It just wasn't important anymore. She couldn't understand that. She thought I was an emotionally messed-up little girl who wanted a mommy. What I wanted was a somewhat normal life, but without the artificial atmosphere of school. I felt like we were being warehoused. Betty became the embodiment of the Establishment in my mind: that of the public school system, the medical system, the legal system and every crushing aspect of what it was like to be a child with no voice and no choice.

I liked Betty because she was my mother's sister, but never felt close to her. She expected me to be like her daughters, or maybe she expected me to somehow be like what Lillian's biological daughter would have been. I always felt she was trying to shape me into something more respectable, more demure, more "Christian." It frustrated her that I did not conform.

Sometimes she came in the house to track me down. Once as I lay on my bed reading, having no intention of going to school, she barged in. When I told her I wasn't going, she spouted, "Lil isn't going to get better, you know!" I never knew what to say when adults randomly blurted out statements like this, so I said nothing. My lack of response infuriated her.

If anyone had bothered to ask, I would have told them I preferred the quiet of the house when everyone was gone. I drank tea, gazed at the mist hanging on the evergreen trees, listened to my mother's many records (my favorite being *Peer Gynt / Finlandia*), read our *World Book Encyclopedia* set cover to cover, played piano, studied and designed many house plans, and pored over Dad's extensive collection of *National Geographic* magazines. I learned more then, on my own, than I ever learned in school.

Although Mom had a full-time nurse, it took a staff of people to care for her. She needed to be lifted from her hospital bed to the wheelchair, from the wheelchair to the commode. Her liquid diet had to be prepped, put into a bag attached to a tube that was put down her throat for every meal, then the bag and tube needed to be sterilized. Mom endured all this in sight of everyone. I think that must have been the worst – having to use a commode right there in the living room, being unable even to wipe herself. Of course she couldn't speak, only moan or cry, so she could not articulate her feelings.

Besides Gramma and the nurse, many others helped on a regular basis: her sister Betty, sister-in-law Evelyn, old friends from church and more. All with that Scandinavian matter-of-fact kind of vibe with underlying love. I was especially impressed with Evelyn's nonchalance because there had always been contention there concerning the family dynamic. I think Ev wanted to be Gramma's favorite. She told me once her siblings used to beat her for fun. Joining her husband's family must have been a relief. Maybe she needed to secure her place – make sure she was wanted and needed. Mom never said a bad thing about anyone but had confessed to Dad that she just flat-out didn't like Evelyn. It's possible Ev didn't like Lillian much either. They had very different personalities. Even so, they were in each other's weddings and both Mom and Betty drove Ev to doctor appointments without complaint when she couldn't drive herself. Ev took care of me, a very upset toddler, when Mom broke her back. And now she was cleaning up her sister-in-law's waste. It's just what family did.

Even though I had cared for Mom alone when I was as young as eight, I was not asked to do so now, and for that I was grateful. I wasn't strong enough. I couldn't handle her sad, staring eyes, the constant sick smell, seeing/hearing her swallow that awful tube. Instead I tried to keep the house up next door and entertain her as I could. Even that was hard because we were never alone.

There were many visitors. Family and friends already stopped by at Gramma's on a regular basis, now even more were added to the throng. A group from Mom's former church came and prayed over "Sister Lillian" with laying on of hands, asking God for complete healing. Complete healing from a stroke that would eventually kill her. Mom cried so hard she nearly choked. When Dad heard about it he told Gramma those people were not to be allowed back. He did not suffer fools gladly, Christian or not.

That Christmas we were at Gramma's, as always. Same people, same comforting food, same gift exchange, Uncle Clarence reading the second chapter of Luke. All the same, except Mom in that horrible condition. Later, Clarence played chess with her and claimed he did not let her win. That made her laugh, in her sad, throaty way. I so appreciated him at that moment.

Finally, Mom was allowed back home. She had progressed (or, regained ground) enough that she could sit in a wheelchair on the main floor and go up the stairs with the help of a railing and at least one strong adult.

Her nurse, Mary, came with. She was a no-nonsense retired RN who knew Clark Gable. Old as the hills. And Catholic. Mom's family had little to do with Catholics, thinking they weren't "real" Christians, instead just going through the motions of religion. To be a "real" Christian meant to be born again, to ask Jesus into your heart to be your personal lord and savior. Otherwise your faith was dead.

I once asked Mom what "reciting the Rosary" meant. She said it was a Catholic thing but that it didn't mean anything because it was something repeated, not said from the heart. I asked: Then why do we recite the Lord's Prayer? She didn't want to discuss it further.

But when it came down to it, if the Catholics were the only game in town, they were Christian enough. Like Maria in *The Sound of Music*. There was no talk about the nuns belonging to a dead religion. When there's a bigger enemy to deal with the petty differences no longer matter.

So we had an old Catholic nurse living with us who went to school with Clark Gable. Who smoked. And was happily divorced. Mom must have just reeled at all this. I had very little experience with divorce at that age and couldn't understand how someone could be *happy* about it. "You can't get blood from a turnip," Mary said cheerfully. I had no idea what she was talking about.

Keith was home at some point during this, between stints in detention. He was under the impression that Mary was a servant there to do our bidding. It amused me no end to hear her set him straight.

The day Mom came home, our German Shepherd Mitzi was allowed in the house to see her. Although all our dogs were loyal to us, they really belonged to Mom. We were afraid Mitzi would jump on her in excitement, but instead she quietly walked over to the wheelchair and laid her head in Mom's lap. Mom laid her one working hand on Mitzi's head and sobbed.

That night I noticed the old mantle clock, which had not worked since Mom went to the hospital no matter how I tinkered with it, started again of its own accord.

Time dragged on. The summer before I was to begin high school Dad put our travel trailer next to the house and ran an extension cord to it. It was my vacation getaway. We hadn't been anywhere in years. I pretended it was my apartment, with art nouveau and potted palms and a yellow tiled bathroom. I stayed up until the wee hours of the morning listening to the radio and reading my beloved Taylor Caldwell books. I had a new appreciation of classical music – including opera – and theater. I watched old movies, the older the better. If it wasn't in black and white it wasn't old enough. I listened to radio theater as well. And I loved ballet. My cousin Britt and I insisted on watching Mikhail Baryshnikov in *The Nutcracker* every Christmas Eve at Gramma's. With Kim or Britt (or both, as they were friends as well), I saw *The Turning Point, The Sting,* and several other movies we probably had no business seeing at our ages.

Some Swedish cousins came to visit. Now the cute girls were beautiful teens, turning heads wherever they went. It was fun hanging out but I didn't have the same connection to them as the others did. I felt markedly different. I had wanted to fit in, to be Swedish, but instead was just a tag-along. The brown-eyed step-child.

They took sad pictures of themselves with Mom, who resembled a living skeleton at that point. They knew it would be the last time they saw her.

Visiting Gramma one day, our old cousin Eleanor remarked sadly over her coffee: "I cannot understand why I'm sitting here when I have no one and Lillian's up there suffering."

Every day, I walked the mile to the store to buy a can of Tab, then drank it walking home. That's as much as I got out. Late that summer, my cousin Linda complained to me that, because of my mother needing care, they had not been able to take a vacation. She "only" got to go to the east coast with a friend and her family made the usual trip to their beach house.

"Do you know where I went this summer?" I challenged. "The store."

I needed new clothes for school. Dad gave me his credit card with a note giving me his permission to use it and dropped me at the mall. I had no idea what I was doing but managed to find a few things, including a huge stuffed dog. I don't know why I thought I needed that except maybe as a last grasp at childhood. Dad certainly wasn't impressed, but it sat on my bed for years to come.

We had one last mother-daughter moment, Lillian and me. I finally started menstruating and ran to find Mom sitting quietly in her wheelchair. I knelt next to her and whispered, "Mom, I started my period." She searched my face with her sad eyes, trying so hard to talk, but could only cry. In her eyes I could see the longing of everything she wanted to say. Time was suspended. I endured reality.

In late August, Mom developed shingles. I considered this the final insult. As if she didn't have enough pain, now she moaned constantly. "Isn't there *anything* that will help?" I asked Mary when I thought I would go mad hearing Mom cry. Mary said no.

One night soon after, I heard Mary come into the room next to mine (where Dad slept), say something, then Dad's sharp response, "What?!" I fell back asleep. That morning things were different, but in my groggy state I couldn't figure out what it was. Finally it struck me.

"Where's Mom?" I asked when Dad came in, looking haggard.

"She... she died."

"Why didn't anyone tell me?!" I exploded. I hated being the last to know, as if I didn't matter. My mother died and they're just getting around to telling me? But I was also disturbed about something else and couldn't articulate it. In fact, I didn't want to think about it.

"I thought you should sleep. There was nothing anyone could do." He obviously didn't understand. I just needed to *know*.

I walked the mile to my cousin Jerome's for my summer babysitting gig. I told them what happened.

"You didn't have to come today," they exclaimed.

"That's okay. I wanted to." Dad took me going on as usual as a sign that I was taking it well, but I really just needed the quiet. I knew the phone would be ringing nonstop and people would start dropping by. I needed to prepare for the onslaught.

Later Britt, Linda, and Laurie came over. We vacillated between making prank calls, to sad, serious discussions.

"You were actually related to her. I wasn't," I said.

"That's not true, Noelle! She was your mother!"

Then why didn't I know when she died? I demanded, only to myself. For years I had experienced flashes of insight, dreams, and psychic feelings about a variety of things. I always thought I would know when Mom's time had come. Instead I slept through it, as unconcerned and unconnected as a stranger. The door had been shut with no good-bye.

Nearly as many came to her funeral as her wedding with many of the same names in the guest book. My friends and their mothers attended as well: Kim and Mrs. Kelemen, Renee and Mrs. Tanaka. Mrs. Bessette played piano. I know this but do not really remember. My only clear memory is looking over at Dad as we sat behind the privacy curtain to see him openly weep.

Before the burial Dad suddenly came into my room. "Do you want Lillian's ring?" She had a near-flawless emerald-cut diamond in a double platinum band. It had never been off her finger, even at the hospital. It was like a part of her. I couldn't imagine it anywhere but on her own hand and declined the offer. Only two days later I deeply regretted that decision but it was too late.

At some point I noticed that the mantle clock had stopped again. She was gone and so much was gone with her. She was right – She really did live in the Last Days. We just didn't realize it was exclusively for her.

I started high school, determined to make it work for me this time. But I was still sick so often I flunked some required classes due to absences. If it had been just the usual viruses (I caught all of them) and even the tonsillitis that developed twice a year, it may have been okay; but it was also the debilitating periods.

"It's not *normal,*" Dad kept saying, like if I would try just a little harder I would be healthy and by not doing so was a character flaw, a moral failing. I was taken to doctor after doctor.

I tried to explain how heavy the flow was, how bad the cramps were, how I felt sick and bloated and tender all the time. And there was something else.

At the beginning and end of each period there was a strange mucus that stunk. I found it on the tampons I had to wear along with the pads to confine the flow. It had a yellowish-green tinge and it was always in the same place, upper tampon, right side. I tried to explain it to Renee's mother one day when she took us shopping.

"That's not normal. You should see a doctor," said Mrs. Tanaka. Well, yes. This is how those appointments would go:

"Does this run in your family? Did your mother have periods like this?"

"I don't know. I'm adopted."

"Oh, well it really doesn't matter."

"Then why did you ask me?" There was never an answer to this question. They quickly moved on.

"Have you experienced any trauma recently?"

"My mother died," I would respond, wanting to be truthful. I could have added, "I watched her die for two years and before that my so-called brother violated me and I feel completely rootless and lost as an adoptee," but I felt freakish enough.

"It's a reaction to her mother's death," they would tell Aunt Betty, my designated mother-substitute. In other words, they had no idea. If they couldn't figure it out, I was emotionally unbalanced. My respect for the medical profession was not improving.

"If I broke my leg would that be a reaction to my mother's death too?" I shot back bitterly.

One doctor prescribed Valium, which I flushed down the toilet. Another (who never did one single thing right, down to misdiagnosing a heat rash on my arm) had me come in after hours for counseling. It didn't last long as we really had nothing to say to each other. Once, during another long wait in the exam room I saw my medical file that had been left by the nurse and was reading how dysfunctional I was when the doctor walked in.

"You're not supposed to look at that!" he said, snatching the folder from my hands.

"Why not? It's about me."

"But it isn't for you to read," he sputtered sternly. Amazing. Information about me, that could only matter to me, but I wasn't supposed to see it.

I endured many pelvic exams, always done by men and always done badly. I nearly went into shock from the first one. I told them – *I told them* – the spot was on my vaginal wall but all they looked at was my cervix.

No one really listened and no one took me seriously. No one.

I wanted to find my birth mother. But it didn't matter because I was fourteen and had absolutely no idea how to go about it. Not only that, I had no rights. I only knew I had an ever-deepening need to connect with someone biologically.

If I could find my birth mother she would understand my health problems, most importantly my periods.

If I could find my birth mother I could look at someone who actually looked like me and I would know where I came from.

If I could find my birth mother I would no longer feel adrift.

I mustered up the courage to tell Dad. Agitated, he paced the living room. "Why?" he demanded.

"I…I just need to see her," I said, suddenly unable to explain.

"If we hadn't gotten you, someone else would have!" he shouted, seemingly out of nowhere. I was always taken aback by these random things adults would say. His words cut me. He continued pacing.

"The day we were supposed to bring you home, the doctor told us we had to wait. *'Oh, that woman!'* he said." Again, I grappled with the meaning of this remark. I took it to mean there was something fundamentally wrong with my birth mother, or at least that was the doctor's opinion.

"Could I just see my birth certificate?" I said, finally. I knew they were kept in the safe. I had the idea there would be some clue on it that would lead me to her. He opened the safe and handed it over, warning me it wouldn't tell me anything I didn't already know.

I held it with trembling hands. For all appearances I was born to Walter and Lillian Ardahl. All the info was there, but altered to tear out the actual parents and replace with the legal ones. Signed by the doctor who delivered me and arranged the adoption, and stamped with a gold seal. It was all official. I was like a maple branch that had been ripped off and grafted onto a birch tree. At least if I was a tree, no one would insist I was a birch with no business wondering about the maple grove I came from. But since we were such a civilized society…

Tears ran silently down my face. I neve felt more alone.

Soon after I overheard Dad discussing this with Aunt Betty. "Of course she wants to search. She lost her mother and wants to replace her," Betty said with authority. I seethed. It was all so simplistic, so black and white to them, as long as it gave the answer they wanted. The problem was me, not the fact I was thrown into this bizarre social experiment called closed adoption and forced to play an endless game of pretend. Because that's what we were doing: pretending to be normal.

We were pretending the "as if born to" clause worked. Pretending genetics didn't matter. Pretending love conquers all. What did that get my adoptive parents? Two sons who never graduated from high school, one of them a violent criminal, a daughter who was constantly ill, a wife and mother dying an agonizingly slow death, a husband and father left alone to carry on.

And yet the game continued.

It became a burning need within me to find my birth mother. If this had been during the age of the internet or if at least my adoptive family would talk about *anything* I could have found support in a search-reunion group. My cousin Britt told me she heard you could get information from Remann Hall, the juvenile detention center. We called. I was informed by a sympathetic but firm woman there that no one could search before the age of eighteen. Four more years. It may as well have been fifty.

I had heard of people looking for others in classified ads. Maybe my birth mother would leave a cryptic message in the newspaper on my birthday? For some reason I was *sure* there would be a note for me. Even though I had no idea if she was still in the area, or if she thought I was, I was positive there would be a message. As Christmas neared I scanned the personal ads, looking for something in the tiny font that would give me hope.

"Learn to dance" said one in the short list. I scanned further.

"Divorce only $75," "Discreet Escort Services," and several other advertisements that were not so discreet.

Nothing. There was no message. I looked again and again. I checked every day. I was so sure something would be there. How could I have been wrong?

At this same time my uncle George decided to die. He simply went to bed one day and wouldn't get up. Dad called two of his nephews to come to the house, one being Jerome, the cousin I babysat for, the eldest son of the eldest son. I saw them standing just inside the door of George's room. Jerome said, "Why are you doing this, why won't you get up and eat?"

"I just don't want to," Uncle George said simply. They told him they'd be forced to take him to a hospital. He said he didn't care. It didn't take long. He died the week after Christmas. A very small service was held with only immediate family attending, not even cousins being informed. I think Dad and the others were embarrassed he had willed himself to die. They couldn't understand it.

Not long after that, Dad came to me with a troubled expression. He held Uncle George's will. "He left everything to Lillian," he said, bewildered. I looked and he had done just that, with no explanation.

When Mom had died an anonymous note for Dad came among the hundreds of condolence cards, urging him to make right his parents' estate. I was the one who opened that card and wondered what it could possibly mean. Dad was infuriated. He had a house built for his parents on his property. Their "estate" must have been a very meager one, with mostly just some furniture to divide. There was nothing to "make right." Dad confronted who he considered the most likely suspect (one of my aunts) but I never knew what happened afterwards.

He didn't need more trouble. Saying nothing to anyone else he had the will changed so the assets would be equally dispersed among the siblings. If he had left it alone, George's small estate would have gone only to Dad, being Lillian's next-of-kin, and if anyone complained they could have read the will themselves.

But Dad was practical to a fault. Although he worked hard for his money he was not greedy. The will was changed. We never spoke of it again.

I would sometimes go to the mall just to sit and watch people walk by, wondering about their secret lives. I had never considered someone like George, a casualty of battle fatigue, a mere shell of who he might have been, could have a secret life as well. Was he in love with Lillian? Or had he hoped to die first to show his gratitude to her for sharing her home all those years? She cared for him only out of a sense of family duty. Did he know that? He died almost four months to the day after she did. They were both in their early fifties and had not truly been alive for years.

As the long, dark days of winter set in, I took refuge in my room where I'd sit at my desk, reading and drawing. When I was deep in thought it started. My stereo wandered off-station, as if someone turned the knob. I got up and adjusted it. Settling in to my daydream, it happened again. The setting moved to the next station over. Then a book on my desk fell over on its own. I jumped. I felt someone watching me.

I whirled around in my chair, half-expecting to see a ghost. There was nothing – just my room as usual. I decided to calm my nerves with a cup of tea. The house was very quiet as I was the only one home. In the kitchen I tried to make sense of what happened. Although I believed in paranormal activity my dad was firm that the source of anything mysterious could be found "in a bottle of wine," while Mom believed ghosts were demons impersonating loved ones, because *When we are absent from the body we are present in the Lord.* (2ⁿᵈ Corinthians 5:8)

So what was happening? Was Mom trying to get my attention? She had died here in the house, in her bedroom; some part of her – a memory, a remnant – could still be here. Did she have a message for me? Was she finally trying to say good-bye?

I jumped again as a baking pan rattled on the counter. "What? What is it?" I said aloud, looking all around, hoping to see a misty figure, or for a note to suddenly appear. I waited, straining every sense, but there was only silence.

The radio would wander off-station often after that, when I was alone and deep in thought. And small objects such as pencils would roll on my desk. "Stop it!" I finally said. I was angry. What was the point? Where was the message? All I had was irritation followed by silence, as if I was being teased by an unseen little brother. If this was Mom telling me I wasn't alone she had a strange way of showing it. Still, I held onto the idea that she was reaching out through the Cosmos, only to me.

New Year's Eve we went to Gramma's. This was unusual. We usually didn't do anything for New Year's. Maybe they needed to get together one more time because they were missing Lillian and took comfort in each others' presence. Whenever we gathered in that first year after she died they would openly weep at the mere mention of her name.

It was a dull affair. That much I remember. At one point we went around saying what we were thankful for. I said something mildly snarky (which would be considered *normal* for a teenager, I'd like to point out) about making it into high school. A cousin's distant cousin was there: Tammy. She was about my age, adopted, and a spoiled brat.

Once I asked one of my aunts point blank if Tammy was actually her adopted parents' granddaughter, a child of their much older biological daughter. I asked because of the remarkable physical resemblance between all of them. I knew back in the 1960s parents could "order" babies with coloring similar to their own, but this went far beyond that. You cannot predetermine bone structure or expression.

"Don't even say that!" was the response.

"Why not?" I reasoned. "She looks just like them."

"She does *not*." Okayyyyyyy. The fact her face was nearly interchangeable with her adopted mother's seemed to be lost on them. Or the obvious needed to be ignored.

At the time Tammy and I were born it was very important to hide pregnancies of unmarried daughters. It was not far-fetched that if a young daughter became pregnant out of wedlock that the parents would create a ruse; in fact quite often the "parents" people grew up with were really grandparents with an older sister being their birth mother. That was true for musicians Bobby Darin and Eric Clapton, both of whom were devastated at the discovery of the deception.

On the other hand, when actor Jack Nicholson was informed by a reporter that his deceased older "sister" was actually his mother, he absorbed the news without trauma, saying it actually "made…things clearer" and felt relieved to finally know the truth.

Judy Lewis, "adopted" daughter of actress Loretta Young learned as an adult she wasn't adopted at all, but was conceived on location of *Call of the Wild* by her mother and actor Clark Gable. Ms. Young's reputation was on the line. While she couldn't bear a child as an unmarried woman in the 1930s, she *could* adopt one and so, following Ms. Young's "mysterious illness" in Europe, the baby was put in an orphanage and "adopted" a year and a half later. At twenty-three the daughter felt she couldn't marry because she knew nothing about her background. Her fiancé was the one who told her the truth. She was the only one who did not know; everyone else did but kept the secret.

When we were adopted in the 1960s it was all about honesty (even though there was scant information given) but to say the child was "chosen". "Other parents have to take what they get. We got to *choose* you!" As if we were produce at the grocery store.

By then the mother/grandmother switch was not encouraged. But if the original family did not want to adopt the baby out and at the same time did not want their daughter's reputation tarnished, it was still a possibility.

Tammy was completely undisciplined. There was no evidence of that with the older daughter. Why would a happily married couple raise their biological daughter the "right" way then turn around and raise their adopted daughter the "wrong" way? Guilt? They wanted different results? I don't know.

But even if I was completely wrong – even if she was adopted because they could have no more children and wanted another, even if Tammy was born to total strangers of no biological relation to them – why deny the glaring physical similarities? Usually people go out of their way to find a resemblance, almost as a concession that adoption really *is* like birthing your own. They did the opposite.

Back at the New Year's Eve party. Tammy's answer, in syrupy tones:

"I'm just grateful I was adopted."

Murmurs of approval went up from everyone but me. I felt bile rise in my throat.

"Aren't you grateful?"

It came back to me as fresh as that day in first grade. What did I have to be grateful for, again? Death? Separation? Violation and pain? Was it supposed to be because I was rescued from my lowly state of being a bastard? "Given a name?" Dad threw it in my face that if they hadn't adopted me someone else would have. I was a commodity. We were never given the "chosen baby" story, but now I had to think about how I could have ended up anywhere, that there was no Grand Design. *"God has great plans for your life."* Yeah, sure He does.

And I was supposed to be grateful. Eternally grateful. It was my first encounter with the Good Adoptee. Even though she acted "badly," Tammy was a Good Adoptee. Good adoptees are grateful. They ask no questions. They spend their lives trying to be good enough to belong to their parents. Bad adoptees act as though they really do belong. They ask inappropriate questions. They challenge. Ironically, they act "as if born to" with their sense of entitlement. I was a Bad Adoptee. Society wants to play this game until it comes to the adoptee being as ungrateful as a "real" child. Then it becomes a problem. And the problem is the child. And the child is never allowed to grow up.

For what seemed like a very long time, days ran together endlessly and I can only remember select scenes. I was in a constant state of near-despair. Every night I went to bed hoping I wouldn't wake up in the morning. No thoughts of suicide – I didn't want to kill myself – I just wanted to go away, disappear, cease to exist. When you feel as if you've come from nothing (adopted, not born) it's almost a comforting thought to go back to nothing.

The pencils and radio knob stopped moving of their own accord. I was both relieved and wistful. That phenomenon lasted just a few months and never happened in the presence of others. I had wanted my mother to say good-bye; if she had been haunting me she never made the reason clear. I missed her but it was obvious I was not going to get closure. Apparently missing someone is not a good enough reason. I was waiting for something. Waiting, and not knowing if it would ever come.

Whenever Keith wasn't around, John and I could relax. He had his drivers license and an old station wagon, both of which I made good use of. I cajoled him into taking me to see *All That Jazz* at the movies, *Anything Goes* at a community college and even *The Nutcracker*, performed by a local ballet company. It was the first time I had seen ballet live. I was riveted. John was bored out of his skull.

Aunt Betty didn't approve of me hanging out with John. She openly blamed Keith as being the source of stress that caused her sister's fatal stroke. And no one would disagree with that but she was one of the few bold enough to verbalize it. She didn't stop there, though. "John's not lily-white, either," she warned, meaning I-don't-know-what. Without Keith around, John could really be himself: a quiet guy who loved animals and motorcycles and *Looney Tunes*. He certainly wasn't a threat. He just didn't match the rest of the family, but that was why I liked him. Besides being my brother and childhood playmate, we were both "different" in the same way because we didn't fit in. We didn't really have conversations; we were just together. Of course John didn't talk much anyway. Dad nicknamed him "The Shadow" for his ability to seemingly appear and disappear from a room. He walked quietly, spoke little, and had a calm demeanor that made all animals love him.

At the beginning of my sophomore year I had a boyfriend. I had decided, as a mature fifteen year old, that I would never date anyone from my own school. I didn't like the gossip and the drama. As it happened I met a boy from another school (our dreaded rivals, in fact) at a wedding reception.

Knowing just about everyone leads to a lot of wedding invitations. One family Dad knew well was Italian. All their weddings were at the Catholic church in the valley. That's where I met Mark Rossi.

He was a year older than I was and had a car. He was funny and easy to talk to. He asked for my phone number and I was over the moon when he actually called me. Our first date was to the Puyallup Fair. Before I left, Dad gave me

$10, "So you won't owe him anything," he said, simply. I tried not to smile at this. When Mark dropped me off that evening I gave him the money. "You don't have to do that," he said, rather taken aback. "Try explaining that to my father," I replied.

My grandmother was concerned. "Is he a Christian?" she asked. "He's Catholic," I answered, not knowing if that answered her question. She shook her head. "*Oj-oj-oj.*"[2]

Our relationship lasted four months. It involved movies, pizza, and a lot of kissing on the couch in the rec room. A lot of kissing. Some of it in a horizontal position.

It ended when he suddenly stopped calling me around my birthday. I didn't know what happened, in fact I still don't. But there had been no declarations of love or promises made. And with that there were also no regrets. It really was the perfect first relationship. It had been fun but now it was over. I was secretly relieved to know I could experience sexual arousal from another person. It made me feel...normal.

I liked some aspects of high school. While junior high felt like a prison, this was more like involuntary servitude. I liked being able to take classes I was interested in but at the same time despised the required ones. It wasn't the classes or teachers themselves (okay, sometimes it was), it was the fact I had no choice in the matter. If I didn't take these classes I would not get credit and if I didn't have enough credits I would not graduate. And that meant being a Failure to Society. The senior class when I started high school had a lower credit requirement and they seemed to me as intelligent and worthy as anyone. I resented how we were forced to stay in class longer while they were allowed free time, enough to hold jobs during school hours.

One class I liked was American History, because it was taught by a man who wasn't afraid to speak his mind. Instead of teaching from the dry textbooks he told us outright why the internment of the Japanese was wrong and gave us

---

2 "Oj-oj-oj" is the Swedish equivalent of the Spanish "Ay-ay-ay" and rhymes with "boy". Both translate to "Oh!" and are often used when one is at a loss for words.

personal accounts of growing up in a segregated society. I got the feeling though, that I sometimes knew too much.

We were learning about the Iron Curtain following WWII and he said three European countries were absorbed into the Soviet Union as if they didn't exist: "Latvia, Lithuania and..." He drew a blank.

"Estonia," I offered.

"What?"

"Estonia," I said. I knew this from National Geographic magazines and my love of maps.

"Why do you know that?" he said. I was confused by the question. Why? *Why* did I know that? Not "How" not "Oh thanks, that's what I meant," but "*Why* do you know that?"

"Why don't *you* know that?" I finally responded.

There was a reason I specifically knew about Estonia and such. These countries had a double status. To the West they were still the Baltic States. To the Eastern Bloc they were republics of the USSR. I felt an affinity to them with their dual identities and their long fight to be recognized as individuals. Fighting to be themselves.

I attended a mother-daughter tea with my grandmother, aunts and cousins at the Baptist church. I had been to many teas there with Mom. She used to make us matching dresses, which I loved. Now instead of a special dress I was given a white corsage, signifying my mother was dead. It made me feel very alone in a crush of family.

I wondered – If my birth mother was alive and everyone knew it, would I still be wearing a white corsage? As long as I was with these familiar faces there was no other mother. But I was two people: one born to and one adopted. We were pretending only the adopted one was real.

After Mom died, Dad merely existed. He continued to work every day, both at the shop and at home but was really just going through the motions. Friends and family stopped by almost daily. I attempted to play hostess.

Dad hired a housekeeper: Della. He wanted someone to cook dinner and keep house so I could concentrate on school. About all I remember about Della was her black hair and her stories about how hair dye causes cancer and that they used kerosene to get rid of head lice. And that she was completely ineffective as a housekeeper. She was soon replaced with Stella. Stella made me long for the days with Della.

She was one of those women of a certain age. Completely colorless. While Della bragged about her shiny black hair and how she looked twenty years younger than her actual age, Stella could make no such claims. Her complexion resembled uncooked bread dough; her oversized glasses made her eyes nearly disappear; and her hair seemed to have no color at all. I cannot remember if she was widowed or divorced, but she had an adult daughter.

She quickly inserted herself as the alpha female. Or, she tried.

She insisted on a certain cleaning product that was found only at the mall and we bought it for her. She then spent the better part of one day scrubbing a bathroom door with it. Dad was not impressed. Nearly every day upon coming home from school I'd find her on the phone. "Well I have to go," she'd say to the caller, cheerfully, as if it had been a five-minute coffee break. Even though no matter when I arrived I'd find her there, just getting off the phone. Then she tried making friends with me.

Being in school all day is hard enough for an introvert. When I got home the last thing I wanted to do was "chat" and "get to know each other" with some hideous old bag. I wanted to be left alone, have a cup of tea and maybe watch *The Three o'Clock Movie*. This offended her. I soon found out why.

She kept asking questions about Dad, about Mom, about our lives in general. I answered unenthusiastically. One day she asked to see a picture of Lillian so I showed her a colored 8 x 10. The next day when I walked in her otherwise blasé hair was a brilliant shade of red.

"You...um...colored your hair," I managed to say, not knowing if I should laugh or be angry at this blatant attempt to usurp my mother's memory.

"Yes, do you like it?" she replied. Too stunned to answer, I took my tea and wandered to the living room, hoping *The Three o'Clock Movie* was a good one.

Stella followed.

The movie was *Showboat,* which I loved. Stella kept talking. I wanted to hear the movie and not have to think about what she was up to. I gave monosyllable replies. Finally she talked through "Old Man River" which should be a crime because it's one of the best songs ever written. To get my attention she tried to talk about music, calling "Old Man River" a Negro spiritual.

"It's a ballad," I said flatly.

"Of course, it's that *too,*" she replied, encouraged she had me engaged in conversation now.

"No, it's not a Negro spiritual if it wasn't written by black slaves or at least their descendants. This was written by some white guys to sound something *like* a Negro spiritual."

She got up and went back to the kitchen, furiously chopped vegetables, then stormed back.

"I know! I certainly know the difference between a ballad and a spiritual!" she declared fiercely, shaking the paring knife for emphasis before stomping back to the kitchen.

Well good for you, I thought. That night Dad glanced nervously at Stella's red hair but said nothing. Not long after he confided, "Stella asked me to drive her to eastern Washington for some family reunion. What does she *want?*"

"It's obvious she wants you, Dad." And she wasn't the only one. As a handsome and healthy widower in his fifties, he was in high demand. His reaction to the unwanted attention was to dig deeper into his work. He rarely left his shop. These forward women made him uneasy. He did not drive Stella to eastern Washington or anywhere. When the end of the school year came he told her I would take care of the place for the summer. And when summer was over she was informed her services were no longer needed. She brought her daughter over to see for herself. I had the place spotless since I knew how to keep house by then.

"Don't you need some help?" she asked hopefully. Her daughter nodded encouragingly.

"No, I think we're fine. Thanks." We gave her some canning jars as a lovely parting gift and that was the end of our housekeeper era.

I found my niche in the music/drama department. Not that I was a gifted musician, but passable, and I enjoyed being with the others. I had taken piano lessons from Mrs. Bessette for years, even continuing after Mom died. I really didn't need it anymore but found the weekly 30 minute sessions with my old teacher a pleasant ritual.

"You're going to be a teacher," she said proudly. This was a high compliment in her opinion. I had no desire to be a teacher. In fact I couldn't think of anything much worse.

My group of closest friends formed during the musicals and plays. I was okay with performing but would much rather be "in the pit". Either genetically or via my Nordic upbringing, I did not like to draw attention to myself but at the same time felt a heavy responsibility to not let anyone down. If I made a mistake that affected anyone else I could barely sleep that night.

My taste in music expanded again. Now besides classical, gospel, blues and jazz, I also liked what is now called classic rock. Back then it was just rock and we liked it loud: Van Halen, Pink Floyd, Fleetwood Mac and U2. But I had a special affinity for Led Zeppelin. It was more interesting to listen to, more complicated, like jazz.

I was known for being, alternately: nice, a bitch, friendly, stand-offish, funny, serious, sarcastic (what teenager isn't?), smart, or a smart ass. That last one was leveled at me by another student during what must have been the worst class in all my years in high school. A required social studies course whose sole point seemed to be to make us hate ourselves as Americans. When I once again could not refrain from correcting the teacher, a boy turned to me and asked me if I liked being a smart ass. I considered for a moment then said I'd rather be that than a dumb one.

I discovered something important one day in the school library. Three other girls sat with me at a table. We weren't talking, we weren't reading, we were together but we were alone. I was struck by this. No matter how we presented ourselves in other situations, here – with others like ourselves – we were resolutely silent. We had a certain seriousness, a posture, a set of the jaw, and a shell we had to leave whenever we interacted with others. Then it hit me: We had all lost our mothers. One in a crash, one to a heart attack and two to strokes. No matter how long it had been, if the death was expected, or if a step-mother was now in the picture, we were all still somehow changed. Steeled as if for the next blow.

My friends' mothers didn't like me at this point. Or at least they did not approve of me. Even the ones who knew my mother and had treated me like their own daughter in years past seemed to think I was now a bad influence. They thought I drank, used drugs, and slept around, when I did none of those things. Maybe it was the steely resolve combined with missing out on a normal adolescence that made me appear "bad" to them. I wasn't like their own daughters any longer. I was tainted. I was different. I was dangerous.

The band room became my new safe haven. And Mr. Donaldson, band director, became my new favorite adult. Although he was married and a father, he considered himself to be a kid like the rest of us. He loved music, loved to laugh and enjoyed being with us as much as we enjoyed being with him. He welcomed us into his home and his life and seemed not to separate his work from his family. We would have followed him anywhere, like the charm of *The Music Man*'s title character Harold Hill. He wrote in my senior year book:

"I've tried saying it from time to time – I shall miss you much – you have added personality, charm, beauty and most of all a very nice person that has made my job a real pleasure. It is these talented people that strive, dig in, work, care, and are not afraid to give their time and talent that makes it all count. I sincerely hope that you have many, many great memories. Let me know how you're doing from time to time but most of all may your shadow fall in the nicest of places. It indeed has been an honor and a pleasure knowing you."

He tragically died soon after. He was so young – younger than my mother when she died. The first time I watched *The Music Man* years later I had to stop the tape, overwhelmed by the memories.

In my circle of friends I found family. Brothers and sisters. And I could have (and maybe should have) left it at that.

Dad and I were out to dinner and he had a lot on his mind. Keith had been thrown in jail again. I don't know what for, I didn't try to keep track. Could have been theft, drug possession, assault or a combination of all three. I was always more at ease whenever he was incarcerated so I hoped he would just keep screwing up. Dad didn't have it so easy.

"Should I bail him out?" The question was torturing him.

"No," I said firmly.

"If I do he'll just get into trouble again."

"That's right."

"But if I don't he'll hold it against me." (translation: take revenge)

"He'd find something to hold against you no matter what you did."

"Leaving him there is the right thing to do," he said.

"You're right," I said.

He bailed him out the next day.

Chapter 5
~Love, again~

Without Mom it was like Dad had lost a limb. Their marriage was very traditional – she had been his helpmeet. They needed each other and each was a compliment to the other. Without a spouse, it was like part of him was missing.

He was not the type to date, though. Or to look for dates. And the women who pursued him sabotaged themselves by doing so because he didn't like being chased. Besides, they weren't his type. He liked vivacious women who did not necessarily need him. Enter Carol Edmonds.

I had known her all my life. She was part of the neighborhood. Once Dad and I drove past her house.

"See that place? Carol Edmonds lives there. She takes care of her two kids and her mother all by herself," Dad said with much admiration.

The first time I remember meeting her I was very young. She came to the front door because Dad was going to work on her car. Even after deciding to no longer service his customers at home, Dad always took care of people who were alone in some way: elderly, widowed, never married or – in Carol's case – divorced.

There she stood, slender and petite with her wavy silver-blonde hair, youthful yet tasteful outfit and the ever-present smile. "Hi, I'm Carol!" she said while doing a little twist, pulling herself up straighter. I liked her. She was happy. Not like the grumpy, frumpy middle-aged women I usually encountered.

She had been divorced as long as I had been alive. How she managed to stay single all those years was by focusing on her mother and kids. Nothing was allowed to take priority over those relationships. Besides, she was their sole support. She didn't date. I doubt anyone suggested she wasn't "serious" about her job as it often was said to women in the 1960s, but when she was a new-hire, her male co-workers thought she was a hot divorcée there with the objective to get laid. They rudely asked what happened to her marriage.

"My husband got sick of me and left. Someone has to feed the kids," she answered simply. After that they looked after her like a sister. She also earned their respect. If it snowed she slept on the couch in the break room so the weather wouldn't keep her from coming in. She didn't gossip and didn't complain, just minded her own business, did her job and did it well. She earned more per hour than Dad.

Her kids were also adopted and that was another reason why I liked her – we had something in common.

Some time after Stella was banished, Carol was having trouble with her Chevrolet. "Take it to Walt. He'll fix it," advised her friends. "Oh, I don't want to bother him," she said, knowing people were forever dropping by for car advice. But the problem remained and finally Carol brought it over.

Dad quickly remedied the situation and started to walk away. Then before she knew what she was saying, the committedly-single Carol blurted out: "Would you like to come over for dinner?"

"He just looked so *sad*," she told me later. Carol fixed the troubles of the world with food. If she fed you it was her way of saying she loved you.

Dad wouldn't be sad much, if ever, after that moment. Or hungry. Love had unexpectedly arrived.

It took some adjusting, of course. Especially for Carol. The first morning after they were back from their honeymoon I was at the kitchen table reading the paper. Dad was already up and had started his morning routine. Carol tore down the stairs, yelling, "Fire! Fire!"

"Carol, there's no fire. Dad's making toast," I said casually of the smoke billowing from the toaster.

"Well I hope he doesn't expect *me* to cook like that!" she said, recovering. I hated to tell her but actually, yes, he did. His one complaint about Lillian's cooking was that it was never "done" enough. His idea of done was to cook something until all the flavor, texture, color, and nutrients were destroyed. Otherwise, bread was just "warmed-over dough."

"Dad, if it was supposed to be that way it would be called 'incinerate', not 'toast'," I tried to reason. He kept eating it black and smoldering regardless. It was good to be able to see the humor in things again, even if unintentional. And over time, Carol did get Dad to eat food less…charred.

She had two kids: Shelley and Tom. Both adopted. Tom ruggedly handsome, smart, and athletic. A real All-American. But Shelley, while a natural in subjects like computer programming, struggled. She was attractive but didn't seem to think much of herself. Maybe it was too difficult living in her little brother's shadow, maybe it was because she didn't resemble her adopted family at all, or maybe it was because she battled alcoholism, but she had a hard life. They were already out on their own when Dad and Carol married. But one night Shelley came by, drunk, and needing to talk.

I didn't want Carol staying up by herself so I joined them in the rec room, where Carol kept awake by exercising and even standing on her head. It was surreal – Carol on her head and Shelley rambling on about her life and how it was in shambles.

"I think everything would have been different if we hadn't lost Susan," Shelley said suddenly. That got my attention.

"Who is Susan?"

They looked at each other. Carol giggled nervously. Shelley said, "Oh, she was another kid we had, but she wandered off," and laughed shortly.

The truth was there had been another daughter, the youngest child. By then Carol's marriage was falling apart, but she kept a brave front. When it came time to divorce she said, "Just let me have the kids – that's all I want!" and didn't even get that. Her selfish husband couldn't be bothered to come to court to make Susan's adoption final. The judge heard of the impending divorce and with stunning cruelty the baby was taken. A daughter, sister, granddaughter, niece – gone – as suddenly as if she had been kidnapped.

Carol broke down. She threw away everything associated with Susan, not keeping a single photo or token. She couldn't eat or sleep and dropped to a mere eighty pounds before pulling herself together with the thought that her two remaining children needed her. People were already put through hell to qualify for adoption. To think she had proven herself three times only to have the baby taken – by the State, not even the birth mother – still leaves me reeling. She was deemed worthy of motherhood until her cad of a husband left her for another woman, then she wasn't good enough anymore.

I didn't know her prior to this. I only knew Carol as being fiercely loving and loyal to her children and that they were obviously her reason to live. And it was very important to her that we were included into the fold. She fussed over us, making favorite dishes, even for Keith, who repaid her with crude insults. She was born to be a mom and was determined to mother us. Especially me.

When Carol married Dad, her mother didn't believe we were adopted too. She thought Carol was the only woman on earth who couldn't have a baby. After getting to know us, she revised her stance:

"Well, Keith and John might be adopted, but Noelle isn't. She looks just like Lillian and acts just like Walt!" I liked Gramma Millie. She was a funny little thing.

I didn't ask any more questions about Susan because the mere mention of her name made Carol cry and I couldn't stand to see her cry. I did think about Susan though, like I did with my "almost siblings", the ones our doctor offered but my parents did not take. I wondered if we would have known each other in school and if we would have been friends. Would Carol still be married to Dad? Does everything align in the Cosmos to make these things happen regardless? And was Shelley right – would her life have been so different that she would not have taken up alcohol as a teen? It must have been bewildering for her as a little girl trying to make sense of having a baby sister and then not, as if Susan had never existed. No funeral, no good-bye, just *gone*.

And I wondered where Susan was now, what her name was, where she lived. Was she secure in the knowledge she had once been the beloved child of another family or did she feel twice abandoned? The cruel irony of adoption is that one parent's joy comes at the expense of another's grief. In the case of a baby known briefly as Susan, two mothers were left grieving.

Keith finally screwed up bad enough to go to prison. I'm fairly certain it was for when he slammed some guy's head in a car door. Several times. Dad blamed it on "dope," meaning any sort of illegal drug, as if this behavior started when he was a teenager. But I remembered an eight-year-old boy peeling the shells off robin eggs. Frankly I didn't care why he was put away as long as he stayed there. I could breathe again.

Gramma never really changed, except her hair went from gray to silver to white and she shrunk as she aged. She came to America as a young bride, not expecting to stay. Her husband told her it was just a visit. The visit was rather extended, lasting seventy years, although she did return to visit Sweden several times.

She ran their egg business with hundreds of chickens, milked cows, harvested apples from the orchard to make applesauce and cider, put up vegetables from the garden, kept house, raised three children, and still had time for church and socializing.

She had worried at one time that she would not live to see grandchildren. The first did not arrive until she was sixty-five. She married "late" (in her twenties) and had children late as well. Then her children went on to do the same. Still, being Swedish they could take their time, being a long-lived lot.

With a mischievous twinkle in her green eyes, she would blithely cheat at board games and yet she was the most honest person you'd ever meet. Never in a hurry and yet never idle. Unconcerned about worldly affairs but prayerful of all. No matter what she was doing, if company stopped by (as they often did) she had time for coffee and cookies.

She always wore a dress with a light sweater – wool in the winter, cotton in the summer. Never pants, even when gardening. Her daughter Lillian got her to don a modern pant-suit in the 1970s and Gramma wore it just long enough to provide photographic evidence. One snapshot. She looked extremely uncomfortable.

Next to her old brick house was a little garden containing a riot of flowers: roses, lilies, dahlias, lilac, snapdragon, daffodils, gladiolas, tulips, forsythia and interspersed everywhere were tiny blue forget-me-knots. She loved flowers. Her daughter Betty often brought her bouquets to display indoors as well. Even now when I see a wild-colored mix of flowers I think of her.

"I'm going to Gramma's," I'd say in passing to Dad on my way through the woods leading to her back door. If I timed it right she would just be taking bread out of the oven. She made sweet, dense bread on baking sheets. In Sweden it was called simply *bröd*, but we grandkids dubbed it *mor*[3] bread and the name forever stuck. There was no recipe, she never made it the same way twice, and yet it was perfect every time. It was a necessary staple at every holiday dinner but it was available almost always.

When any of us would stop by we would make ourselves at home: watch TV, snack, read the old books and magazines she never threw away, color on the butcher paper she kept in the kitchen cabinet, collect eggs from the chickens, or help around the house or yard. She carefully paced herself all day, doing fine crochet work one moment, gardening the next, then having a cup of coffee and reading her *Guideposts* magazines. I think because she never learned to drive she did not feel pressured to always "go do something."

When we grandchildren were old enough to drive we took pleasure in taking her to church or out to eat. She discovered pizza in her eighties, her favorite being pepperoni. She enjoyed unusual food combinations, like baloney with tuna sandwiches. Considering how she ate, I'm not sure how she outlived all her siblings who followed a traditional Scandinavian diet and lifestyle.

Her only health concern even in her nineties was shortness of breath and developing bronchitis every winter. I asked her about that because everyone else I knew with chronic bronchitis had been raised around cigarette smoke and she certainly hadn't.

"My mother smoked a pipe," she told me with a gentle wheeze. "They thought it was healthy – kept away worms."

I loved her for the same reason I loved my father: She never treated me as if I was adopted. Beyond recounting how "Lillian was as proud as a peacock" that Christmas Eve when I debuted, the only thing she ever said about adoption was to express bewilderment at how any woman could relinquish a child. It was

---

3 *Bröd* = bread. *Mor* = mother, pronounced "more". *Mor-mor* = grandmother, or "mother's mother".

completely beyond her. "How could a mother give away her baby?" she would say, shaking her head. Of course I didn't have an answer since I knew nothing about my own relinquishment beyond the fact that my biological parents weren't married. Gramma's solution was to "get married, then." I suggested there could be complications; maybe one parent was already married, or was a criminal, or they were impoverished.

She just shook her head. No reason existed that made sense to her.

Everyone loved her. When she turned ninety a crush of people descended on her house to wish her well. She was Maria, Mom, Mor-Mor, Tant Maria and Auntie but most simply called her Gramma if she was a relation or not.

I remember her prior birthday even more clearly though. I stopped by, expecting to find at least a few others there, but we were alone. She was feeling reflective and told me about her will. "A third and a third and a third," she said in her pretty Swedish accent, "And Lillian's third divided by three. That's fair," she said, nodding, satisfied. A third of her farm to each of her three children, with Mom's share divided between Keith, John and me. I didn't think much about it. What would I inherit, an apple tree and a cow? But I appreciated how she wanted to keep it fair. She then told me she had offered my dad Lillian's share when Mom died but that Dad wouldn't take it. It came as no surprise to me that Dad wouldn't accept such an offer. He also liked to keep things "fair."

Dad didn't mention that to me but he did tell me Gramma came to him some time before with her will, worried. She asked him to look at it because she didn't think it was what she had asked for. She loved her son Clarence like Lillian had loved him: wholeheartedly but with eyes wide open. Either she asked him to have the will drawn up or it was his idea, but when it was done it was her son-in-law she approached for advice.

Dad reminded her he was a mechanic, not a lawyer. "But I'll take it to a friend at the bank. He'll understand it." The banker's opinion: "This will was written for Clarence." He was to get nearly everything, with only a small mention of his living sister and none at all of his late sister Lillian. Dad reported back to Gramma. She had the will redone. That was when she was eighty-nine.

I was horribly nearsighted, diagnosed at age twelve and given thick, ugly glasses – so heavy they gave me a headache to wear them. Instead I went without and asked to sit in the front row for all my classes.

With the onset of menstruation I started having low back aches. No amount of pain killers or stretches or use of a heating pad helped.

As in elementary school, I caught every cold and "flu bug" going around. I was assured that this was actually making me stronger, building my immunity. "I should be immune from everything soon," I said, ruefully. I couldn't wrap my brain around the idea of being sick as "good for you". Wasn't that the idea behind immunizations, that we couldn't take the chance of getting a disease because it made us *weaker*?

Starting in junior high, I went to the doctor for tonsillitis twice a year on average, where I was assured the antibiotics would clear up the infection. I kept asking, "Why not just take them out?" and was told having tonsils was good for me. I could not see how something that became inflamed and infected every six months could be "good for me." Also the antibiotics stopped working. First I was given sulfa, then tetracycline, and finally a form of penicillin. When one stopped being effective I was given another. If it was strong enough to work it made me sick to my stomach.

And of course my periods had not "settled down" as doctors assured me they would. I was sick from one thing or another nearly all the time. I couldn't remember what it was like to feel healthy.

My younger cousin Laurie said to me about my absences, "I miss about two days of school a year, so I figure that's normal." Thank you. I didn't feel nearly weird enough already.

While looking for more pain reliever in the kitchen cupboard I came across a bottle of iron tablets. My mother's. It had been there at least five years, untouched. I had heard iron was good for the blood so took one. The next day the backache was gone. To see if this was a coincidence I didn't take the iron for a few days. The backache returned. Took the iron = backache gone. After that I took one every day. I told my doctor on the next visit about my wonderful discovery. "That couldn't possibly make any difference," he stated. "There's no connection."

I had less regard for doctors with every appointment.

When I was seventeen I was talking with another girl in band and the subject of bad periods came up. She told me she had the problem opposite of mine – she almost never menstruated. To normalize her cycle she was put on birth control pills. "I can't believe your doctor never suggested it. You should try them," she said. Somehow I *could* believe my doctors did not suggest something that might actually help, so I made an appointment with a gynecologist. I came out with a prescription for Ortho Novum 35 and a name for my condition: dysmenorrhea, combined with menorrhagia.

All those terms mean are a painful period and excessive bleeding, simply describing the symptoms, not giving a cause for the condition. Though it sounded like a junk diagnosis I didn't care. Just to have someone say, *Yes, this is really happening and no, you shouldn't have to live like this* was all I needed. Feeling triumphant, I told my cousin Laurie.

"You mean there's really something wrong with you?" she replied. I let it go. Like Dad, if she couldn't personally relate it was highly unlikely to be real.

At first when I took the Pill it was like driving into a brick wall then throwing the car into reverse. Eventually my body adjusted and I had a single period every twenty-eight days with much less blood flow. I couldn't believe it. I felt *healthy.*

Around the same time I got soft contact lenses. Suddenly I could see. Trees had leaves again. I didn't have to sit in the front of class to see the blackboard. The whole world opened up.

And at some point the spot on my tampons disappeared. I was so accustomed to seeing it that it took me awhile to realize it wasn't there anymore.

The passing viruses and tonsillitis remained. But for the first time in years I really felt there was something worth living for. The nightly wish to not wake up in the morning was gone.

Carol was finding her way in this new family. Dad's side treated her as if she had always been there. But she also had to integrate into Lillian's family. She lived in "Lillian's house" with "Lillian's things" and on the same plot of land as

Lillian's immediate family.

We had not made the house into a shrine, but we did tend to leave things as they were. Mom's cookbooks, special tablecloths and dishes, holiday decorations - all were just as she left them. I would take things out occasionally to wash them then put them back. It never occurred to me to do anything else with them. Carol brought some of her own furnishings and décor, although most was left with her mother in the house across town.

Before they married, Dad bought new carpet, curtains, and furniture for the living room. I picked it out. It was needed but Gramma asked with a twinkle in her eyes, "Is someone getting married?" Carol was so friendly no one could help but like her and everyone attributed the positive change in Dad to her. She and Gramma really took a shine to each other. Just as Mom used to go next door on Saturday nights and "put up" her mother's hair, Carol now took over that duty. Sometimes I'd go along and watch; Gramma at the dining room table, Carol standing behind her, expertly twisting the wispy white locks with Dippity-do and securing with bobby pins, the air filled with chatter and laughter. Although Carol did not resemble Lillian at all, in this one way it was almost like reincarnation.

The mere mention of Lillian's name still made her sister's eyes well with tears. But at a church-sponsored bridal shower for cousin Christie, Betty introduced Carol as her sister-in-law. I later overheard the woman on the other end of the introduction ask if Carol had "taken Lillian's place." I interjected, "No, she's just expanding her own."

It actually seemed harder for Aunt Evelyn. I think she was jealous of the instant camaraderie between Gramma and Carol. Evelyn was like the Prodigal Son's forgotten brother – the one who stayed and didn't realize he was being rewarded constantly by doing so. Evelyn kept her own house and yard immaculate, grew a garden every year, and was a wonderful cook. She also worked just as hard on Gramma's farm and everyone knew it. Her position was secure, but she was resentful. When Gramma "gave" Carol one of her apple trees, saying anything that came from that tree was hers to use, Evelyn was ready to spit nails. We were all in Gramma's old cellar-type basement one evening in the fall, pressing cider, when Ev tried to pick a fight with Carol. Gramma told her in no uncertain terms to knock it off. No one else would dare talk to Evelyn that way, but no one in their right mind would argue with Gramma either.

Another time Aunt Ev tried to fight with Dad. Gramma wanted to give something to Dad and Evelyn didn't want him to have it. Turning her tiny but powerful frame toward Evelyn, Gramma declared, "Walter is as much my son-in-law as you are my daughter-in-law!"

And that was the end of that.

Carol and I were very different, just as Lillian and I were very different, but we found our common ground. The one thing we never agreed on was how to load the dishwasher. If she had it half-done I'd take everything out, rinse, and reload. It had to make sense to me, have some order. Carol couldn't be bothered with such niceties. She liked everything done *fast*; she had no time for anything else. Her housekeeping was "a lick and a promise." She had Thanksgiving dinner cleared, washed and put away within thirty minutes of us finishing the last bite. Even her way of serving food was rushed. After taking the time to make a huge meal, she would shove it all on the table at once: appetizers, salad, main course, and dessert. Dad was used to eating on the run from working at his service station, but this paled in comparison.

She cheered wildly for her sports teams. She loved them all, but especially the Seattle Sonics. Dad got a kick out of her enthusiasm, quietly smiling at her shrieks of triumph or fury. She taught Dad card games and they'd have lively competitions with friends. The only activity she did that forced her to sit quietly was knitting afghans. She needed to be busy.

She didn't "believe" in sickness. Not that it did not exist, but that if she wholeheartedly ignored it, it wouldn't affect her. So she would go to work sick, probably infecting everyone else in the office. When I would point out that these viruses were contagious, her defense was "I didn't have a fever." Her own mother had been "dying" for over forty years (or so she said), leaving Carol to care for her various neuroses. Carol was used to taking care of things herself – fast. Her answer to everything was either food or bleach. If she couldn't feed it, she'd bleach it. "Hospital clean" she called it. I shuddered, knowing how dirty hospitals really were. Our towels inevitably lasted only a few months.

We created a ritual where we'd sit at the kitchen table, drink tea, and talk after I got home from school. No matter how bad of a day either of us had, she was unfailingly happy. Or, as I would describe it to friends: depressingly cheerful. I had the Nordic penchant for dark moods even if I could find the humor in nearly any situation.

She wanted me to call her "Mom" and I tried, but it never came easily. While I would write "Mom" in birthday and Mother's Day cards, she was always "Carol" in my mind because that is who she was my entire life before she married Dad. She would sign cards "Mom Carol" as well, as if unsure I would welcome her taking the title. Years later I realized the name "Carol" had become synonymous with "Mom" to me.

I first became aware of Brian Reid in French class. Madame hit the lights for a film, and a voice mimicking Maurice Chevalier (or maybe Pepe Le Pew) came from the back, saying in low tones, "Oh, *ma chérie…*" Everyone cracked up. It's what he lived for.

He was slender, blue-eyed, blond and just barely taller than me. With an abundance of hair that made me jealous. Handsome, with a great smile, and the strong jaw line I found attractive. The genetic lure was there. But I wasn't interested in a relationship. I held fast to my rule of not dating classmates. I had broken that once or twice since my first boyfriend with tepid to disastrous results. Never again. Still I was drawn to him. Our characteristics complemented each other. He was an extrovert, I was an introvert. He was spontaneous while I over-analyzed. He was young and idealistic. I felt old and disillusioned. I liked being around him just to soak up the carefree atmosphere. I soon discovered he was incredibly smart as well as funny.

He wrote essays in one sitting, going back later to create the required rough draft because he had no patience to do it the "right" way. He could turn a phrase or compose a poem in mere seconds. He was a natural at math, so much so that once the teacher interrupted us as we labored over a geometry test to hold up Brian's paper from earlier in the day, which he was now grading:

"That Brian Reid – what a show-off. I said show your work on the last question and he wrote three different ways to get the same answer."

He had a great voice and was in swing choir even though he never learned to read music. Instead he relied on those around him and a lot of charm to get by. He loved the Who and the Beatles as well as Pavarotti and jazz and the blues.

He joined drama club as a freshman and lived for performing, having absolutely no fear of being on stage. A terrific mimic, he had me in stitches with his impressions. He and best friend Christopher introduced me to Monty Python by reciting, in its entirety, *Monty Python and the Holy Grail*. They were so good with accents that an English-born waitress at a café once picked up the tab for their lunch because, "It was so nice to chat with someone from home."

He wasn't in sports but then neither was I. I never liked team sports, with a special loathing for basketball stemming from (what else?) PE requirements. He played soccer (goalie) as a child and was a junior fencing champion, but his family had the tendency to blow out their knees so most gave up sports by puberty.

He loved science fiction and always seemed to be reading some huge book. Electronics and computers made perfect sense to him while they mystified (and bored) me. He even enjoyed the primitive computer programming course offered in school.

While he was all these things he was also immature, impulsive, and had a rather grandiose sense of self. He was sure he was going to be a great photographer working for *Vogue* magazine. He also bragged incessantly about his family. He was full of drama and often spoke or acted before thinking. In fact he never stopped talking; silence made him nervous. I chalked it up to him being a normal teen, figuring he'd mellow and mature. Besides, normal is good, right?

Something I did not understand about him was why he liked me, unless it was simply chemistry or because opposites attract. I didn't want to get involved but he was persistent. This flattered me. We started dating. Very quickly it moved into something exclusive. Soon after that he started telling people we were going to get married, only he didn't bother telling me because he figured I knew.

I should have ended it there, but I decided he was just shooting his mouth off so let it go.

He professed his love to me. I really didn't want to hear it. I wanted something I could walk away from. And I knew that once the line was crossed there would be no going back to the brother/sister relationship I had enjoyed before. I tried to look at it logically and rein in my feelings but he made me feel beautiful and wanted. When you are forced to see and interact with someone every day and they love you it's hard to maintain a safe distance. As doomed and cliché I imagined all high school romances to be, I found myself having one.

I stated my rule: Whatever we may or may not do romantically, it was between us and not to be discussed with anyone. He then proceeded to tell not only all our friends, but also his favorite teacher the details of our developing physical relationship.

I should have ended it there, but by then I was in love with him.

Dad did not approve. He never said so but it was obvious. "That boy," he called him. When Dad didn't like someone he either mispronounced their name or did not say their name at all. "Are you going out with *that boy* again?" I was embarrassed because for all of Brian's genius he was immature and grandiose. Dad didn't like immature and he didn't like grandiose, so if he was impressed at all with the genius part he didn't let on.

Carol was more understanding. She liked seeing me happy and since Brian seemed to make me happy, he was okay in her book. The only time she said anything was one night when Brian and I parked, hidden on a dark rural road. Our relationship was just starting to get physical and involved a lot of passionate kissing. We lost track of time. Unbeknownst to us, his mother was worried sick because it was so late and drove up and down the roads trying to find us. Since these were the days before cell phones there was no way to track our whereabouts. She called my house to see if he was there, waking Carol who had to get up early for work the next day. When I finally walked in the front door, Carol stood imposingly at the top of the stairs and gave this edict:

"If you're going to stay out all night with Brian, *call his mother!*" and with an impressive sweep of her robes went back to bed.

If Lillian had been alive there's no way I could have gotten away with it. But Dad had a hands-off approach with anything involving boys, dating or sex.

In other words we never talked about it. Once I went camping with Brian's family and we stayed an extra night. Dad forgot I told him we were doing that and called Brian's mom when I didn't return the day he thought I would. We stopped at her house before I went home and she told me in worried tones that my dad "knew" Brian and I spent the night alone. I reassured her that he only mixed up the day I was coming back. When she looked dubious, I reminded her I was eighteen and that my dad figured my sex life was my business. Sure enough, when I got home there was no mention of the sleeping arrangements.

It's not that he didn't care; he just didn't want to think about it. If he never spoke the words it was something he could ignore. Although he gave me a car to drive and discussed important financial matters with me, he still thought of me as a little girl for the most part. Once we had an early-morning crow problem. I asked him to borrow a shotgun so I could finally get some sleep. As I patrolled the orchard one sunrise, just dying to blow a stupid crow to smithereens, Dad watched from the kitchen window and said to Carol, "I just can't get used to seeing Noelle with that big gun." The crows were too smart for me and moved on so I never had the chance to use it. But that he would trust me with a firearm when he didn't even believe in keeping any in the house amazes me. He either figured I was such a good shot that there was nothing to worry about or (more likely) I was such a lousy shot that no one was in any danger, including the crows.

My family and Brian's were polar opposites. My parents married in their thirties and became parents via adoption closer to age forty. Brian's parents had to marry out of state because her father would not give permission, since Joan was a teenager and pregnant and Dennis was just a little older.

Now my parents consisted of my adoptive father and step-mother while his were a double set of parents. My dad twenty-five years older than Brian's step-dad, old enough to be his father. Brian's parents divorced when he was a little boy and went on to have many failed relationships. They both found soul mates in new spouses, so much so that I could not imagine them ever being married to each other originally.

They had three children together. I felt Brian and I had an affinity in that we were both the youngest of three. But while I was treated like a para-adult by my own parents, Brian was not. He constantly had to prove himself to be taken seriously. This infuriated me. It was the same manipulation we received from so many teachers: Expect the students to act like adults while treating them like children.

Ironically, while my father was in denial that an adult relationship was happening between us, Brian's mother accepted and actually encouraged it. "When are you going to make an honest man out of my son?" she'd tease. Brian's father liked me but wanted Brian to "play the field" instead of settling down so young.

It was a combination of those opposing viewpoints that cemented it for Brian: He wanted us to marry as soon as possible. He never really got over his parents' divorce and the instability of his life in the years until they ultimately married other people. He wanted us to be like his grandparents, his dad's parents, a feisty long-married couple I grew to adore. I met them at Brian's father's wedding. "This is Noelle and I'm going to be married to her as long as you two have been together," was Brian's introduction. Gram and Gramps Reid looked a little taken aback but welcomed me nonetheless. They were good that way; accepting of every stray that came along. They still called Brian's mom "our little Joanie." On more than one occasion I witnessed Gramps putting his arm around her affectionately and saying, "Dennis may have divorced you but we didn't." That's the way it was: Once a Reid, always a Reid.

It was a long, hot summer. That was one reason. Also we had been dating for about six months and Brian convinced me we were spending the rest of our lives together. Even without that promise, I had decided that whoever I had my first consensual experience with, I would not regret it later.

From what I understand, it's not usually the girl who feels the need to apologize. Brian was gallant, assuring me the pain was because my hymen had broken. He didn't seem to notice the lack of blood. I laid there, arms sprawled above my head, and wondered if I'd ever know what it is like to feel normal.

It wasn't only intercourse, and if Brian had been more experienced he probably would have realized there was something wrong with me. One day his hand slid down my bare pelvis and between my legs. I grabbed his wrist.

"No. I don't like that," I said quietly.

"Okay," he acquiesced, startled.

There were a lot of things I could not tolerate. Everything hurt. He bought personal lubricant and while it helped, it did not solve the problem, because the problem was me.

I felt guilty. He deserved better. But he never complained. Instead he called me "delicate" and treated me as such. One day though, he playfully pulled me to the living room carpet and I nearly hyperventilated. We were both unnerved. "I would never hurt you," he said. But he didn't ask questions and I didn't offer explanations. All those years of not talking about it made that easy. A few times I alluded to it among friends but never really came out and said anything. The word "rape" was never spoken. I wasn't even sure it would be considered as such because it did not involve stereotypical intercourse. It was in sex ed class that I first heard rape defined as violence using sex as a tool. That it wasn't about sex as much as it was about power and control. And in Keith's case, inflicting pain.

I decided not to tell Brian, as there would be no point. I did not want him to be angry with Dad for not getting rid of Keith and I didn't want to try to explain/defend because that would mean actually talking about it, which was too painful. I blocked it out for the most part. Just seeing the word *rape* made me flinch and I couldn't stand to see it even hinted at in movies. Brian forced me to watch *A Clockwork Orange* with him, calling it a great film. I nearly threw up. Nothing but an endless series of violent acts, including (of course) rape. I was gratified later to hear the author hated the movie as well for the same reasons. But I could not deal with a depiction of sexual assault in any form, be it movies, books, TV, or newspaper. I knew I was different that way and hated it.

Another reason for not telling Brian was because he came from a long line of law enforcement. Their idea of a fitful punishment for rapists was to nail the guy's dick to a log and set him afloat in a lake. They never actually did this of course, but it exemplified their feelings on the subject. I did not want to protect Keith – I wanted him dead – but I wanted to protect both Dad and Brian from bad feelings about each other. There was nothing anyone could legally do at this point and I did not want someone explaining that to me either. It was too late. Too late for vengeance, too late for justice, too late for anything.

Chapter 6
~The So-Called Real World~

In my quest to be Swedish, I asked Gramma if I could be there the next time she made mor bread. We all previously asked for the recipe and she just laughed. There was no recipe; she would not know where to begin if forced to write it down. Even her daughters never learned to make it. It was called mor bread for a reason: it was hers, not theirs.

But I showed up at six one morning, notebook in hand, and followed her around like a puppy.

She took a bottle of raw milk out of the refrigerator and poured it into a big pot on the stove.

"Wait," I said. "How much milk was that?"

"Oh, I don't know. Whatever was there," she said in her Swedish lilt.

She poured some salt into her hand and threw it in.

"Wait. How much salt was that?"

She showed me her palm. "About that much."

"Gramma, I'll never get this right if I can't write it down."

"Well, we didn't do it that way. We just...*made it.*"

"Then how did you know?"

"You'll learn," she promised.

So whatever Gramma did, I copied. I learned we needed to add sugar until it smelled like this, and mix the flour until it felt like that. "*Verk* the dough," she instructed. "Like this," and expertly turned and kneaded, making a perfect oblong loaf every time. I made something more...abstract.

"Does this look okay?" I asked, hopefully.

"Sure," she said, while shuffling away, not even glancing my direction.

Somehow, it turned out perfectly. I wrote vague instructions with a very wide tolerance of measurements. Over the summer I attempted it at home four times, and four times failed miserably. I kept a record of measurements and timing and technique. Four times I threw the entire batch in the trash, frustrated beyond words. I went back to Gramma's to bake with her again. This time without the cheat sheet.

I tried on my own once more. It was perfect.

I could now do something none of my adopted relatives could do, something vitally important to our family. I trumped them in Swedish-ness. If I could have, I would have congratulated myself in Swedish. Instead, when they asked for the recipe I replied, "We don't do it that way. We just make it."

When I finally accepted (at Brian's insistence) we were indeed a couple I let Brian know our life would include church. None of this "Mom takes the kids to church while Dad sleeps in and watches football" garbage. So we went church shopping.

My father was born into the Lutheran faith but now only went to weddings and funerals. Brian's father grew up without much religious instruction but now regularly attended his wife's Lutheran church. We both liked how it was predominantly Nordic. It was the only common thread between our families so we tried it on for size and discovered a perfect fit.

Once we got the hang of the service: standing, sitting, kneeling, the strange psalm tones, liturgy, and sharing a common cup for communion – we liked it. We liked how the entire service revolved around scripture interwoven to create one message. We liked the vestments and paraments. We liked the ancient Kyrie, Creeds, and Great Thanksgiving. And though we were still teens we preferred the traditional, formal service over the contemporary. I felt I had enough Praise music to last a lifetime; the old hymns (minus guitar and drum set) were a relief.

And so we decided to be confirmed. To those raised Lutheran, confirmation classes usually start around age thirteen, lasting two arduous years. Because we were coming in as "adults" we were fast-tracked. One part of Luther's Small Catechism I specifically remember is when the pastor read from Ephesians 1:5:

"In love He predestined us for adoption to sonship[4] through Jesus Christ, in

---

4 Sonship translates to full legal rights as a child and heir in ancient Roman (and Greek) society.

accordance with His pleasure and will," then asked if anyone present was adopted. When I didn't respond, Brian nudged me.

"Oh. Yeah. I am," I said lamely.

"Were you adopted as a baby?"

"Yes."

"Were you asked if you wanted to be adopted?"

"Not that I'm aware of."

"Did they wait until you were old enough to understand before legally adopting you?"

"No."

"Did they adopt you to be their daughter out of love?"

"I…suppose," I said, not feeling qualified to answer on behalf of my parents.

"It is the same with God for all of us. It was with love and by His pleasure that we were chosen and adopted as children of God. Even if we didn't understand it. Even if we weren't asked."

I absorbed this with no further comment.

I used to think of adoption in the Bible only concerning people like Moses, Esther and Jesus. In the case of Moses it was a matter of life or death. His Hebrew (natural) mother hid him in a basket in the river because she couldn't bear to hand him over to be killed, per Pharaoh's orders. Ironically it was Pharaoh's daughter who adopted the baby. More ironic yet, after she found him she gave him back to his birth mother to nurse – for pay – with the condition he be brought to her when weaned to be raised as her own son, an Egyptian prince. Since children were breastfed until at least age three at that time, it meant Moses knew and would remember (at least in a rudimentary way) his birth mother. There is no record of him being shocked upon meeting his siblings Aaron and Miriam again in adulthood.

Adoption is an ancient practice. Apparently, even God does it. It is the Western method of closed/secret adoption that is new.

Of course being adopted by God is not the same as being adopted by humans. The main difference being adoption is almost always Plan B for couples who are infertile. If they had been able to birth their own, there would be no need to adopt. And God doesn't seal original birth certificates.

Brian and I completed our class and were confirmed as members of the Lutheran Church. We invited our closest family to attend the service. Brian's father was pleased. Brian's mother didn't care one way or the other. Dad seemed happy but it was hard to tell. Carol was happy that we were happy but she herself was satisfied to have just "a gut feeling for the Lord" and not bother with church.

I also invited Aunt Betty and Gramma Nelson. Although they must have felt I was taking a step backwards, they attended and did not express their disappointment. In Gramma's youth at the turn of the century, many Swedes began following more evangelical denominations such as Baptist, Covenant, Methodist, etc., all "free churches," breaking away from the state-mandated Lutheran church. Only a few decades prior that would have been illegal. They fought for the freedom to make another choice, to be something other than Lutheran. And here I was running right back to it.

I wondered if Lillian was turning in her grave but this felt right. I had been a reluctant Baptist but was now a wholehearted Lutheran. I hoped she took comfort in the fact that this is what I chose and that I was happy.

My senior year of high school was the best since I was in Mrs. MacKenzie's fourth grade class. Once again I had straight A's, even a few A+'s, most shockingly one for PE-Running. We jogged every day, no matter the weather. As when I was a child I excelled in running; I had both speed and endurance. Nothing prize-worthy but good enough to be asked to join track. Being non-competitive, I was not interested. In fact I was anti-competitive; if there was a contest I would routinely throw it because it just didn't matter to me to win. But for this class I wanted to prove to myself that I was good enough.

In seventh grade I received my first F courtesy of a PE teacher. Young and bitter, she had no business teaching pre-adolescents anything, much less anything having to do with their bodies. I wasn't able to do some required sport due to absences so she told me I had to run laps during the next free day instead. Her student helper was to watch to make sure I did them all. The girl was not pleased to have to stand with a clip board and count me doing laps while everyone else got to have fun inside. There wasn't much time and we could not be tardy for the next class. That was the rule. I ran and ran. My sides ached, my chest hurt to breathe, my legs felt like lead. Only one lap to go. The bell rang. I knew I couldn't continue or both the helper and I would be late so I stopped. I figured I would run the final lap (or laps, if the teacher tagged on more) later.

"Did she finish?" the teacher asked the helper in the girls' locker room as if I wasn't there.

"No," she said, simply.

So she flunked me, the bitch. Since I had no one to advocate for me, I felt there was no fighting it. The F went onto my report card.

My high school PE teacher, however, proudly wrote, "Here every day!" on the transcript along with other accolades. She knew perfect attendance was my greatest achievement after nearly failing previous semesters due to absences. Dad was so proud he posted my report card on the refrigerator, like I was seven years old instead of seventeen.

I took an architectural drawing class. I had always loved drawing houses. Even in the back of my music theory notebook I sketched floor plans. As a senior we were expected to think about college. I wanted to be an architect. The career counselor tried to let me down easy:

"That takes eight years of college, including a heavy load of math." He knew I didn't like math, at least not the way it was taught in school.

"But it's what I like to do," I said.

"How would you pay for it?" he asked, knowing I had not applied for any scholarships.

"My dad would pay for it. He thinks college is important," I said confidently.

Turns out, while Dad did think college was important, he only thought it necessary if it led to a life-long career. And he kept seeing articles in the paper about out-of-work architects, all of whom had college degrees they had yet to pay for. If he read it in the newspaper it was true so he told me to think of another career. He then lamented about women who had four year college degrees who "wasted" it by getting married and having children instead of getting a job.

He had nothing against marriage or children, just what he considered waste. He admired women who were bright, successful, even owning a house before getting married and *long* before becoming a mother. I tried to tell him not everyone can wait until they're forty to start having children. He countered it worked out fine for him. I didn't attempt to point out that all of us were adopted and that neither he nor Mom went to college anyway.

The fact was, if he wasn't going to shell out money I wasn't going to college. I had only worked picking berries and babysitting up to that point. I never considered scholarships because I wasn't great at anything or even in the top ten in my class. Maybe I could have been if not for the absences but it was too late now. And even though I could play piano I wasn't like those who were musically gifted. Sports were completely out of the question. So to even pay for community college (which I had no interest in) I would need a real job. Lots of my friends, including Brian, worked at local burger joints in the summer. I couldn't see how mastering the art of cooking French fries was going to further any career plans.

"You should be a professional letter writer and write letters for other people," joked my friend Christopher. I was known writing for amusing notes to those in my circle.

"You should be a professional writer, period," said one of my favorite English teachers. He encouraged me to join a local writers group after I was in two of his classes. But I didn't feel old enough or good enough. After being treated like a child so long I wasn't ready to be taken seriously now. Thirteen years of public school indoctrination had done its job; I couldn't imagine being anything but a student. Under the guise of preparing us for "real life," we had been stifled. Held in an artificial environment of perpetual childhood, we were not trusted to leave campus on our own and needed a note from our parents to excuse absences even if we drove and held jobs. Besides, I felt I had nothing to say.

"You should be a teacher," said an old teacher and student advisor, firmly. I shuddered. Why did people keep saying that?! The teachers I knew certainly did not seem fulfilled in their careers. I couldn't imagine *choosing* to be trapped that way. Besides, it meant more college.

Brian was not nearly so conflicted. Instead he was overwhelmed with options. First he wanted to be a photographer. I said, "Fine." Then he considered joining the Air Force. I said, "Okay." Then he decided to be a cop like his father. I said, "If you become a cop we're not getting married." Because Brian becoming hardened like his father was exactly what I was afraid of. He was taken aback but because he loved me he dropped that idea and came up with a compromise: He'd be a firefighter. *That* I could live with.

I kept thinking about architectural drawing. If I couldn't be an architect, then maybe a drafter working *for* an architect? I imagined happy days at a drawing board, drafting the plans for beautiful houses. I could do that.

We had to write an essay as a final English project before graduation. I did mine on adoption, specifically the right to search. There was nothing in the school library that helped so I went to the public library where I discovered the works of Betty Jean Lifton. Just her book *Lost and Found* would be enough to sway most anyone toward the reunion movement and open adoption. But although her book was packed with information, it was the only one out there. The few others on the subject were memoirs. The movement was still in its infancy – the idea too new. The lack of "experts" in the field made my argument look weak. Also, I tried to do too much with it. Suddenly there was *too much* to say. My final essay was shaky at best. I did not feel much like a writer. Drafting was sounding better all the time.

Doing the essay reminded me I was now considered old enough to ask for my adoption records to be opened. No one got to have them for the asking, though. We had to request on bended knee, as if acknowledging we were not worthy to own information about ourselves. Even a senior citizen, a war veteran, a grandparent would not be considered "old enough" to know their original name and circumstances of their birth. We were forever "adopted children." I discovered during my research that Washington State had a unique system where a court-appointed confidential intermediary could petition for the records to be opened and from there could search and ask the other party if a reunion was welcome. The searching party was given no identifying information until written permission was granted. That's as close to our own search for self as was allowed.

I had a dream:

I gave birth in my bedroom only I didn't know I was pregnant. The birth was painless but the baby had no features, no face. It was like something less than a doll. Even less than an adoptee. Even less than me.

I had to search. I could not have children until I did.

I wanted as much information as possible, even if it was non-identifying. From the privacy of the school office I called Dr. Clark, my old pediatrician. I did not tell him I was interested in searching, only that I wanted medical information. For instance, did my birth mother take DES?

(Diethylstilbestrol, commonly called DES, was a synthetic hormone sometimes given to women from 1940-1970 in the mistaken belief it lessened the chance of miscarriage. Instead it was discovered to be a carcinogen for both the daughters and sons of women who took it, plus could cause malformations of the reproductive organs. With all the trouble I had with menstruation I wondered if this could be the reason why.)

He reassured me that he never prescribed DES to any of his patients. I reasoned later she probably would not have taken a drug to prevent miscarriage for a child she was relinquishing, but since I knew nothing about her or what led her to Dr. Clark in the first place it was still a possibility, however remote.

I asked if he remembered anything about my biological mother that I should know. He said it was a long time ago and he did not know her that long but that she appeared to be generally in good health. I wasn't going to get anything useful out of him. Finally I asked about my ethnic background.

"Well, what do you look like?" he said.

"Swedish," I said, purely out of habit.

"That's what you are then. You're Swedish."

You ass, I thought. I wanted answers, not a pat on the head. I wondered if he even bothered to write down the non-identifying information he gave his clients or if he just casually mentioned them upon transferring the commodity. Was the information he gave my parents correct? What was my birth mother told? Had other adoptees contacted him like this? Did he ever consider "the baby" would grow up, or were they forever the grateful child in his mind? After I hung up the thought occurred to me that I should have asked him what he meant when he said *"Oh that woman!"* to my father but I knew he would not have told me even if he remembered.

About to graduate from high school, I was expected to have a plan for my life. Only I didn't. I knew what I wanted ultimately: a house, a husband, and children. But there was no college for that in the 1980s. I kept thinking about drafting. It was artistic yet practical. Dad would like that. I liked how it was something I could walk away from.

I called all the community colleges, figuring they'd be my best bet. I told them I didn't really care about a degree or going on to a 4-year college, I just wanted a good job as a drafter. I figured they'd jump at the chance to enroll me.

"Have you tried Tacoma Voc-Tech?" was their unexpected response. No, I had not considered TVTI. It was a vocational/technical institute, considered lowly for secondary education – very blue-collar. But when the *third* community college rep asked me the same question, I finally checked into it. I figured I'd see it, say no, then wonder what to do with the rest of my life.

It was an old brick building on Tacoma's Hilltop. A lot of very non-collegiate-looking people wandered in and out. Honestly it looked like some sort of work release program. What I was doing here? This was crazy. Carol went with me to meet the "drafting teachers" who were actually engineering instructors. We met the instructors for architectural and structural engineering which only confirmed I was not going to school there. Finally we met the instructor for mechanical engineering (a subject I had absolutely no interest in) only because his classroom was on the way out of the building. And I was hooked.

Mr. Granville was one of the nicest men I ever met. Like a more jovial version of my dad and around the same age. Previously a ski instructor, now a teacher with a less physically-demanding job. Madly in love with his wife of four decades, calling her alternately "the boss" or "the bride," jogging to the phone across the hall whenever she called. He loved his kids and grandkids, jazz, and good food. His wife was always trying to put him on a diet, in an attempt to make him "slim as a gazelle," he would lament. I found myself imagining spending the next two years of my life in his class, learning to draft and letter, drinking tea at my drawing board, chatting with Mr. Granville about his grandkids. I made the decision.

"I cannot believe you're going to a *trade school*," Aunt Betty said fiercely. "You're college material!" My older cousins had gone off to college and the same was expected of me. I tried to tell her I had no passion for anything and this was a compromise but the explanation fell flat. I could barely understand how I ended up at TVTI myself. I could blame it on feeling inadequate, having no single interest, or the rootlessness that plagued me, but there was something more. It was like I was *put* there. It was stupid to think of that sort of place as Destiny so I stuck with my story of "It's good enough to land a job."

I made friends there. I was particularly close to Elizabeth. A couple of years older than me, centered, calm, and ageless. She was working in retail but wanted the engineering credentials to fall back on. We hung out – going to lunch, shopping, walking at the park. She put up with my occasional flashes of teen histrionics.

The other students were an odd mix. Men and women of all color, background, and age. Some older, learning a new trade. Some young like me, just starting out. Some were just plain weird and I'm not sure why they were there, but maybe they thought the same of me.

Like I used to watch people at the mall, wondering about their secret lives, I pondered the others at school. As I drank my tea and practiced the fine art of lettering, I imagined what they were like outside the classroom. One in particular caught my attention. He was in the class next door and a complete mystery: Craig Evershaw. Tall, slender, blonde, in his mid-thirties, I admit I was attracted to him. But for all his pale coloring he was a very dark figure. Never smiled, wore black and moved with the ease and power of a panther. He seemed so out of place, like a caged exotic animal. The more I saw him and talked to him the less I knew and that fascinated me.

When I first started attending TVTI a horde of men descended, wanting to know my availability. Even if I had been "free" there wasn't a single person I was interested in. Except Craig. And he was the one who didn't ask. Instead he started casually hanging out with me during breaks, telling me wild stories I thought he invented for amusement – his or mine, I wasn't sure. I decided early on to believe only half of what he said, whatever half I found more interesting. When I told him this he nearly smiled.

Brian had given me a "promise ring" the prior Christmas. It was a sweet adolescent trend for those who wanted to show commitment but didn't have the money for a real engagement ring. It was also a visible reminder to anyone that I was taken. Craig was unimpressed but never made a move on me. He did make a lot of inappropriate comments though, usually in the form of a joke.

"Not if I was the last man on earth, huh?"

"Oh Craig," I said sweetly, "If you were the last man on earth I would… seriously consider it."

This was our usual banter. He regaled me with tales of adventure, of travels to Europe and Asia, of mysterious interactions with even more mysterious figures, of close-calls and unsolved crimes and mistaken identity, of foundlings and acid trips and fleeting moments with the famous and infamous. He also talked about art and music and movies. He was an artist. I saw some of his work so I knew that much was true. I didn't understand what he was doing there at TVTI, since he was obviously so unhappy. He said it was punishment for not paying taxes he didn't owe. My work-release impression wasn't that far off, it seemed. He was as surprised to find himself there as I was. But I was killing time; he was serving time. He really was a prisoner, even without barbed wire and guards in towers to keep him in.

He called me "Kid," as if as a reminder he didn't take me seriously. Still, he seemed to prefer my company to that of anyone else. He was angry and bitter and rarely found the humor in anything, unless it was black humor. I created an alter-ego for him called "Caustic Man" who used his super-caustic powers to bring everyone down, saving them from inadvertent happiness. I didn't tell Craig about Caustic Man.

Although I socialized with many others, including men, it was seeing Craig and me together that concerned people. People like Mr. Granville, who did everything in his power to keep us apart. I'm sure everyone could see the chemistry, but what they did not know was we only saw each other at school. We knew nearly nothing about the other's life. We didn't even exchange phone numbers. But there was always a smoldering sexual tension between us, one we did not acknowledge. His voice, the way he moved, the way he looked at me...

I have wondered how different life would have been had we acted on it.

At nineteen I got my first "real" job, at a candy store in the mall. I figured I could earn money and support my chocolate habit at the same time. Dad was ridiculously proud and his story of how I landed the job got better every time he told it. In truth it was just a few hours a week and for minimum wage, but I had plans for the money.

When I had saved $175, Brian and I drove the hour north to Kirkland and with the help of a Thomas Bros map, located the office of WARM – Washington Adoptee's Rights Movement. I don't know if they ever had a nineteen year old walk in with cash in hand before, but they acted professional and nonchalant. I signed the forms and gave what little information I had. Now it was up to them. When the time came, my assigned confidential intermediary (CI) would take my case in front of a judge and ask for my records to be opened. From there she would search for my birth mother. Those things I knew would happen. After that it was a huge unknown.

The thought overwhelmed me at times. I had a dream:

I was outside old St. Joseph Hospital but there were no doors or windows, only brick walls. All my records and information were inside. I ran around the building but there was no way in. I pounded on the walls, yelling at those inside to let me in, to give me what was mine. I pressed my ear against the wall only to hear a voice say the records were sealed.

I told only my closest friends about my search. Remembering Dad's stinging words, *"If we hadn't gotten you, someone else would have!"* I said nothing to family members. I needed positive thoughts, not negative what-if's clouding my mind.

Brian was refreshingly casual about it. "Of course you should know your mother," he said. Maybe he wasn't thinking of the ramifications – because there are always ramifications – but I appreciated the support nonetheless.

I checked out every book on adoption the main branch of the Tacoma library had to offer. I re-read *Lost and Found* and *Twice Born* by Betty Jean Lifton; *The Search for Anna Fisher* by Florence Fisher, founder of ALMA; *Orphan Voyage* by the great Jean Paton, the first to write on rights of the adopted, and any other I could get my hands on.

I was standing on the edge of a cliff and any little breeze or shifting of the ground could make me fall; and only then would I know if I could fly.

As enlightening as the books were, nothing could compare to WARM meetings. And once again, Tacoma seemed to be my destiny. The meetings were held in the old Carnegie library just down the hill from school, which was just down the hill and from St. Joseph Hospital. I wondered if I just kept walking down the hill toward downtown if I would run into my birth mother. Maybe at the Pantages Theater we'd accidentally sit together for *The Nutcracker*. Or we would get coffee in the same shop. But even if we met, would we recognize each other? Had I met her already? The idea that I could have met my mother and not know gnawed at me.

WARM met in the old part of the library, under the copper dome. There I found life-long friends in other members of the adoption triad: Men and women of all ages, adoptees, birth parents, adoptive parents, significant others. We were so different but had among us the common thread in the need to reunite, and the belief it was not only our right but right *morally*. It was good to see not only adoptees but adoptive parents who believed that. These parents impressed me. If they were nervous about their baby searching, they didn't let on. I was the only young adoptee who came without parents in tow. Independence accelerated by my mother's death, I expected to do things on my own. I often found myself thinking *It's better to ask forgiveness than permission*. Sometimes I didn't bother with either.

For the first time I could say anything I felt about adoption and have my comments met with nods of acknowledgement instead of blank stares. They "got it" before I even articulated it. We were experiencing the same journey. I finally could tell the "Grateful Story" from first grade and have complete understanding.

I could explain my fear of Dad being angry if he knew I was searching. They told me he was probably only concerned about me getting hurt but I couldn't quite believe that. At the same time I did not feel guilty because this wasn't about him. It was about me. I had to do this like I had to breathe.

One girl there was also a good friend from high school: Jenny Miller. She came to the meetings with her adopted parents. Although I physically longed for children and one of my reasons to search was to know my genetic history, she wanted no part of motherhood. She liked other people's kids and was a favorite auntie to many. But it was something she absolutely did not want for herself. She insisted it was from her mom running a daycare in her home. I felt there was something more.

We met monthly, discussing where we were in our search, how we felt, obstacles and how to overcome them. I learned sleuthing techniques from those who had enough information to do their own search: how to find an address, the best day/time to go to a records office, how to get more than you give in a phone call. I tucked the information away, both relieved and irritated my CI would do all the work for me.

I expanded on my people-watching skills at the candy store. I looked for anyone who bore a resemblance to me, studying things others took for granted: bone structure, posture, gestures. I wondered who else had my small skull, baby-fine hair, dark eyes, unusually white skin, laugh, fatalistic humor, or love of dark chocolate with raspberries.

One day an older white woman came by. She had huge, watery brown eyes and a deliberate air about her, as if testing every sight and sound. She said something to my co-worker, an observation of some kind that made her say half-jokingly, "Are you psychic?"

"I have feelings about things," the woman answered.

"Will I find my mother?" I interjected. My co-worker's jaw dropped as she had no idea I was missing a mother.

The woman considered me with her staring eyes. "Yes," she finally said.

"When?"

"Not long." That aggravated me, since "long" is a very subjective term.

"Does she look like me?"

Now most posing as someone with extrasensory perception would default and just say "yes" since chances are in their favor. Besides, I'd never see this woman again. But she studied my face and finally said, "Not really."

Not really? Are you kidding?

She added, "She has brown eyes, but not like yours." Then taking her bag of candy she slowly and deliberately departed. My co-worker took a cigarette break to calm her nerves. I was left wondering who I looked like if it wasn't my mother. Or if I could trust the visions of a random, candy-buying psychic.

I couldn't completely discount her either, since my own flashes of insight and premonitions seemed to be getting stronger. I had "feelings about things" also. And one thing I felt was that my birth mother was in Tacoma. Not just anywhere in Tacoma, but Bayridge, one of the nicer neighborhoods. The more I explored the city in my incidental travels, the more I felt it. It was one of the reasons I took the job at the mall, hoping our paths would cross.

There was no good reason for me to believe my mother was there or any particular place, or even that she was alive. I did not know where she came from, if she already lived here or was just passing through when I was born. No one ever mentioned that detail, if they knew. All I was told was she was married or divorced, possibly had other children, and was an "educated professional" with Swedish, English, and Irish blood. Maybe.

Brian took it in stride. He liked having a future wife with a knack for knowing things. It drove me crazy because although I *knew*, I had no proof. No mother to show for it. What is the point of knowing without the having?

Then there was "the voice." The first time I heard it Brian and I were on I-5. Just ahead of us was a station wagon with a wood rowboat tied to the roof.

"Move," a voice commanded. Barely glancing at the mirrors I swerved into the next lane, just as the boat came loose and flipped, crashing down where we had been only a second before.

"Jesus!" Brian said, twisting in his seat to look back at the splintered remains.

"Did you hear that?" I said, hopefully.

"Hear what?"

"You didn't hear someone say 'move'?"

The look he gave me answered my question. But I already knew, because I heard it in my head. It wasn't my own thoughts, it wasn't a feeling or vision, it was a voice – just a voice. Not male or female or with any distinguishing characteristics, but when it spoke I obeyed instinctively. It never occurred to me to do anything else.

It happened again. And once again I was driving. Elizabeth and I were going to lunch. Approaching an intersection on one of the many streets that run along side a hill, I had the green light.

"Hit the brakes."

I slammed on the brakes. Elizabeth started to say, "What—?" when an out of control car came barreling down the hill, through the red light and on. If I had not stopped they would have hit us exactly where she was sitting. It was the only time I ever saw Elizabeth unnerved.

I was still pounding on the brick walls of the hospital. But now it was the Berlin Wall and I was in the Eastern Bloc. My mother was living her life on the free side, blissfully unaware that I ran along the barrier separating us, pounding it with my fists and screaming, "I'm here! I'm here!"

The old St. Joseph Hospital was torn down while I was at TVTI. I passed it every day as it fell. I considered taking a brick as a tangible link to the place where I was born, but before I could the hospital started *selling* them as commemorations. I decided the hospital had taken enough from me already; I wasn't going to give them money for a lousy brick.

Chapter 7
~Standing on the Edge~

Life continued outside my search. Brian took fire fighter training and became a volunteer. Nothing made him happier than to run into a burning building. Soon he was a resident volunteer, meaning he lived at the station for no pay but also for no rent. He worked a variety of part-time jobs with his eyes on ultimately being a paid firefighter. At church he ran the sound system and had no fear of helping in the nursery either. He also refereed soccer for little kids. On the sidelines a proud dad once asked, "Which one is yours?"

"The one in black and white with the whistle," I answered.

We decided to marry when we made enough money to rent an apartment. Brian was impatient. He wanted to set a date. I said no, there was no point in setting a date we didn't know we could keep. His mother wanted to know what we were waiting for. My father wanted to know what the hurry was.

His father wanted him to see other people and not settle down so young, which was understandable because he had married (and divorced) young, but it did not endear him to me either. I really liked his wife, kids, and step-kids and already considered them family. I figured if anyone should be digging in their heels it would be *my* father. Brian's mother, meanwhile, asked me to call her "Mom" and I was included in all the family gatherings, including that of her husband's enormous family.

Brian and I were together for every holiday, family get-together, wedding and funeral. I was equally in awe and horrified by his family's extrovert tendencies. While I had not hugged my own father since I was a child and could not remember ever kissing anyone in my family besides my mother, it was like running a gauntlet of hugging, kissing fiends upon arriving at any Reid gathering. I mentally steeled myself before walking through the door so I wouldn't feel I needed to curl up in the fetal position in a quiet corner somewhere. But they were such happy, welcoming people that I could not fault them this one flaw.

Brian's paternal grandparents were the real characters. Once while visiting their home of forty-plus years, we were joined by Brian's brother Eric and his young wife. Brian and I had been together at least three years at that point and the Reid clan was getting impatient. The subject of children came up and Eric joked that any children we had would be the result of the second immaculate conception.

It was on the tip of my tongue to say it was Mary who was the Immaculate Conception and he was confusing that with the Virgin Birth, when Gram put her arm around me and said in genuine consoling tones, "That's okay, honey."

Then I was on the verge of spouting, "Are you insinuating that I don't have sex with your grandson?!"– very offended – when the humor of the situation struck me and I managed to say nothing. But in reality our sex life wasn't funny. I could still barely tolerate it. I knew Brian truly loved me because he never complained. He didn't even act as if anything was wrong, instead seeming satisfied with what little I could give. What other handsome nineteen year old male would put up with that? Of course I loved him. How could I not?

There was no one I felt I could talk to about it and doctors didn't have a clue, so we just continued on, pretending to be normal.

Afraid I would have tonsillitis twice a year for the rest of my life, I finally saw a specialist. "How long have they been like this?" the doctor asked, shocked. "Seven years," I rasped. "That's when they should have come out: Seven years ago," he muttered. And so I was off to St. Joseph Hospital. I wasn't concerned until that morning when Dad awkwardly patted my shoulder and said, "We'll see you later."

I'm going to die, I thought.

Carol drove me there and stayed the entire day, even while I was unconscious. Coming out of the anesthetic, I vomited violently. Carol calmly called for the nurse and helped clean up. Driving home, she carefully avoided potholes or sharp turns. And once home she continued to dispose of my vomit like it was no big deal, and offered chipped ice and liquid jello or anything I could manage to swallow while balled up on the couch.

Besides nurturing, Carol was also fearless. One night I stopped at the end of the driveway to get the evening paper. With my back to the street, I felt something approach and whipped around just in time to see the neighbor's big black dog lunge for my throat. We waged battle in the middle of the road: me kicking, yelling, and hitting with the newspaper, the dog lunging and snarling, both of us advancing and retreating, over and over. Finally a passing car broke up the fight and the dog ran home.

When I told Dad and Carol they were quietly appalled. I figured that was the end of it. But the next day, unbeknownst to me, Carol strode across the street to confront the dog's owner. Mrs. Jansen was a force to be reckoned with. A tough old farm wife who had lived through many trials; you did things her way or you didn't do them at all. The entire town admired her with a healthy dose of fear. Lillian, who was a favorite everywhere, never felt welcome in their home, despite having lived on the same street for forty years. Lillian's father shot the Jansen's dog long ago, mistaking it for a wolf, but if there was ill-will it was not discussed. Feuding was done silently in Nordic communities. They seethed quietly and decades passed before offenses were ignored if not forgotten.

For all her fierce exterior, Mrs. Jansen loved many things, and her dogs were at the top of the list. They could do no wrong. So it was unforgivable that her dog was shot while on another's property, even while looking as if it was there to kill chickens. Now Carol was going to tell her another of her precious canines attacked someone unprovoked. Most people would have left looking as if they had lost a war. Most people aren't Carol.

"If Noelle had gotten hurt I don't know *what* I would have done!" Carol exclaimed, leaving what she might have done to the imagination. Mrs. Jansen's beloved dog was locked away. I never saw it again.

At TVTI we had the option of taking a night class specifically to study for the state certification test. Several of us did, including Elizabeth and Craig. Once a month though, it interfered with the WARM meeting. I wasn't going to miss that so vanished half-way through and drove down the hill to the library.

I told only Elizabeth what I was doing. I didn't feel comfortable talking about my search to anyone but close friends at that point. But Craig noticed my absence and said the next day, "Where did you disappear to? If I have to stay here and suffer, you should have to stay and suffer." So I told him. He didn't appear impressed or disturbed, but he seemed to make a point of never being impressed with anything. Still, after that he was in on it.

Craig didn't have a car then, so often I drove him back to where he was staying during his "detention", the upstairs apartment of a friend's house in the Bayridge neighborhood. More than once as we neared it I said, "I know my birth mother is here. I can feel it." He didn't argue but he had such a low opinion of humanity in general that he couldn't imagine I would find anything worthwhile. I mainly kept my comments confined to the WARM meetings, where I didn't need to explain.

Meanwhile I had been assigned a CI, a very sharp yet friendly woman named Lorraine. CI's are specially trained and sworn to secrecy. That was the arrangement when the confidential intermediary system was created by the founding members of WARM and Judge Norman B. Ackley, who was also an adoptive father:

"Under the confidential intermediary procedure, the (birth) parent is simply asked and more than 90% of them answer that...they just want to meet their child. Almost all these contacts have been successful, resulting in many warm, new relationships which do not harm the relationship with the adoptive parents."[5]

CI's gather their petitions and go to the judge in their jurisdiction, hoping he/she is friendly to their cause. Even having no compelling reason to do so, the judge could simply say "no," leaving the CI and the one searching with nothing but a door slammed in the face. If the judge said yes and the records are opened, the CI would search for the individual being sought by any means possible (mainly public records). If/when locating the individual, she would discreetly approach, usually via phone, and ask the all-important question: "Will you agree to a reunion?" If the answer is "yes," great. If the answer is "not yet," the waiting game begins. If the answer is "no," she would ask for more time or at least

---

5 Norman B. Ackley, King County Superior Court Judge, June, 1979

for medical information. She could release no identifying information without the written consent of the person being sought. (I say "she" because my CI was a woman, as most are.)

The first snag in my search was that my CI couldn't find me being relinquished in Pierce County, even though I knew I was born there, my adoptive parents lived there, the doctor who handled my adoption practiced there, and I was sure my parents told me they went to court there. Adoptees already feel as if they were not born, so being told I did not exist according to records was not a good feeling. I vented at the meetings. They listened patiently. They assured me I existed, that this was just a mistake that would be rectified. Meanwhile I had to wait until my records could be found before the process could really start.

While in this limbo, I lived vicariously through the searches of others. Like all marriages have similarities and differences, all searches have a common thread but vary wildly. Emotions roller-coaster with each step, new realization, rejection and acceptance. At one meeting someone spoke on grief and loss and how this applied to every adoption. The adoptive parents had to grieve over the loss of their phantom birth children. The birth parents grieved over the loss of their biological child. The adoptee grieved over the life they would have had with their birth parents. It was a huge paradigm shift for me to hear it put into those terms. It did not make out all of adoption to be a tragedy but here was the reality: In adoption, the joy of the adoptive parent receiving a child comes at the grief of the birth parent relinquishing the same child. And beyond that, there is sorrow for all that "might have been." Sorrow not in the forefront, not determining every aspect of a person's life, but something missing, and the absence of which was felt every moment, sometimes keenly, sometimes at a low ebb. The road not taken.

Blessed are those who mourn, for they shall be comforted. (The Beatitudes, Matthew 5:4)

But what if you do not mourn? Jesus said, "those who mourn," not "those who pretend there is nothing to mourn about." If those in the adoption triad do not recognize there is something to grieve, how can the wound be healed? And, as is often the case, how can these feelings be resolved in an adoptee when the adoptive parent feels threatened by the phantom birth parents and/or guilty over getting to *be* the parent? If there is a perceived threat of losing the adoptive parents, often an adoptee will not search, in fact won't even admit to having the need.

In fact, most don't search. None of my adopted siblings did. If in denial, authentically having no need, or feeling antagonistic towards their birth parents, most adoptees never make the move. Birth parents search even less frequently, feeling they do not have the right since they were the ones who relinquished, even if under coercion.

Even though so few reach out, when they do there is nearly always a "yes" waiting for them. Those who are met with "no" are often dealing with someone deeply wounded by the adoption process. The humiliation of the birth mothers can be extreme. Sent away to homes for unwed mothers, sometimes left to birth alone or without anesthetic to "teach them a lesson," forcing them to sign relinquishment papers against their will, being promised they can get their baby back in a few months, or told to just forget because they can always have other children…these stories were all too common.

One birth mother at the WARM meeting said she sobbed over the relinquishment papers because she had to sign a statement that said, "I am an unfit mother."

"Why can't I just write 'I'm too young?'" sobbed the then-sixteen-year-old. But rules were rules.

Birth mothers were both revered and reviled. An older man at the meeting memorably stated, "It's a beautiful thing that immoral whore did," referring to his wife's birth mother. Saintly whores these women, as long as they give up the baby. Because to keep their own child would be selfish when there are *good* women out there – married women – who cannot have children. By default, infertile married women were good, unmarried pregnant women were not.

Equally irritating was the belief that all adoptive parents are superior. Because they obviously wanted children, even to the point of raising others' babies as their own, this made them better. "Adoptive parents are the cream of the crop," said our group leader, looking around the table to heads nodding in agreement. While I thought my own parents were terrific, I could not add my vote. I knew adoptive parents were as human as anyone. Adopting doesn't make that person a better parent, it makes them a parent, period.

Another pervasive myth is that all adoptees feel abandoned. I never felt abandoned. Possibly because of the matter-of-fact way my parents presented adoption, or because in my child's mind it was against the law to have children without being married; but for whatever reason I did not have that issue to overcome. I harbored no resentment. I had no score to settle. I just had to *know*. Know where I came from, know who I looked like, know my genealogy as far back as humanly possible. Maybe this is why I felt free to search while my adopted siblings did not, because I had nothing holding me back.

I turned twenty. Then twenty-one. The wait continued.

The most consistent thing about Brian was his inconsistency. It was the one thing that made me hesitant to marry him. He would firmly state one thing one day and the opposite the next. Even when his friends or I would point this out, he was unmoved. It was as if he couldn't see it.

I was as unchanging as a glacier in comparison. Dull and predictable. I didn't *want* to be dull and predictable but it seemed to happen in order to form the necessary balance. Brian called me his memory. He couldn't or wouldn't remember things because he knew I would. Birthdays, deadlines, events – it all fell to me.

But he was also romantic, giving me a dozen long-stemmed red roses on my birthday, when roses are decidedly out of season and expensive. And he was there when I awoke at the hospital after having my tonsils out even though I knew he had other places he needed to be.

We agreed on all the important things: Politics, faith, goals in life. We wanted a house with a big yard, three kids, a cat, a Golden Retriever for him and a German Shepherd for me. He would work and I would stay home after the first baby was born. This was all in the nebulous future but it was the plan. We envisioned ourselves as his grandparents fifty years down the road, still in love and with a bevy of grandchildren to spoil.

His family was boisterous and happy and liked to do things like camping. My idea of camping was sleeping in a plush trailer complete with electricity and running water, eating quiet dinners outside and going for walks. Their idea of camping was sleeping on the ground and having uproarious gatherings worthy of being ejected from the campground (in one case being asked never to return). I decided I was an anti-camper and didn't care who knew it. Still, I admired their high-spirited nature. And they put up with me, with my pumps and pearls and devotion to Miss Manners.

I was well into my second year at TVTI. My routine was to have lunch with Elizabeth and to drive Craig home after school. At first I only played taxi a few times during the incessantly wet winter-spring so he wouldn't have to walk in the rain. Soon it became an expectation. As summer approached and the sun came out we did not alter our arrangement. Sometimes we stopped at a park or the waterfront and just talked. Or more accurately, he would talk; I would listen.

The topics were often outrageous, such as his tales of sexual conquest. Although never crude, I found his motivation shallow, as in "because he could". There had been a long line of lovers who seemed to want the same as he did: sex, no strings attached. Nothing perverse, just an endless number of women who got into bed with him. Such is the life of an artist. He half-jokingly suggested I should try it. Meaning, try him. He had no idea how close I came to saying yes.

Of course saying yes would have been disastrous. Not only concerning my relationship with Brian but the act itself. I had only told a select few girlfriends about the pain during intercourse and they were as mystified as I was. I knew no one who could relate. All the women who fell into bed with Craig certainly didn't have that problem. Or did they? One day when we were alone I summoned the courage to ask.

He eyed me curiously. Had I talked to a doctor? Several. Did I ever have a pelvic exam? I had lost count of how many. Was I tested for sexually transmitted disease? With every Pap smear.

He considered this quietly. Then he wrote "serology" on a slip of paper and gave it to me. "Have this done. Have it tested for everything." – "What is it?" – "A blood test." My heart sank. I had hoped that he knew just one other woman who had the same problem. Instead he thought another test would give the answer. I knew it wouldn't.

It couldn't be called frigidity because the desire was there. I had read about vaginismus, a condition common among concentration camp survivors who were physically unable to endure penetration, even to insert a tampon, but this did not apply to me either. I had hoped taking the chance in asking Craig would solve the mystery. Instead he now knew something about me I didn't want anyone to know. Confiding in him had been my last chance. I pushed the whole thing to the back of my mind again, but I knew then without a doubt I was a sexual cripple.

One day as I drove him home, Craig asked if I would ever have an abortion. "You mean, if the baby was healthy?" I asked.

"Yes," he said.

I could see in my peripheral vision he was gauging my expression. He often did that. I don't know why he asked except maybe for the shock factor. He was always trying to catch me off guard. I knew he never wanted to procreate; he loathed his own genetics. To him abortion was a mercy. To me it was something altogether different.

"Only if I really hated the father," I answered after some consideration.

There was no way I could destroy what would be my child unless I hated the father so much I thought the baby was better off not to exist. It was an odd thought and it stuck with me. I wondered if my mother hated my father. I wondered if she ever considered abortion. And if she knew that I would have one in extreme circumstances, would she be ashamed of me, the baby she didn't abort?

It was summer and I was supposed to be done with TVTI but I was afraid to move on. I had been in school since I was five years old, and as much as I hated the constraints it had become everything I knew. I wasn't ready for the "real world." I asked Mr. Granville if it would be okay for me to stay through the summer. He said yes.

While pretending to be busy there I also still worked at the candy store, still went to the WARM meetings, still waited for something to happen with my search. I was stuck in the waiting.

Then it was August and I had to leave. There is no ceremony, no graduation, no "good-bye and good luck" party at a voc-tech. Students just pack up their box, say "Bye" and that's that. I didn't want to leave the comfort of Mr. Granville's class. I also did not want to leave Craig, but I couldn't tell him that. I couldn't tell anyone. I drove him home as usual. He was in a black mood. I pretended not to notice. Halfway there he told me to pull over.

I don't remember where we were or what he said. I just knew he was angry. He told me everything that was wrong with me. I sat in stunned silence, unable to absorb what was happening. I heard only bits and pieces:

"…your childish morals…"

Why are you angry?

"…find out too late…"

Why are you saying this?

"…marriage and brats…"

Why won't you kiss me?

"…sexually frustrated…"

Why won't you kiss me, just once?

"…with that stupid hurt look…"

And getting out of the car he slammed the door and strode off.

Don't leave.

I watched him walk away.

Don't leave me.

Time stopped. Reality stopped. I was standing on the edge of a cliff and any little breeze or shifting of the ground would make me fall. And I knew I couldn't fly.

That Sunday I sat quietly at church and begged God to take away my desire for Craig – to make me forget about him completely.

Life went on, somehow. I endured reality.

I was at the mall when I found myself following a woman I had never seen before. As she walked past me I didn't actually look at her, I just put the clothes I was holding back on the rack and trotted after her like a puppy. Fortunately I realized what I was doing before she did. Drawing myself up short, it came to me I had done it as a reflex – she smelled like my mother. Chanel no.5 is slightly different on every woman who wears it, but this woman's scent was so close to Lillian's that my olfactory sense recognized her as my mother and I followed her like it was the most natural thing in the world.

I stood awkwardly, watching the woman-who-was-not-my-mother walk away, breathing in the last trace of her perfume. It seemed I was always watching people walk away.

I loved many things because they were a tangible reminder of Lillian: purple orchids, coiffed auburn hair, styles from the 1950s, a table set with fine china, white gospel music, left-handed cursive, even Roquefort dressing.

I stumbled across a theory that what was called a poltergeist ("noisy ghost") is actually telekinetic activity caused by an adolescent girl during times of stress, when her hormones are more than her physical body can contain. It hit me that what I thought was Mom trying to communicate with me after her death wasn't her at all. It was me. I was chasing a ghost that I created.

I couldn't let go of that relationship, even though she had been dead for years, what seemed a lifetime ago. Carol could not replace her. Not even my birth mother could replace her. I needed *that* connection, with *that* mother. Getting married, even having children, would never fill the void. I would always miss her. I would never "get over it."

Some months later, a postcard arrived from Germany. Addressed to me but at my cousin Jerome's place a mile away. The postman knew better and it was correctly delivered. On one side was a photo of Neuschwanstein Castle in Bavaria. On the other side was Craig's familiar script in black ink that merely said, "Ludwig's castle" and where it was located in Germany. There was no return address.

He escaped at last. And he thought to write to me from Europe. He must have looked me up in the phone book before he left and not knowing my father's name, copied the most likely Ardahl in the listings. But *why* did he write? Was he taunting me? Did he want to prove at least this wild story was true? Was he apologizing for the way he left? I had too many other things to think about, so tucked the postcard away with the letters from my other well-traveled friends and family. This had to be the final post-script. I relegated Craig Evershaw to the back of my mind again, determined that this time he would stay there.

Chapter 8
~Reality Shifted, Part 1~

Then everything changed forever. My search took off. Lorraine, my CI, called to say she had located the family, who in turn gave her my birth mother's new surname and phone number.

"Does she still live in Tacoma's Bayridge neighborhood?" I asked casually.

There was the slightest hesitation before Lorraine replied, "I never said that." I could almost hear her thinking, *"Did I say that? Did I actually tell her that?"* And I knew my feelings were correct. She was there.

Lorraine said she was going to attempt contact and would do her best to get a "yes". She called back, saying "She wants to say yes but needs time." I sweated it out for a week, imagining going door-to-door in Bayridge, asking every middle-aged white woman if my birth date meant anything to her.

Then it happened. Lorraine called. "Do you want a name?" I could hear her smiling. I still remember sitting at the kitchen table, writing everything she said, as if afraid this information would somehow be taken from me because my birth mother changed her mind.

Pamela Linden Mathias. She was married and had three children (besides me); Sharon, twenty-four and married with a baby of her own; Paul, eighteen; and Teresa, ten. *Ten?! A little sister after all these years?*

She was from Spokane but had lived in Tacoma since I was born.

She was a teacher, as was my birth father. (I picked my jaw up off the floor.)

He was married, she was divorced. *"Get married then,"* said my grand-mother. *"Maybe one is already married,"* I said.

And she wanted me to call her.

She wants me to call her. My mother, Pamela Mathias, wants me to call her. I made arrangements for the next day, so I had plenty of time to panic/rejoice/have hysterics beforehand. I called co-adoptee Jenny Miller and asked her to help me find an address. We drove there in the dark, missing the street several times, finally turning the right corner, and cruised slowly past the house. It was not as I had imagined, not a craftsman-style, but it was old and classic. I liked it. A young man – a teen – parked his car and walked toward the house, eyeing us briefly. "That's your brother!" Jenny whispered dramatically. I sank down in the seat, then wondered why I was hiding. I wondered if my siblings knew about me. On the way home I realized I had been driving within two blocks of her house every time I took Craig home from school.

I could hardly sleep, knowing the next day I would actually speak to the woman who gave birth to me. When the time came I went to Jenny's house for privacy. I still had not told Dad or Carol; it was all too new and I was afraid of their reaction. Besides, this wasn't about them. This was *my* journey.

I sat alone in Jenny's room, notepad in my lap, and made the call. Her voice was familiar but I couldn't place it. She was as nervous as I was, which was strangely comforting. We talked for over an hour. I cannot recall the exact conversation, only that we tried to fill the other in on our lives. There was just one thing I remember she wanted to make clear: "About your father – It was not a love relationship." She spoke warmly, carefully, articulately. A lady.

I remember asking about my ethnic background. She said she was Swedish on her father's side and English, Scotch-Irish, and German on her mother's. And my birth father?

"He had a German name: Havner." Great. I was only a quarter Swedish and half German – even more if Pamela had German blood also.

We agreed to meet in two days time. But where? Not her house, not mine, not a restaurant. I thought of the perfect place: The library, where I had spent so much time during my search.

I asked Brian to drive since I was a nervous wreck. We pulled up to the curb and I saw a nicely dressed woman carrying a shopping bag and purse, walking in the direction of the library's main entrance.

"That's her!"

"How do you know?"

"I just know. I bet she has photo albums in the bag!"

"She could be an axe-murderer for all you know. She could have an axe in the bag."

Still, Brian knew better than to argue. I jumped out of the car and ran up to the woman, who (it happily turns out) *was* my birth mother and not an axe-murderer. And who did have photo albums in the shopping bag. We stood and looked at each other. The Mall Psychic was right – I didn't really look like her at all. There was a resemblance but it was hard to pinpoint. Different coloring even though we both had brown hair and brown eyes, and completely different bone structure. After absorbing this, we went to the Rare Book Room where we were sure to have privacy. Only it was full of people. So we found a quiet corner in another part of the library and proceeded to get ourselves thrown out for being too noisy. It was the only time either of us had been ejected from a library. We were oblivious to the commotion we caused, we were so wrapped up in our conversation and in each other.

Brian was long gone, not expecting to pick me up for some time. We were back to looking at each other on the sidewalk, wondering what to do next. Pamela threw caution to the wind and asked me come to her house. In the car she told me briefly about my father and how I came to be. "I feel now I was set up, like a goal he was determined to achieve. I didn't love him," she cautioned, as if to not get my hopes up. I never had the feeling they were in love so this didn't bother me. "He loved sports, loved coaching." I shuddered. The one thing I was never interested in.

"Let me guess - His favorite was basketball."

"How did you know?"

"It's the one I really despise."

There in her home, on her living room couch, we really talked. She showed me album after album of photos. Of her children, of her parents, of herself and her husband. I kept looking for a resemblance – to anyone – but found them only in the vaguest of terms.

At some point her son came in. The one I saw two nights before. My brother, Paul. I wasn't the youngest anymore, at least not here. Pamela explained in our phone call that Sharon and Paul had not known about me until she told them two days prior. So they were all still letting it sink in. And Teresa still didn't know, because Pamela wanted the moment to be right.

Paul and I sat and stared at each other. He really didn't look like me either. None of my half-siblings did, as far as I could tell.

Pamela was concerned about people recognizing I was her daughter if I was seen there. She was not ready to bring it all out in the open – not yet – after more than twenty years of secrecy. Hoping to put her at ease, I asked Paul:

"If you saw us walking down the street together, would you know we were related?" He said no.

"But you have the same voice," he added.

What?

"You sound exactly the same."

That's why her voice sounded familiar on the phone, it was *my* voice. We looked at each other and laughed. I asked her if she also loved coffee and chocolate. "Oh, absolutely," she answered.

"And reading?" Yes.

"Writing?" She had kept journals for years.

"And music?" She could play piano and sing but didn't claim to be great at either.

"And art?" She came from a long line of artists and had been an art teacher. "What is your favorite medium?" Pencil sketches. Finally, *the* question:

"Favorite art style?" French impressionism.

This was my mother. There was absolutely no doubt.

Then she pulled out something I didn't expect: The yearbook from the school where she and my father taught in Idaho. In the black and white photos I saw how my parents and their world looked the year I was conceived. She opened it to the only candid shot, catching him by surprise as he leaned on his desk. I looked closely.

"There I am," I said in wonder. In the grainy photo I saw the male version of myself: the compact bone structure, dark eyes against pale skin, the casual ease missing from all the posed shots. It was me.

"What? Oh, you don't look like him. Not at all," insisted my newly found mother, completely dismissing the idea. I said nothing, trying not to smile. Sometimes the obvious needs to be ignored.

We talked numerous times in the beginning. It was overwhelming for Pamela but at the same time she welcomed it. After decades of hiding and secrets, she was cautiously coming out into the light. This is what she told me over the many meetings, lunches and phone calls:

It was the early 1960s. The era of *Mad Men*, Kennedy's Camelot and the Space Race. A brave new world that was still highly conservative, still easing out of the Red Scare. The anti-war movement, civil rights, and "women's lib" were barely on the horizon. The Pill was new, high-dosage, and available only to married women with her husband's and doctor's approval. Pamela White (née Linden) was a young divorcée and mother of one little girl, Sharon. Her husband had emptied the bank account and vanished, leaving Pamela to rely on her parents for help and guidance. She'd had a very traditional upbringing in Spokane with upper-middle-class parents, married young, and did all the things expected of a young bride. When her husband disappeared, it was her mother who encouraged her to go back to college. A photo of Pamela in her graduation cap and gown after earning her bachelor's degree, toddler on her hip, made her mother very proud. Pamela always listened to her mother.

And so she found herself just over the border in Coeur d'Alene, Idaho, teaching art at the high school. She rented a little place for herself and her daughter and settled in to stay. She made friends with another female teacher who was about her age, single, and lived in an apartment. She didn't know anyone else in town.

Enter Glenn Havner. He was slightly older and had a master's degree in education, but what he really cared about was sports, mainly basketball. Even with his slight build, he loved sports and was an excellent coach.

He also loved his wife. That was why Pamela trusted him. She figured a happily married man would be safe to socialize with. ("Those are the ones you need to worry about," said Dr. Clark, much too late.) He was charming; he made her feel attractive. After being abandoned by her husband the attention was like a soothing balm. She had no idea how vulnerable she was.

The school and all its activities became her social life. She attended football and basketball games even with little interest in either. As winter melted into spring, Glenn tried to melt Pamela's resistance, little by little, but as close as she came to crossing the line, she held back. She liked having him around, craved the attention, but he was married. Not only that, she liked his wife. Shirley was friendly, smart and beautiful. It was obvious Glenn was in love with her, but apparently that wasn't enough.

Once he stopped at Pamela's place, casually sat on the bed and patted it, asking her to join him. "What about your wife and kids?" she challenged. He jumped up then but it was just a small set-back. He'd win eventually. He made sure of it.

(Pamela was deliberately vague about what happened next. Partly to protect me from the graphic nature of it, partly to protect herself from the long-buried feelings, and partly because she was a lady and ladies don't talk about these things.)

They both had been drinking. They were alone. She didn't want it but was unable to stop him. When telling her mother this later, she was admonished, "A woman can always get her leg up there," meaning: she wasn't really resisting. I knew my grandmother was wrong and that there was more to the story, but I wasn't going to press for details. I could tell it was difficult enough for Pamela to say this much.

Although she felt used, she still had mixed feelings about him. Classic victim scenario. Not long after, they were alone again and he pulled her to him. She resisted.

"Come on, nothing's going to happen," he whispered reassuringly.

"I think something already *did* happen," she blurted out. He released her.

"You're just saying that," he muttered, but did not touch her again.

At spring break Pamela went home and to her doctor, who confirmed what she already knew: She was pregnant. Her father demanded to know who did this to her. *"What is his name?!"* he shouted, pounding the table, but she resolutely shook her head and said nothing. She wasn't going to be a home-wrecker. Still, she had to go back and finish out the school year. How could she do that and have no one suspect?

Her mother said, "You'll have to be a good actress." Pamela always listened to her mother. She did as she was told.

Back at work, Glenn found her. "Well?" he demanded.

"Oh, it was nothing," she said as casually as possible.

"Ha, I thought so," he said.

You son of a bitch. You get to stay here and go on with your life and I have no idea what I'm going to do, she thought. But she couldn't deliberately hurt Shirley or their children. She didn't care about him, but she cared about them.

By June, word got around that Pamela was not renewing her contract. One day, while stopped at a red light in their little town, Shirley ran up to Pamela's car.

"Is it true you're not coming back next fall?" Pamela confirmed it was true. Then something she never expected:

"Is it because of Glenn?"

Pamela's mind went blank. *How much does she know?* Pamela grappled for a response, something truthful without giving away more than Shirley already knew. She finally said,

"Partly, yes."

The light mercifully turned green and she drove away.

The school year over, Pamela was back in Spokane with Sharon and had decisions to make. "Therapeutic" abortion was quietly available to women of means. But it was still risky, and having lost a baby to late-miscarriage early in her marriage and now as a mother, Pamela knew what it was to carry a child and could not bring herself to end the pregnancy.

As a single woman, long since divorced, she could not have and keep a child out of wedlock, at least not without being punished. She would be shunned in society, unable to work, the child labeled a bastard, and even Sharon would carry the stigma.

Her father knew a man who was in love with Pamela and would agree to marry her and take the child as his own. As noble as this seemed, Pamela could not enter into a marriage with a man she did not love. It would be a lie.

There was one last choice: Give the baby up for adoption.

Pamela entered the WARM meeting to thunderous applause. WARM had been my rock during the two year search and the members were now my friends. Even if their own search was not resolved and never would be, they were sincerely happy for me. And they liked Pamela, but then, how could they not? The whole thing was overwhelming to her since the reunion came out of nowhere. She had no time to prepare. I was The Secret she swore to keep and now suddenly she was explaining how she had four children instead of three. I told her she didn't *have* to do that if she didn't want to, but she was adamant she wanted no more secrets, that there was nothing to be ashamed of. Gray Panthers founder Maggie Kuhn's famous line "*Speak your mind, even if your voice shakes,*" is a quote I apply to her at this stage. She was very brave coming out into the light. Speaking her truth, even with voice shaking.

She wrote to her elderly aunt, the matriarch of the family:

"I am experiencing a sort of rebirth…"

She said she felt God's hand in my adoption because I went to a Swedish and Christian home. Great-aunt Nora could not have children herself and was displeased at her brother (my grandfather)'s choice of spouse, since Pamela's mother was decidedly *not* Scandinavian. I never had the chance to meet Aunt Nora but Pamela was pleased she at least knew of my existence before she died.

Meanwhile, I was trying to keep the peace. The reason it took Pamela a week to say yes to the reunion was her husband's opposition. She told him about the relinquishment five years after they married because she decided there should be no secrets between them, no matter what the "experts" advised. He replied in so many words: *Fine, now we never need mention it again.* Jim Mathias did not take to change or surprises. He had married this woman and adopted her little girl as his own and they settled down to a normal middle-class life. There was no room and no need for surprises. Then I come along.

He gave Pamela an ultimatum: She could have the reunion or the marriage. She didn't tell me exactly what he said, but that seemed to be the gist of it. After a week of agonizing, she decided if their twenty-year union could not survive this upheaval it wasn't worth keeping.

Maybe that shocked him – that she was willing to put everything on the line, that this wasn't some passing whim. He did not leave. Neither did she. They adjusted. I did my best to be pleasant but it was like being presented to a disapproving father-in-law every time we were in the same room. Finally, I wrote a letter. I addressed it to Pamela but it really was to Jim:

"…I do not expect to be included in 'family' events. I won't say no if you ask, but just know I do not want to disrupt any family traditions." He seemed placated by this but it would be years before he was comfortable having me around.

My new siblings reacted in various ways. They had their lives and I did not change that but I was a new reality – the sister that wasn't there before.

Pamela did not have *too* much difficulty telling Sharon or Paul about me, but with Teresa she kept it quiet for awhile, saying just that I was her "special friend." Finally when she could not suppress it any longer, Pamela prayed, "God give me the words," and it just came out, perfectly. She cried. Teresa cried. Teresa had given me several drawings, of flowers and cats and whatever little girls like to draw. They were always addressed to "My Friend Noelle". Now she gave me a new crayon masterpiece: "To My Sister Noelle" and it was my turn to cry.

I did not meet Sharon for a few months because she was married and out on her own. Her husband's career required near-constant relocation and my appearance happened when they lived across the country. But she took the time to write a gracious letter introducing herself and welcoming me to the family.

She was home that spring and when we met it was as if we had always known each other. She was beautiful, gentle, and articulate. Her life centered round being a wife and mother yet she made a point of doing things for herself. She loved beautiful clothes and art and dance. In fact she had taken ballet for years. It's even possible I even saw her dance when I forced my brother John to take me to see *The Nutcracker*, but I did not keep the program and couldn't remember the year, so have no definitive proof. I like to *think* I saw her dance.

She was so young when I was born that she never realized our mother was pregnant.

In Paul I finally had a "little brother," though he towered over me. He was a true mix of both his parents – the embodiment of his father's work/family ethic and his mother's Nordic moods, his father's dark European coloring and his mother's Celtic bone structure. He loved sports and cars and hanging out with his dad. We didn't have much in common. But it became "okay" between us when he decided I was his little sister, not elder. I told him that wasn't really fair, since I never had a little brother before and he already had a little sister, but he stood firm. He had a quiet sense of humor and loved to tease, but not in a mean way. In a nice, big brother sort of way.

Finally, there was Teresa, the unexpected blonde. Although Pamela was half-Swedish, there were no blondes in the family as far as anyone remembered. Jim joked if he hadn't been there when she was born, he would have wondered if they got the right baby. In truth she looked just like the others, only with very fair coloring. Pamela reasoned if recessive genes didn't win out once in a while, blondes wouldn't exist. Teresa was downright cherubic with her golden hair and green eyes but she was a very real kid as well. Still liked to color and play with dolls. I saw in her the childhood I might have had.

A certain amount of reorganization took place. I had not expected that. I did not expect to be included – grafted in – almost immediately, if at all. I had no idea what to expect, really. I had hoped to be friends but they surprised me with much more. After getting over the shock of my existence they welcomed me.

One night when everyone was there, we watched a slide show of family photos. While they laughed and chatted I sat transfixed, completely pulled in, mentally inserting myself into each shot, the would-be me. The trip to Disneyland: *"Sharon is ten so I would have been seven, with that awful pixie haircut."* I imagined what I would be wearing, my height next to my siblings. Would I still have been afraid of the "Microscope" ride? Would I have complained about the heat? Would I have been allowed a chocolate milkshake with nearly every meal? Now Christmas: *"Teresa is a toddler so I would have barely been thirteen."* Here I tried to place myself in the picture and couldn't. That time of my life was so dysfunctional, so *wrong* I couldn't even imagine being here instead, with a healthy mother and intact family.

Of course this other-me may never have happened, even if Pamela some-how kept me. Maybe she would have stayed in Spokane to be near her parents. Or if she did move to Tacoma, maybe the circumstances that brought her to-gether with Jim Mathias never would have occurred. And if that didn't happen, no younger siblings. Or at least not the ones I knew now in the form of Paul and Teresa. Would I have been jealous of Sharon, the perfect older sister with her thick silky hair, beautiful eyes, talent and grace? Probably. Would I have been overlooked, the forgotten middle child? What talents would I have honed to be distinguishable, to be noticed?

As a mental exercise I imagined myself as a Mathias or at least a Linden. Raised Presbyterian instead of Baptist. A middle child instead of youngest. Tak-ing ballet instead of piano. But it was just fantasy. Although I was a Linden (and Havner) by blood, spiritually I was an Ardahl. The adoption worked in that re-gard; I was a maple limb successfully grafted onto a birch.

There was not much difference between my original and adopted families on the surface. Both middle-class, white, Christian, conservative. I was adopted out because of the mores of the time, not because Pamela wasn't a perfectly ca-pable mother.

I never felt abandoned, in part because my adopted parents never made me feel unwanted, but there was something more. Pamela felt a measure of peace with the adoption and somehow I knew it, even before I knew her.

Pamela had already surprised me with the gift of the school annual, es-sentially giving me a snapshot of the era when I was conceived; but she had an-other gift and I don't know if she had any idea how powerful it was when she gave it to me.

It was a newspaper clipping, yellowing but carefully preserved. Dated only six years prior, yet a lifetime ago, entitled *A Christmas I Remember:*

Editor's note: The following entry contains no byline – as its writer noted – "for obvious reasons." But, she added, "I hope it is printed. It is true."

AS CHRISTMAS drew near so did my due date. "Why me, Lord?" was all I could think. Little did it matter. I was trying to do what was best.

I couldn't forgive myself and thus wanted God to share the blame.

She arrived a few days before Christmas. As I came out of the anesthetic, a nurse came and asked if I had seen the baby.

I told her "No." Her expression changed from smiling to shock. I didn't know what sex the baby was, if it was alright, or anything about it. I'd received a general anesthetic so I wasn't awake during the birth.

It was terrible, the feeling of unexplainable depression. When the doctor came in, I asked the baby's sex. "A girl." Could I see her? A pause as the doctor searched my eyes and said, "Usually it's best not to."

I shook my head. Then he added, "If you're sure you aren't going to change your mind…" I shook my head again.

"Well, I'll see," he said, and he went out the door. I'd made my decision long before this moment. The decision for her future had rested in my hands. I'd felt like King Solomon. A wise decision had to be made.

MANY FACTORS had to be considered, but the one which tipped the scale was the choice of whether she would be raised in an atmosphere of shame or one of pride. Attitudes were much different then.

I don't know who the doctor had to convince, or if he was the one who had to be convinced, but after a time a nurse walked in carrying a tiny bundle. My baby!

My depression immediately changed to unbridled joy. What a beautiful, perfect baby! The nurse left the room, trusting me with this little creature. And fifteen years ago this was rather unusual, too. Those five days in the hospital turned from days of utter despair to days of unparalleled joy, even though I knew it was temporary.

I SAVORED every minute with her, drinking in her sweet aroma. Hour after hour, I gazed into her tiny face and whispered, "I love you…enough to give you up."

What a wrenching. Elated with the miracle of birth and the precious baby I balanced too precariously in my two hands – at the same time devastated by the fact of not being able to give her the home and life she deserved.

Did she understand? Would she ever understand? How can anyone who has not been through this know how much love it takes to give up the beloved.

As I sat searching her face, mentally trying to touch her innermost soul, her little eyes opened. She was looking straight at me! Dear Lord, maybe she does know; maybe somehow, someway, beyond which we on earth can comprehend, she knows.

I SAID GOODBYE to my baby later that day, leaving her in the care of those at the hospital until her adoptive parents came to take her home.

Christmas was a little sad that year. However, I was thankful there was someone who would take my baby and love her. Each year the return of the "joyous season" brings back memories of those days in the hospital, when I said goodbye, making a total commitment to the secret I'd have to live with forever.

My breath left me. *Here* is what I had looked for. On my fifteenth birthday, as I scoured the tiny print of the personal ads, looking for a hidden message, a secret code – this was in plain sight. If I had not been looking for something hidden I would have seen it. My father's relatives busy with my uncle's slow suicide, my mother's family still deep in grief, all buried in pre-holiday activities, no one saw this who could have put the clues together.

Here was the reason Dr. Clark sputtered, "Oh that woman!" Here was the explanation for the one day delay in bringing me home. Here was the message from my birth mother that I *knew* was there…if I had just turned the page.

I knew I had to tell Dad. Everyone knowing except him wasn't sustainable. I was sure he'd be furious; he'd feel I had betrayed him and Lillian. I thought and thought of a good way to broach the subject. It had to be perfect. I stalled so long, God intervened. This time it was while I was at work. I had a job closer to home, at an ice cream shop, and when I closed one evening, I found I had a flat tire. It was okay when I went in but was now completely out of air.

"I can handle this," I thought and went to get the lug wrench out of the trunk. Ha. No matter how I twisted and turned it, I couldn't get a single nut to budge. I envisioned standing on the thing and jumping up and down. Finally I stood, looked to the skies and said, "Fine!" I called Dad.

As he easily removed the lug nuts, saying, "I don't know why you think this is so hard," I figured this would be a good time, being he was busy doing what he did best.

"Dad, I've met someone and I hope you'll think it's okay." He barely slowed in removing the tire, but absorbed this and said,

"Why, who is it?"

"I found my birth mother." I waited for him to explode. I waited for the ground to open and swallow me. I waited for the disownment proceedings to start.

"Well. That's...that's fine," now putting the new tire on.

I was still waiting for some cosmic retribution, or at least a more non-Nordic reaction from him, then realized none was forthcoming.

"Fine?"

"Sure."

Fine? *Fine?!* I had tortured myself all these years, apprehensive for this very moment, and it's *fine*?

He asked about her and her family. I told him I had an older sibling and two younger.

"Why did you get left out?"

"She wasn't married then."

"Hm," he said, understanding. The tire was replaced, lug nuts tightened to ensure no mortal could remove them. "Well, that's fine," he repeated.

I could hardly wait to tell my friends at the next WARM meeting how "fine" everything was.

It was actually harder with Carol. I was at the kitchen table while she fussed around, wiping the counter. I barely got the words out of my mouth when she burst into tears.

I tried to say something reassuring, like "This doesn't change anything with us," and she nodded but kept crying.

"Your dad figured you would be the one to do it," she said, when able to talk. I wished Dad would tell me these things himself.

"I've always wondered if Susan would search for you—"

Renewed sobs. "No, no..." was all she could say.

"Why?" I asked, bewildered. But she only shook her head.

It was some weeks later when I approached Dad as he watered the rhododendrons.

"Hey Dad, would you like to meet Pamela?"

"Sure. That would be fine," he answered casually.

"Good. She'll be here in fifteen minutes."

I wanted Pamela to meet Dad and Carol as they really were, not in some stiff, formal way and I knew they'd try to make things "perfect" if they knew she was coming. They rose to the occasion. I think Dad had time to only wash his hands before Pamela drove up. I made introductions in the living room, the same room where Dad had paced and angrily warned me, "If we hadn't gotten you, someone else would have!" and "Oh, that woman!"

My birth mother and my adoptive father grasped hands. My mother and my father who I thought would never meet in this life. They stood, looking straight into each other's eyes. Pamela spoke.

"Thank you for adopting Noelle."

"Thank you for giving her to us."

My father – my stoic Norwegian father who avoided making any statements that bordered on emotion – said this readily, without the usual stammer or hesitation. The woman who gave birth to me thanked the man who raised me and he in return thanked her for her sacrifice.

Time stopped. There was no one else in the room. If Carol was crying, I didn't notice. All I could see were the two people who were the very center of my existence. The vision seared into my psyche.

Later, Carol remarked that Pamela seemed anxious. "Well, she was nervous about meeting you," I reasoned.

"She was nervous about meeting *me*?" Carol said. She visibly relaxed. It disarmed her that Pamela had put her in the position of the mother, not the stepmother.

I told all of my family and friends over time. It only seemed to matter to those who knew Lillian. Brian's family didn't care in the slightest. But when I asked Aunt Betty, "Have you heard the news?" tears welled in her eyes.

"You found your mommy," she said, voice breaking.

"No. Lillian was my mommy. I found my birth mother." At this she regained her composure.

She asked some questions to be polite, including, "Where does she live?" When I said Tacoma, she burst out, "Tacoma?! She was supposed to go back to Idaho!" *Oh, there's an interesting tidbit of information – they knew she was from*

Idaho. Water under the bridge, but I found the outburst interesting: She was "supposed" to go back to Idaho. As if she did not have the freedom to live where she wanted. She had no reason to go back. There was nothing to go back to. Yet to the adoptive family – who had completely anonymity like the birth mother – she was obligated to disappear. To do anything else was a threat.

Aunt Betty told me that when John was born, one of my aunts on Dad's side published a celebratory notice in the newspaper, mentioning he was adopted. Lillian was livid, afraid John's birth mother would somehow see it and put two and two together. She made sure there was no such public notice with me. When I relayed this to Pamela she laughed shortly, saying it had never entered her mind to try to find me that way or any other way.

Soon after this, my sister-cousins and I were at Gramma's. We had just presented her with a studio portrait of the four of us in Swedish folk costume. (I had, as always, been positioned nearest the light so looked like a specter. My cousins exclaimed, "You're so *white*, Noelle!" – "Yes, well, I'm Caucasian," I wearily pointed out.) Gramma was in her easy chair, dressed as always in a floral print dress and a light cotton sweater, her white hair set in tiny curls, her green eyes bright. The rest of us sat scattered on couches or chairs. It was relaxed like it always was. By this time, everyone had heard I found my birth mother, and nothing had changed. In this family I would always be Lillian's daughter. I wanted Gramma to hear the "A Christmas I Remember" newspaper article and this seemed an opportune moment. Linda volunteered to read it aloud. Gramma listened thoughtfully; I was unable to interpret her expression as she gazed into the distance. There was profound silence as we collectively held our breath, waiting for her response. Finally Gramma said:

"It must have been very hard for her."

We exhaled.

No more "How could she?" Because now she understood how she could and why she could and why she *had to.* It was possibly the biggest paradigm shift of my grandmother's life and she dealt with it with the same quiet acceptance as she handled everything.

Chapter 9
~The Actual Real World~

That summer Brian and I traveled to Spokane, to Pamela's childhood home. I knew my new grandparents only through what Pamela had told me and the photos she shared. They were in a state of decline even though they were both younger than Gramma Nelson and even though my grandfather was also Swedish. She was physically infirm yet sharp. He was ambulatory but had dementia. I wished I could have known them twenty years earlier.

The house was in an old, tidy neighborhood circa the 1920s, brick with wood siding additions. No yard to speak of, just old evergreen trees. Pamela said her father's solution for lawn care was to "pave it over and paint it green." Inside it was crowded with old furniture and bric-a-brac, as if decorated when they first moved in and never changed except to add more stuff. Stacks of magazines with a small tablecloth thrown over made for a new end table and soon there were piles on top of that as well. The interior had the dull, dark coloring that slowly afflicts old houses not periodically updated.

The story went that when they decided to move to Spokane, my grandmother found this house and bought it, informing her husband after the transaction was complete. Instead of being angry at not being consulted, he was proud of his wife's strong decision-making skills. A true Proverbs 31 woman: *Her husband has full confidence in her and lacks nothing of value.* He indulged her in every new luxury and convenience and she in turn created a beautiful home. But that was over fifty years ago.

Pamela first introduced me to her mother. The way she was hunched over in her favorite chair made her look like a soft, round ball. Wearing a house dress one would expect from several decades prior, her formerly lush auburn hair now white, she did not resemble the proud woman I saw in photos. Pamela told me her mother's hair had been so thick in her youth her doctor ordered it cut because the weight of it gave her headaches. She promptly had it bobbed and never grew it long again, much to her mother's horror, because only "fast" girls bobbed their hair. The most striking thing about her though, were her huge brown eyes. These remained the same. Pamela and Sharon inherited that trait although I did not. And I certainly did not get the hair.

Pamela told me her mother was a society lady. She had belonged to every fraternal organization known to exist, serving as an officer in most. She inked letters in beautiful cursive on stationery after composing a rough draft on plain paper. She insisted on a properly-set table. An excellent seamstress, she made dozens of outfits with matching hats, gloves and shoes. She never went out – even to the grocery store – unless appropriately attired. Being the eldest, she was forced to help to raise her younger siblings, which left her with little regard for babies or children. She allowed herself only two. Once they were born she doted on them properly, feeding them modern, "scientific" formula and keeping them dressed to the nines. They were known as the best-dressed children on the block. She was always proper; formality was her natural state.

And so proper introductions were made. "This is my mother, Helen Rose Linden. You can call her Mrs. Linden or…" I knelt down so we were eye-to-eye. "Hello Grandmama," I said. I didn't come all this way to call my grandmother "Mrs. Linden."

"I always wondered what happened to you," she said matter-of-factly.

After talking with her for a few minutes, Pamela brought me to her father who sat on a couch nearby. They had needed round-the-clock care for some time, partly due to her inability to get around and his ability to do just that. He was at risk for wandering off, unable to find his way home again. Before a respected businessman, now an octogenarian preschooler.

Pamela said, "This is Palmer, your grandfather, but he won't know who you are." He was tall and slender. I could now see where Pamela got her Bain de Soleil complexion and almond-shaped eyes. I sat next to him on the couch and said hi.

"Hi!" he said cheerfully.

He was born to Swedish immigrants but allowed no folksy Scandinavian culture in his home. In order to preserve their heritage, his parents made him believe they could not speak English. When he discovered they were indeed bi-lingual he never spoke Swedish again. One reason he was attracted to Helen was that she was so mainstream American.

Ironic that my adopted parents asked for a daughter with Nordic blood when the one it came from ignored it completely. Although he was full Swede and I was only one-quarter, I was more Swedish than he was. He spent his life trying to squelch his background while I spent mine trying to cultivate it.

I had brought some photos to show them. Pamela took out one of me in a provincial folk costume, age three. "Does she look like a little Swedish girl, Dad?"

"She sure does!" he again exclaimed cheerfully. I wished I could talk to him. Brian would often say he wished he had known my grandfather in his prime. It was obvious he was well-spoken and educated but it was all in shadow now. The one person he really interacted with was his wife and he tried her patience with his constant shows of affection:

"I love you, Honey. You're beautiful. You're more beautiful today than you were yesterday."

"Shut up, Palmer," she'd say wearily.

"Okay." Then with a sly smile he'd walk away, clapping his hands slowly and deliberately. It was comical yet sad. Helen certainly didn't find it amusing. Her constant aches and pains did not allow it.

Pamela showed me around the house. On the main floor was a living room, dining room, kitchen, bedroom, bath, laundry, and between that and the kitchen, a "sling room."

"Sling room?"

"It was a bedroom but Mom wanted it for storage. It's where she slings stuff." It certainly was well-utilized for that purpose, but I wished it was still a bedroom. The entire house was packed with papers and things in every possible nook and cranny.

The kitchen originally had a breakfast nook but that was also converted to storage. It was in a charming spot by the window. I tried hard to see past the stuff to imagine my grandparents sitting there drinking coffee in the mornings.

Upstairs in the half-story there were gabled ceilings, which I always found cozy. My grandfather had an at-home office there and on the other end was Pamela's childhood bedroom. Like my own bedroom, there were huge evergreen trees outside the window, only hers were much closer to the house, making it almost invisible from the outside. It was like a secret room. I liked it.

But I had envisioned something much different overall. I wasn't sure what that was or why it was so important to me but this was not what I expected. Disappointed, I went downstairs.

Stepping into the main floor bathroom I switched on the light. Yellow tile. A beautiful tiled bathroom made of the best materials. This was the one room where things weren't stored in perpetuity so I could see it as it really was, the way it had been when my mother was a child. The vision came rushing back – the potted palms, venetian blinds, gabled roof, breakfast nook, art nouveau – it was all here. It was just buried under years of accumulation. Although the house was not a craftsman in that it did not have the heavy beams and wood siding exterior, the floor plan was that of a bungalow.

Now looking past the clutter I saw the wool carpet, the original furniture, the glass art deco. Pamela had said her mother always bought the best. The exception was the dining set: a whimsical drop-leaf table with lyre-back chairs and matching buffet. Although cheaply made and used daily it had lasted decades, a testament to their care.

It really was the sort of house I had dreamed of since I was a child.

I felt completely at home. I felt I *was* home.

I was home.

Pamela and I liked going to lunch and shopping. Specifically shoe shopping. At our first lunch together we reached for the same dark chocolate raspberry torte off the dessert cart. The first time we went shopping together she gave me a tile trivet meant to be used as a wall hanging. She said she felt drawn to it and that she should buy it for me. It was in the colors I planned to use for my kitchen when I had my own place, only I had never told her my color choices.

There was very little difference in tastes or opinions between us, only she was more conservative. I had a more cutting wit and was always ready with a smart remark. Only my Nordic introvert nature kept me from saying every "clever" thing that came into my head. I would instead release it in telling stories to friends over drinks or in letters. My adoptive family never got my sense of humor. I thought my birth family would, but it was my friends who really understood me or at least put up with me.

One day as she drove me home after a visit, she told me what Dr. Clark had said. That I would be going to a good family who lived in the country who had two children already. It pleased her that I would have an older sibling like I would have if I had stayed with her. We pulled up in front of the house. She went on to tell me how glad she was that I ended up where I did. I said nothing.

"You were happy, weren't you? Except for losing Lillian, of course," she added.

"If Keith hadn't existed, yes, I would have been very happy." I hadn't told her about Keith. I didn't want to tell her now, but she didn't want any secrets. I had a gut feeling I needed to say it now. I explained Keith was "off", that he was some kind of sociopath.

"Did he…hurt…you?" she asked quietly.

"Yes," I said, unable to lie.

"He…molested…you?" she asked even more quietly.

"Yes."

She burst into sobs, like Carol did when I told her I had searched. "I'm sorry. I'm so sorry. I didn't know," she cried.

"Of course you didn't know. No one did. It's not your fault," I said, enduring reality but wishing I was anywhere else at that moment.

"But they took you to a doctor. You got therapy," she said hopefully.

"He got therapy."

"Why?! Why him and not you?!"

I had never really thought about "why" before but the answer came easily, "I guess because they knew there was nothing wrong with me."

Pamela would have to forgive my parents for this. I could only imagine how hard that was. She herself sought therapy after this and I was asked to accompany her on one occasion.

The therapist did not impress me. A "Christian counselor," she made up her mind about me before ever laying eyes on me. She told me I felt abandoned. All adoptees do, she said. *Don't tell me how I feel,* I thought fiercely. I told her even if every other adoptee on earth felt that way I never did. It irritated me that she was feeding Pamela lies masked as generalities when she came to her for comfort and counsel. I told her I knew dozens of adoptees and the abandonment issue was a myth. She finally let it drop. Then the real reason we were there:

"Why haven't you gotten therapy about being molested?"

"I feel I worked through it on my own." A lie, but I clung to it.

"How can you work through something so traumatic without help?"

"Because I know it wasn't my fault."

"But you won't even tell Brian," interjected Pamela.

"No, I don't want him to feel he has to 'do' something about it."

"But you're protecting Keith!" they said in unison.

"I'm protecting Brian. And my dad. There's nothing anyone can do at this point. To bring it up would just cause bad feelings. And Brian's dad's a cop. They'd feel they'd have to do something and there's nothing legal they could do."

The therapist wearied of my logic. What it came down to was I refused to be a victim. This was the era in the 1980s when everyone was a victim of something. Every TV talk show had a victim of this, a victim of that. I refused to play along. To be a victim was weak. To need help in the form of therapy was weak. It wasn't normal. And damn it, I was going to be normal.

Feeling free to pursue a "real" job, one beyond the coziness of the ice cream shop, I applied at Boeing and was soon lost within the vast catacombs of offices, shops and engineering groups. One worker among thousands.

I made friends there, most notably Cecelia Vaughn. We had much in common but were vastly different. She was Swedish also but mixed with exotic blood that gave her a more striking look. She had grown up in a Nordic family and understood subtleties like "nearly laughed out loud," why trash had to be neat and the superiority of white-on-white food.

What was different about her from all my previous girlfriends was that she understood men. While we muddled along she had them figured out. Her husband was completely in love with her and she with him, but every man she so much as smiled at acted as if they had been given a gift from God. She also understood my adoration of classic clothing styles – hats, silk, pearls. And she introduced me to champagne. Good champagne, with hand-dipped chocolates, steamed artichoke, delicate brie or just more champagne on the side.

Over time I was able to talk to Cecelia about nearly anything. But I never felt it necessary to explain myself to other co-workers. One day the subject of siblings came up in the office. "How many brothers and sisters do you have?" an engineer asked.

"Twelve," I answered.

"Twelve?! Are you Catholic?"

"No, some of them are Catholic but I'm not."

"Are they your real siblings?"

"Define 'real'."

"You have the same biological parents and grew up together," he said after some consideration.

"Wow, I'm an only child!" I exclaimed and walked away, making the mental note never to ask an engineer to define anything ever again.

As one Mother's Day approached, another man in the office asked what I was doing that weekend. "We'll make the rounds. See the moms," I said.

"Your mother and your husband's mother?" he asked.

"Both of my mothers and my fiancé's mother and step-mother, yes."

He looked at me with something akin to pity and said as if explaining to a child:

"You can have only one mother."

A sharp remark was on the tip of my tongue but I stopped myself just in time. I opted not to make myself the office conversation piece. "The girl with three mothers." I could just see it.

After working out one evening, I passed two women in the health club locker room. One was holding the hand of the other, who was very distraught.

"…and I said, okay, but you can't call her *Mom,*" her voice breaking on the final word. The friend nodded in understanding. Even with my proper up-bringing, it took everything I had not to interrupt with, "Would you say that if she was getting married and wanted to call her mother-in-law 'Mom'?"

It was obvious this was not a case of "losing" a daughter to marriage. It was "losing" a daughter to reunion. And this woman was afraid of losing her sta-tus and power of being the mother, the one and only. Afraid of losing the love of her child, now adult. She didn't know she would only "lose" her daughter if she shoved her away or tried too hard to cling to her. But I couldn't say any of this, because these were strangers having a private conversation in a very public place.

My friend Jenny Miller's search, meanwhile, had resulted in a non-re-union with more questions and frustration than resolution. Neither of her birth parents had any other offspring and didn't seem to care about the only child they did procreate. Her birth mother felt when Jenny was twenty-one she would be mature enough for a reunion. I said, "So, when you're twenty-one, *she* will be mature enough to meet you? Great." But even when the arbitrary milestone was reached, there was no contact, no reunion.

She never met her father either. Instead his brother came as a stand-in and a rather strained relationship was formed. The uncle seemed to take it as his duty to meet this stranger who was his biological kin. He promised to make her part of the family, to include her, even if her parents couldn't bring themselves to do the same.

One day Jenny called. She never called me at work so had my attention immediately. She said in a quiet, shocked voice:

"My birth father is dead."

I expressed my own shock, because he was very young, barely fifty. I asked what happened.

"He had a heart attack."

"I'm so sorry, Jenny. I'm sorry you never got to meet him. Will you go to the funeral?"

"He died three months ago."

I was sure I had heard her wrong so asked her to repeat that. She said again he died three months earlier and her uncle – the one who promised to include her – had only just informed her.

"Your father died and they didn't have the *courtesy to tell you?!*" I railed, as if being angry on her behalf could somehow change anything.

If I had to sum up Jenny in one word it would be "friend". Always there for others, always supportive, always caring. She never wanted children and was ambivalent about marriage, but fiercely devoted to the families of others. My own birth family took her in along with me and included her as her uncle should have included her in theirs.

I could barely imagine how she must have felt, to be treated as an afterthought. After her adoptive father also died, she moved to the other side of the country, entering into a bad marriage with all of us protesting, but it was with a man who wanted no children either. It's possible that's all they ever agreed on.

With Brian now working at a fire station and me at Boeing, we nearly earned enough to get by. Having no clue as to how broke we really were, we set a date for the wedding the following spring.

Brian called me a wedding groupie. There was nothing I loved more than a well-put-together wedding. And there was nothing I despised more than a badly planned one. The 1980s saw a revival of formality, but in excess. The dresses, the hair, the jewelry, the details, and especially the cost, were all done in a big way. I didn't want trendy, I wanted classic. Something I wouldn't be embarrassed about in ten years. Every wedding I attended I appraised like a society-page reviewer, needing to see reoccurring themes and flattering styles. There were never enough weddings to attend (or, as Brian would say, "critique"). He teased that he expected to find me on a street corner, wearing my best dress, holding a sign written in calligraphy:

Will Be a Guest at Your Wedding

To me, weddings were the last bastion of proper society. No one wore hats or gloves anymore. No one cared about proper table settings. Everything was a casual affair. ("Why be so formal?" I was asked. "Because change is refreshing," I replied.) Being both analytical and a devotee of Miss Manners, it was of the utmost importance to me to do things The Right Way. And weddings seemed to be the only place left where people were willing to even try.

But it wasn't an excuse to put on a big production. It was going to be "big" only because of the number of people involved. This would be the first time all our family would be together in one place. I cannot adequately put into words what this meant to me.

Pamela cautiously asked if they would be invited.

"Well since I'd like Paul to be an usher and Teresa to be a bridesmaid, I certainly hope you'll be there," I answered.

I wanted everyone represented in the wedding party. So the ushers included someone from each of our families, with the obvious exception of the Havners. The bridesmaids were my closest friends from school. While I had once dreamed of having all sisters and sisters-in-law as bridesmaids, most of them couldn't be there. My childhood friends – including Kim Kelemen, Renee Tanaka, and Jenny Miller – were like sisters to me. We had our fallings-out, growing apart and finding each other again, bonding in difficult times. They were my sisters.

Gramma was affronted that I didn't include my sister-cousins in the wedding party. They had other important roles, but for them not to be bridesmaids was beyond her comprehension. That's what cousins were *for*, she said.

"Gramma, if I put all the cousins in, there'd be no one left in the pews."

Dad dragged his feet. Although he had grown to like Brian he couldn't understand why I was rushing into marriage after a mere five years of dating. I tried to explain that this terminal engagement was becoming embarrassing.

We sat in the living room: Dad, Carol and me.

"You know," Dad reminded me, needlessly, "I was more than thirty when I got married."

"You didn't meet Mom until then," I counter-reminded.

"I got to pal around with my friends," he continued.

"All my friends are in college or getting married," I said.

"No receiving line," he said, abruptly changing the subject. I gladly ceded on the receiving line. I had already decided not to have one after one of my cousins never got to attend her own reception the summer before, trapped instead in an endless greeting of guests in the doorway.

"You'll need a new suit," I mentioned as casually as possible, relieved that negotiations were finally underway.

"There's nothing wrong with the one I have."

"It needs to be a dark suit. This will be an evening wedding."

"It's a waste of money."

"Oh Dad," I said cheerfully, "when you see how much this whole thing costs you'll have a heart attack and die and then we can bury you in it."

At this point Carol, who had been quietly listening, nearly fell on the floor laughing. Dad didn't even crack a smile.

"You know, my pa was buried in the same suit he was married in," he seriously mused, as if this was an economical epiphany.

And then he really surprised me. He opened a bank account dedicated to the wedding and handed me the checkbook. All I had to do in return was promise to be a good shopper.

Not long before this, I found Lillian's wedding dress, carefully preserved. I loved her dress. I had always loved looking at their wedding album. The black and white photos showed her at her best – tall and elegant. Betty, her sister and maid of honor, told me she didn't remember where Lil found the dress, but that when she saw it she knew it was the one. To me, it was the definitive wedding gown because it was hers. In her scrapbook she had copied an advertisement:

"Simple elegance of pure silk dupioni, with lace, sequins and seed pearl appliqué at the bateau neckline, enhancing the beauty of the bouffant skirt."

The bodice and sleeves were very fitted. It looked in the photos as if it had been made exclusively for her.

I knew it wouldn't fit me. She was 5'- 9" with a movie-star figure. I was smaller and less endowed. And from the few color snapshots I knew the material was bright white, which I couldn't carry off either.

Still, I wanted to take it out and actually touch it. It would feel like she was there for a moment. It would be a good omen. I knew the dress was in a heavy vinyl garment bag in the back of Dad and Carol's walk-in closet, where it had hung for nearly thirty years. Finding it and unzipping the bag, a memory rushed back:

Mommy and I were in her closet. I loved playing there because I could pretend it was a little house. It was a completely square room, carpeted, with a delicate light fixture on the ceiling and a tiny window on Daddy's side, behind the hangers. I liked looking at Mommy's "fancy shoes" and Daddy's belts and ties that hung on the wall. I would shut myself in and pretend a thousand things: It was a castle, a fort, a secret room and only I had the key. On this particular day, Mommy unzipped a large bag hanging there and said,

"This is my wedding dress. Do you like it?"

I made a face and shook my head. She sighed. Immediately I felt bad but all I saw was a huge dress made of strange fabric. I couldn't imagine it on me just as I couldn't imagine myself as an actual grown-up, but I didn't have the words to explain.

I laid the bag on the bed.

Gently lifting the dress I saw the silk had mellowed to a soft ivory. There was slight deterioration under the arms from the alcohol-based antiperspirant she wore. And the tulle under the skirt had predictably lost its fullness. But other than that it was flawless. I was wistful, thinking even though it was now a shade I could wear I wouldn't possibly fit into it.

I almost put it back, but something made me ask Carol to help me try it on. Misty-eyed, she fastened the buttons up the back. It hung loose all over. I looked like I was still playing pretend like when I was little and would try on Mom's dresses. The rich material shimmered. It was so beautiful I didn't want to take it off, even though it was obvious it would take multiple alternations to make it fit and I didn't want to ruin it by cutting it down. Suddenly Carol thought to grasp a handful of dress at each shoulder and simply pull it up. We looked in the mirror and drew in our breath. Except for the skirt length it was perfect. I do not know how, but it was.

I had my dress. And Lillian would be at my wedding after all.

The summer I was in Spokane, Pamela and I did a lot of shopping. The Crescent was the twin of the upscale Fredrick and Nelson's department store back home. It had a very classic look and of course it was Grandmama Helen's favorite.

I could imagine her in a luxurious coat and stylish hat, shopping for a new pair of gloves after "lunching" with a friend. Pamela and I were in our element.

We stopped at a bridal shop. Pamela didn't want to usurp Carol in the mother of the bride role, but I told her Carol wasn't much into shopping and wouldn't mind. I wanted to try on veils and headpieces. I had the dress but nothing else. I found a tiara. There is no woman alive who doesn't want to try on a tiara at least once. It was really lovely. Although I admired traditional Swedish and Norwegian wedding crowns – tiny coronets of gold or silver – we did not have one in the family and I did not want to be the first to wear one. Not to mention it would make my tiny head look even smaller. I felt beautiful in the tiara and Pamela said it suited me, but it was made of white crystal that clashed with the dress. I described the muted silk and seed pearl appliqué to her.

"I'll probably need to have something made," I said. Then jokingly added, "Do you know any crown-makers?"

She started to say something, but stopped. When we were back in Tacoma she pulled out a photo album I had not seen before – from her first wedding. And in it, a very young Pamela was wearing a circlet crown made of seed pearl.

"That's beautiful. Where did you get it?"

"My mother made it."

Hope rose within me.

"Do you still have it?" Carol had burned her wedding dress, claiming it was damaged with mold. I figured there was just as much sentimental value tied to Pamela's first marriage.

"Mother does. I asked her to find it and send it here."

After what seemed like a very long time, a small box arrived in the mail. I lifted Pamela's crown as gently as I had first lifted Lillian's dress out of safekeeping. Delicate loops of ivory pearl strung on wire. I was afraid I would break it just by holding it. As that thought crossed my mind a few tiny pearls fell but for the most part it held securely. I put it on. She smiled.

When I got home I took out the gown again and laid the crown on it. It was as if they had been made for each other.

Chapter 10
~Wedding~

It was time to address the invitations and Dad was causing trouble. I wrote up the guest list and included all his siblings. He crossed out his sister Pearl. She owed him money from years before and he took it as a personal affront that she seemed to have forgotten about it. I wrote her name again. He crossed her out again. Finally I just left her name crossed out but sent an invitation anyway. I wasn't going to start excluding people now, after all the effort to bring them together.

My cousin Christie asked gently about Keith – if I had invited him.

"Incarcerated people don't get to go to weddings," I answered serenely. He could rot there as far as I was concerned. I had received a letter from one of his cell mates at the state prison, genteelly introducing himself, saying Keith had told him what a wonderful Christian girl I was. Apparently it wasn't enough for Keith that he had destroyed my childhood, now he wanted to pimp me out. Carol, not knowing the depth of my hatred for him or the reason for it, laughed over the letter. To her it was pathetically funny. To me it was a reminder of how sick Keith really was.

I asked Pamela to give me a list of people she wanted there. She felt she was intruding, overstepping her bounds. Her immediate family was already invited but that added only a few while other sides of family were counted in the dozens. Eventually I coaxed a short list out of her – a handful of her closest friends. All of them knew about our reunion except one. Vicki was a granddaughter of the woman who lived next door to Pamela and Jim. They had been neighbors for over twenty years, the families seeing each other in passing every holiday. Vicki and Sharon had also been friends at school but had not seen each another for years because Sharon often moved, following her husband in his career. In fact Sharon couldn't be at the wedding because she on the other side of the country and couldn't get away – which may have been part of the reason that out of that entire sprawling clan, only Vicki was extended an invitation. It would almost be like Sharon was there.

A note that was supposed to be included to explain Pamela's connection was somehow missed. So when Vicki's boyfriend walked into their apartment one day he found her looking at a piece of mail with consternation.

"I got this wedding invitation and I have no idea who these people are!"

Craig Evershaw took the card from her hand, read it and said, "I know who they are. And I think I know why you got it."

The three of us met at a restaurant Craig and I used to frequent downtown. She was beautiful – a slender brunette with an exotic flair. But then all of Craig's girlfriends were beautiful. I sat across from them. Vicki kept exclaiming, "You sound just like Pamela! You look just like Sharon!" I knew I didn't look like Sharon but took it as a compliment.

Craig and I had spoken by phone after Vicki got my number from Pamela. He finished his stint at TVTI soon after I did, got a lot of residual checks for past art projects, went to Germany, (sent me a postcard), came home, met Vicki and soon moved in together. It was the longest relationship he had ever had and he seemed comfortable with that.

"Are you – dare I say – monogamous?" I teased. He feigned insult that I would find this amazing. He was much more relaxed; the simmering anger was gone. He didn't bring up our last meeting and neither did I. He also didn't seem surprised that out of the hundreds of thousands of people in the area we would cross paths this way. The improbable happened to Craig on a daily basis.

Back at the restaurant they looked at me and I looked at them. Craig lounged with his usual coolness. Vicki couldn't get over my resemblance to Pamela and Sharon.

"Those crazy genetics," I shrugged.

I told them about my search, about Boeing, about Brian. Much had happened in the past year and a half and there was so much I wanted to say to Craig, but it would have been inappropriate. He was in an actual relationship now and I was two weeks away from being married.

I can't remember how it came up, but Vicki said she'd had an ectopic pregnancy that needed to be terminated after not aborting on its own.

"She was really sick," Craig said.

"No one knew what was wrong," Vicki added.

"*I* knew," Craig insisted. "At the hospital they couldn't find a cause until I said, 'What if she's pregnant outside the uterus?' Then they rushed her into surgery."

"I'm so sorry," I said, sincerely. They looked at me like I was suddenly speaking Greek. "You lost your baby," I explained, trying to make myself clear. Apparently Vicki wanted to be a mother as much as Craig wanted to be a father, so my condolences were unnecessary.

I watched him walk away again, this time with the beautiful Vicki on his arm. It was if they had been made for each other.

One week later Brian was given a bachelor party by best friend Chris and the three day hangover he suffered and shared nearly ended our engagement. I rationalized he hadn't planned the party and this one incident shouldn't determine our future. Still, I was angry at the way he treated me. Then I came down with a brutal stomach virus and he took time off work to care for me. I forgave him.

At a bridal shower given by his side of the family, I winced when Carol, feeling nervous and out of place, make a thoughtless remark to my almost sister-in-law, who later recounted it to her husband in tears. Eric tracked me down, saying he wouldn't be in the wedding if Carol didn't apologize. The situation was tenuous but I just couldn't hand Carol over; I knew she didn't mean to offend and would be distraught if I told her. Instead, I sent the offended couple a bouquet of flowers and a written apology. This appeased them. I prayed nothing worse would happen.

The day before the wedding, Brian called. His grandmother, his mother's elderly, frail mother, suddenly died.

"Do you want to postpone the wedding?" I asked.

"No."

I breathed a sigh of relief. I don't know what I would have done if he had said yes. Out of town guests had already arrived, everything was paid for and the wedding party was assembled. We went ahead with the rehearsal. Afterwards we were doing what we could to decorate the blasé church hall for the reception when Brian and several close friends disappeared.

"They're outside smoking pot," Jenny hissed. I went back to what I was doing. "What are you going to do about it?" she demanded.

"What am I supposed to do about it?" I answered.

The next morning was worse. Dad paced. Although he had become distantly fond of Brian there was very little love for Brian's parents. Years earlier Brian had found himself without a place to live after budget cuts took his residency at the fire station. He resorted to sleeping on our couch for several weeks until finding other arrangements. His parents found this hilarious. Dad seethed. Here Brian was working hard, trying to make good, and when he had a temporary setback his parents did nothing. "Don't they *like* him?" he finally said, jaw clenched. When Dad clenched his jaw he was really angry.

Now Dad was pacing, telling me everything he didn't like about Brian's father. The list was long but it boiled down to how he found him stingy. I had no idea what to say. "Am I supposed to call off the wedding because you think Dennis didn't serve enough food at the rehearsal dinner?!" I railed. Carol intervened, told Dad to leave me alone. I had done the same for her when her son married years earlier. Dad didn't like Tom's fiancé because she was a dark-skinned Hispanic ("Mexican", Dad insisted, although her family had lived in America longer than his). The morning of that wedding he paced also.

"I don't like it," he spat. We were alone. I was putting on my make-up.

"Dad," I said finally, "Tom has been Carol's son for over twenty years. You've been her husband for six months. Don't make her choose. You'll lose."

The wedding went on, then and now. And my step-brother's subsequent perfect children melted Dad's otherwise unbending heart.

After things calmed down now, Dad said wistfully, "Noelle's had that bedroom twenty-two years." To which an exasperated Carol replied, "For heaven's sake Walt, she's not dead!" What it came down to was Dad was not ready to let me go. I realized I had lived there even longer than Lillian, even though it was "her" house. I had become an expected component.

I had been plagued by dreams where things went wrong and one was of me dragging my father down the aisle. ("Dad, get up! You're embarrassing me!" I whisper desperately. "You're too young!" Dad wails from the floor.) With the day actually here I wondered how much more could happen and still see me wed by evening.

I was surprised with a call from Sharon. Because she couldn't be there she wanted to at least give me her best wishes by phone. Before hanging up she said, "I love you." I let this sink in. My sister who did not even know of my existence one year ago just said "I love you."

"I love you too, Sharon," I managed to say.

At the church, Aunt Betty burst into tears every time she looked at me. Brian, who was surprisingly perceptive at times, sidled up to her and said gently, "It's the dress, isn't it?"

"The last time I saw it, it was on Lillian," she sobbed. She continued to be a soggy mess the entire day. We didn't get a single picture of her.

I had warned the photographer I was not photogenic, that he'd need to catch me in a good shot rather than asking me to pose, but he didn't seem to believe me. Brian couldn't take a bad picture. White-tie looked great on him. The entire wedding party looked terrific. But it took shot after shot to get a decent one of me so I didn't look like a mannequin. As I sat on the steps in front of the altar, bouquet in my lap, waiting for more instructions, I heard my cousin Britta say: "Hey, Noelle," and looked just in time to see the flash. It was the best photo taken of me, ever.

A myriad of things continued to go wrong, but the ceremony itself appeared perfect. Most of the mothers and grandmothers were escorted properly, although a few slipped in beforehand. Pamela's entrance was accompanied by excited whispers from my family's side of the aisle and confused murmurs from everyone else. All of the mothers looked lovely. Brian's mom, newly grieving for her own mother, held up bravely and lit a candle representing the Reid side of the family. Carol lit one for my side. Brian and I would use these to light a unity candle during the ceremony. The symbolism was important to me.

My dream did not play out and Dad walked me down the aisle with dignity. But at the front of the church I suddenly found I could not let go of his arm and spontaneously embraced him, after no physical contact between us in over ten years. Aunt Betty sobbed anew.

Part of the ceremony was inviting everyone to take communion, with the wedding party serving. Guests told me later they liked this but something I was not prepared for was the sight of my devout Baptist grandmother standing before me, ready for the wine, which really is wine in the Lutheran church. Discretely leaning forward I whispered, "Take just a little sip, Gramma." As alcohol passed her lips for the first time in her ninety-plus years her eyes opened in shock but she gave me her mischievous smile before returning to her seat.

At the reception I worked out a system. If people came up and introduced themselves they were new relatives I did not know. If people came up and kissed me without introduction they were relatives I *should* know. I stole strawberries from guests' plates. I figured being the bride they couldn't stop me. I went to get myself some punch when Aunt Ev intervened. "No, I'll serve the bride!" she insisted. It was about the nicest thing she ever said to me.

Out of the corner of my eye I saw Craig and Vicki enter the room. Craig had no use for churches or weddings but was apparently willing to come to a reception. He stood before me wearing black. I faced him in bridal white.

"You're a knockout," he said in his way where it's impossible to tell if he was serious or joking.

"Thanks. So are you," I replied.

My cousin Christie complimented Dad on the festivities. "Noelle did everything," Dad insisted, unwilling to take any credit. Dad's sister Pearl cornered my mother Pamela and told her several times, "I wish you could have met Lillian." Pamela assured her that she wished she could have met her as well. Aunt Betty continued to cry every time she looked at me. Brian's grandparents congratulated us and slipped us some cash for the honeymoon. My little sister Teresa, as bridesmaid, was determined to stick to me like glue so I entertained her with a quick game of tag. Mr. Granville complimented me on the cake and went back for seconds. I knelt on the floor to show wheelchair-bound Grandmama Linden how her crown had been attached to a custom-made veil; I felt like I was being presented to the Queen. She confessed some time later that she had mixed feelings about sending the crown, which accounted for the delay; she was disappointed Sharon did not wear it for her own wedding. But now, she said, she was satisfied that I did. Friends from WARM asked, "That girl who did the guest book – that's one of your sisters, right? One of Pamela's daughters?" I laughed, "No, that's my adopted cousin, Britt. We're just both Swedish."

Craig and Vicki quietly exited the same way they came in. Once again there was no good-bye. I knew he wouldn't correspond now that I was married. I told myself he knew how my search turned out and he was happy with someone like I was. Letting relationships go, even when they were over and done with, even when there was no definable relationship in the first place, wasn't my forte. Once someone was in my life I needed them to stay there. For the third time I watched him walk away.

Brian and I took a short, pitiful honeymoon after I was back from the ER with a severe case of "honeymoon urethritis" and Brian had served as a pallbearer at his grandmother's funeral. We then officially joined the ranks of the working poor. Our whole lives were ahead of us. The future looked bright.

Brian's mother wanted to know when we were going to start a family. It had been three months since the wedding and she couldn't see what we were waiting for. Trying not to act taken aback by the highly personal question I pointed out we earned just enough to get by with both of us working full-time.

"When Stephanie was born we used a dresser drawer for a crib," she said, almost proudly.

"You really think we should duplicate that scenario?"

"You should have babies when you're young." My father thought I was too young to be married and my mother-in-law seemed to think my biological clock was already ticking at the age of twenty-two.

"But…to deliberately bring a child into the world knowing we can't afford it?" For that she had no answer.

Brian was no help. He asked me to stop taking the Pill as a gift to him on his next birthday. I said no. He had this eternal optimism, or more precisely: obliviousness to reality. He made it easy to believe anything. But we weren't ready to be parents in any way, shape or form. If one of us had to play the heavy I was willing to be it.

Dad couldn't get used to the fact I was married and not living at home. Once Brian stopped by without me to ask about the car. Later he said, "You'd better go see your dad." I asked why. "When I walked in and he realized you weren't with me his face just fell." Since I couldn't afford a washer/dryer or the prices at the Laundromat, I brought our laundry home once a week instead.

Dad jokingly complained we must be the dirtiest people he knew because we do so much wash. I said, "No, we're the cleanest people you know because we do so much wash." I would visit every Saturday, sharing a meal, then go next door to see Gramma. It was a pleasant ritual.

Feeding me there wasn't enough though. The first time Dad and Carol came to the apartment they called ahead to ask if they should bring pizza. I had made coffee cake and was pleased to finally be treating *them*. I said, "No, you don't need to bring pizza." Carol relayed this to Dad. There was a perplexed silence.

"Does she want hamburgers then?" I heard him say.

"I don't want you to bring anything," I said. "Just come over."

They sat awkwardly at my dining table, Carol's old metal kitchen table dressed up with a nice tablecloth, one of their wedding gifts. They reluctantly ate the coffee cake, as if taking food from my own mouth, and made small talk. I gave them a tour, which took approximately one minute. After I again declined a meal out they went on their way. That night going to bed I thought, "I did it. I actually fed my parents for once and they didn't pay for anything." Satisfied, I laid my head down, only to hit something hard. Reaching under the pillow I pulled out a can of tuna fish. Carol Feed-the-World Ardahl wins again. She was thereafter referred to as the Tuna Fairy.

We had a new, top-floor, all-beige apartment centrally located between our work and families. The bedroom faced the parking lot but the back looked over woods that had not (yet) been torn down for development. The best times were spent watching the rain fall on the evergreens and ferns in the woods, and Sunday mornings when Brian and I leisurely read the newspaper in bed, sunlight streaming in, sipping our coffee. Sundays were often the only time we had together. Our work schedules mostly kept us apart.

We couldn't afford a pet deposit so left my beloved cat Tigra at Dad's. But another made itself available, a silky Himalayan who just showed up one day. I don't know why she preferred our apartment to hers. I'm sure the fresh tuna and chicken had nothing to do with it. Brian dubbed her "Queen of Leisure." She'd be by the door when I came home and stay several hours to be fawned over. Before bed I'd put her on the doormat and she'd disappear, only to be there again the following afternoon. Finally one day there was a woman along with the cat. The woman, a neighbor, said she figured "Azure" had been visiting someone and followed her. She loved her, "But obviously she prefers you, so if you want you can have her." I explained about the pet deposit. She said we could just continue on as we were. An open adoption.

During that first year I saw more of the cat than Brian. This is not how I had envisioned marriage. After one especially long day at work I laid on the bed, just staring at the ceiling. We had no TV, all my family and friends were busy with their own lives and Brian wouldn't be home until after I was asleep. What's more, Brian seemed to prefer the company of Chris or Eric on his day off instead of me. When we were single, he pushed for marriage. Now that we were married he seemed determined to act single. It was like I was a convenience he could bring out once in awhile. And this is what it was going to be like, day after day.

Silence weighed down on me. I had never felt so keenly alone. Azure lay next to me purring, curling and uncurling her beautiful tail. Hugging her to me, tears started to stream down my face. A long-forgotten pain welled up from my heart. I sobbed as I had not done since I was a child. Azure continued to purr. I endured reality, barely.

Keith was out of prison for the moment and Brian bought me a gun. He knew Keith was violent and dangerous and that was good enough reason for him. We never had guns back home. Dad believed chances were too good for the bad guy to turn the weapon against us. I felt a gun was the only thing that would level the playing field. My friend Jenny asked what the point was, if I wasn't willing to kill with it.

I said, "Who said I wasn't?"

"You would really shoot Keith?"

"Given half a chance."

She didn't know what happened. As much as she disliked her own adopted siblings she couldn't imagine shooting them. I could, easily.

Brian and Keith had never met. But Brian was already great friends with John. As different as these two slender blonds were in personality, they became as close as brothers. Soon Brian knew more about John than I did. And one day he had quite the story:

John had beaten Keith to a pulp. They were now in their mid-twenties, their prime. I don't know what started it, but witnesses would attest that the usually passive John clearly had the upper hand. He had to be pulled off of Keith because once he started punching him it was clear he was not going to stop. John had him on the ground and just kept pummeling, way past the point when it was obvious he had won. John told Brian that Keith, for all his size, hit like a girl.

"Is that what happened to you?" he taunted Keith then. "Were you somebody's bitch in prison? Were you were fucked so much you're a girl now?"

Keith had often written to John while in prison. He must have thought they were close because when they were children, he could get John to do almost anything. John was, as Dad would complain, a follower. That was now forever changed. I was glad. In fact when I relayed this to Cecelia at work, she chided, "Noelle, you're practically giddy."

I didn't say so (because I never talked about it), but even if it wasn't the case, I felt John had finally avenged me. He didn't kill Keith but he completely humiliated him in front of his peers. I don't know if Keith was raped in prison but the sick thought gave me some satisfaction. I was finally able to forgive John for not rescuing me before. He had been just a child himself, under Keith's power. Now the tables were finally and permanently turned.

Chapter 11
~The Putative Father~

Lorraine, my CI, unexpectedly sent my original birth certificate. And with it, a copy of my birth father's wedding license. She said since I was successfully reunited with my birth mother there was no reason not to give me these things. My original birth certificate looked nothing like my legal, amended one. The amended was white with official gold seal and misinformation. The original was green and down-to-business. My name was "Infant Girl Linden," my mother Pamela (Linden) White. No father listed. Pamela told me she had given that information but apparently they did not find it necessary to record. In the 1960s putative (reputed, presumed) fathers did not need to be notified or give consent. In the box to show whether I was real or not, it was checked "illegitimate". The rest of it was mainly medical. I was born at thirty-nine weeks. It was my mother's second live birth.

I found it almost funny to be holding this forbidden document in my hands. I knew everything on it and more, but if I were to go to court to ask for it, I would be refused. If my adoptive parents – the legal parents – asked, they would be refused. My birth mother, who gave all the information for the certificate, would be refused. Even if my birth mother, my adoptive father and I – all three parts of the adoption triad – stood together before a judge and asked, we would be refused. The only people it could possibly matter to were disregarded. It was instead entrusted to a stranger.

I turned my attention to the marriage license application. Glenn Havner and Shirley Johnson married in Idaho, both twenty-one years of age. They successfully passed their blood tests.

I knew from Pamela that Glenn had a master's degree in education, that he and Shirley married in the Catholic church, and that they had several children. She couldn't remember exactly how many, but thought it was three.

I had this document, the school annual, and what Pamela had told me.

I was ready to search for my birth father. And this time I would do it myself. Searching for the father is often called "the mini search" because it is generally the second search and most of the emotion is invested in the first. But this would be the only search I would be doing on my own. Because chances were good he did not know about me (unless Shirley figured it out and told him), it would be tricky. I was determined to do this quietly as so not to upset Shirley or their kids.

My friends at WARM understood. I still went to the monthly meetings whenever possible. Step-mom Carol didn't understand. "What do they talk about?" she wondered aloud to daughter-in-law Raquel. While Raquel herself was not adopted and her husband Tom seemed to have no inclination to search, she had keen insight and said, "It's like belonging to a church. You go because you have something in common; you believe the same things."

Carol seemed to think once I found my birth mother that it would be over somehow. That I got what I wanted and would be "done." When I told her about the "Christmas I Remember" article and how I wish I had seen it at the time it was published she said,

"Well, what difference would it have made? You couldn't look for her."

"It would have made all the difference. I would have known she was *there*," I said, not knowing how to explain any better. For six long years I keenly felt an absence. Carol didn't want to think about this.

I started my search for my birth father in the most logical place: the phone book. At the main library I looked up Havner in the Coeur d'Alene, Idaho directory. Only there were no Havners. They must have moved away at some point. Pamela suggested I contact Bob Richardson, the principal of the school where they had taught. "He was a nice man. If he knows where Glenn moved, he'll tell you."

I looked up Mr. Richardson and found he had conveniently stayed put. Remembering to give only enough information and no more, I wrote a short, to-the-point letter asking if he knew Glenn Havner's current whereabouts and enclosed a self-addressed stamped envelope for good measure.

Pamela was right. I soon received a cheery note from Mr. Richardson, saying Glenn had moved to Boise some years prior, was teaching there, and included his home address. Next I needed to know if Glenn and Shirley were still married. That would give me some indication how to proceed. I found the phone number and called, having some ruse in mind if Shirley answered.

Instead a young man – possibly a teen – picked up. I asked if Shirley was available. "No, she's not home," he laughed. I heard a girl giggling in the background. Apparently I had caught whoever answered in a good mood. A brother, probably. And maybe his girlfriend. Or sister? But they sounded so young – younger than me. How many siblings did I have, anyway? I thanked the-voice-who-might-be-my-brother and hung up.

So Shirley was still in the picture. I imagined her as the long-suffering wife and wondered how many other transgressions she tolerated.

Because they were still married, I couldn't write him addressed to their house. I needed to find out where he worked. But Boise in the 1980s was much bigger than Coeur d'Alene in the 1960s. I couldn't very well call every school within driving distance. Then I thought of the IEA, the Idaho Education Association. Within a minute of calling I had the name and address of the school where Glenn was teaching.

Now I was struck with anxiety. With Pamela everything was out of my hands. A professional searcher was doing all the work, taking all the chances. This time it was on me. I had to do this right.

I wrote a short note, saying only I had something of a private nature to tell him and that I would call on a selected day and time. I signed with my name and city.

The following weekend I paced in the apartment, alone. At the appointed time I sat with my notebook and pen, picked up the phone, took a breath and made the call.

"Hello!" a man's voice said brusquely. Music played in the background.

"Hello," I said, trying to sound pleasant, "this is Noelle Ardahl Reid calling from—"

"What? Wait a second," he snapped. "Let me turn off this music." The music abruptly stopped. "Now, what is it?!" He sounded like an angry drunk. I wondered if he *was* an angry drunk. I tried again:

"This is Noelle Ardahl Reid, calling from Washington State—"

"Is one of my kids in jail?!"

"Um, no, I hope not."

"Then what is it?"

"Did you get my letter?" I said, trying a different approach.

"No!"

Now I had no idea what to say but I had the feeling he did get the letter. Maybe that's why he was drinking. Maybe that's why he was angry.

"Well, I'll send another one," I offered.

"No! Don't send another!" and the phone slammed down.

I sat stunned, staring at the phone. Absolutely nothing was written on the page of my notebook. I had just had a one minute exchange with my birth father – the first time I ever heard his voice – and I couldn't even call it a conversation. It was a disaster.

It was also a disaster as far as Pamela's husband was concerned. My sister Teresa was privy to most phone conversations between Pamela and me and knew I was going to attempt contact with Glenn. One day she innocently asked in her father's presence: "Did Noelle find her dad yet?" And so much like his perceived rival, Jim stormed out of the room yelling, "No!"

I told Pamela in rather short terms that Jim could relax, that there was no contact and that I didn't foresee any either. But I also couldn't leave it this way; my search wasn't over. At the next WARM meeting I asked for advice.

They found it interesting he was hostile to a note and phone call from a stranger who wasn't asking for anything. "Maybe this has happened to him before," they joked. "Maybe he'll ask you to take a number and get in line." – "Or maybe he thought you were a former student with a crush."

"Or a paternity suit," I offered ruefully.

They told me I needed to be more direct. That the next time I called I should say, "Don't hang up. This is your daughter Noelle." But I couldn't drop a bomb on him like that at home, even if he did suspect. What about Shirley?

"She knows," they said.

I said, "She probably does, but it doesn't feel right to call like that."

Then a letter. Sent registered this time, so his signature will be proof he got it. But what would convince him I'm his daughter? What evidence do I have? What proof? Then it came to me:

My face.

I composed a one-page letter, stating who I was in the first sentence: the daughter of Pamela White and himself. I did not give any current information on Pamela, including her current married name. I told Pamela to let Jim know that.

To make it as easy as possible for him I enclosed a list of questions he could answer and send back: names and ages of siblings, any diseases or conditions that ran in the family. I told him I didn't expect a relationship from him, just information.

I chose the best pictures of me I could find, from early childhood up to the present. Since copying photos was only done by professionals then, I had to sacrifice the originals. I hated to do it, but knew one certain snapshot would convince him if nothing else would. I was about four years old, in my favorite red "cherry" dress, putting puzzles together at the kitchen table. My mother must have asked me to look up because there I was with the same natural pose and expression he had in the yearbook when someone asked him to look up as he leaned against his desk. My expression was his expression. My face was his face.

It was now November. Four months had passed since I wrote to Mr. Richardson. I had to send the package right away or it would be too close to Thanksgiving. I knew better than to try something so dramatic during the holidays.

Letter read and re-read, photos sorted, I carefully addressed the manila envelope to Glenn P. Havner c/o the school. Hugging it to my chest with eyes closed, I prayed it would be accepted with the same openness I was mailing it and sent it on its way.

Approximately one week later the signed receipts arrived. I had his signature. He got the package. I waited. He'd want to contact me on a weekend. The weekend came and he didn't call. Of course it was too soon. He'd wait until Thanksgiving break. Come Thanksgiving there was no letter, no phone call. He needed more time; it was too much of a shock. Certainly by my birthday...by

Christmas…by New Years…

There was no call. There was no letter. He received my note and photos – he must know I'm telling the truth – but he didn't respond.

Time went on. After losing his job at the fire station, Brian faced the fact there was no future for him there. The market was flooded with volunteers but paying positions were scarce. We made the decision for me to work while he went to school for computer programming, the new career of choice. I wrote to Glenn (care of the school but regular first-class mail this time) when we moved to a shabby townhouse so he'd have my new address and phone number. I wrote again when we moved to an even more run-down trailer the country. I wrote whenever I had a new phone number at Boeing. There was no response. I endured reality.

A friend at WARM was trained as a CI. "He's getting your letters. He's reading them," she assured me. This made me feel worse. I decided if he wasn't going to be forthcoming with information I was going after it myself.

First, I ordered his birth certificate. With this I made several discoveries: He was firstborn of his parents, both in their early twenties. His father's name was definitely German but I couldn't place his mother's. Both of Glenn's given names were Irish. Was he named Glenn Patrick because his mother was Irish, or just because he was born in the month of St. Patrick's Day?

His father was listed as a musician. I wondered how a musician eked out a living during the Depression in a small town in Idaho. I also wondered what happened to them. Pamela told me Glenn's mother lived in an apartment in Coeur d'Alene but had a different last name, remarried after being either divorced or widowed – she couldn't remember which.

Then I considered Glenn's birth date. Counting back thirty-nine weeks from my own birthday I realized he turned thirty around the time of my conception. I wondered if that meant something. An early midlife crisis? Was his obsession with Pamela some brief madness? Or was it just the times, the way it was, when married men had affairs with divorced women, that being the safest source because there was no angry husband in the wings? Besides, as Carol could tell you, young divorcées in the 1960s were considered fair game: promiscuous and practically "asking for it." Was that his justification?

I needed to go to the source. But I wanted information, not confrontation, so going to Boise was out. Instead, co-adoptee Jenny Miller and I drove to Coeur d'Alene that summer, stopping first in Spokane to visit my grandparents. Grandmama sat at the dining room table, regal in her housedress, looking at the lunch sandwiches set on fine china. "What this table needs is a good centerpiece," she muttered to herself.

Over coffee in Coeur d'Alene, I told Jenny what I knew. His name and birth date. His parents' names and approximate ages. That they were Catholic, German, and that he had a master's degree in education. I knew from searching Polk indexes (city directories) some names of relatives and their vocations. And that Coeur d'Alene was still crawling with Krenns, Glenn's mother's side of the family. While we chatted casually I looked around the diner and noticed several people looking at us. I wondered if they had caught any of our conversation or saw a resemblance and thought it best if we did what we came to do.

First we explored the high school and looked up every annual from the late '50s through the mid '60s. It looked as though Glenn moved to Boise not long after I was born. Then we drove through the old downtown and in the surrounding neighborhood to see if we spotted anyone who looked as if they might be a relative. I had no actual plan, since that never seemed to get me anywhere anyway. I was just going to take it as it came. I had the addresses of some of Glenn's relatives and we cruised past their houses. Then we came across the oldest-looking Catholic church in town. Jenny and I looked at each other. "Church records!" we said in unison.

We went in to find a pleasant middle-aged woman in the office.

"I'm doing genealogy research for my mother," I explained, smiling. "She told me if I was ever in Coeur d'Alene to try to look up Glenn Havner."

"Glenn Havner? Sure, I know him," she said brightly. "My husband and I go fishing with him and Shirley nearly every summer."

I resisted a strong urge to bolt.

"Really? That's...*great,*" I said, managing to keep smiling. "So you can tell me something about his family—"

"Wait. How are you related to him?"

"Hm? Oh, distantly." (Coeur d'Alene and Tacoma are very distant from each another.) "I've never met him."

"But your mother wants you to research his family?"

"Yes, she's quite obsessed with genealogy. You know how some people get." I looked at Jenny knowingly, as if sharing an inside joke. She smiled and nodded.

"Well, some relatives live right down the street. Bill and Cathy. Really nice people. I'll just call—" she said, reaching for the phone.

"No! I don't want to bother anyone. Anyone *else*. Since you know Glenn and Shirley, that's perfect. I was just wondering what's in the records?" *Oh God please put the phone down I'm so close.*

She gave me a curious look but put the phone back in its cradle. *Please do not notice the obvious resemblance,* I prayed. *And please, no one from the diner stop by.* Jenny sat in the chair next to mine, casually poised like this was the most natural thing in the world. I tried to copy her relaxed posture.

"And you want information about his family?"

"Yes, and anyone related to him. My mother wasn't quite clear on the lineage so I'd better just get everything so I don't miss anyone. We came all the way from Tacoma and won't pass through here again."

This must have sounded crazy enough to be plausible because she got out the record books. As she went through them page by page, year by year, I wrote in my notebook at a furious pace. She explained as she went:

"Glenn's younger sister is Jean. Glenn's daughter Heather Jean is named after her. I can't remember Heather's last name – she's been married a few years now." *Heather. My sister's name is Heather.* I recorded her date of birth.

She gave two more names with birth dates. My younger siblings, Kelli and David. Another sister – I couldn't believe my luck. I must have been speaking with David the time I called to see if Shirley and Glenn were still married. Eldest were Ryan and Joseph. Heather came next. Then me. I was sandwiched between my sisters Heather and Kelli like I was between my cousins Linda and Laurie.

"Shirley wasn't Catholic before they got married," the secretary informed me. She was pregnant though. I knew that from Pamela. Shirley must have told her, or maybe Glenn did. Suddenly the secretary looked up and said:

"Do you want to know about Shirley's family too?"

"Sure."

She rattled off the names of her parents and siblings and other factoids.

"Do you know anything about Glenn's father's family?" I asked.

"No, nothing about them. But a lot about the Krenns," which she pronounced *Kreens*.

I said, "*Kreen*? I thought it was *Kren*." No, she said, it's pronounced Kreen. I asked if she knew where the name came from. She didn't. I asked if she knew Glenn's mother. (I could not make out her first name written in cursive on the birth certificate or the town where she was born.) "Was her name Anita?"

She didn't know. She moved away a long time ago to live with her daughter Jean, she said. But her brothers all stayed. And before I knew it I had page after page of names, dates of marriage, birth, baptism, death, even godparents of the Krenns. She concluded with my great-grandparents. *I had the names of my great-grandparents:* Eli Krenn and Flossie Martin. I asked if the surnames Krenn or Martin might be Irish because there seemed to be a lot of Irish first names in the family. Either that or they were just very Catholic. She said she didn't know but, "You know what? Bill and Cathy would know. Let me just give them a call," she said, reaching for the phone.

"*No*. Really. We don't want to bother them. And," looking at my watch, "gosh, look at the time. We need to go. Long drive. Thank you so much for all your help."

Jenny floored it out of town.

When the laughter finally died down at the next WARM meeting, someone said (wiping tears from their eyes) the church secretary will no doubt tell Glenn and Shirley, so then what? Maybe this will jolt him into contacting me, I reasoned, just to keep me from actually showing up in Boise. (I wouldn't actually do that, but he didn't know.)

But as before, there was no phone call. There was no letter. Using my list-making skills from childhood, I dissected all the information I had and created a family tree, listing all my siblings – adopted, step and birth – in family groups and

chronological order. I looked them up in phone books and Polk indexes, sometimes discovering spouses or new jobs. I remembered their birthdays and kept
them in my prayers. I held onto these scraps of info like they were precious clues
to a mystery. Because that's all I had, really: names, dates, and theories.

I could have written to any of my brothers but my gut said no. I had
learned to follow these instincts and regretted any time I didn't. This was too important to do wrong. My sister Kelli was still living at home. Her natural loyalty
to her parents would keep her from responding to me. I tried to find Heather but
kept hitting dead-ends. I was at an impasse. Time continued on.

Then I was pregnant and decided Glenn Havner didn't deserve to know
this grandchild existed. When we moved again, this time to a 1920s craftsman
in Tacoma, I didn't write. Soon I was busy with the house, husband and baby I
always wanted and I tried to forget I had a father who didn't care enough to send
one note, even if to tell me to drop dead.

Chapter 12
~Parents and Grandparents~

When Brian and I decided he should go to school for computer programming, it meant we'd be living off my paltry income, so we had to vacate the nice, all-beige apartment with the view of the woods. We moved into a run-down town-house with no trees or shade in the middle of a heat wave. On one side of us was a battling neo-Nazi couple. On the other side, your stereotypical drug dealer and girlfriend, black tank-top and all. And across the narrow parking strip was a quiet Korean family who fermented kim-chi in the sun-drenched kitchen window that faced ours. In the unrelenting heat there was no escape from the smell. Lord, it was awful.

The consolation was that my brother John moved in also and shared rent. My co-workers asked if it was weird living with my brother. "I lived with him for over twenty years. What's hard to get used to is living with my husband." John and Brian got along famously. They only parted ways when I felt nostalgic one night and made stuffed green peppers like Mom used to do. Brian wouldn't be in the same room with such an atrocity and instead walked to a café. John and I ate alone. After, I asked how he liked it. "It was okay," he answered. That was what he always said, whether he ate everyone's share or hid the discarded remains under a crumpled napkin: "It was okay."

We were there only a few months when John told us he had found a bet-ter job and housing offer, quietly packed, and left. There was no way we could afford to stay without him and soon we found ourselves in an even more run-down abode: a falling apart, ten-foot-wide trailer in the woods. It had belonged to Brian's great-aunt. We struck a deal with my father-in-law to live there rent-free as long as Brian was going to school and signed a paper to that effect. My dad quietly clenched his jaw that we had to sign an agreement to live in a filthy old trailer.

I cleaned it as best I could, putting the ugly green curtains through the wash five times to remove all the nicotine, cat fur, and grime. When scrubbing the fake tile in the bathroom, I discovered the tan walls were originally pink. There was a spot in the living room where we couldn't step or the floor would give way. Aunt Cora had been a cat-lady, childless and long-time widowed. Her once tidy trailer was packed end to end with absolute junk. I methodically sorted and donated or threw out nearly everything, keeping just a quaint ceramic pitcher and a wood end table. I found a note from her husband, a career Navy man, written decades earlier. A Mother's Day card to a woman who would never have a child: "I'd rather have you than anyone, even with a mess of kids." Once, years before, while Brian mowed the grass, Aunt Cora told me she had had two miscarriages in her youth. Instead of babies she filled her home with cats but there was only one left when we got there: Baby, an enormous Maine Coon. It was a year before he trusted me enough to let me pet him.

We had brought two cats of our own: Tigra, an elitist domestic shorthair and Azure, a silky Himalayan. I loved those cats. I had so many growing up I had nearly become accustomed to the pain of losing them. But I'd had Tigra for seven years – longer than any other – and Azure had just shown up at our apartment and was a great comfort to me when I was lonely.

At our place in the woods, the cats were free to run, and they enjoyed being outdoors as much as in. They supervised as I planted tulip bulbs and watched TV with us at night. Both were always there by the door when we came home. A dog could not have been more faithful.

Then we learned all about feline leukemia. Tigra got it first. The day she was diagnosed and put down all I could do was cry, wracked with sobs. Then Azure got it. I took her to the vet myself and asked to hold her while she was given the lethal injection. The last thing she did was to curl and uncurl her beautiful tail as she always had, then she was gone. There was no more cat to greet us at the door. No more cat to sit on our laps. Because Baby never associated with the others he seemed to avoid the disease, but he was Aunt Cora's and only tolerated us, so it was like not having a cat at all.

Meanwhile, my grandparents in Spokane were in rapid decline. After traveling back and forth for months, Pamela finally went to stay in order to give her brother a respite as well as to exert control. They were very different in personality, these siblings, as far apart in age as they were in opinion. Sharing responsibility for their parents pitted them against one another. They agreed their parents should have the best available care. Everything else was war.

Grandmama went first. On her deathbed, Pamela (a born-again Christian) asked Helen Rose if her salvation was secure. "The promise," her mother whispered, holding to her belief of predestination, the chosen elect.

Unlike when Lillian died, this time I felt it before I was told. Sad at the loss but comforted by the connection. My sister Sharon and I drove to Spokane together. It was winter. I tried to make myself useful by cleaning, once finding my grandfather putting dirty dishes in the cupboard. "What are you doing?" I asked gently. "Just putting things away," he said.

My cousins there remarked how young I was when I lost my adoptive mother. It had been ten years; a lifetime ago. "That's not an easy age," they sympathized. "I don't think there is an easy age to lose your mother," I reasoned. Our parents didn't seem to be having an easy time of it, anyway.

They reminisced how their mother liked things "just so." How the table had to be properly set. That she resolutely refused to gossip. How she kept her children "dressed to the nines." And the story of when she was a little girl, how she would pat the sofa and politely say, "Come sit 'side me."

At the funeral, Granddad looked sadly at the casket and asked no one in particular, "What will happen to me now?" Even with dementia he knew she was gone. He required round the clock care and though he accepted help he didn't recognize anyone. Only one time the fog partially lifted. Going to bed he stopped on the stair landing and asked, "Where is that little girl? The one who always helps me?" meaning his granddaughter Teresa. Like I stayed home to care for Lillian, Teresa stayed to help care for her elderly grandparents rather than leave her mother.

Before heading home, Pamela asked Sharon, Teresa and me into her mother's bedroom. Several hats were on the bed. A select few of her mother's vast collection, each having a story. Sharon was very becoming in Grandmama's black "traveling hat." Teresa chose one with a veil. A brimless royal blue number was more my style. I was also given a hat box from The Crescent to keep it in. At that moment, I had everything.

That summer we were back for a brief stay at the lake place. If he realized it or not, my grandfather kept one Swedish tradition in having a summer house. It was very rustic and intentionally so. Although it had electricity and hot and cold running water, he never allowed a telephone to be installed. It was meant to be an escape. The first time I was there, Pamela showed me her mother's favorite tree. Favorite because of the way sunlight shined through the branches. I smiled. I had favorite trees for the same reason.

Granddad seemed to know the place even if he didn't remember his own name. He would appear lost then would suddenly respond to conversations like he had been keeping up the entire time. I wondered if he was happy. He seemed blissfully unaware, if that's the same. I wished once again that I could really talk with him.

Later that summer, he vomited blood. Pamela rushed him to Emergency where it was discovered he had a bleeding stomach ulcer. It must have been terribly painful but he never showed a sign.

"Dad, how do you feel?" Pamela asked, when informed of the ulcer.

"Fine…And you?" he replied politely.

I had a dream:

My grandfather spoke to me. There was no dementia. He knew who I was. He was saying good-bye.

That morning the phone call came. I went back to Spokane.

Palmer Linden did not want his daughter to relinquish me, "the baby." Pamela told me as much. He had encouraged her to marry a man he knew was willing to take us as his own, but she couldn't do it. After she held me for that one day in the hospital she sketched a picture of my face. At her parents' house for Christmas, her mother advised her to get rid of it, get rid of the memory and move on. Pamela always listened to her mother, even when her heart said no. She threw away her only memento. Her father was quietly depressed over the holidays and Pamela knew it was because he had not been able to help us. Because his grandchild was out there, somewhere. She said he was more of a father-figure than a father, typical of his generation, but this event obviously cut him deeply. When we were first reunited, I wanted to tell him I was okay, that everything turned out alright, but he was trapped in dementia. In death, he knew.

At the funeral home, I talked with my brother Paul. We found out our grandparents had not updated their will in decades. In fact, Pamela was not yet born in the only copy they could find. I told Paul my dad updated his will regularly, whenever there was a major change of some sort, and that he always kept me informed. And that my adoptive grandmother's will was changed as late as age eighty-nine and how glad I was to have that settled because I could envision a bloodbath otherwise, even if it did involve just cows and apple trees. Legally I was entitled only to inherit from my adoptive family. I was actually relieved I would have no part in the disaster waiting to happen that was our mutual grandparents' estate. In stark contrast to my adoptive family's affairs, my birth grandparents' will, properties and taxes were a complete mess.

My grandmother was a farm wife.

My dad was a mechanic.

Our grandfather was an estate planner.

I was surprised to be included in the dispersion of the personal items. I never expected that, and in fact asked Pamela to make sure her brother knew I didn't want anything of sentimental value to the others. The most memorable thing I came away with was the inexpensive yet classic dining room set, the one used every day for over fifty years. It did not have much monetary value, in fact it was rather scratched and worn-looking, but that's not why I wanted it. I knew my mother and grandparents sat at that table for every meal. And I knew how important a well-set table was to Grandmama. It was central to her daily life. This would be like having a part of her with me. Whenever I sat at that table it would be as if she was there.

Brian nearly finished college before landing a job. Employed and impatient, he wanted to start a family. I wanted that also but knew two things: I needed a house first and women in my family did not "try" to get pregnant. So this was going to happen quickly.

I confided to Sharon at the lake place that summer that we were going to have a baby within a year. Thanks to her example, I knew I wanted natural childbirth with a midwife. It became of the utmost importance to be in a house before then because I was not going to give birth in a dilapidated trailer. At least getting pregnant would prove to be easy.

I was privileged to witness Sharon give birth to a handsome boy that winter. I knew then I had found the midwife I wanted to attend me: Janet Brooks. Well-known and respected in the medical community, she had delivered over 2000 babies. My sister's strength and ease in labor combined with Janet's quiet confidence was the go-ahead I needed.

I knew the moment it happened on a weekend getaway to Seattle. Brian didn't quite believe it but didn't argue. I was the wife who "knew things," after all. I also knew the baby was a girl. Our parents had a variety of reactions at the news. Dennis Reid seemed resigned, as his other children had already provided him with grandchildren. But upon Brian saying, "I'm going to be a father," his mother exclaimed, "With *Noelle?*"

"No," I said. "With his concubine. I want to keep my figure."

Pamela, who loved babies, thought it was wonderful. But Dad did not speak for three days. It's not that he wouldn't speak to me, he just couldn't speak, period. His baby was having a baby. Not even adopting one, *having* one. Carol was just a little more resilient since her daughter-in-law had already birthed two perfect grandchildren. She knew it was survivable.

But she gave me a pregnancy and childbirth book circa the 1950s that read like a horror movie. Women were expected to put themselves completely in their doctor's hands and not concern themselves with the birthing process. After all, they'd be unconscious. I'm not sure what Carol's motivation was. Maybe she didn't realize medical culture had changed that much in thirty years so really thought it was valid information. Or she wanted to scare me into having a hospital birth for my own good. If it was the latter, it had the opposite effect. There was no way I would surrender myself to the medical practices of the day. And that decision *was* for my own good, and that of my baby.

My pregnancy was absolutely textbook. I was healthier than ever before, even having the "glow" some women experience. Even though I knew I was pregnant and felt every change, the first time I heard the hummingbird-quick heartbeat, tears ran down my face.

No matter how I played the scenario in my mind I could not imagine relinquishing this baby. I tried to put myself in my birth mother's place but the constrictive mores of the 1960s were thankfully beyond my comprehension. To have to move across state to hide from anyone who knew her, to birth unconscious on a day chosen by the doctor, being made to feel criminal for wanting to see her child just once, having to sign away all rights to a baby that had just been rudely taken from her body, forced to allow others to decide the child's fate, never knowing what happened from that day on…The "loving choice" was truly barbaric. Pamela's strength amazed me.

Only one internal exam was required by my midwife. While she checked my birth canal, searching for abnormalities, I winced. Janet was looking across the room at nothing, concentrating, pressing gently with her fingers. Her finesse made it bearable.

"Hmm," she said. "There's a hard ridge there, like a shelf."

"What is it – a deformity?"

"Everyone is different. I don't know what caused this."

"Will it complicate things? Will the baby get stuck?"

"No, when the time comes I'll press it down so the baby can get by."

I relaxed. Everything had to be right. I took excellent care of myself and readied as much as possible. Brian and I took a birthing class and I read every book I could find. I slowly stockpiled supplies, keeping them in the closet of my old bedroom at Dad's because there was no room in the trailer. And besides, we were going to move into a house before the baby came.

Let's just say everything that could possibly go wrong in buying a house, did. When we finally found and fell in love with a quirky 1920s craftsman we had already lost months of time and thousands of dollars, money we did not have to spare. Only the quest to find my roots was as powerful as my quest for a house. As summer approached, I was on edge. The deal had already fallen through once.

The sellers were reasonable; they said we could move in when we liked and pay rent until it actually sold. This was an unsettling prospect to me, but the thought of having a newborn in a moldy trailer was worse. We agreed to move in a month before the due date.

Dad, once he found his voice again, was supportive of home birth. He and his siblings had all been born at home, after all.

"You know," he said, "Frank Haugen's daughter had a baby on his birthday. A boy."

"Dad," I said firmly, "I am not due for over a month after your birthday. We won't even move until after your birthday. I am not having a baby on your birthday so just forget it."

Very early in the morning one day in midsummer I woke to a twinge. It just came and went. I figured I should use the bathroom since I was awake anyway. I sat on the toilet and went. And went. And went. Every time I thought I was done I had to go more. I let out an exasperated sigh.

"What's wrong?" Brian called from the bed.

"I don't know. It's like I can't stop going. It's like—" and the phrase *it dawned on me* became real.

"What?! It's like what?!"

"Like…amniotic fluid." I caught some in my hand. It smelled sweet. Another twinge hit and I knew it was a contraction. I told Brian to call Janet.

"But it's too soon! It must be false labor," he reasoned. He ran to get me a glass of wine as I staggered to the living room. I knew this was real but was afraid he was right, that it was too soon. Too soon to give birth outside a hospital. I took a sip of wine he handed me – the first in seven months – and promptly spit it out on the floor. It tasted like vinegar. Stronger contractions were coming now. Brian called the midwife.

One way for Janet to gauge where a woman is in labor is to speak with her. Brian put me on the phone. As distracted as I was I noticed how awake she sounded when it was still dark outside.

"I'm only at thirty-six weeks. What should I do?" I'm sure she could hear my panic.

"It's okay, honey. You're healthy and so is your baby." Just hearing her voice calmed me. And at hearing her words I relaxed. "You can come here or go to your parents'." That was my back-up plan, to have the baby at Dad's if we hadn't moved yet. I just never imagined I'd actually have to use the back-up plan. I told her we would call again when we were there to give her directions.

Although Brian had worked as an EMT and had actually stood by once as a woman gave birth in her home, he couldn't quite accept this was really happening. He needed something to do. I told him we were going to Dad's, so he got dressed and gathered everything he thought we might need. Meanwhile I hung on the front of the refrigerator, moaning through the next contraction. Turning my head I found myself facing the wall calendar.

"I don't believe it," I groaned.

"What? What now?" Brian exclaimed.

"It's Dad's birthday."

After Brian broke all speed limit laws we discovered no one home at Dad's. I was glad I still had a key. I readied the bed in my old room while Brian called Janet. Coming upstairs he said, "She's delivering another baby right now. She'll be here as soon as she can." I again tried not to panic. I realized what I needed was a doula, another woman who had given birth. I had wanted Sharon to be there but she was gone for the weekend. Then I thought of the most obvious choice.

I called Pamela, who came right over with Teresa. The instant she walked in I felt my stress levels drop. Pamela believed in gentle birth, something she herself rarely received. And she had helped her daughter Sharon through several labors. She now helped me breathe through the contractions and moan deeply. At one point I hung from her neck and shoulders for balance. It was now mid-morning. Janet was still helping with another baby somewhere.

Dad came home from having breakfast with a friend. He walked into the kitchen to find Brian making a sandwich. When Brian told him what was happening Dad started pacing. He heard me moaning upstairs and paced some more. Finally he stopped and thundered, "Isn't this taking an awfully long time?!" It was happening much too fast to suit Brian so he couldn't think of a response. Dad retreated to the safety of his shop.

Brian called his brother Eric to come over to help "pass the time." We suddenly had four more in attendance, as Eric brought his wife and their two young children. I had no idea what Brian was thinking, maybe that we were going to play cards between contractions? And Eric didn't know any different since his children were born by c-section.

The midwife arrived. And she brought an apprentice. There were now nine people in my room not having a baby…and me. Janet shooed everyone out of the room except the midwife-in-training, and checked my progress. She found the spot – the ridge – and pressed down hard, stretching the skin to its limit.

"Ow," I said involuntarily. She had that far-away look in her eyes again, concentrating, and kept stretching the tender area.

"Ow!" I said, tears welling in my eyes, grabbing her arm to get her attention. She shook herself out of her trance and said, "I know, honey. It's over now." She called Pamela in and asked for a trash bag. Pamela in turn looked at me and said, "Noelle, where are the trash bags?" Janet looked from her to me and said to Pamela, "Isn't this your house?" I started to say something but could only manage single-syllables, so let Pamela explain. I did manage to say, "Kitchen."

I tried walking and squatting but the only place I was comfortable was on the bed, so settled there. After starting so quickly, labor now slowed to a crawl. To motivate me, Janet had Eric hold a full-length mirror at the end of the bed. "See? There's the baby's head," they encouraged. I lifted myself long enough to see dark hair (thinking, "Wow, my baby has hair," but was mostly captivated by the look of wonder on my brother-in-law's face), said, "Uh-huh" and laid down again.

Janet wasn't going to rush me but didn't like dawdling. With Brian acting as one stirrup and Pamela as the other, she instructed me to keep pushing after the contraction was over. "Push past the pain," she said. Only there was no pain, only what could be described as a powerful pull, being swept away and pulled back, swept away and pulled back, like the ocean tide. I allowed myself to ride the waves, not purposely birthing but just letting it happen.

Suddenly, she was there. My daughter, my child. Tiny and beautiful and perfect. With dark silky hair matted down in creamy vernix and eyes a mysterious blue. Brian cut the cord under Janet's direction. The baby – my baby – was then weighed and measured and wrapped up warm like a little burrito in a pink blanket and laid next to me. I stared at her. She stared at me. I didn't touch her. I was in shock at what had just transpired. I couldn't believe my baby was outside my body. Just a few minutes ago I was pregnant, my due date over a month away. We weren't ready and yet, here we were: parents.

Brian ran to tell Dad, finding him grinding some hapless piece of metal into dust. He approached the bed with an uncertain yet hopeful look on his face, like a child on Christmas morning.

"Happy birthday, Dad. I guess the air hose we got you is kind of anti-climatic."

"I can always use a new air hose but this is fine," he said. Fine. That word again.

Janet encouraged him to hold his granddaughter but he never holds new-borns, leaving that to the expertise of the mothers. She said, "Touch her then," knowing now how momentous this was.

"My hands are dirty," he protested.

"You're not dirty," she said calmly.

He reached out a blackened, calloused hand and just barely touched the baby's head with the tip of one finger. He seemed pleased with himself.

"What is her name?" someone asked.

"Lillie Carol Reid." I knew my first child would be a girl and that I would name her Lillie. I knew it absolutely, yet to watch it unfold was incredible. I was in my bedroom where I had spent so much of my childhood alone, along with my father, my birth mother, my husband, and my daughter. It was perfect. The act of birth washed away the stain of Keith molesting me, overriding it with something far more powerful. I almost wished I had labored in the living room, but this was meant to be. This house had now seen birth, death, violence, and love.

Carol came home to find her house filled with people, so she fed them. No matter what I needed she did it. I apologized again and again for the mess and she said again and again, "It's fine," and she meant it. Dad called relatives I had never heard of to tell them what I gave him for his birthday. Before she left,

Janet cautioned them, "She needs rest and privacy. No visitors for a week at least."

Dad must not have heard because there was a veritable parade of guests beginning that day. What stressed me wasn't so much the visitors but having to take the baby somewhere every day for one medical exam or another. Because she was early she was prone to jaundice and got it bad enough to need to go under the lights. She also never latched on to breastfeed. After that first hour of life outside the womb, she promptly went back to sleep, rarely opening her eyes for the next month.

"If you were in such a hurry to get here, you could at least stay awake now," I gently chided, but Lillie continued to dream. I poured precious amounts of expressed breastmilk into her mouth and except for swallowing as a reflex she did not stir.

"She doesn't know she's been born yet," Janet said. I felt I was caring for one of my baby dolls from childhood. I went to the midwife, the pediatrician, the lactation consultant, the lab to get yet another foot tap; it was never-ending. One day I passed near the cemetery where Lillian was buried and something made me pull in. Leaving Lillie in the car I walked over to the grave. I usually visited only on Memorial Day, to lay flowers with Dad. This time I was completely alone.

I stood and looked at the gravestone. It had been eleven years. As long as I had been with her before she had the first stroke that changed her forever.

"I named my daughter after you," I said aloud and was surprised at the bitterness in my voice. I named Lillie after Lillian and Carol, with Lillian first. Not my birth mother, not Brian's mother…Lillian. She was first in my memory. If someone asked me who my mother was, she was the automatic default.

I wondered if she knew I wore her wedding dress, loved red hair, followed a stranger in the mall who smelled like her, gave birth in her house. I wondered if she meant more to me than I ever meant to her. I wondered if I was still chasing ghosts.

She never said good-bye. And now there was only silence.

Back at Dad's in my old bedroom, with Brian and Lillie sleeping on either side of me, I had a dream:

We were in the Chrysler. Mom was driving, as always. I sat next to her. Colors had never been so vivid. I could feel myself there. I could almost smell her Chanel no.5. Her hair was vibrant in the sunlight. She was well. She was beautiful. She pulled into the driveway, drove up the hill, and stopped in front of the house. I was happy for a moment. Then, still looking ahead she drew in her breath and blurted out, "I would have killed myself you know – if I hadn't died." We drove up the driveway again. She stopped in front of the house. "I would have killed myself you know – if I hadn't died." We drove up the hill. "I would have killed myself you know – if I hadn't died."

"Stop it! Stop saying that! I heard you!" I screamed.

I woke up, heart pounding.

Chapter 13
-Breakdown-

We moved into the house as the second deal fell through. Our opinion of real estate dealers and bankers could not sink any lower. Reams of pointless paperwork and ever-changing regulations. And it all cost us more money.

I couldn't stand to have Lillie in the trailer even for one night. It was so damp, I was afraid with her under-developed lungs she'd get RSV.

And we couldn't stay at Dad's any longer either, because Keith moved into a travel trailer on the property the same week. Even though I never had to interact with him, I could barely sleep at night knowing he was there. Brian patrolled the grounds and slept with his gun on the side table. The only time Brian and Keith ever met was in the kitchen: "You've got a kid, huh?" was all he muttered.

Shelley also stopped by. I was in the living room, once again trying to get Lillie to nurse, when I heard Carol tell her excitedly at the door:

"Noelle had her baby!"

"So?" she replied, sullenly. I never had a sister in Shelley, as much as I would have liked to.

I spent my days at doctor appointments, or after-the-fact baby showers, or packing things at the trailer. And trying to navigate the maze known as home ownership.

Giving Dad and Carol a tour of the house, Dad found fault in nearly every aspect. It was too small, it cost too much, it was too old. I finally snapped:

"It doesn't matter! The deal will fall through again and we'll be thrown out in a few months!" Carol shushed Dad, told him to leave me alone. I was on edge, not knowing if we'd ever be able to buy the place, but having no where else to go.

Dad never had a mortgage, in fact couldn't stand the idea of one, so had no idea how to help. He offered to put $5000 toward the down payment if Brian's father would match it. Dennis held out, demanded stipulations, said we never thanked him for all he had done for us, meaning allowing us to live in his aunt's filthy trailer. Apparently he had not heard any of the many thank-you's we had offered. We were infuriated. They had a shouting match on the phone and Brian vowed to tear up his father's check in front of him and drove over there to do it. Instead they reconciled over a beer. I wished he had stuck with his original idea. I couldn't imagine fighting with my father that way. It literally made me sick. But the idea of "owing" Dennis anything was worse. And that's what we did – the worse thing.

Try as I might, I could not get the sleepy Lillie to breastfeed. After a perfect birth, I was a failure with this. I talked to La Leche League, was handled like a dairy cow by a lactation consultant, rented a $1000 pump from a hospital, and weeks later, I still could only eke out a few ounces at a time, and never got her to latch on. I supplemented with formula, never knowing what kind was best, or if there was a kind that was even good enough. "I couldn't nurse my firstborn, either," my midwife consoled me.

We had been told by the vet that although Aunt Cora's beloved Maine Coon showed no signs of feline leukemia, it was only a matter of time until he succumbed, and now that we weren't living in the trailer there was no one to feed him. It had taken over a year until Baby trusted me enough to let me pet him. Now I was going to betray him.

I put a can of cat food in a laundry basket on the porch of the trailer and waited for him to jump in, petted him as he purred, then put another basket upside down over it, tying the two together. Baby panicked. He had never been trapped before and reacted like a caged bobcat. I drove the mercifully short distance to the vet's office and begged them to euthanize him right then, because I couldn't stand his cries of terror. Shaking and through tears, I signed the death warrant. They took him in the back room and almost immediately he went silent. In the parking lot I unceremoniously vomited.

Due to an addressing error, Boeing never sent the $50 a week short-term disability owed me, and not working those weeks had us strapped for money. Brian had to keep working, not only because he did not get parental leave but because we wouldn't afford it otherwise. He could only help with moving on weekends. He had always hated moving and was nearly insufferable about it in the best of circumstances. These were not the best of circumstances.

It was a Saturday. Brian had borrowed his step-father's truck to move furniture when he called from a pay phone to say the axle broke and he was stuck miles from anywhere. I sat in the rocking chair he bought for me and the baby in our otherwise-empty living room, rocking Lillie in the spreading twilight, and had my first nervous breakdown.

Dad and Carol were horrified at the sight of me. Shaking and silently crying, I balled up on their couch, Lillie snug beside me in her little car seat, oblivious to the drama. Carol made some tea while Dad paced, jaw clenched. I could barely speak but choked out words to the effect that everything was wrong.

I did not endure reality as much as I simply kept existing. Time wasn't measurable. My life was counted from one crisis to the next and I was swept along with it like debris in a river. But when I finally snapped I knew of only one place to go: Home. Dad didn't know how to help, there was nothing that money could fix, not even the house while it was in ownership limbo.

Eventually things calmed enough that mundane details were no longer insurmountable. We moved in and paid rent, waiting for the sale to finally go through. My milk dried up completely with the breakdown and I resolutely bought a set of baby bottles for Lillie, who thrived regardless of how I felt. Brian got over moving and settled into the house and fatherhood. He was a terrific father when he wasn't distracted with something else.

Before going back to work, I put together a proper reception for Lillie's baptism, finally getting Lillian's silver and Eleanor's china out of safekeeping from Aunt Betty. Months earlier, I had gone back to the dressmaker who put together my bridal ensemble, asking her to take the lace off my veil and put it on a traditional silk baptismal gown. In our new home we had all sorts of desserts and coffee and champagne. It was, as Miss Manners would say, a lovely post-script to the wedding. I think Lillian would have been proud of my hostessing, if not the infant baptism or champagne.

Nearly everyone was there at the Lutheran church where we married years before. My adoptive family, birth family, and Brian's family by both blood and marriage. I asked my step-brother Tom and his wife to act as godparents. Family and friends mingled while Lillie slept through it all. Despite my exhaustion I was happy. It was as it should be.

I went to my midwife to be fitted for a diaphragm. I joked that I hoped I would have better luck with this than I had with contraceptive sponges. Used for three months after going off the Pill, they would inevitably turn sideways. Janet gently slid a practice diaphragm in to try for size and released. I froze. It felt as if I was being wrenched open.

"Take it out! Take it out!" I gasped, my arms paralyzed at my sides. Janet quickly removed it.

"What is *wrong* with me?" I said, breaking into a sweat and shaking.

"It's that ridge."

"I guess I'm just built wrong," I said quietly. Deformed was more like it.

"You still make great babies," she smiled.

I went back on the Pill.

Because the sale on the house had not gone through, I had to keep working so we'd look good on paper. Not only was I working full-time as a drafter, but also part-time as an instructor. The idea originally was I would work only a few hours a week after having children. My co-worker and friend Cecelia Vaughn found the job for me, run through various voc-techs, and although I balked at being a "teacher" I was surprised to discover I enjoyed it. The problem was I was once again stuck in the waiting – waiting for the deal on the house to close, not knowing if it ever would or how.

Being a mother heightened my senses. I would wake in a cold sweat after dreaming the bank lost the paperwork and we were out on the street. I couldn't completely relax, ever. My focus was closing on the house. I needed to know it was really ours.

When Lillie was still an infant, Brian brought home a bedraggled Siamese cat. She was on "Last Day" at the Humane Society and Brian couldn't just leave her knowing she'd be dead by morning. She was starved and crawling with fleas and had an incessant meow that was more of a Yiddish "meh," and believe me, she had a lot to say. Besides that she had a mottled color that made her not look like a proper Siamese at all. She was so trashy looking, in fact, we named her the worst Asian thing we could think of: Kim-chi, after the stinking cabbage that fermented in our Korean neighbors' window several summers before.

If all that wasn't bad enough, she was jealous of the baby, as if she had been there first and the furless thing was an interloper. I did not have much hope for this cat. After we got rid of the fleas and she filled out a bit she wasn't so bad looking, but there was still the sibling rivalry. She wanted to be the baby. I would find her in Lillie's stroller, car seat, even her perfectly white crib.

One day I gardened in the backyard while Lillie took a nap upstairs. I had the baby monitor with me and all was quiet until Kim-chi came to the screen door, meowing loudly. "Oh what, Kim-chi? You can't come outside, you spoiled cat." She pawed the door frantically and meowed even more. "What is the matter with you?" Then she actually yowled – something she had never done before. This finally made me get up and go to her. "What? Is something the matter with the baby?" I asked in mock-dramatic tones, as if we were in a Lassie movie. I opened the screen door, but instead of bolting outside she raced up the stairs to the baby's room. I felt my blood run cold and scrambled after her to find Lillie in her crib silently choking on vomit. If that miserable cat hadn't alerted me, Lillie could have died. Kim-chi's place in our family was forever secure.

Unlike her paternal cousins, Lillie did not resemble the Reids at all. My sister-in-law and I had resigned ourselves to being mere vessels to produce Reid children but Lillie surprised everyone by looking nothing like me *or* Brian. Instead she carried on my birth mother's traits with her Bain de Soliel coloring and almond-shaped, hazel eyes. There had never been anything other than blue-green eyes in the Reid Clan before.

We were sometimes mistaken for babysitters. People would analyze the baby's face then gaze at me and Brian and say, "She looks like...?" I finally started carrying a photo of my sister Teresa as a small child so I could show them the baby looked like someone, even if not her parents. Brian was very glad then that I had searched. Lillie would have been impossible to explain otherwise.

For a time, Pamela and I co-led a local search/reunion support group. During one of the more memorable sessions, a woman was there with her long-suffering adoptive mother. Monopolizing the meeting with her drama, pounding the table and screaming as her mother quietly sat by, she was trying my patience.

"I know I'll end up just like her! Just! Like! Her!" she screamed, referring to her birth mother, pounding the table at each word for added emphasis.

"What do you mean, exactly? What are you so afraid of?" I interjected, trying to get her to think about what she's saying.

She looked at me in disbelief. It was apparent she imagined her mother (or maybe all birth mothers) to be an irresponsible whore. It was also apparent she did not realize I was sitting next to my birth mother at the time.

"Aren't you afraid you'll turn out like your mother?" she demanded.

I turned to look at Pamela being her serene ladylike self, back at the crazed adoptee, and said, "You mean…Presbyterian?"

One day at work, I had the sudden thought to look up my paternal grandmother's surname in the supplied Seattle phone book. There was a Krenn listed, so I called. A young man answered. He sounded pleasant so I got right to the point:

"I'm doing some genealogy research and wondered if you knew where the name *Kreen* is from?"

"You knew the right way to say it." He sounded surprised.

"Yes, but that's all I know."

"It's German. If it's pronounced *kreen* it's from southern Germany. If it's pronounced *kren* it's from northern Germany."

More Germans. Oh well. I thanked him and added this to my notebook.

Nearly a year and one more deal falling through later, the house was ours. I quit Boeing before they fired me; my enthusiasm plummeted when my job was rendered meaningless during yet another restructuring.

I finally settled into the life I always wanted. I worked as an instructor just a few hours a week, took Lillie for long strolls, read to her, wrote letters to friends, and puttered in the yard. Even though we were chronically broke and the house a constant mess, when the children were small was the happiest time of my life.

Chapter 14
~Last Will And Testament~

Carol's former mother-in-law died. They had remained close despite Carol's divorce from her no-good son because of mutual fondness and wanting to stay involved in the children's lives, even though the kids' legal father was completely uninvolved.

In going through her things, a photo was unearthed of Susan, the baby who was wrenched away from Carol many years before. It was Christmastime and Susan was crawling toward the camera, the tinsel-laden tree in the background. As far as I know it is the only surviving photo of her. Carol showed it to me, tears in her eyes. She would get misty at the mere mention of Susan so I was careful not to bring up the subject. Carol had destroyed all reminders of the baby's existence when she was taken, but she did not dispose of this unexpected memento now. It was carefully put away. I wondered how often she took it out of her desk to look at it and what she thought/felt when doing so. But I couldn't bring myself to ask.

I was very pregnant with my second child when Gramma passed away. She needed care only in the last year or so of her life and that was only in the form of someone staying with her. Since her children lived next door this was not a problem. Or so I thought. I would often visit with Lillie, who thought this white-haired grandmother was a character from one of her books.

One day she fell in the kitchen and broke a hip, necessitating her first-ever confinement to a hospital bed. This signaled the end. She died just after her ninety-seventh birthday.

Then it happened. Intellectually I thought it couldn't, but instinctively I knew it would. In Gramma's will, my brothers and I did not receive our shared third as promised, but one-third of one-tenth. Clarence and Betty split the other ninety percent. Dad asked about it, knowing how the will was written eight years earlier. Hesitantly I showed him the papers. He exploded.

"A tenth! A tenth! That's all she was worth to them!" he raged, pacing back and forth in the orchard. Carol and I watched from the kitchen window. I had never seen him so angry. Carol winced at the sight. Dad had never trusted his brother-in-law but always held Lillian's sister in high regard. She now came crashing off the pedestal Dad had made for her, knowing she was part of the scheme.

Aunt Betty caught wind of this, probably through her husband – the only one Dad was still on speaking terms with. She asked for a meeting. We sat in my dining room, at the table that had belonged to my grandparents in Spokane. I never expected to be included in that estate. But even more I never expected to be excluded from this one. I told her I wanted the truth: "What happened?"

Aunt Betty felt righteously justified. "I *sacrificed*. I gave up my *life* to stay with her. Lisa practically raised herself!"

Lisa was eighteen and for the past year had been with either her father at their house or with her selfless mother next door, whose "sacrifice" consisted of sitting with her own mother. I effectively had no mother from age eleven through sixteen. I knew something about "raising oneself".

Gramma needed no special care, just assistance you'd expect for someone of her advanced age. The fact that she and Clarence planned this, *years* before their mother needed help of any kind – and could not have known if she ever would – seemed to be lost on her.

She further validated: "I owed Mom $10,000 from an old loan. That will be taken out of my share and put back into the estate." She said this as if I should congratulate her on her honesty. Apparently the thought that she could pay her mother back by caring for her never crossed her mind. She needed her inheritance promised "and then some." This gave her as much as an upper-level professional's salary – more than what Brian earned – even after repaying the loan. Not bad for one year's pay as a part-time companion.

I could not be impressed with her sacrifice since I was never given the opportunity to help. I would have gladly sat with my grandmother several days a week. Since no one asked, I assumed no help was wanted. If I had known how put out they felt I would have insisted. Gramma's mind was clear, she would retell the same stories again and again, but there was no dementia. The idea of her being a burden was laughable. She was an easier charge than my toddler. I could have cared for the both of them with no trouble. But no one asked. They didn't ask because then they would have owed me.

Gramma would say in her gentle wheeze: "I have no pain." She just became smaller and slower and more delicate. She outlived all her siblings and most others of her generation. "I think God forgot me," she said, almost wistfully.

There was just one hint something was wrong after she told me on her eighty-ninth birthday that the will was amended to "a third and a third and a third." She had said several times in recent years, "I don't want to be a burden." I assured her she wasn't. Obviously her son and daughter convinced her otherwise. Gramma never mentioned it; I think she was so worn down by her children that she allowed the will to be changed. She never alluded to Clarence's interference before, just asked Dad to examine the document. This time Clarence got his way and Betty went along for the ride.

I said to my brother John, "You know they wouldn't have dared if we weren't adopted." We weren't "real".

Then there was a certain degree of revenge. *"None of us will ever be so bad off that we can't take care of Mom,"* Lillian said firmly to her brother when he tried to draft an unnecessary plan for their mother's care. It must have stung having his sister throw that in his face. She knew it was self-serving and would have no part of it. Betty made for an easier accessory. She could justify it with her "sacrifice". Maybe she had the twisted idea that helping to care for Lillian after the stroke was worth two-thirds of her sister's share, even though it took a staff of people, including a full-time nurse, and Betty played only a small part. I didn't ask. I didn't want to hear any more.

I said nothing to my uncle or anyone else, including the cousins, just consoled myself that this would one day benefit them and that they had nothing to do with it. Dad told me, jaw clenched, that if I wanted to fight this in court that he would financially back me. This offer was only made to me, the daughter. As usual, the women were to handle it. I told him I didn't think it would be worth it after the cost of court and lawyers. And I was about to give birth. I needed a peaceful atmosphere; I couldn't have this hanging over me.

I decided some people never got over the Great Depression, the fear of never having "enough". A strained, unspoken truce went into effect. I had to forgive them over and over in my mind to be able to interact with them at all. I doubt Clarence knew the difference but my relationship with Betty was noticeably stand-offish. Some time later I was making small-talk and asked about our old cousin Eleanor.

Betty pounced: "She's dead. But she didn't have any money, you know!" Once again I was left reeling, blindsided by this declaration. Even her birthday greetings were that way. Her advice when I turned thirty: "Look at it this way, Noelle: You're not dead." I had no idea what to do with this information. When I asked about Eleanor, she was ready; it was apparent she expected a fight. She could not have known how fearful and guilty she sounded.

Dad and Carol and I had made the special trip to Seattle to take Eleanor to lunch on more than one occasion, and Dad always took care of her old Plymouth while she could still drive. She moved into the special care section of her posh retirement home when her memory and reflexes started fading. I wish I had made the effort to see her then, even if she couldn't recognize me, but what was easy with one child was complicated with two and I let the time slip away. I thought of her every time I had occasion to use her china. Sometimes I would send a card to be read to her. She was special to me – the queen mother who never had children. The time I spent in her house was pivotal to my childhood. But when she died I wasn't informed.

Dad did not mention the will again but did not speak to Betty or Clarence for years, even though they lived next door. We never celebrated Christmas or Easter with them again. Dad never forgave how Lillian was slighted.

Gramma was the only person besides my parents who never made me feel like I was adopted. Being adopted doesn't make you grateful. Being made to feel you're not adopted does.

My second child came into the world with many of the same witnesses as the first but this time in our own home. Midwife Janet Brooks was so efficient that she had cleaned up and left within fifteen minutes of arrival.

If people thought I wanted a boy since we already had a girl they were wrong. I wanted another daughter. We named her Chloe. She was beautiful and delicate and absolutely perfect. Suddenly, our lives changed forever in the form of this tiny, incredible human being.

Chloe was a serious baby. We never knew what was going on behind those steadfast blue eyes. Even when she was old enough to make a joke, she was so deadpan it was hard to tell how she meant it. She and Lillie were inseparable. Even while being very different in temperament they preferred one another's company over that of anyone else.

Lillie loved books. If I didn't read aloud for at least an hour daily she thought she was being punished. One series she enjoyed were the Frances books by Russell Hoban. But I couldn't just read it as written – Lillie had to be substituted for Frances and Chloe for little sister Gloria.

One day we sat on the bed and read *Best Friends for Frances*:

It was a fine summer morning, so Lillie took out her bat and ball. "Will you play ball with me?" said her little sister Chloe. "No," said Lillie. "You are too little." Chloe sat down and cried.

And with that, the real Lillie and Chloe burst into tears.

"That's mean!" Lillie cried. "I wouldn't say that to you, Chloe! I would play with you!" Chloe continued to cry. I suggested we finish the book to find out what happens. When Frances/Lillie decided Gloria/Chloe was indeed her best friend, all was right with the world again.

As natural as it was, their bond amazed me. I tried to imagine what it would have been like to grow up with Sharon and Teresa – to have sisters – but my life had been so different it was inconceivable. That other me was a ghost, a would-have-been-me, with a different name, different parents, different everything.

Dad and Carol invited us to stay at the lake for a few days. Since we had only one car, I left it for Brian to commute to work and join us on the weekends. Carol picked us up – the kids and me – and we stopped at a grocery near our destination so I could buy camping treats: s'more fixings for the kids, wine coolers for me. Camping was the only time I drank wine coolers. As I put the 4-pack into the cart, Carol exclaimed, "Well I'm not going to pay for *that!*"

I replied smoothly, "Since I'm thirty years old, I thought I'd buy it myself." She made a sour face. Whenever she was on my territory, such as being a guest in my home, she treated me as an adult. But when the tables were turned and I found myself in the dependent daughter position, I may as well have been five. Because she was driving today, she was in charge.

"I get to be the mother!" she'd singsong, giggling, as if playing pretend with dolls whenever the occasion would allow. "I get to be the mother!" when she was overriding her adult offspring. "I get to be the mother!" when making the final decision, settling any argument.

I had always viewed her as being so competent, always doing the right thing. I wondered now how much of that was a bluff because she needed to be the mother.

For a year or so I babysat for a friend. Michelle was a single mom of one daughter who was the same age as Lillie. Since they got along, I agreed to let Amanda spend her day with us, joining in on whatever we were doing while Michelle worked.

One day Michelle was upset. She was pregnant, again, and by Amanda's father, again. When she told him he took off. She briefly considered hunting him down, then sensibly decided he wasn't worth it.

Then she shocked me. She said she planned on adopting the baby out.

"It worked out for you, didn't it?" she asked, hopefully.

That was a huge question and I wasn't sure how to answer, except that I hoped she was leaning toward open adoption.

Open adoption is more of an ideal than anything, and not enforceable. Still, it was a big step up from the adoptions of my time, which were closed, sealed, secret, and shameful. Because of the dwindling number of healthy white newborns available for adoption starting in the 1970s, potential birth mothers were increasingly catered to, told what they were doing was selfless and wonderful, and were given any number of promises, just as long as they relinquish that baby.

Fortunately for Michelle, she had a good therapist to help her sort things out. The father of the baby was not going to help and Michelle's family, while sympathetic, couldn't offer much more. Michelle herself was stuck in a job and made barely enough to get by. She didn't want to separate Amanda from a sibling, but she wanted what was best for them, and she knew she couldn't provide for both. After considering every option available, she decided on open adoption, just not *too* open. While she wanted to meet the prospective adoptive parents, she didn't want to know their last name or where they lived. That way she wouldn't feel compelled to avoid them or seek them out.

A couple was chosen who agreed to the semi-openness.

After giving birth to her second daughter, Michelle wrote *Sarah Christine* on the birth certificate, even though it would be the adoptive parents who would choose the name that would go on the "real" (amended) certificate. Michelle said she did it only because she felt bad leaving the name blank; it looked like she didn't care.

But when the parents-to-be saw what she wrote, they said, "We like that. That's what we'll call her: Sarah Christine." And after being brave for so long, Michelle burst into tears.

"You're...so...*nice,*" she said through sobs.

One year later, a package arrived via the agency that arranged the adoption, containing the agreed-upon update from the adoptive parents. It would be a week before Michelle could bring herself to open it. Photos of Sarah throughout her first year, with cheerful stickers and captions written by her adoptive mother fell out of the envelope. Sarah playing at the park. Sarah playing with her toys. Smiling, always smiling, just like Michelle. "Happy Sarah," it said on the final picture. And she really did seem happy. I just hoped she stayed that way.

When Lillie was four, she was asked to be flower girl at the wedding of my friend Renee Tanaka in Los Angeles. We made a vacation of it, driving down the coast.

Before we left, I attempted to contact my birth father's only sibling, his sister Jean Havner. She lived in Los Angeles as well and I knew this would be my only chance to see her. Since Glenn did not see fit to respond in all these years, I hoped to have better luck with someone not so close to the situation. The tricky part was that I knew her mother – my grandmother – lived with her.

I sent an overnight letter, explaining myself, telling her I would call on a certain day and time when I was in town and that I hoped to speak with her.

On that day, I took little Chloe and found a pay phone in Jean's area. There, on an unfamiliar street in an unfamiliar state, I hoped to God this aunt of mine would just pick up the phone. The answering machine clicked on instead. I left a message but I knew she would not call or contact me. I had come up against a wall of silence.

Chapter 15
~The Ghost Child~

Chloe was out of toddlerhood when we set our minds on having our third and final child. We had always wanted three. Now that I had two amazingly different daughters, I was finally ready to have a son. But since this would be our last, I wanted to make sure, so read a Choose the Sex of Your Baby book. Seemed plausible, so I planned the timing very carefully, knowing my cycles averaged twenty-two days rather than the usual twenty-eight. I figured even if we missed the mark, we'd have another daughter; so it was impossible to lose.

Like clockwork, we conceived again on the first try. But an unexpected bonus was to discover my sister Sharon had conceived on the same day. With my other children I had been pregnant along with sisters-in-law, cousins or close friends, but never with Sharon and never having the same due date. Our mother was more excited than we were, if possible. To top it off, Sharon and I were both seeing midwife Janet Brooks.

At my first appointment Janet needed a blood draw, completely routine. But this time the room went dark around the edges and I wanted to curl up in the fetal position. Janet helped me down the hall to where Brian was waiting with the kids. She told him to keep an eye on me and make sure I drank a lot of water. Tunnel vision continued and I started shaking. I picked through dinner then shivered under a blanket on the couch. I figured I just wasn't in shape to give blood; before having children I could rarely donate because of low blood pressure. I got better. Life went back to normal.

Two weeks later, on Valentine's Day, I was very introspective, nearly in a dream state. I turned in upon myself, creeping silently throughout the house.

In the bathroom a single drop of blood fell into the toilet. "I'm starting my period," I thought dully. I stared at the drop as it sank and realization slowly came over me. I called the midwife.

"How do you feel?" Janet asked. "I don't know," I answered honestly.

"Honey, put your feet up. There's nothing you can do at this point." I wrapped in a blanket and watched a movie. I used the bathroom again. A trace more blood. Brian came home. I told him. He tried not to show he was upset.

The next day: more blood. And the next day: even more. I called Janet again. "Honey, you're miscarrying. I'm sorry." I called a few friends, then my birth mother. In denial, Pamela said I should go to the hospital in an effort to keep the baby. At that very moment the cramping started and I knew it was over. Next there were clots. Every visit to the bathroom was another small death.

In the winter mist I took a long walk alone. Brian understood.

Finally, after almost a week, the final piece appeared – what would have been my baby. So tiny, not even a human form yet. In the back yard, under the apple tree, I buried my grief in the cold, wet ground.

A dark heaviness consumed me. My body killed my child. The same body that nurtured two daughters rejected my only son. Did it happen when I moved that heavy garbage can? Did I miss some essential nutrient? But the bigger question was Why? What was the point? I was angry with God over the stupidity of the entire phenomenon.

Some were sympathetic. "I heard what happened…" Dad's voice trailed off. Gram Reid sent a note of condolence. It was my friend Michelle, whose daughter I watched, who said exactly the right thing:

"I'm sorry. I know you really wanted that baby."

Others were less helpful, including those who should have known better. "It's God's plan." – "Be happy. You have two healthy children already." – "It's nature's way – it wouldn't have survived." Or, the most thoughtless: "It's not like it was a real baby."

I stood with my neighbor Gail while the kids played in her front yard. She happened to be going to her car with her son Zach when we strolled by. Zach was the same age as Lillie, adopted from Guatemala, and one of the most handsome little boys I ever laid eyes on. But the kids played together only by chance like this; Gail decided long ago, and I reluctantly agreed, that Zach and Lillie together were like gasoline and fire, both dominant first-borns. And I don't think Gail liked me. I couldn't pinpoint why and I didn't want to come out and ask so we just kept up the neighborly routine.

She asked how I was. I mentioned as nonchalantly as possible what happened, including the indifferent remarks. In silence we watched the kids play as we stood there on the sidewalk. I looked up at the sky, arms folded, breathed in deeply and shut my eyes. Suddenly all the anger, pain and grief that had been simmering in me exploded:

"What is *wrong* with them?! Can't they see it *hurts?!*"

And Gail, an adoptive mother who would never know miscarriage, much less pregnancy and birth – a woman who owed me nothing, didn't like me and had every right to just walk away – put her arm around me and gently said:

"They're stupid. Let it go."

The rage drained from me. I would come to think of miscarriage as a small sorrow, something not to be talked about, just quietly endured. I will always be grateful for Gail in that moment. She had empathy when there was no basis for her to have empathy.

Time dragged on. In early spring, bluebells came up around the apple tree. They were planted before we moved in and sprang up every year with no help from me. Most blue, but some pink. When I would pull weeds, the tiny bulbs would come up as well so I'd casually throw them back in the ground.

One morning, I sipped coffee, looked out the kitchen window, and saw it: A wave of blue flowers crashing against a wave of pink. The colors had never been segregated like that before. It must have happened when I pulled weeds and accidentally separated the bulbs. My gaze was drawn to where the colors met. Something else was there. Coffee cup in hand I investigated. There, where the blue and pink converged was another tiny flower, one that had never been there before. A forget-me-not.

Gramma's garden had been covered in tiny blue and yellow forget-me-nots. I thought of her every time I saw one. They sprang up in every available space in her yard, including the window wells and cracks in the front steps. But any attempt of mine to transplant them here had failed. My neighbors didn't have any so I couldn't ask their advice. Then this one just shows up, unbidden. It was a gift. But why? Then I realized it sprang from where I buried what I believe would have been my son.

I told no one. It was too *Where the Red Fern Grows*. I didn't want anyone to cheapen this supernatural offering.

The kids knew I had been pregnant and that the baby didn't grow right, so died. Lillie was very spiritual as a small child. She sometimes said things that made even the adults at church take note – sudden insights. She could also take me by surprise with her questions.

"Mommy, is the baby in heaven a baby?"

God, give me the words, I thought, using Pamela's prayer, and without forming an answer heard myself say: "He's everything he could have been."

Sometimes God is saving us from something worse. But the question there was no answer for was, Why does God allow it to happen at all?

We tried to conceive several more times after that and for the first time in my life, I caught a glimpse of what infertility felt like. Even after two healthy, very-planned children, I felt like my body was failing me. First by the loss of the last pregnancy and now by not procreating at all. Months went by. I was tired of stumbling over my box of maternity clothes so loaned it all to Sharon. I thought that was smart until I saw her in one of my favorite outfits. Then I felt like I had been slapped in the face.

On the phone with best friend Cecelia Vaughn, I choked out, "I wasn't... *done*." Cecelia understood. There is no logic attached to biological need. If a woman has not met her desired number of children, her body instinctively craves the very feel and sound of an infant; it does not matter how many other children she has. The need is there; that is the reality.

I could not begin to imagine my adoptive mother's pain at being unable to carry and birth her own child, not even once. Not even a miscarriage. When I was little I had wished I was Lillian's biological daughter, in part because even then I knew adoption was second-choice, a substitute. I wanted to make her pain go away. I wanted to be Real, like the Velveteen Rabbit.

When depression convinced me I would have no more children, I said to Brian, "Is it okay if we stop with two?" because I just couldn't go on hoping.

Surprised, he said, "Sure," because he knew there was no right answer.

Then we had our first unplanned pregnancy. I didn't want Brian to know until after I was past the point where I had lost the last one. I had to be sure, even if that meant hiding morning sickness. We were walking alone in the woods on a mountain when I finally told him. He pulled me down to the mossy ground and we made love in celebration.

Our final child was a beautiful girl we named Dagne. She was absolutely perfect. Her birth was so quick the midwife couldn't get there in time. Brian and I caught her ourselves. This is when I stopped "well baby visits".

Because of job or insurance changes, we went through pediatricians like TV character Murphy Brown went through secretaries, only in our case it wasn't funny. The latest was not supportive of anything I did, such as think for myself.

On my last visit with Lillie and Chloe in tow, she was irritated that I correctly diagnosed an allergy in Chloe that she had missed, so then took an adversarial approach to homeschooling, which I had done with the kids since birth.

"What books have you read on the subject?" she challenged.

"All of them," I replied evenly. "How about you?"

She fumed, and told me I was overly involved with my children. "Overly involved." With my three year old. Then she started in with various arguments against self-education, which she obviously knew nothing about.

I finally wearily interrupted, "You know, you're just the pediatrician." It was later apparent she never forgot the sting of that remark.

She never said she was anti-homebirth and I never asked her opinion on the subject, because it was none of her business, but her body language spoke volumes. On my first visit with newborn Dagne – a week old and thriving – she grilled me with questions, checking them off on a form and getting testier with every answer:

"Number of weeks?" – "Thirty-eight."

"Length of labor?" – "Less than an hour."

"Apgar score?" – "We didn't do one, considering the midwife wasn't there until twenty minutes later. She was fine, though—"

"Vitamin K shot?" she interrupted. "No," I said, and regretting it immediately. She slammed the pen down.

"Why didn't the baby get a vitamin K shot?!"

"Why would she? She didn't need one."

"Every baby needs one. They're completely routine."

"Why should they be routine if they're unnecessary?"

"It could save the baby's life if there's a problem with bleeding."

"There was no problem with bleeding."

"There still could be. I'll call the hospital and you can just walk—"

"Hold it." This time I interrupted. "Why should this baby get a shot when her sisters didn't and my midwife did not see the need for one?"

She did not try to hide her disgust of my ignorance. "There is a disease," she said in serious tones, "where people bleed from every orifice of their body. And the condition is fatal."

I looked at her and said flatly, "You mean *Ebola?* In *Africa?*"

Now she was really angry. She said I could get the shot at the hospital or from my midwife ("assuming she has it," she added contemptuously) but Dagne was getting a vitamin K shot. She said she would have the office call me to make sure it's done. I am fairly certain I was red-flagged with Child Protective Services at that point, thanks to the good doctor. She had her revenge.

I called Janet Brooks. Hearing her calm voice was just what I needed. I told her that while the shot may be harmless, it was also unnecessary and I didn't like being bullied into it. Janet said, "She has more vitamin K in her body now than she'll have at any other time in her life[6]. But if there is a problem when I give her a foot tap, we'll know she needs the shot and I can give it to her then."

There was no problem drawing blood and when the pediatrician's office called, I said, "I took Dagne to my midwife and she got everything she needed." I then found a new pediatrician, lowering the bar to: Just don't piss me off.

We had a full house by then. Life had become a flurry of Play-Doh, walks to the park, finger-painting, ballet, swimming, church, bike riding, lessons, dress-up, and birthday parties. The entire upstairs and most of the main floor were bur-

---

6   Vitamin K naturally peaks just after the first week of life, which is thought to be why the eighth day is the mandated day for Jewish circumcision.

ied in kid activities. The broom closet was a rocket ship. The couch was an island. A bush in the backyard was a camp hide-out. Their imaginations endless. Their energy boundless. I was starting to realize why my mother needed naps.

The three girls were very different from each another, in appearance and personality. But they were also fiercely loyal. If one was hurt by another child, the other two would come to her defense. They loved their cousins and their friends but no one was closer than their sisters. Something so normal was foreign to me.

The kids, being kids, never asked why they had so many grandparents or why I seemed to have brothers and sisters who weren't related to each other. One day though, Lillie said, "When was Papa Walt married to Grandma Pam?" She knew Papa was my dad and Grandma was my mother and she also had a vague idea what divorce was. When I told her they never were married and didn't even know each other until I was twenty-one she was dumbfounded. I explained as best I could, but for years the kids would pair up the wrong grandparents.

Chapter 16
~The Surreal Summer~

It was an unusually hot, dry summer. The air was thick with dust and noise from road construction work. The heavy machinery was parked directly across the street from our house, so there was no escape from it. With no rain, the noise echoed all day, giving the weird effect that we were under attack.

Our next-door neighbors, a nice young couple with two little ones, had just moved back east after he completed his studies. They were the first spirit-filled Catholics I had ever met. When I told Moira we were having difficulty finding another house, she said, "I'll pray to St. Joseph to intercede on your behalf." And she did. It wasn't just an empty promise, a passing, "I'll pray for you," that is quickly forgotten. They were spiritual in a tangible way. They were also thoroughly Irish. Beyond wearing green to avoid being pinched, I'd never celebrated St. Patrick's Day before. Now I can't imagine March 17th without corned beef and soda bread. I introduced Celtic crosses and triquetras to my Sunday school classes. The more I learned, the more Irish I felt, as if coming home to a place I had never been.

When they drove away I couldn't watch. It was just too hard. I was tired of watching people leave.

Between the construction and the weather, many opted to go on vacation so the neighborhood felt abandoned. I kept up the usual routine with the house and kids, but the weird atmosphere kept me on edge.

As a news junkie, if I don't watch local broadcasts and read the paper every day, I feel disconnected from my community. The month before, I was annoyed because I was often too busy to do either; a martyr sacrificing myself for the kids' summer ballet and swim lessons, only I wasn't very gracious about it. Now on TV was the tragic story of a young man who died while camping. Slipped and hit his head on a rock. He looked so athletic and handsome in his photo; it was hard to believe he could die from a simple fall. Then something happened that had not happened in years. The voice only I could hear said:

"Pay attention."

That was all. Pay attention to what? Brian, who loved camping, did not have any trips planned. What did I have to worry about?

"Pay attention."

You can't argue with a voice that's in your head, so I checked the story every time it came on TV. Still I couldn't see what I was supposed to notice. Then I read his obituary and understood.

He was Shirley Havner's nephew. The church secretary in Idaho gave me the names of Shirley's siblings but not their locations. One apparently lived here in the Tacoma area and this was a son. My mind raced.

Had Glenn and Shirley visited here before? Would they come now? It had been more than ten years since I first contacted my birth father. I never told him I moved to Tacoma, never told him about my children; because he never responded, I felt he didn't deserve to know.

"This is your only chance," the voice said.

For what? But I knew. I called Pamela.

"Could you watch the kids for me? I need to crash a funeral."

I dressed in a nice black skirt and beige jacket. I wanted to arrive just before it started, so if Glenn noticed me he wouldn't have time to bail. I had no plan in mind. Nothing ever went according to plan anyway.

At the funeral home, I asked where Mike's service was being held. The woman at the desk said it started in the chapel in ten minutes, but would I like to view the body first?

Didn't expect that. Heard myself say, "Yes, of course," and next thing I knew I was alone in a darkened room with the body of someone I had never met.

I suppose I should have expected to be punished somehow, I thought ruefully, and approached the open casket to gaze at this stranger's face: *Young. Handsome. Should be alive.* I wondered what he would have accomplished had he not gone on that camping trip. I wondered if it mattered, if this was just "his time" and would have died regardless. I wondered why things happen the way they do. I apologized to him silently for being there with ulterior motives and departed.

The chapel was standing room only. This worked well for me because I was forced to stand in the back where I had a view of everyone, even if it was just the back of their heads. In the front rows sat the family. I examined everyone. That must be his father. That must be his mother…one by one, row by row. About the third row back I stopped. There was a man about the right age with dark silky hair. Is that him? Is that Shirley sitting next to him? There was no way to know from my vantage point. With the crowd, I wasn't sure there would be a way for me to maneuver to see his face.

But the opportunity presented itself. When the service concluded we were invited to pay our respects to the family, starting with those standing in the back. The rest were asked to remain seated, i.e. trapped. I walked to the front and joined the line of mourners leaning over to talk quietly to Mike's family in the front row.

Waiting my turn, I casually looked up to where I thought I saw Glenn and Shirley from the back of the room and locked eyes with a couple staring at me in utter shock. She was a beautiful blonde. He was me, only thirty years older and male. They could not look away and I resisted the urge to do just that, forcing myself to level my gaze into theirs. They didn't move – didn't even look like they were breathing – just sat frozen as if seeing a ghost.

Only a moment had passed, but it was my turn to give my regards. Offering my hand, I murmured my condolences and walked through the adjacent door leading outside.

It was over. Nothing had happened yet everything had happened. I went to retrieve the children.

"How did he look?" Pamela asked with great curiosity.

"Older. A lot more mellow. And…surprised." But their matching expressions gave me some information: Shirley knew. She knew about me. I was not The Secret, I was The One We Don't Talk About. He must have shown her the photos and letters because it wasn't just shock, it was the shock of recognition. They knew me. The only other possibility was that she saw the resemblance, but if that was the case she would have nudged Glenn and pointed me out. Instead they sat as if pretending to be invisible – like deer in the forest – hoping I wouldn't see them.

Beyond that, their friend at the church in Coeur d'Alene must have mentioned the strange girl from Tacoma who wanted genealogy info. They knew I was capable of showing up in unexpected places. They looked afraid of what I would do next. But I had already done what I came to do.

I wanted to see my birth father, just once. I had gotten what I wanted.

Pamela came over the next day. She needed to further process what happened. She told me things about her time in Coeur d'Alene bit by bit over the years, whenever something would trigger a memory. Once my sister Sharon mentioned to her how I thought I was conceived in the house they rented. Pamela had called me then, wanted me to know that wasn't true, and would I like to hear what actually happened?

Wincing and holding the phone away from my ear, I said, "Sure." What could be better than hearing about your parents having sex?

She told me they had been drinking. Nearly everyone smoked and drank then. What she added now was that they had gone to see a school basketball game somewhere on a Friday night. He drove. They made an evening of it. Away from the pressures and constraints of their roles as teachers, they were enjoying themselves. Glenn said, "I want to see where you grew up," and drove into Spokane, past her old house. She asked if he wanted to meet her parents, figuring it was an innocent offer, but he declined. Then they stopped at a diner where they didn't know anyone. They had drinks and danced. Pamela felt she was just out with a co-worker, a happily married co-worker, and all this was fine.

Suddenly, the alcohol really hit her and he helped her to the car. They started back to Coeur d'Alene. Then, on a dark road somewhere on the border of Washington and Idaho, in the front seat of his Corvair, Glenn Havner finally had his way.

"It wasn't...awful," she assured me when I muttered something about date rape through gritted teeth. "I just didn't want it. And I couldn't stop him."

I wondered if he had been proud of himself. If it mattered to him, or if the thought even occurred to him, that his "conquest" had to be drunk to succumb, even after months of grooming. She thought his love for his wife was her protection. She had no idea at the time she had been set up.

She didn't talk about that now. Instead we discussed how people change, how times change. She no longer seemed to hate him. She would never like him, had no respect for him, but the simmering anger was gone. Left behind was mainly disgust. She had moved on.

Then she said she had seen the aftermath of a horrific car crash that morning. Brian said he heard it on his emergency scanner and it sounded bad. The voice nudged me: *"Pay attention."* But I didn't want to pay attention. I wanted to further process what had happened at the funeral. I avoided the news that night, something I never did.

The next morning was peaceful. No construction work. Brian and I were enjoying our first cups of coffee. Turning on the TV, the news anchor said, "Mother of four killed in hit-and-run." I was about to sarcastically say, "Oh, great," when the beautiful face of my friend Andrea came on the screen.

My coffee cup crashed to the floor. I heard my own voice, *"Andrea! No! No! Oh my God, not Andrea!"*

But it was Andrea. Just two blocks from her home, she was hit by a speeding SUV and killed instantly.

"The babies won't even remember her! They won't remember their own mother," I gasped. Bordering on hysteria, I paced with nowhere to go, clutching my stomach. I kept closing my eyes and then looking back at the TV, hoping it wouldn't be there, that it wasn't real. Brian was upset as well, even though he didn't know Andrea. He had never seen me like this.

Andrea was my physical therapist after I hurt my back slipping on ice. That's how we met. She had a calm, professional manner and knew instinctively what to do. I got to know her well in that year of treatment. But more than just therapist/patient, we were contemporaries. We married around the same time, had children around the same time, bought old houses in the same neighborhood. I would run into her grocery shopping, at the park, strolling through town. We knew many of the same people. Our kids played together. She was a terrific mom – very involved – but never looked haggard like I did. After her last pregnancy I told her she had no business looking that good. She just laughed.

It wasn't fair for Andrea to be dead. It was wrong. Unnervingly wrong.

Unable to believe it and too distraught to drive, I put Dagne in her stroller and walked there. Brian understood. Already there were signs, flowers, candles, cards and a banner made by her church saying, *"Lo, I go before you."* Kneeling in the awful rut left by her car, I laid flowers. It would be two years before I could steel myself to drive through that intersection.

It could have been me. It shouldn't have been Andrea – it shouldn't be anyone with little children – but why her? And overriding all of it: They won't remember her. The little ones won't remember their own mother.

The rest of the day was surreal. My senses were raw. Just the usual noises of the kids playing put me on edge. I needed evening to come to escape the harsh brightness of the day. The air was too hot, too loud, too close. Making dinner I opened all the doors, hoping for cross-ventilation, when I heard wailing. Horrible, agonized wailing. I went to the front porch to see the elegant black woman who lived across the street emerge from her house with arms raised as if in supplication. Her daughter had just arrived and was getting out of her car. At the sight of her mother the girl began to scream, fell to her knees and rocked. The older woman continued to wail as if she would never stop. The girl screamed as if in agony. I couldn't take anymore and shut the door on the sight, but was unable to shut out the horrible sound.

The woman's son had died in his sleep. She went to wake him and found him dead of a stroke. He was only in his twenties. Scores of family and friends came to grieve together. I walked over with coffee cake, wishing I could feel numb but instead was on edge, waiting for the next blow.

Over the next week, the realization would hit me again and again that Andrea was dead and I would be left grieving anew. It didn't matter where I was, the tears would just come.

I called Pamela again, asking if she could watch the kids while I went to Andrea's funeral. This time she dismissed me, saying she needed to see a friend. I was annoyed. I was going to a funeral, not bar-hopping. I almost never asked anyone to babysit; when I did there was a real need. I called around but no one seemed to be available. I suddenly thought of Michelle, now married, whose daughter I used to watch. She said yes.

That meant driving across town and back so I was one of the last to arrive at the service. Even though the old stone church was massive there were so many people that, once again, I was forced to stand in the back, unable to even get into the sanctuary.

And once again, because we were standing, we were the first allowed to come forward, this time to take communion. As I passed, I laid my hand on Andrea's closed, draped coffin. I don't know if that was permissible, but I had to touch her to accept this awful reality. To say good-bye. I was already a Lutheran taking communion in a Catholic church – claiming my spot – this was more important than rules.

Feeling wrung out, I went to pick up the kids. Michelle emerged from the bathroom with a home pregnancy test and a surprised expression on her face. Even while congratulating her, the thought struck me: When was my last period? With all the recent trauma I had lost track. Weariness replaced with keen focus, I stopped at a drug store on the way home and distracted the kids with candy so they wouldn't see the box I slid into the cart.

Having just one decent bathroom, we had an "open-door" policy, but this time I locked myself in. When the positive sign appeared on the stick I just stared. How was this possible? We've always used birth control. It's not like contraceptives have expiration dates. To prove this to myself, I opened the medicine cabinet, pulled out the box of spermicidal inserts we had been using and made a discovery: Contraceptives have expiration dates. Methodically hitting my head against the wall, I stared at the box in my hands.

When? But before even completing the thought the answer came: When Brian was leaving for that fishing trip in July. I suspected I was ovulating – I had been having cycles for a few months because Dagne was weaning – but figured the inserts would do their job.

I had come to the conclusion years earlier that every woman has her own personal threshold for the number of children her body can handle. My limit was three. During my last pregnancy I was exhausted, couldn't absorb iron, and would sleep eleven hours a day. My legs ached with varicose veins. Keeping up with three busy kids plus my husband plus the house and the yard...I was stretched to the limit.

And now I was having another.

Was this some sick cosmic joke? I had heard the fourth child was often a surprise but never believed it. How can you be surprised after three? Now I knew.

When I was pregnant the second time, Brian's father called and had a long conversation with him. And by conversation I mean diatribe. About how having more than two kids can lead to divorce because the demands of raising them detracts from the intimacy of the couple. He was telling Brian this to save our marriage. We needed to stop having children. Brian recounted this to me in subdued, accepting tones, completely beaten down. When he finished there was brief silence, then I exploded:

"If your father is experiencing latent guilt over abandoning you and your mother, that's his problem, not ours!"

Brian leapt from the couch as if I had attacked him and stormed downstairs, only to reappear minutes later, much calmer.

"You're right," he said. "Screw him. We'll have as many kids as we want."

But I continued to seethe. That Dennis could concoct the idea that his son's very existence brought about the break up of his marriage was bad enough. That he would actually say it aloud to him disguised as fatherly advice sent me over the edge.

I admired my father-in-law for many things, but his track record as a husband wasn't one of them. His kids didn't make his marriage fall apart, his habitual infidelity did. Thankfully he was much more mature by the time I knew him and he went on to have a long and happy marriage with Brian's step-mother. But that didn't stop him from applying a heavy dose of "creative memory" to his history. The Reids were famous for it. So I did not look forward to announcing this blessed event.

I kept the news to myself for a few days, pondering how to tell Brian. Meanwhile, it occurred to me that our old neighbors (also expecting) may have known Andrea since they attended the same church. Maybe they would like a clipping of the obituary. It was Brian's habit to take the newspaper downstairs when I was done. I ventured to the dungeon.

The basement was so rustic we didn't allow the kids down there. It was dirty, with cement walls, an exposed crawl space, a huge scary furnace, full of boxes and cobwebs, and a workbench that Brian covered in moldy beer bottles. He'd hole up there in his robe, listening to his police scanner, reading magazines about guns or hiking or naked women, although I don't think much reading was required with that last one. The one good photo of me – the one my cousin Britt took at our wedding – was pinned to the wall above the workbench. We never got around to having it touched up or copied. I liked that it was the only thing Brian bothered to display in his "den." I went downstairs only to do laundry and otherwise tried to stay out of his space.

I picked up a random newspaper from the pile and seeing the right date, opened to the obituaries. Only I didn't realize it was the right date but from the month before, and scanning the page for Andrea instead found my old engineering instructor, Mr. Granville.

I did not have time to read the paper the month before. It irritated me, but other things took priority. Now I realized that during those weeks of righteous self-sacrifice, my favorite teacher had died and I missed the funeral. He had been a guest at my wedding. I attended several special occasions with him and Mrs. Granville over the years. He always remembered to send a Christmas card. I cared for him like I did my own father and now he was gone. Furious, I threw the paper down and buried my face in my hands.

Over the span of nine days, I learned four people somehow connected to me had died, I saw my birth father in the flesh, and found myself unexpectedly pregnant.

Reality shifted under my feet, again and again. Reeling, I stop looking for Andrea's obituary and climbed the stairs back into the harsh light of day.

I wrote Mrs. Granville a condolence letter. She graciously wrote back, saying he was cracking jokes right up to the end and went quickly. That gave me some comfort.

I informed Brian in a birthday card that he had waited a little too long to get that vasectomy. After feigning a heart attack he adjusted faster than I did, but he didn't have to figure out the details. That was left to me, as always. But we both had to face the derision that comes with a bonus baby:

"Have you figured out what's causing that yet?"

I knew I could count on my father-in-law. Looking at him wide-eyed I replied, "No, what?" and continued to stare, unsmiling, as he laughed. My own father's reaction was worse.

"Oh, for crying out loud!" He loved his granddaughters but knew they were a handful. While he admired my sister Sharon with her little brood – he always admired vivacious women – he knew I didn't have her stamina. He remembered how wiped out I was when pregnant with Dagne, who Dad now fondly called "a going concern" with her non-stop activity.

"Are you trying for a boy?" I was asked again and again, as if I felt somehow incomplete with my daughters. "Unplanned" just doesn't compute with some people. No, I wasn't "trying" for a boy. I wasn't "trying" at all.

"How did this happen?" my friend Jenny Miller asked with sincere surprise.

"The usual way," I replied. We both laughed. After a few months, I was able to laugh. Jenny, my cohort in adoption adventures, knew I took bringing children into the world very seriously. That I could have a surprise pregnancy shook her as much as it did me.

If I had seen Mr. Granville's obituary in July, or if I had known the contraceptives had gone stale, or if Brian had gone ahead with the vasectomy, this baby would not have happened. I knew in my soul that there were no "accidents". This baby was needed.

There were practical concerns, the main one being the house. As much as I loved its quirkiness and charm, it was going to be very small very soon. It was already wall-to-wall beds in the one spare room for the girls. We just couldn't put child another in there.

The major obstacle was finding something big enough that we could still afford. Prices had shot up dramatically since we first moved in. And although Brian earned more now than he ever did, we never got ahead of our expenses. We were always on the verge of some financial crisis. Money was the main thing we fought about.

My brother John nearly provided an answer, albeit unintentionally. John and Brian were as close as brothers, even as polar opposite as they were in personality. They would go camping, take potentially crippling bike rides, or just hang out nearly every weekend. John lived in a run-down rental with a lone cat. A construction worker, it was always feast or famine; overtime with frequent bouts of unemployment.

John smoked cigarettes from the time he was a teenager, even though our parents never did and it was not allowed in the house. Brian grew up in a cloud of smoke, developing bronchial pneumonia nearly every winter thanks to the smokers around him, but never took up the habit himself. John quit drinking in his early twenties after a few nasty hangovers while Brian continued to expand his repertoire, hangovers be damned. We grew up in the stoner era and they both enjoyed smoking pot, which I hated. So John smoked while Brian drank and both indulged in marijuana between miles-long bike rides in the fresh air. They were a bundle of contradictions, those two.

Brian called John one day, telling me after: "John sounds like Darth Vader. If he isn't better by tomorrow, I'm taking him to the doctor." But the next day when he tried to call, there was no answer. Brian went John's place to find it locked. Knowing he was inside, Brian pounded on the door and windows and called to him, getting a weak murmur in response. It took John ten minutes to drag himself – crawling – to the door. Brian rushed him to the ER where the doctor told Brian that his brother-in-law would have been dead in a few more hours, the pneumonia was so severe. He spent weeks in ICU, getting antibiotics and oxygen. Even his blood was infected.

Still, he took up smoking again immediately upon his release.

I stood guard in the ICU, openly glaring at the women who would visit. John had the same girlfriend over and over – all broken-winged sparrows with a drug problem – they just had different names. They'd visit and force him to carry on a conversation, making his oxygen levels plummet.

"He shouldn't talk. He's too sick," I'd say to their blank stares.

Once he needed to give a urine sample and since the staff was busy, I brought it to the nurses' station myself. The nurse who took the steaming cup from my hands said, surprised, "What a good sister!" to which I grumbled, "I certainly am."

Because we were the ones to call John's employer to let them know what happened, we became the official emergency contact. Twice in the years after his near-death experience, they called because he didn't show up to work and wouldn't answer his phone. Both times he was delirious with fever from pneumonia, not even knowing what day it was.

The second time it happened, the receptionist suddenly said, "Are you the eldest?" Surprised, I said no, that John was older. "Oh, well you seem like the eldest," she said.

Dad was grateful to Brian, although he never said as much. But when Brian jokingly suggested we should buy a place with a "brother-in-law" apartment for John so we could keep an eye on him, Dad wholeheartedly supported the idea. Until that moment we never seriously considered it. Suddenly it made sense. I started looking for accommodations.

I had a dream:

I was standing in the kitchen. Boxes were haphazardly packed around me. The cupboards and drawers stood empty. Slowly turning, I looked at the incomplete stencil above the archway – the one of ivy vines that I never finished. I felt empty. And angry. And defeated.

"Why would I feel like that?" I asked myself and others when describing the dream. "We *want* to move."

The question haunted me.

One way I house-hunted was online. This was when home computers were still just coming into vogue, the advent of the Internet. As I stumbled around, getting used to the technology, I found a few places with a spare house on the same property, but nothing was within reach financially.

Navigating a real estate site, I accidentally clicked on something and the following window popped up:

ARE YOU LOOKING FOR SOMEONE?

I stopped and pondered the question, waiting there on the screen.

"As a matter of fact," I answered, "I am."

I had kept up with the Havners over the years as best I could, checking Polk Indexes every so often at the main libraries in Seattle or Tacoma. Polk Indexes are hard-bound city directories that also include the profession of those listed and sometimes where they work as well. That way, I knew one brother was a teacher, another a store manager. I knew my younger sister Kelli worked in a restaurant when she was still living at home. I wanted to contact her but couldn't bring myself to do it as long as she lived under her parents' roof. If there was anything I understood, it was loyalty to parents. I never learned Heather's married name so couldn't trace her. I felt a woman would better sympathize with my situation so I waited for Kelli to be out on her own or for Heather to turn up rather than contact one of my brothers. It had been over ten years since I discovered my siblings' existence. Kelli would be a full-fledged adult now.

I looked at the screen again and considered. Seeing my birth father ("our father", I reminded myself) at the funeral last summer seemed eons ago, so much had happened since. I was almost certain Shirley knew and it was painfully obvious Glenn wanted nothing to do with me. But I had brothers and sisters. I loved my siblings from Pamela's side of the family, never thinking of them as "half". I had a richer life knowing them. I was now just an old shoe in their midst instead of a sort of glorified in-law. I liked being an old shoe. I knew that sort of relationship would be impossible with the Havners, but my need to connect was just as strong. They represented half of my genetics.

The pop-up window patiently waited for a response.

I hesitantly typed *Kelli Havner, Idaho*. And just like that, I was looking at three possible matches. Seemingly overnight, every phone book in the country was just a click away. It happened so fast I was stunned, not sure what to do next.

I decided to write a letter, to-the-point without giving too much away, asking if she was Kelli Havner born on a certain day and if so to please contact me – giving my name, address, phone number and email address. I hand-wrote the letter three times to send to the three Kelli Havners, said a prayer over them and dropped them at the post office before I could change my mind. With any luck, one would find the right Kelli and she would be intrigued enough to respond.

And she did, in a way. I was at my computer one afternoon a few weeks later when an email appeared from a Detective Larson of Ada County, Idaho. Ada County: Where Boise is located.

I don't believe it, I thought, *She called the cops!*

Heart pounding, I opened the message. It was polite, but somehow that didn't help. In it, Det. Larson asked why I was searching for Kelli Havner, that she asked him to contact me to know my intentions before she would be willing to respond to me herself.

Great. She has a cop friend. And not just a cop – a detective! I imagined my father-in-law: a tough, grizzled officer with no patience for mysterious letters or guessing games. Someone who would want to protect a nice young woman like Kelli from predatory people like me. I had to end this now and promptly typed something like:

"This was just a mistake. Sorry for your trouble. Okay. See ya. Bye."

It was possibly only slightly more coherent than that. Moments later, a much more relaxed email arrived. I could almost hear him laughing:

"Don't worry, no one is going to arrest you. Kelli was just afraid this might be a scam of some kind and asked me to check into it."

He seemed younger than I first imagined. And friendly. Maybe I had a chance. Taking a deep breath I wrote that I was Kelli's half-sister and that she and her other siblings did not know about me. I said our father worked with my mother at one time in Coeur d'Alene and that I was born and raised here in Tacoma. And I would like to make contact, even if through an intermediary. Could he tell her that, please?

He answered: Yes, he would do that.

A few hours or days or decades later, after all my nerves were shredded, Det. Larson emailed again. He had asked Kelli to come to his office so they could talk privately, face to face. He said when he told her what I wrote she was surprised. Not shocked, not angry, not disbelieving, just surprised. After quietly absorbing the information, she said, "I guess the family just got bigger."

It was my turn to be surprised. Not: "What does she want?" Not: "Why should we believe this?" Instant acceptance. I was stunned. Det. Larson said I should expect a call from her tomorrow afternoon. He relayed that Kelli wanted to tell her sister Heather first. I barely dared to believe this was happening. It just couldn't be this good.

But true to her word, Kelli called. I holed up in my bedroom, paper and pen in hand, with the thought that this might be the only contact I ever have with that side of the family. I had to make it count.

I needn't have worried. She was warm and articulate, with no trace of suspicion in her voice. Once we were past the initial "I don't know what to say," remarks, we had no trouble talking. She said she asked her friend the cop to contact me in case I was some sort of con artist. In turn I told her I would have no problem providing a DNA test if she wanted one, but she dismissed the idea.

I gave her a brief life history. She gave me hers, including the fact she had just married, so went by both surnames for now. If I had not searched for her when I did, I might not have been able to find her, like I couldn't find Heather. I explained why I didn't try to contact her sooner. She agreed she would have been too loyal to her parents to respond, and disbelieving. When I assured her I was the result of a one-time sexual encounter that involved alcohol – not a love affair – she said she could imagine that since her dad was an alcoholic. I remembered my one phone call to him: *An angry drunk?* Apparently so. It was unfortunate.

She and Heather were very close. She had to tell her sister about me before contacting me herself. Upon hearing the news, Heather exclaimed in mock-offended tones, "Why didn't she write to me? I'm older." Kelli smoothly retorted, "Well, obviously she likes me best." I had the feeling I was about to discover where I got my sense of humor.

I told her what I knew about them and where I got the information. She was surprised that I knew so much, but I told her that was all I had: names, birthdates and a couple of factoids. Nothing personal. So she told me all about her siblings and their spouses, what they did for a living, where they lived, the names and ages and interests of their children. They seemed so well-rounded: academic, athletic and productive. I tried to assimilate the information as I wrote at a furious pace. There was a pause. My mind went blank. I had run out of things to ask. Kelli gently suggested: "Do you want to know what we look like?" – "Yes!" I exclaimed, feeling stupid, and the ball was rolling again.

She said everyone had brown hair except her and her mother. They were blonde. And everyone had either brown or green eyes. She promised to send pictures.

Then she relayed something shocking. Her father – our father – had dementia. And that it began after he had a stroke some years ago. Kelli said her mother retired early in order to take care of him, because while he was ambulatory, he was losing his sense of reason.

Dementia? He was too young for dementia.

I considered my memory of him at the funeral. He did not look like a stroke victim, but my frame of reference was Lillian. Was this why he didn't respond to my letters? But that wasn't possible, because he could not have been working in that condition. I didn't have time to stop to speculate further; Kelli and I had too much to say.

I said I would write a letter to her and Heather to share and send photos as well. And that I would do it soon since I was close to giving birth. I told her then and would say it several more times in the months ahead, that she could consider me her auxiliary sister, a spare waiting in the wings if she needed one. I wanted her to feel there was a safe distance between us so she wouldn't worry about being open with me.

Heather called as well. She and Kelli were much alike, but if I had to find a difference I would say Kelli was more family-oriented while Heather was more mindful of a career. And even with Kelli's quick wit, Heather's was even more cutting, like mine. Something that impressed me was how positive they were about any situation. And gracious concerning my unexpected appearance. The word "gracious" would come to mind again and again when conversing with them. I attributed this to their mother.

When I wrote to them, I explained again how I tried to contact their dad (I finally decided to call Glenn "their dad" to avoid tripping over myself with "our father") while avoiding their mother. And why I opted not to write to their brothers. I said I left the decision to them if they wanted to say anything to anyone; that what I hoped for was a window into their worlds. Every time I received an email, letter or phone call, my reality shifted a little more. I recognized myself in them. I knew more about myself by knowing them. I could scarcely believe my luck.

Chapter 17
~The Last Baby~

After Dagne's quick entrance into the world, we joked with our midwife that she would need to move in so she'd be present for the birth of our fourth child. The pregnancy was textbook, at least for a geriatric mother like me.

Both Chloe and Dagne were born exactly two weeks early, which was perfect as far as I was concerned. Full term without the extended wait. We had "nudged" Dagne out, which worked a little too well, but we agreed to call the midwife with plenty of time to spare for this one.

Two weeks before the due date, we prepped the house and got labor started. Janet Brooks was called. Everyone assembled. This was it – my final labor and delivery, my last baby. Janet checked me.

"This isn't happening today, honey."

"What do you mean?" I said, with consternation.

"It's a false start. The contractions will die down then stop. I can't force it – you're not ready."

Watching with disbelief as she packed her bag and started toward the bedroom door, I exclaimed, "Well, how long? Tomorrow?"

"Maybe longer than that."

"More than a day?"

"Maybe a few days. Maybe," she said, reaching for the door knob behind her, "a week."

"A *week?!*" But she was gone. True to her word, the contractions petered out and for the first time in my life I waited on a baby. Even with the EDD over a week away I felt overdue.

One long week later, contractions started on their own. The troops reassembled. This time Janet broke my water, which really sped up the labor. But something was wrong. Even though the contractions were intense the baby barely descended. The head had come out, finally, but that's as far as it progressed.

Brian told me later, much later, that at this point he looked at Janet's face and saw something he had never seen there before: grave concern. She told him and Pamela, who were acting as my "stirrups," to drop my legs. She pulled me to the very edge of the bed and had someone help me sit up part-way. It may have been Brian; I have to rely on others for the memory because I was nearly having an out-of-body experience at this point. My only fully-formed thought was: *I'm going to die, the baby is going to die and Lillie and Chloe will see the whole thing.* Dagne was mercifully taking a nap upstairs but Lillie and Chloe were trapped there in our room – there was no time to think about their welfare at this point. The midwife knew instinctively what she had to do. She was concentrating solely on me.

Bracing herself against the end of the bed with her knees, she slid her hands in under the baby's armpits. She said to me: "Push with everything you have and *do not stop.*" Although she doesn't look it, Janet is a powerful woman with great upper body strength. She has even helped carry laboring women to her car in the event of emergency transport. Brian said as she squatted there, knees against the bed, her arms shook with the controlled effort of pulling the baby from my unyielding body.

I was only aware of intense pressure and hallucinated colors and flashes of light. I pushed harder than I thought possible, knowing on some primal level this was a matter of life or death. Everyone in the room held their breath. Lillie and Chloe covered their eyes. Time stopped.

Suddenly: release. "Oh, thank God. Thank God," was all I could pant. "It's a girl," Janet said triumphantly, placing her on my lower stomach. I reached down to take her, barely able to move my arms, but Janet said, "Wait," and quickly clamped and cut the cord. Usually she let it alone for awhile, allowing the placenta to vacate first. I didn't understand what was happening.

For all the seeming brutality of her birth, newborn Sophie did not show any ill-effect. She was absolutely perfect. As I finally held her with shaking arms, Janet checked her over and pronounced her well and healthy. Then she asked me to nurse the baby to help dispel the placenta. This proved to be nearly as painful as the birth itself. Again, I did not understand.

Every time we had a baby we always offered Janet a glass of celebratory champagne. Every time she politely refused. Except this time. Not only did she take the alcohol, she sat down with Brian to debrief him. Janet had a rule – she never discussed anything disturbing with mothers, so she never told me this. Instead she told Brian and he finally relayed it to me three days later, when he could talk about it without losing his composure.

When the baby did not come quickly, Janet knew something was very wrong. This should have been another fifteen minute birth. Instead, something was holding it back. Obviously it was not a matter of unusual presentation or shoulder dysplasia. When the baby was out as far as the shoulders and could not go any further, Janet knew the umbilical cord must be too short. The baby was literally tethered to my uterus, since the placenta does not release until after birth in a normal delivery. She knew she had to get the baby out immediately in order for her to take her first breath. With her head out but her chest and lungs still trapped in the birth canal it was truly a dire moment.

Janet confessed to Brian that she never had to pull a baby that hard before and really did not think Sophie would live through it. It is a testament to her expertise that, not only did Sophie survive, there was not a mark on her and no evidence of birth trauma whatsoever.

Janet stayed about an hour, massaging my stomach to promote the healing of my uterus. She also gave me a vitamin K shot to help with clotting. Whatever Janet did I knew was necessary and did not question. After seeing Sophie was fine and admonishing everyone to make sure I took it easy for a few days, she departed.

Later, when I told step-mom Carol what had transpired, she said, "So is she going to stop now?"

"What?"

"The midwife. Is she going to quit?"

I had to think about it to understand what she was saying. To her, this was proof that homebirth was dangerous – that we should have had a doctor in a hospital. Instead of applauding Janet for literally saving the baby's life, Carol thought this would give her the sense to give up her life's work. I looked at my perfect newborn and shuddered to think what could have happened at a hospital, with someone attending who did not have Janet's skill and instinct.

"She did everything right. There is nothing they could have done at a hospital that would have been better."

Carol shook her head. She must have thought I was playing fast and loose with my children's lives. The opposite was the truth. My daughters were too important to allow inept doctors anywhere near them. I had suffered enough for all of us.

Pamela loved babies, especially her own grandchildren, and even more so when she got to hold and admire them without having to babysit. We had provided her with a passel of them. And Sharon – the show-off – had another just before I had Sophie. While I staggered around in post-partum fog, my older sister serenely did everything she did before while exuding youth.

In truth, I liked having "honorary twins" with siblings and friends. They were natural playmates, being so close in age, like my girl cousins were with me growing up. My daughters had cousins wherever we went.

When Sophie was still a newborn, Sharon came over with her newest addition along with our mother Pamela. It was the first time all of us had been together since Sophie was born. While we sat enjoying the babies, the mail arrived. And in it was the promised package from my "new" sister Kelli.

I sat on the couch in the gentle spring sunlight. Pamela held Sophie. Sharon held her new daughter. I opened the large manila envelope and out poured dozens of color photos, with attached captions. Suddenly, they all had faces. Suddenly, I knew them even without meeting them. Thanks to Kelli's vivid and amusing notes I could almost place myself there with them, picture by picture. Most were current but she managed to find a few from her childhood, from family vacations or Christmas. She made a double copy of her wedding photo with everyone on the church steps, using arrows to identify them by name, relationship and age: Glenn and Shirley, Kelli and her husband, Heather and her family, the brothers with their wives and children.

I couldn't help but notice I looked more like Glenn than any of his "legitimate" children. But there was also a strong resemblance between Heather and me. I finally knew where I got the baby fine hair. And the lithe figure. But they all had a healthy, athletic look that I did not acquire. And they were just good-looking people. They didn't only come across as "successful" when described, they looked the part as well.

Kelli included a letter. Every message from her and Heather was like an unexpected sunny day, they were so naturally positive. It was hard to believe our father suffered from alcoholism and the depression that goes with it when reading his daughters' relentless but authentic positive spin. Pamela's family had a tendency toward depression, or at least the moroseness that comes with being Scandinavian. I hoped to avoid that, and tried via osmosis to soak up my sisters' attitude and incorporate it into my own life.

Feeling I was hogging the photos and ignoring my guests, I passed some shots of Glenn to Pamela. She remarked how much he had changed but how little Shirley had. She was lost in her own thoughts for a time. Sharon serenely nursed her baby. I read Kelli's letter:

"If we lived closer, Heather and I would be over there holding that little girl all the time," Kelli wrote in her cheerful cursive. "We love babies." I looked at Sophie, now in my lap. I looked at Sharon and Pamela. I looked back at the letter and the pictures. A powerful feeling swept over me, a connection, as if these paternal sisters were really here in my living room along with my maternal sister and my mother, as if I could reach out and touch all of them, creating a circle. It was perfect – a perfect moment – and it took my breath away.

All these years later, after so much has happened, I can still remember exactly how I felt then, as if it was really possible for the Cosmos to be in alignment.

We were back to our idea of normalcy. Brian continued to excel as a programmer, rode his bike on even more challenging trails, and watched a lot of loud sports on television. Kelli once hopefully asked in a letter, "Do you like any sports at all?" Coming from a family of enthusiasts, as both participants and fans, she was looking for common ground. That side of my genetics centered on beer and basketball. The side I gravitated toward was more champagne and ballet. I told her

Brian liked sports enough for the both of us.

Meanwhile, I continued to shuttle the children to theater and art lessons and became even more involved in church. I was teaching Sunday school and emphasized art as part of the program, much like my birth mother had. Apparently I was doomed to my fate, because even as my birth father discouraged his other children from a teaching career, I was teaching children and back to instructing for the technical colleges part-time as well.

Try as I might, I could not find a suitable yet affordable house with an attached brother-in-law apartment. And as always, we teetered on the edge of financial disaster. If it wasn't property taxes it was something else. I barely got the bills paid every month. Brian worked at better and better jobs but it never seemed to translate to more money. Or at least his income couldn't keep up with his appetites.

Finances were a strained subject between Brian and me, and it pointed to a much larger problem, but I was too involved to see it. I thought it was Brian's responsibility to earn the money and my job to manage it. I was guilty of being a slowly boiled frog – I didn't recognize what was happening. He kept me off-balance with guilt, accusing me of mishandling the funds. The only time I ever hung up on him was one day when I checked the bank account to find it nearly empty, so called him at work, only to have him sneer maybe I shouldn't have "blown it all."

I was so incensed I couldn't speak and slammed the phone down. He called back sounding arrogant, thinking he had the higher moral ground. I said through clenched teeth I had "blown" the money on the mortgage payment before slamming the receiver down again.

That evening he tried turning the tables. He knew if he could get me to the point of crying in frustration he would have the upper hand. But that night I used my anger to back him into a corner, wielding the checkbook in his face like a switchblade.

"Do you want it? Do you want to pay the bills?" I said with dead seriousness. He practically ran from the room. I knew the threat of abdicating control of the checkbook would scare him if nothing else would. Although he had a natural ability with math, there was a mental block when it came to money. More than once when he used his debit card for cash, leaving us overdrawn, he exclaimed: "But I haven't spent it!" as if the bank would know the difference.

When we were teens he called me his memory. It was charming then. Now I fielded terse phone calls from the dentist office, from family members, wanting to know where he was, why he hadn't kept his appointment.

The real frustration was that he expected me to keep him in line and then would be angry with me if he strayed. But at the same time he would not do the simple things I asked, like signing up for direct deposit or jotting events on the kitchen calendar. He had evolved into my fifth child and I had no idea what to do about it.

My sister Kelli finally got email, and along with Heather, we began a cheerful correspondence. Heather liked the expediency of email while Kelli preferred handwritten notes. I liked both. Every so often we would call, but being they were in Idaho and this was before free long-distance plans, we saved that for special occasions.

After Kelli sent the package of photos I wrote: "Did your mother make a pact with Satan? She's stunning." It was the truth. Not only was she beautiful, she didn't seem to age.

They didn't ask questions that scrutinized too deeply. I told them upfront that my conception was the result of a one-time act fueled by alcohol. Since our father was an alcoholic that made sense to them.

It was ironic Glenn had this host of health problems now, since he had built his career on sports, and his entire family was athletic and just oozed youth. My life had been one stupid health problem after another: allergies, bad back, disabling menstrual cycle, near-sightedness, soft teeth. And I despised competitive sports. It went against my nature. I'm sure I would have been a real disappointment if he had known me.

Kelli often mentioned how much they enjoyed getting together: her parents and all the kids, spouses and grandkids. They even vacationed together when possible.

In our exchanges, they filled in details of their dad's life. The most dramatic change happened with his stroke. Everything changed with that. Shirley eventually had to retire from a job she loved in order to care for him, because he was a danger to himself, like Granddad Linden had been. They were afraid he would wander off.

"He's driving Mom crazy but he's very funny. I guess when your memory goes you don't have many worries," wrote Kelli in a letter.

"You know how there's Type A personality? Well, Dad was Type Double-A." Heather emailed. "But he really mellowed out after that stroke."

"When did it happen?" I thought to ask one day. "How long ago?"

"Ten years. No, maybe twelve now," replied Heather. She recalled the year. I stared at the computer screen. Tentatively, I typed,

"What time of year?"

"In the fall. Around Thanksgiving."

I felt punched in the stomach. I could barely breathe.

What have I done? What have I done? He had a stroke the very month I sent the letter. *He had a stroke because I sent the letter.*

Even if he had wanted to respond, could he? Was the shock too great? Did my letter finally make it all impossible to ignore and overwhelmed him to the point of a traumatic cerebral event?

Then came the realization that not only did Shirley know, she must have been the one to read the letters – all of them – because they would have been redirected to her even though I sent them to the school. I had tried so hard to circumvent Shirley, to protect her. Pamela's only request was that I try not to involve her; she didn't want her to be hurt. Not only did she know, her life was forever altered. In what should have been their prime, she had become her husband's caregiver. Because of me.

"I'm sorry. I'm so sorry," I emailed Heather.

"Why? You don't have anything to be sorry for."

"He had the stroke because of my letter."

"No, you didn't cause it. He was a stoke waiting to happen."

But the timing was inescapable.

Whenever I thought of Heather and Kelli the word "gracious" came to mind. The way they handled my unexpected appearance and everything that involved left me both awed and humbled. This was just another example of their exceptional nature. I wondered how long it could last.

Chapter 18

~Miscreant~

Keith never really went away, of course. In his youth, I could breathe whenever he was incarcerated. Now I prayed for him to find work far, far away. Across state lines was almost far enough, but a time zone away was better. He was a laborer. I don't know if he acquired any skills beyond that, for all his supposed intelligence.

When he was around, I avoided visiting Dad because I didn't want any encounters. I had that luxury; Dad and Carol did not. For their own safety they had to keep him at arm's length, instead of divorcing themselves from him altogether.

Many years before, Dad mentioned that the subject of disowning Keith had come up once. Not in the dramatic sense of cutting someone out of a will, but legally. He and Mom actually discussed rescinding the adoption, so he would no longer be their son. When Dad told me this, I realized from Keith's age at the time that it must have been after I was raped, only Dad never alluded to that. He never acknowledged it at all. But he did confess to this one conversation.

"Why?!" I exclaimed. "Why didn't you do it?"

"It was too late. We were afraid he would come back and burn the place down." But it wasn't only that. I knew in spite of everything, Dad loved Keith. And Mom had loved him too. As sick and twisted as he was, he was their son, their much-wanted first-born, even if not born to them. Dad never gave up on him and tried so hard to find good in him, even if that simply meant the temporary absence of criminal activity.

At this point, Keith only seemed to care about having enough money to have the creature comforts he wanted: a vehicle, a place to live, to fish, and the usual vices of beer, cigarettes, and weed. If there was more, I'm not aware of it. He didn't care about any of it being "nice" or about bettering himself. He just wanted what he wanted. And he wanted the world to give it to him.

Somehow he found a girl who liked him, enough to live with him and have his child. I doubt it was planned, but they had a daughter when Sophie was small. She was due on my birthday. Thankfully she was late.

Having a would-be wife and child made Keith harder to avoid. Now he had good reason to be there for holidays and extended visits. But both John and I made it clear we did not want to see him. I wasn't the only one who detested Keith; John had no use for him either. We weren't too afraid of him doing violence any longer, but he was just disgusting. Brian called him a "shambling mound" à la *Dungeons & Dragons*, and that's what he was: a big, hideous *thing*.

The first time I laid eyes on Hannah ("my niece" I reminded myself), I thought, "What an unfortunate child." Not so much because of her own appearance but because of the two rotund human beings who were her parents. How intelligent could the mother be if she chose to have a relationship with Keith? I got no impression from her at all; she seemed completely devoid of personality. We spoke a few times, but never had a conversation. I wondered if she had come from a highly dysfunctional family for someone like Keith to seem normal to her. I wondered what she saw in him, what hopes she had for her life. They mostly just sat and smoked, and since smoking was not allowed in the house, that meant if I stayed inside I could avoid both of them for the most part, so I did.

"Who is Keith?" Lillie asked on the way home from Dad's one day. The question startled me. I mostly kept my thoughts about Keith to myself. I had never mentioned him to my children. John was their uncle. Eric was their uncle. Paul was their uncle. Brian's best friend Christopher was their uncle. And they had lots of other uncles beyond that. But Keith wasn't their uncle. Over my dead body would he be that.

"Supposedly he's my brother," I answered evenly. They looked at each other, pondering this silently. Lillie, speaking for all of them, said, "Is he Uncle John's brother too?" I said yes.

"Why haven't we ever heard of him before?"

"Because I don't like him."

That left them both mystified and satisfied. They couldn't imagine having a sibling they did not like, but they understood it was possible to not be friends with someone. They didn't ask anymore questions about him.

I had a pet name for Keith: "Miscreant piece of filth." It amused me to use it as a title. Instead of "William Smith, attorney at law," he was "Keith, miscreant piece of filth" or just "that miscreant piece of filth" with no name at all. I would only say it in my mind, except in the company of close friends like Cecelia. She understood, even though I never told her why I hated him. After decades of not talking about it, it was easier to say nothing.

One summer Keith and his little family (as I would think disparagingly, only to myself) stayed at Dad's for a few weeks. Somehow we were obligated to come to dinner. At least the kids and I were. I think Brian got out of it by making an excuse of some kind. By then he was always making an excuse not to socialize, even with his own family. The only exception was John; Brian would hang out with John if no one else.

When we walked in the door, toddler Hannah shrieked, "Cousins!" like it was Christmas morning and we were Santa with the presents. Carol had apparently told her she had all these girls to play with and loved the kids on sight. Mainly Dagne and Sophie obliged, being closer in age. They played dress-up, built towers with blocks, rolled on the living room carpet.

I sat in a chair, watching them play. Keith sat on the opposite side of the living room. We watched our children play on the floor, the same floor where he had violated me almost thirty years earlier, when I was a little girl, like my daughters were now. I perched there, guarding my children, not willing to leave them in his presence for even a minute. I looked up to see him staring at me. I stared back. We sat there, time suspended, silently glaring at each other.

A few days later the phone rang. By then we had Caller ID, and I saw it was Dad's number. I answered only to hear Keith's voice mumble, "Oh, sorry," and hang up.

I froze. He knew my number. He knew my phone number and called. All these years I made Dad hide my phone number and address so Keith would never know where I was, where my daughters were. But he knew. And he called to show me he knew.

Brian was home and saw I was concerned. "Who was it?"

"Keith," I managed to say. He jumped up, immediately pacing.

"What should we do? What did he want?" Of course I had no answer to either question. Brian was nearly beside himself, looking around wild-eyed as if Keith was about to burst in and slaughter us all. Brian never used to be like this. He was the one who patrolled Dad's property at night after I gave birth to Lillie, because Keith was there. His reaction now only served to magnify my own fear.

I knew Keith was staying at the house while Dad and Carol were on vacation. While that would have been unheard of before, now that he had a live-in girlfriend and child, Dad hoped he was more stable. Before this, they never knew what he was capable of from one day to the next. Sometimes helping Dad with heavy labor around the property, sometimes telling Carol her cooking (which he ate voraciously) tasted like shit, or siphoning gas from their cars.

"Who is *Keith*?" I was asked by the nice young man who, with his family, house-sat for my parents a few summers earlier. He asked as calmly as one can after being raided by SWAT team. A dozen heavily-armed officers descending on the house in full view of his little children, all because they mistakenly thought Keith had taken up residence. I don't know what Keith had done to inspire this. Dad tended not to talk about anything unpleasant or anything he deemed unnecessary; that made it less real. As much as the young man liked my father, he never house-sat for him again.

Now Keith was there, watching over the very house he had burglarized and vandalized so many times. I couldn't believe it when Dad told me, but this was evidently his way of keeping Keith in line, by entrusting him just so much and no more.

Brian was nearly hysterical, pacing and saying, "What are you going to do?" I despised him at that moment. I despised his helplessness. In a pattern that was to be repeated many times, I made the decision. I called the police. I told them that a known criminal just called me in a threatening way, to make sure I knew he knew where I lived. And that I had young daughters and so help me, I would shoot him on sight if he came anywhere near me. So they had better confront him to let him know.

A few hours later Keith called again. This time he did not hang up. He wanted to know if I had called the cops. Said the police had been there and told him to stay away from me. I said yes I had. He said, "Why?"

I countered, "Why did you call here?"

"I *69'd about a job. I don't know how it got your number," he said, sounding more articulate than I had ever heard him, even with his disgusting mumbling.

"That had better be true," I said through gritted teeth, while Brian whispered loudly for me to tell him to stay away. I turned away from the sight of my husband jumping around like a child, trying to get my attention.

"Why the animosity?" Keith said.

("Well, I was shocked," I later recounted to Cecelia. "I had no idea he knew the word 'animosity'." Cecelia laughed appreciatively.)

"Really. You don't know? Just stay away from me. Stay away from my children."

"Is this about me playing doctor with you when you were little?"

Time stood still. I no longer saw Brian, or the street from where I stood on the front porch, or anything. The air was sucked out of my lungs. Stitches ripped from my psyche. Everything went black. Then I realized Brian had gone inside and I was alone. The phone was still to my ear.

I heard my voice say thickly, "Is that what you would call it if someone did that to your daughter?"

"Well, I'm sorry. I apologize."

"Stay away from me. Stay. Away. From. Me," I rasped through clenched teeth and hung up.

Dad happened to be outside when I arrived with the kids for a visit, after Keith was gone. My car had not been serviced in nearly a year. Brian used to see to these things, but he never seemed to think of it now, and I was busy with everything else. When I drove up, Dad heard the engine knock. He clenched his jaw. Dad only clenched his jaw if he was really angry. Before I could even get out of the car he ordered me to take it to his shop in the back.

I felt stupid that Dad had to take care of my car like I was still a teenager living at home. Sometimes when I was with Dad and Carol, I felt like a five year old. When we went somewhere together, Carol drove and Dad paid. If I tried to tell Carol anything, from childcare to computers, she dismissed me. I couldn't possibly know more than she did because she was the mother. So I would never know more and certainly not know better.

Because I did not do everything the same way they did at my age, I was doing it wrong. Dad praised me when the kids took swimming lessons but sadly shook his head when I opted for ballet over piano. Carol and I battled over the babies going barefoot. She insisted they would learn to walk only if they had "good, stiff shoes." I told her they'd learn to walk if Dad would put them down once in awhile. It was funny sometimes. Today nothing was funny.

I ventured back to the shop. Dad had not only changed the oil, he put new brakes on and rotated the tires, which he warned me were in dire need of replacement. He spat something about Brian letting his wife and kids ride in a death-trap while spending money on "gingerbread" for his truck.

While he was giving me a piece of his mind, he asked me about calling the police on Keith. It set my teeth on edge whenever Keith was mentioned. I said at least it was just one cop, not a SWAT team. He grimaced a smile and said, "What did he ever do to you?"

Before he even got the words out, he knew he had made a mistake. It was like throwing a lit match on gasoline. I exploded. I didn't plan it, but now couldn't stop it. I screamed at him, screamed with all the rage I had kept in for over twenty-five years:

"WHAT DID HE DO TO ME? WHAT DID HE *DO* TO ME?! HE TOOK MY CHILDHOOD! HE DESTROYED ME! HE MADE ME UNABLE TO RELATE TO MY HUSBAND! I CAN'T HAVE NORMAL SEX! I WILL NEVER BE OKAY! I WILL NEVER *GET OVER IT!*"

The words were torn out of me. I could feel them being ripped from my body like my innocence had been ripped away. I didn't know what I was saying until I was saying it and only then realized it was true. As much as I refused to be a victim, I was broken. The brokenness was always there. Even as a grown woman, a wife, a mother, inside I was a destroyed little girl. And I hated Keith for it. Hated him and would never, ever forgive.

"Okay. Okay," Dad said quietly, putting up his hands in protest. His face registered shock. His voice nearly trembled. I stood there shaking. That was all there was. I don't know if he ever said anything to Carol – I certainly didn't – but he treated me with more deference after that. He always made sure I knew when Keith was around so I didn't have to see him. He mentioned him only if absolutely necessary.

A few days later at home, the voice said, *"It's okay to think about it."*

I said in my mind, "Think about what?"

"It can't hurt you anymore. You can think about it."

I was walking across the kitchen. It was the middle of the afternoon. I remember that. I stopped and shook my head slightly, trying to clear it away, but ignoring it was impossible. Taking the skeleton key from the kitchen windowsill, I staggered to the bedroom, as if walking through fog. Locking myself in, I sat on the bed.

"It's okay to think about it. Put it together. It's okay to think about it," I told myself. And piece by piece, like a puzzle, like a chain, it came to me.

The feeling of being torn, the black mucus, the spot on my tampons, the pain during intercourse, the ridge on my vaginal wall…When Keith raped me, he tore my vagina with his dirty fingernail, leaving a wound that did not heal. The black mucus was old blood. The spots on my tampons were from the tear reopening, weeping with every cycle. A side-effect of taking so many rounds of antibiotics for my tonsils was for this infection to finally heal also. But it left behind scar tissue, making a hard ridge. Sex hurt because this ridge was hit over and over, like a permanent hymen on one side of my vagina, making intercourse nearly impossible in some positions. It was also why I couldn't use a contraceptive sponge – the ridge would always force it sideways. Doctors didn't see it because they put the speculum past it, looking at the cervix. The midwife found it but did not know what it was.

The birth of my first child caused the scar tissue to finally be stretched flat but I did not know this. When I was being fitted for a diaphragm, I mistook my tenderness for a deformity. I didn't know the ridge was gone. In my mind it was still there. It did not occur to me that the midwife did not have to push it down for my subsequent babies. I thought they somehow made it past because I no longer had an "untried pelvis." Where I should have finally enjoyed sex, I held back, expecting the pain.

Psychologically, the damage was done.

Rocking there on the bed, arms wrapped around my legs and face buried in my knees, I realized that for the last twelve years I had cheated myself and Brian out of what could have been a fulfilling sex life because I didn't know the problem was gone. My body had healed years ago, but my mind and my soul were scarred. All because I couldn't think about it. Now awash with grief and guilt, I promised to make it up to my husband. I still couldn't tell him, but I could show him.

The next time we made love, I gave myself to him. He didn't ask questions but afterwards went to the basement and cried. And I cried too. I cried for the twenty years that should have been that way.

Chapter 19
~A Glimpse of Myself~

Heather made casual mention one day that she would be in town for a work project. I wrote: "Can we meet?" I couldn't let this opportunity slip by, knowing there was no way I was getting to Idaho anytime in the foreseeable future. I never went anywhere.

We agreed to meet at her hotel near the airport. Though we had spoken by phone and wrote often, I was nervous. I wanted her to like me. Having a great relationship with my siblings on Pamela's side, I was afraid I was asking too much for the same here.

I remember wearing a casual silk outfit. I was partial to long jackets and scarves. I hoped she wouldn't think I looked ridiculous.

I waited in the lobby. She emerged from the elevator. My sister, Heather. We stood looking at one another, trying not to stare so long to feel awkward. My observation was correct: I looked like her more than any of my other siblings, on either side of the family. Same small face, dark brown eyes, baby hair that would not grow past the shoulders, and the same slight figure. She resembled me more than my own daughters. But there was a decided difference in her attitude. She stood straight and sure of herself.

After a brief embrace, I asked if I could take her to dinner. We went across the street to The 13 Coins. I had not eaten there since childhood, as my parents thought it too expensive. I figured this occasion was worth it.

It was crowded, so we waited for a table along with some businessmen. One made eye contact with me. I did as I was taught (smile slightly then look at the floor), then heard Heather say, "Hi," and looked up to see her smiling pleasantly at the men, like they were acquainted. The one she directed the greeting toward broke into a warm smile as well. "Where are you from?" she asked. He gave some response. They chit-chatted. He looked as if this was the best thing to happen to him all day.

I am in the presence of greatness, I thought. And I knew this was a glimpse of our father's charm.

"I like people to feel appreciated," she said when we finally opted to eat at the counter. I made some remark – I can't remember what – and she looked at me, head slightly tilted as if studying me, making sure.

"That's exactly like something Grandma Anita would say," she said in quiet wonderment. "And how she would say it."

"Genetics," I shrugged, not wanting her to think this was weird.

"A lot of what you say reminds me of her. She's really sharp," she added, to make sure I knew this was a compliment. Compliment, confirmation, I would take either. I told Heather how I was forever having trouble containing my thoughts. I was known as the Queen of Quip, always ready with a smart remark. My birth mother's family was not this way – the women especially were more genteel – and I often felt too sharp-tongued around them. Dad was constantly admonishing me for being "sarcastic," even when I was making a comment completely devoid of sarcasm. Growing up in a silent, Nordic family, it was near-torture trying to keep the witticisms to myself. Heather assured me both our grandmother and father were the same way. I finally knew where it came from.

Since she broached the subject of our grandmother, I told her about trying to contact our aunt when I was in California years before, and how I got no response. She shook her head. "No, she wouldn't," she said.

"But why?" I asked. "I was trying to get around your mother. Jean had nothing to lose by talking to me." Heather just shook her head. Then she dropped a hint, the first of several. "Aunt Jean wanted to marry this guy. He was rich and loved to spoil us kids when we'd visit. But Grandma wouldn't let her." Wouldn't *let* her? Did Heather mean our grandmother held so much power, that not only could she force her grown daughter to give up marriage, but also keep her from talking to anyone she did not first approve?

Then I remembered a passing remark Pamela had made. Her best friend in Coeur d'Alene was another teacher who had an apartment next door to Glenn's mother. One day she heard Anita screaming at her adult son, who was visiting. There was no mention of Glenn retaliating.

Pamela told me she thought Glenn said his mother was either divorced or widowed. She sported a different last name in any case. Twice married with no husband in sight and controlling her adult children's lives, I had to wonder if I wanted to be like my grandmother.

Heather travelled to Tacoma for her job several times over the next year. Each time we would get together. Sometimes going out to dinner. Sometimes just for coffee. Or wine at her place or mine. The one time she came to my house, the kids were happy to meet her. Another family member was always welcome as far as they were concerned. Dagne was in a stage where she drew "happy day" pictures with multi-colored crayons. The place was plastered with them, all Very Important in her opinion. She gave one to her new aunt.

Brian, on the other hand, barely looked up when I made introductions. Heather pretended not to notice. We went to dinner.

Every time Heather and I were together, she gave slightly greater insight into the Havner family. Never like gossip or an exposé, but what girlfriends or sisters would share. I was actually relieved to hear that our family was as normally dysfunctional as anyone's. There were problems with addiction, career crises, marital woes – the usual fare. "How did your mom cope?" I asked, knowing it all fell to her.

Heather tapped her wine glass thoughtfully. "With this," she said.

For a moment, I wished my mother Lillian had employed such a method.

What really impressed me about the Havners was their cohesiveness and overall good-nature. They took turns "dad-sitting" so Shirley could get out once in awhile. But she did not use Glenn as an excuse; she was very active with friends and in the community.

Heather completely disarmed the waiter, who fell over himself giving her not only an illegal to-go cup for her wine, but refilled the glass after scribbling his name and phone number on it. She amazed me. I noticed she had rolled up Dagne's drawing and put it carefully in her purse so as not to crush it. She knew what was important to a four-year-old.

As I drove her to the airport, we talked. The wine and past conversations made her comfortable enough to ask how my conception happened. I told her and Kelli previously that I was the result of a one-time encounter brought on by drinking. It satisfied them at the time. Now Heather cautiously asked for more information.

I assured her it was not a love affair. That it couldn't be described as an affair at all. I reminded her how she said her dad was "driven" to the point of obsession. That when he had a goal in mind, he was going to make it. "Well, my mother was a goal," I said. "Even though, obviously, he loved your mom. I think it had nothing to do with her, really." We were silent for a moment as we continued down the dark freeway, accompanied only by the sound of the windshield wipers, lost in our thoughts.

"Has there ever been someone you've wanted," I asked, "even though it goes against everything, and having them could mess up your entire life?"

"Oh, yeah."

"I think that's what happened."

"I can understand that," she said, contemplating. Then after a pause, "How about you?"

There was silence again for a moment before I said, "Let me tell you about Craig…"

I had not thought of Craig in years. There was no room for him in my mind, crowded as it was with children and spouse and all my various responsibilities. And even though his girlfriend Vicki's grandmother lived next door to Jim and Pamela Mathias, I never saw him or heard from him again after my wedding. He just vanished. He was magical that way.

And because he was magic, saying his name apparently conjured him back into my reality. It was not long after when, driving home with groceries and looking very much like the middle-aged mother I was, I saw him coolly walking down the street towards Starbucks. My Starbucks – the one I treated myself to every Sunday for an hour of peace and quiet.

Except for a touch of silver in his hair, he looked exactly the same, as if the intervening years never happened. For a wild second I considered stopping to say hello, then remembered the groceries and a myriad of other reasons why I shouldn't. But the switch had been flipped. He was back in my brain.

My best friend Cecelia had turned into my confessional and therapist since I had the epiphany about the cause of my sexual dysfunction. Our sessions involved her refilling my wine glass and nodding while I talked. I was going through an awakening, a self-realization. This, combined with gaining insight into my birth father's life, was sometimes almost more than I could process. In my mind's forefront were the mundane demands of the day: paying bills, caring for the children, dealing with Brian's ever-expanding neuroses. But in the back of my mind were paradigm shifts. I could talk about them with Cecelia, otherwise I kept them well hidden.

Now, hesitantly, I told her about Craig. He was the path not taken. I was sure I did the right thing, made the right choice, but was now left wondering what might have been. While I did not regret being faithful, I still had conflicting emotions. Cecelia understood.

And there was something else: Constant desire.

"What is wrong with me?" I confided to Cecelia in conspiratorial tones. She laughed.

"Nothing. You're just getting in your grove. Enjoy it."

And I did. Every chance I got. The less Brian and I were able to talk to each other, the more we connected on a physical level. I was determined to make up for all those years of barely-adequate sex. I wanted to show him how grateful I was. I wanted him to be happy. But he wasn't happy.

Sometimes he was euphoric. Out-of-control, no-basis-in-reality euphoric. Other times he was hopelessly sad. Every so often it would fall in the range of normalcy and we could all breathe. But most of the time, he was angry. Anything could set him off. When his breakfast was not absolutely perfect he smashed the toaster, screaming, "It's ruined! Ruined!" If he didn't agree with something said on the news, he screamed at the TV. One morning, he screamed obscenities at me. Because it was sunny.

First thing every morning, he simultaneously smoked pot while drinking espresso-strength coffee. In the afternoons, he drank beer, sometimes scotch, sometimes both. And always more.

Sometimes he was calm and normal. He would make bacon and eggs for the kids, or chocolate chip cookies. We'd stroll to the park. I cherished these fleeting moments. The kids thought Daddy was cranky because "he didn't have his coffee" or because his sports team didn't win, or whatever they could think of that justified what they saw.

I tried desperately to help, but didn't know what was wrong. I made sure everything he needed was in its place – lining up his robe and slippers, keys and wallet every night, kept the bills paid even while money disappeared, took the children out of the house whenever he was especially volatile. He arrogantly stated in his new clipped manner of speaking that I was the one with the problem.

I was a slowly boiled frog.

Heather casually mentioned that our grandfather died.

The comment was so off-hand I had a delayed reaction to it. I knew Glenn and his sister had little contact with their father after their parents' divorce, but it seemed to go against the otherwise cohesive nature of their family to care so little about a close relative. Maybe Heather sensed I was taken aback because she said, "I met him only once, when I was ten. His wife called Mom to tell her he died, but Mom didn't tell Dad. She thought it would just confuse him."

I asked when it happened, and she guessed on the month. I looked up the newspaper most likely to have published the obituary and emailed to request a copy. They promptly sent one.

I knew from Polk Indexes that Johannes Peter "Johnny" Havner married a woman called Barb, who was a nurse, sometime during or just after WWII. I also knew Johnny was a welder. From Glenn's birth certificate, I knew he had been a musician in his youth. I knew these things, yet I knew nothing about him. I did not know, for instance, why he and my grandmother divorced. When I asked Heather, she shrugged. I took from her response that I was the only one who wondered, so didn't ask again.

Now, reading the obituary, I knew where he had lived in Idaho, his parents' names, his high school, that he was a retired welder who loved camping and fishing, that he married Barb after serving in the war, that he had eleven siblings, that he was Catholic, that he died of natural causes, and that he wished for no services.

Besides his widow, he was survived by three daughters and their children. I stopped. This was news. I did not know about these aunts. I read it again, thinking I somehow missed where Glenn and Jean were listed. But they weren't there. They were not mentioned. It was like Johnny's marriage to Anita and their two children never happened.

I was stunned. Never had I heard of expunging family members in such a cold manner. Was this part of the deal when Johnny and Anita separated, that they would treat the divorce as an annulment? Or was there so much hate that there was no relationship, and his widow did not even think to mention his other children, only calling his son's wife long after the fact?

Then I thought of something else. Doing the math, I realized my grandfather's first marriage ended around the time he was thirty. The same age his son Glenn was when I was conceived. But Glenn's marriage survived while Johnny's did not. Did Johnny have an early mid-life crisis like Glenn seemingly did? Or did Glenn, feeling the pain of abandonment, unconsciously follow in his father's footsteps? Or maybe the whole thing was just a strange coincidence.

The next time I saw Heather, I asked about our aunts. She gave me a sideways look, as if seriously reconsidering how much she would tell me in the future. She said nothing except to remind me she met our grandfather only once.

Heather and Kelli accepted me into their circle, including me in group emails, calling on my birthday, passing along a baby gift to our brother, saying just that it was from someone who thought the outfit was cute. Heather always saw me when she was in town. Kelli kept in touch by phone, email, and letters. They were honest about family struggles, not white-washing any of it. I loved them for including me, for trusting me with the information.

But they also held back, and I never knew where or when it would happen. We could discuss our father's infidelity, but not our grandparents' divorce. I could hear about substance abuse and marriage difficulties with siblings, but I couldn't expect even mundane answers regarding these half-aunts, even though the relationship was non-existent.

I wanted to be transparent with them, so told Heather about crashing her cousin's funeral. She did not appear the least bit disturbed. Instead she understood my motivation – that it was my only chance to see my biological father. Heather and Kelli were never defensive concerning their dad, although they could have been. It would have been easier to reject me, to say they didn't believe it. But they not only accepted Life in general, they celebrated what they were given. I wanted to be just like them.

But I did not tell either of them about what was happening with Brian, because I couldn't explain it. My parents gave each another uneasy glances when he would have an angry, unexpected outburst. They took to stopping by with the excuse of unloading a box from a closet, then slipping me a few hundred dollars with no comment. My mother Pamela and sister Sharon also gave each another uncomfortable looks when I would describe some incident, but said nothing. Brian's parents mostly harangued him for being antisocial when he insisted on taking separate vehicles to every get-together, always finding an excuse to come late and leave early.

I was barely keeping my head above water, not knowing it was boiling.

I woke, gasping for breath, but the dream had left me. I knew it was important but the message was gone as soon as I opened my eyes. Shaken, I poured coffee and turned on the morning news. I often woke to a feeling of panic or dread, but this was different. I had a disturbing vision and I needed to remember it. I actually hoped for once to hear the voice, but there was nothing except the TV traffic person making their report. Rain expected. Bad wreck on route—

I froze.

It was night. Raining. That sharp corner near my cousin Jerome's place. A single car in the ditch. Twisted, metallic-colored steel. A mangled body inside. Dad and Jerome ran up to the wreck in the cold rain. Dad sucked in his breath at the sight of the driver. Jerome said, "We want to help you. You need to get up." But the man couldn't move. I saw his face: Craig, covered in blood.

I had to warn him. I ran to the computer. But no matter what method I tried, he wasn't there. Somehow he flew under the radar of the internet. I picked up the phone book. I remembered his parents lived in Tacoma years ago and hoped they had not died or retired to some warmer climate like Arizona. But here they were: Evershaw. We had been living only seven blocks apart.

Before losing my nerve, I dialed. An old woman answered. Now what? What in the world do I say? "Um, hi. My name is Noelle. I'm a friend of Craig's. Well, I knew him in school. I need to get a message to him."

His mother said, "Is this about a reunion?"

"No, I didn't know him in high school. It was at TVTI."

"Well…" she hesitated.

"I know this sounds crazy but I need to warn him of a dream I had about him. You don't need to give me his phone number. Just give him mine."

She took my name and number. I wondered if she thought I was an old girlfriend turned stalker. I wondered if she would even tell him. But that afternoon, Craig called.

"I just want you to know," he said in mock-soothing tones, "I don't think you're crazy."

"Oh shut up."

He laughed. It was good to hear him laugh. It was good to hear his voice. He asked about the dream. I just said he was in a major car wreck in Cedarlake.

"I don't even know where that is."

"Good. Don't go there. At night. When it's raining. Or anytime, just to be on the safe side."

We caught up on the details of our lives. He was with Vicki for five years but moved on. Predictably, there had been a number of women since. He even married one and was currently in the midst of a long divorce.

I told him I had four daughters. He found the idea of any children disturbing but four was completely un-called for. "You must be as big as a house," he said.

"Oh, bigger," I said serenely.

I told him I had seen him outside Starbucks ("*my* Starbucks"). I asked if he went there often. No, he only stopped in looking for someone; he usually haunted other coffee houses. I relayed it was my escape on Sunday afternoons, an hour of solitude. Would he like to get together sometime? He said sure, when? How about 1:00 this Sunday? One o'clock? He didn't get up until at least 3:00 on Sundays. "Back to your decadent lifestyle, I see. Four o'clock then?"

I don't know what he expected, unless he really thought I would be "as big as a house" by virtue of motherhood. But that Sunday I took by his stunned expression he was surprised.

"You look exactly the same."

"So do you," I countered.

We sat and talked. Just like the old days, it was mostly him doing the talking. He told me of his life, his travels, his relationships. I told him my life centered around my children.

"You have *four*? Are you sure?" he asked, still incredulous.

"Pretty sure, yes."

I didn't allude to anything being wrong with Brian. Just said he was a terrific computer programmer. I couldn't explain what was wrong even if I wanted to, barely holding on to normalcy as I was.

I told him instead of how my life seemed to consist of a string of reunions, including this one with him. Then he thanked me. "For what?" I asked.

"For being there at school. It was the worst time in my life. I can't even tell you how much I hated it. But knowing you were going to be there helped." I don't think he remembered our last time there and I didn't bring it up.

He said he started every day besides Sunday "at the crack of noon" at a place in town where everyone knew him. I told him I only gave myself an hour here every Sunday, so chances were we would not be running into each other. Instead we exchanged email addresses.

When we parted he got into his silver Jaguar. I saw the dream again. "Stay away from Cedarlake," I called after him.

There are no coincidences. We met in a place neither of us imagined being. He came to my wedding as the escort of a guest I didn't know. Our lives had crisscrossed for years since, yet we never saw each other. We had nothing in common. We had no basis for a relationship. Yet he had been dropped squarely in front of me in a way that could only be described as something from God. I just had no idea why.

If I needed any confirmation Cosmic forces were at work, I got it a week later. I was late getting out of church, late having lunch. I finally found my way to Starbucks at some odd time late-afternoon, only to find it so crowded there was only one table available. I settled in and tried to concentrate on a book amidst the chaos.

A familiar voice jolted me. I turned to see Craig trying to engage two college girls in conversation. "You *are* his daughters, aren't you?" he was saying. They only eyed him sullenly. Feeling awkward on his behalf I said his name. Startled, then relieved at the sight of a familiar face, he dragged a chair over.

"I thought you didn't come to Starbucks," I said.

"I don't. I'm just looking for a friend because no one's seen him in awhile. I saw his car outside, but his *daughters*" (glaring in their direction) "are driving it – not him – and they won't tell me where he is. And I thought you only came up here early afternoon," he added in mock accusatory tones. I told him how forces were conspiring against me that day. We weren't even half-finished with our coffee when Brian appeared at our table, looking like he just woke up in a foul mood.

I had told Brian about meeting Craig the week before and he didn't seem to care. I only told him as casual conversation, I wasn't asking permission and I wasn't making a confession. I had been having my sabbatical at Starbucks every Sunday for months, an hour by myself to recharge. But in his self-absorbed state he never noticed. Until today. Today he demanded the kids give up information. "She's at Starbucks," they said, dumbfounded by the question. Everyone knew where I went Sunday afternoons. Everyone, except Brian.

"I was wondering where you were," he said. "The kids told me." His voice was quietly accusing, as if he had just caught us coming out of a hotel. I wanted to say, "What the hell is wrong with you?" but instead made introductions. Craig remained seated, as cool as ever, while Brian stood between us, glowering. They shook hands and as they did Craig thought, "He's a younger version of me," Brian thought, "He's an older version of me," and I thought, "I've been set up."

I asked Brian to join us but he said he just wanted to make sure I was okay. Nothing he was saying was making sense. I was embarrassed. I didn't want to explain to Craig. When Brian left I just said I had better get home to make dinner.

At home I ventured into the basement to ask Brian if he'd eaten, since his dietary habits had become erratic as well, only to find him very deliberately cleaning his shotgun. He looked at me strangely and I knew he wanted me to ask him if he was planning to use that on me, on Craig, or on himself, but the whole thing was so stupid I ignored it.

Chapter 20
-Insanity-

A few weeks later, Brian abruptly quit his job. He expected me to be happy about this, because he was free of this millstone around his neck – the thing that paid the bills and kept food on the table. He sent everyone he knew a wild, contradictory email about how his boss lied to him and how his co-workers were also going to quit and they were all going to get better jobs. Only his co-workers did not quit, and days turned into weeks and months with no job on the horizon.

Now he was home all the time, except when disappearing with no explanation. I never knew where he would be or what he would be doing. Nothing made sense.

Desperate to feel in control, he made increasingly bizarre demands and proclamations. He would wake me in the middle of the night to pick a fight or demand sex, or would disappear then be angry if I didn't show proper concern for him. He deliberately hurt himself, like a child wanting attention. Once he even ran away from home. I was constantly on edge, afraid of what was next.

I was also angry. My life had turned upside down. I was now a single mother of five. I vented to a private moms' group online and in emails to close friends. I was teetering on the edge of a breakdown and reached out to anyone who could give me answers or at least anyone who would listen. They were my lifeline. But everyone was as mystified as I was.

I also kept in touch with Craig via email, since seeing him was out of the question, but never confided in him. We kept the conversation light, mainly discussing movies like we did back at school. It was good to have a friend not connected, not in-the-know. Our emails were an escape from reality, like talking to a stranger on a bus.

But Brian started obsessing about Craig and I once found him sobbing. "What's wrong?" I asked.

"I'm lost!" he cried. "I know – I KNOW – you and Craig had an affair.

That's why… that's why I couldn't satisfy you for so long. And now you want him back! That's why I had to quit my job, so I'd be home." He ranted on and on, making less sense with every word.

The whole thing was so crazy I didn't know what to say, except that he had been the only one, ever. I felt insulted, mortified, angry. Yes, as a matter of fact I wish I *had* had a relationship with Craig. But I didn't. Was I supposed to apologize for being faithful?

I told my pastor about Brian and all the stress. He offered to help pay for counseling. I felt I needed to talk to another woman, someone who did not know me already. Someone both knowledgeable and impartial. My pastor knew just the person.

Ingrid was perfect for me in that she was Nordic, so the few words she said were well-chosen. I told her I was there because I couldn't cope, couldn't sort my feelings, was losing my sense of self, trying to salvage my marriage and was sick of trying – trying to fix everything and do the right thing, but I had to.

She asked about my family and friends. I explained as succinctly as possible, including Brian's family and our closest friends, the ones I thought of as brothers and sisters. She scribbled notes at a furious pace. I told her about Craig.

"Do you love him?"

"I don't know. I guess I do. Like I love my brother-in-law or friends who are like brothers."

"Nothing more?"

"I can barely feel anything right now. I can't imagine falling in love if that's what you mean. I need him to be my friend."

"Is that what he wants?"

"He has three girlfriends already. I think he likes having me to talk to with no other expectations."

I don't know if she believed this, but I wasn't there to convince her of Craig's intentions.

She asked if Brian would come in with me. He did, very reluctantly and very arrogantly. He "knew" I was doing this so I could leave him. The counselor pointed out that it made no sense for me to pay for therapy if I just wanted out.

But he was beyond reason. Nothing was accomplished.

The next visit I told her about being raped, how it remained unresolved for over twenty-five years. How I still could not tell Brian.

"You need to tell him."

"I know. I just don't know how. I can't talk to him."

"If your marriage is going to survive you have to tell him."

I asked Brain to go for a walk, just the two of us. Every time I tried to broach the subject, he found something to rant about: the way a neighbor was neglecting their flag, someone else's drug problem, me having coffee with Craig. Finally I stopped him, physically turned him to look at me and said very deliberately: "I've been trying to tell you – The reason why I've been sexually dysfunctional all these years is because Keith raped me."

He collapsed dramatically to the sidewalk. "Why?! Why didn't your father kill him?!" he wailed.

"He didn't understand what happened. I was too young to explain."

"Another man was there before me. Do you know how hard this is?"

I was literally stunned. I just told him I had been raped and it was hard for *him*? He needed revenge for *himself*? I don't remember the rest of the walk. We went home to our familiar insanity.

At the next counseling session, Brian was appropriately subdued. It was all about him, him dealing with the news that I had kept this a secret from him all these years. He was looking for pity. He didn't get any. I told him I wanted him to act like a man, not a child with hormonal mood swings. He was shocked, then furious. He wouldn't come to the next session, my last.

"Your marriage isn't important to him," Ingrid interrupted when I made excuses. She never told me what to do or not to do. She only asked questions and made succinct observations. But she left me with one final remark:

"You expect men to let you down."

That one hit me like a slap in the face. And I was angry, because I knew it was true.

Brian got worse. Now he routinely changed history and reality to fit his delusions. He was paranoid, then passionate, then so depressed he couldn't get out of bed. Mostly he was angry and desperately grappled for control. His grandiose anger was like an inescapable black hole, sucking all of us in. There was no room for us to have our own moods, our own needs.

Sometimes he would be covered in a patina of sweat, eyes glazed, and he would rant. He saw things that weren't there, remembered things that never happened. He once hallucinated that Craig was there. I was terrified but tried not to show it. More and more, I stuffed my emotions down.

Brian's aunt called to check on us. Family and friends knew something was wrong and wanted to lend support. She asked how Brian was doing. I was honest and told her about the mood swings, the depression, but that he was doing okay on that particular day. "And how about you?" she said. I repeated that Brian was doing okay that day. "But how are *you*, honey?" I had no answer. I was nothing, just a conduit for Brian's overwhelming emotions.

A curious insanity was spreading among my contemporaries. People who before were perfectly reasonable were suddenly suspicious, hostile, twisted, and fearful. Marriages broke up, friends no longer spoke, children were neglected. It was as if everyone had a self-destruct switch, and the countdown began at age thirty-five. Some succumbed to it. Others slowly overcame it. But some, like Brian, refused to recognize it was even happening. I didn't know who to confide in or what to confide, so I continued to vent my frustrations to my girlfriends online.

One day as I got up from the computer, Brian sat down. I had just finished an email to someone at church, something about Sunday school. I went about my business and heard Brian muttering. Then cursing. Finally he exploded and started raving about how I was talking about him, how he couldn't trust me, how he read the last email I sent because he was trying to reference something (it made no sense). I said, "What does Sunday school have to do with you?" But he wasn't talking about that – he was talking about a terse and frustrated email I sent to my childhood friend Kim.

"Are you reading my emails?" I said slowly. My account was password protected but he worked with computers so no doubt knew how to hack in. He again tried to justify with a wild story about needing to look up an address and how this was the last thing I had written.

Only it wasn't. What he saw was the last thing I had written *about him*. My blood ran cold. He was spying on me and apparently felt he had the right. Email communication was my last connection to sanity. Knowing I could reach out to friends any time of day was the only thing holding me together. Writing in hard times helped me work through problems. In good times it simply made me happy. I needed it. I needed it like I needed air. And now it was gone.

He stormed off, all righteous anger. I sat down at the computer and composed a letter to my girlfriends and the moms' group I frequented. "Please do not ask about my marriage or Brian. I can no longer speak freely. Bit by bit he has taken everything from me that gave me joy."

He found me weeding in the cool shade of the apple tree in the back yard. Asked if we could talk. "Go ahead," I said, without looking up. I knew he read what I just posted and now wanted to negotiate it to his advantage.

He sighed dramatically. "I mean, can we really talk?" he said. I continued kneeling but sat up and looked at him without enthusiasm. He sighed again. He apologized. He rambled. He explained how he set up his email program to copy any message I wrote containing the words "Brian" or "husband". He insisted on showing me how to secure my email so this could not happen again. He didn't seem to find this bizarre, that the hacker wanted to secure my privacy – from him. I finally said, "It doesn't matter. I'll never feel safe online again." He was crushed, but unstoppable. He was going to save me from himself. He set up the computer to be password protected, but just for me. I knew this was because he wanted me to check his email. That would give him something to blame me for – because then I would be no better.

Instead I took concerned phone calls from friends in the back yard or locked myself into the bedroom. This infuriated him. He found every excuse imaginable to "check" on me, determined to hear my side of the conversations.

I wrote long letters to friends at the library or the park, mailing them before coming home. I tore up the journal I had been writing. I hid the letters friends had sent, regardless of their contents. Our marriage was at the breaking point.

I did not include Craig in the mass email, not wanting him to know the truth about my life. But I knew I couldn't email him anymore. So I went to find him at the coffee shop he frequented.

He was pleasantly surprised when I strolled in. I tried to remain casual, said I happened to be driving by and saw his car. If he didn't believe me he didn't let on.

We sat and talked like old times. Nothing deep, nothing I wouldn't be comfortable repeating to anyone – just conversation. But I had to give some plausible reason for us not to email anymore. Coming up empty, I finally said I'd like to meet him for coffee once in awhile. He looked at me slightly askance and asked why the sudden change?

I said something vague about Brian being uncomfortable with me emailing men.

"You finally did it, didn't you?" he teased, having no idea how close he was to the truth. "You finally drove him insane."

Tears sprang to my eyes, but I smiled and said with complete seriousness, "You're next."

"Life doesn't stop," was a saying of Grandmama Linden's, oft repeated by her daughter Pamela. I just wished Life would dole out events in a more reasonable manner, not bombard me with everything at once. But in the midst of everything else that spring, Gram Reid finally reached the end of her long, full life.

Gramps went quietly and suddenly some years before. At his service, my brother-in-law recounted a conversation he had with him, his wife's grandfather, not long after their wedding:

"I hope you don't mind if I call you my grandfather," he said, being (like me) without one and feeling the void.

"I don't know what you're talking about. I *am* your grandfather."

Once a Reid, always a Reid.

When Lillie was a year old, she spiked a fever. That was the only symptom, but after three days I took her to the latest pediatrician. I was told it could be pneumonia, meningitis, or one other really awful thing I cannot recall, then sent home. Just sent home – a new mother with a very sick baby and no idea what was wrong. I called my sisters-in-law for advice, since they both had children the same age. They in turn called my mother-in-law and various aunts in the Reid clan. Finally, word reached the top – Gram – and I got a phone call. I can remember even now her brash old lady voice, saying with assurance:

"It's roseola, honey. Don't let those doctors scare you."

And it was roseola, also known as baby measles. The rash emerged on the fifth day, just as the fever broke. The disease is so common and generally harmless that most baby books don't even mention it. But a high fever in a baby is terrifying to new parents, enough to send them running to the pediatrician who can collect office visit fees. No diagnosis, advice, or even reassurance was given me. My husband's octogenarian grandmother was the only one with answers. Years later, I went on to tell three other young mothers that their feverish child probably had roseola, and was proved correct each time.

"Why didn't the doctor's office just say so when I called?!"

"Would you pay them if they did?"

Gram was also the one who suggested I add sterilized prune juice to Lillie's bottle when she had difficulty digesting the (doctor-recommended) baby formula. Worked like a charm. The pediatrician du jour was outraged:

"You should have dilated her anus with a baby thermometer."

"You'd rather I put a foreign object into that tiny behind rather than fix the actual problem?" I could just envision explaining *that* to CPS.

Gram Reid's memorial service was packed. Even living to the age of nearly one hundred, she had many, many friends of all ages. I missed them both so much. I missed how Gramps teased Gram to the point where she silently fumed. I missed how they always made up with kisses and Gramps saying, "You know I love you, kid." I missed how they would take care of "old people" when they were both in their eighties. I missed her bright pink lipstick and flowery talc. I missed how she would cuss-out Gramps then apologize for using coarse language in front of me. I missed her "dirty" jokes (A man says to his girl, "Hey, how about I come over tonight?" – "I can't, it's Lent." – "Well, when you get it back, let me know.").

When Brian first introduced me to his grandparents, he told them we were going to be together as long as they had. It was now painfully obvious that wasn't true.

At the reception, family members could tell something was wrong, as much as Brian and I tried to act normal. At one point, while some female cousins and I stood together making small talk, one made a joke about not telling her husband something.

"Not telling isn't lying," she said, and they all laughed.

"Would someone explain that to Brian, please?" I snapped. They gave me sympathetic glances. I went to get another glass of wine. Life didn't stop. It didn't even pause long enough for me to catch my breath.

It was a beautiful summer day. I peered out through the blinds to see a strange car pulled up in front of the house. A rather stout woman emerged. I shuddered involuntarily. Although she didn't look dirty per se, she had an aura of filth about her, as if she never washed but put on a nice dress and a lot of jewelry to disguise the fact. She was looking at a paper and then at my house. She saw me, smiled an ugly smile, and came onto the porch.

I opened the door and faced one of the most hideous women I have ever beheld. Not only did she look dirty, her hair was an unnatural blonde with black roots, eyebrows messily drawn on, and she had horrible teeth – her mouth was like a dirty cave. I couldn't stop staring at her; she was like a car wreck.

With no preamble, she said she'd like to buy my house. I said it's not for sale. She waved the paper she had been looking at in my face. "No, but it's been foreclosed," she said, smiling her ugly smile.

That got my attention. I said, "What are you talking about?" Pleased to have information I did not, she said my house was just listed as going into fore-closure, with a sale date of January 1st. She showed me the list but I didn't really see it. I couldn't see anything. I couldn't take in what was happening.

Still smiling, said she'd give me some time but would I agree to give her first chance? I took that to mean she was only the first of many vultures who would descend. Then I realized she was holding out her dirty, scaly hand – rings on every finger – for me to shake in agreement.

I said nothing and shut the door in her face, but I was really trying to shut the door on a reality that was just as ugly.

Brian and I were barely speaking by this time. Since nearly everything each of us said to the other ended up misconstrued, we avoided conversation altogether. The only way we still communicated was through sex. I figured if we still had that, we'd be okay. The rest was fixable, temporary. I prayed for the day when Brian's problem would be diagnosed and treated. Then he would be gainfully employed again and everything would be okay. Not perfect, but okay.

Only Brian insisted there was no problem. Even when I told him about the foreclosure notice, he didn't seem to care. He only reacted to things that didn't matter, like how people hung their flag, or the fact that the neighbors were painting their house the same colors we painted ours. And how he reacted was entirely inappropriate to the situation.

One night, when Brian was God-knows-where, Chris called.

As bad as Brian was, it paled in comparison to Chris. Whatever Brian did, Chris did first, only on a grander scale. He lost his job, wife, house, and sanity. In that order. When he was finally committed to a mental health facility we knew how serious it was. He told everyone he was better, promised to take his meds, and went out into the world. But he was never the same.

I don't recall most of the conversation. Why he was calling didn't matter. What mattered was his voice. It was completely normal, like so very long ago, a few years ago, before the insanity started. No anger, no distance. It was the warm, friendly voice I remembered and loved.

I recalled a moment at Chris and Brian's apartment, before Brian and I were married. Chris has just finished a stressful shift at work and so had I. Saying nothing, we poured ourselves drinks (scotch for him, wine for me) and sat at opposite ends of the couch, staring at the opposing wall. After a long, slow sip we turned to look at each other.

"Hi," he said, and broke into a warm smile.

"Hi," I said, and smiled back.

Tears now ran silently down my face.

"I miss you," I said.

"It hasn't been that long, has it?" he replied easily. But he didn't understand what I meant.

My sister-in-law Raquel, who I suspected had had a breakdown of her own, like everyone else, emailed in mysterious terms concerning Brian:

"You know what's wrong, Noelle."

"Really?" I shot back, with none of my usual gentle understanding. "I've been told it's everything from ADHD to schizophrenia. If you want to throw a diagnosis into the ring, go ahead. Just don't expect me to believe it, because they all can't be right."

The answer, at least part of it, came to me when a friend put the book *A Brilliant Madness* by Patty (Anna) Duke into my hands. She said that book saved her marriage, because her husband suffers from a form of bi-polar disorder. I didn't know what that had to do with me or Brian, but I said I'd read it.

Opening randomly, I started reading about my life with Brian, only the author was describing herself. Near-mania, sudden depression, wild mood swings, irrational thinking, hyper sex drive then no sex drive, hostility then sadness, huge ego followed by low self-esteem, changes in appetite...it went on and on. Once I started reading I couldn't put it down. It was Brian explained.

When he was in a somewhat peaceful state, I told him what I thought: that he had rapid-cycling cyclothymia, a form of bi-polar disorder. He sat on our bed with his back to the wall, as if holding court, while I stood at the end of the bed pleading my case. Glaring at me and breathing heavily, he suddenly slammed the back of his head into the wall over and over, cracking the plaster.

"What disorder is that a symptom of?!" he demanded.

Standing firm, I told him I was going to make an appointment with his doctor and he was going. He exploded, taking off for John's once again. He often escaped there, which mystified John as much as anyone.

"Don't you have a wife and kids at home?" John asked on more than one occasion. But Brian preferred his brother-in-law's rundown abode. Apparently it was better than being with us.

When he did calm down, he was contrite, even eager to see the doctor, and trotted along like a sad puppy when we went. I did most of the talking. The doctor nodded, asked Brian if he agreed. Brian nodded. The doctor gave him a prescription for depakote, an anti-seizure medication which would supposedly even out his moods.

I had no idea how bad it was about to get.

Brian landed a short-term contract job. It was like a miracle. I had urged him to lose the arrogance, which he saw as healthy self-confidence, causing him to be passed over at several previous interviews. Finally his bravado paid off. He was sure this job would be extended beyond the promised six weeks, maybe even be offered a permanent position. Meanwhile the loan company that had a stranglehold on our lives continued to squeeze.

Knowing we could not catch up without help, I went to Consumer Credit Counseling. Now that Brian was employed, they could act as buffer between our creditors and us – make payment arrangements we could afford. I was hopeful as the counselor called the mortgage broker. Then I saw her expression change to confusion and disbelief. She asked, "Would you repeat that? Are you serious?" She hung up, staring at her hand on the desk phone before looking at me.

"I've never heard of this before but they won't take payments. They won't stop the foreclosure. I'm sorry," she said, offering her hand for me to shake. "Good luck." I sat frozen in the chair, unable to take in her words.

At home I emailed Brian at work: "We're losing the house. We have to be out by New Year's Day. What are we going to do?" He replied in a long, rambling response about my feelings towards him, using the imagery of teaching blind men to play golf. I sat shaking, nearly hyperventilating. The house I had worked so hard for, where three of my children were born, the only home they had ever known, was slipping through my fingers like water. And my husband was concerned about my feelings toward him.

Making sure the kids were okay first, I went to find Craig, desperate for anything resembling normalcy and calm. He was at his usual haunt. As always he made small talk but I wasn't listening. I was like the shell-shocked victim of some natural disaster. Finally he said, "Let's drive through the park," meaning the scenic five-mile drive through Pt. Defiance Park in the north end of town.

I stared out the window of his Jaguar, not seeing the trees, not seeing the bay. We drove in silence in the deepening twilight. I was dully surprised when I realized we were back in the parking lot where we had started. Craig asked me what was wrong. He usually pretended along with me that seeing him was just a casual visit, not a matter of hanging on to my last shred of sanity. He knew his role: he was the distraction, the safe diversion. But he had never seen me like this.

He asked again what was wrong. *We're losing our house. Brian's losing his mind. And there's nothing I can do about it.* I shook my head, whispered, "Nothing," and numbly reached for the door handle.

Electricity shot up my other arm. I looked down to see Craig's hand enclosed on mine. I couldn't take my eyes off the sight, it was so unreal. He gently squeezed my fingers; my wedding ring cut into my flesh. Paralyzed, struck mute, I looked into his face and wondered if his eyes had always been so blue. He didn't let go.

"You can tell me," he said gently. "Whatever it is, you can tell me."

Suddenly, desperately, I wanted to crawl into his lap and sob and tell him everything. I wanted him to hold me and tell me it was all going to be okay. But I couldn't. I couldn't speak. I couldn't move. I silently shook my head.

Just as gently, he released me. I don't remember what else he said. I don't remember driving home. I was only aware of anguish that never abated.

Later, Brian was screaming, ranting and throwing things across the living room. I didn't know what set him off and I didn't know how to make him stop. When he would get to this point there was no reasoning with him. He was completely out of control.

I looked past him and saw the kids sitting on the couch, passively taking all this in as if they were watching TV. It didn't bother them at all.

My God, they think this is normal, I thought. And in that moment of clarity I knew I had to get them out.

Chapter 21
~The "Why"~

The same company that held our mortgage also originated a line of credit and the loan for Brian's truck. They (unbeknownst to us) bundled these accounts so if one went into default, all were in default. Because they seemed intent on taking the house, we did the only thing we could think of: went into bankruptcy proceedings. Following our usual pattern, we chose the most inept attorney possible. He took our money but did not make a move to protect us. He had other clients and liked to present cases together to save (his) time.

So after Brian's truck was repossessed in the middle of the night, leaving him distraught and wandering the house crying as if another child had taken his toy in the sandbox, I called Mr. Brainless, atty.

"The truck was repossessed last night," I said with no preamble. "Would you mind filing before they start carrying away the furniture?"

"Oh. Um. Right away," he sputtered.

I found Brian sitting in his robe on Lillie's bed, his head in her lap. "They took my truck!" he sobbed. As I was trying to absorb this bizarre scene, Lillie patted his head awkwardly and said, "It'll be okay, Daddy." Later she told me, "It felt like I was the grown-up and he was the child." I told her I understood the feeling.

The kids had seen and heard too much already. Lillie had it the worst because she understood the most. I sheltered them as much as I could, but in a small house with thin walls there is no hiding, not for long. And when Brian did things like accuse them of "stealing" his food, there was no hiding at all.

Brian had not sold his old truck, as he had promised to do, and now that was a mixed blessing. He got it running, barely. He went back to work, but the bravado was gone. His truck being taken temporarily emasculated him.

He tried to make up for it with more control tactics. He demanded sex at all hours, day or night. It didn't matter to him if I was sleeping or cooking dinner. If it did not go as he liked, it was my fault. I tried to please him, to connect with him, but what we had just one year before was gone. It was as if we had been walking two paths, intersected for one brilliant season, then continued on alone. Still, I tried. One day he sat sullenly on the bed, propped up by pillows, and said the fateful words:

"You got over your dysfunction just so you could use me sexually."

The look on my face reflected in his own expression. He knew he'd made a huge mistake but couldn't stop himself from finishing the sentence. Ice water poured down my back as I thought, *Using him. Using him sexually. This is what he thinks of me now.* I had wanted to make him happy. I wanted to share the gift of healing I had been given. Instead he threw it in my face. Another bit of my heart was gone.

He tried to counteract with "passion" and "romance" but it made me sick to my stomach. I felt like I was having sex with a child. I could barely tolerate his presence.

All of this distracted him, made him careless. Passing by the piano one day, I noticed a framed photo was missing, the one of my brother John. I looked around but didn't see it. I asked the kids but they had not seen it either. Then I thought of Brian.

I don't know why I needed to know if Brian had taken it or why he would, but I went to the dungeon, his filthy basement lair. Past the boxes he had piled up like a barricade I found his usual collection of moldy beer bottles, gun and porn magazines, radio equipment, other assorted debris, and a small pile of shattered glass.

Why would he break John's picture and hide it? Why would he even have it? I turned on the light over the workbench. John's glass-encased photo wasn't what was broken. The shards of glass were from a small mirror, one I had given to the kids as a toy. The picture frame was there, intact, face-up. And on it was a razor blade, a cheap hollowed-out pen, and a trace of white powder.

I can't remember exactly what happened next, what I said or what I did. My mind went black with rage:

He's played me for a fool. I *am* a fool. I actually believed this was beyond his control, that he was mentally ill. He allowed the doctor to diagnose him with the very thing he fought about with me. "I'm not sick!" he sneered, never telling the truth, even to the point of taking powerful anti-seizure drugs, downing it with alcohol. Risking his life. Risking all of our futures. Did he even take the depakote? Did he sell it? Did he trade it for more drugs?

Smoking pot every damn morning, as habitual as his coffee. Before we were married he thought he hid that too. Friends tried to gently tell me, like I didn't know or wouldn't understand. They were all shocked that I knew but didn't feel I had to "do" anything about it. What would I have done? No one ever had an answer for that. As if, just by me knowing, he would have to stop? That I would put my foot down, threaten to – what? What is the proper ultimatum? He was going to do whatever he wanted. Isn't that what men want – for their wives not to keep them on a leash?

Well, he got what he wanted. I was the perfect wife in that regard. The perfect, deceived doormat who had dinner ready every night at six o'clock, who somehow got the bills paid even as he disappeared with the money, who ran interference with anyone who questioned or accused. Meanwhile, I had no habit to support. No addictions, not even a damn hobby. I was nothing.

But he would still blame me. Because I didn't stop him, even though he went to great lengths to hide it. Somehow it would be my fault. It always was.

"You're *wrong*, Noelle!" How many times did he yell that in my face? Then just hours later contritely confess, "You were right," as if handing me a gift, like I should be relieved to know I was right. "Whatever," I would say flatly, knowing this would be repeated again and again and that it was meaningless. That it was just sucking my life away.

How much of the control tactics were planned? Everything he did to keep me off-balance, how much was a concerted effort? How he must have laughed, knowing he had pulled this over on me. Like lying to his mother when he was twelve. It's so funny when your mother is stupid and you're so smart, isn't it, Brian? You're a consummate liar. A born actor. And now you're twelve again and I'm the mother. You asshole.

Damn you. *Damn* you.

You hate tweakers, despise them. Hate their choice to use this poisonous shit the first time, knowing they'd be instantly addicted. You malign them for grinding their teeth, for picking at sores, for destroying their lives. But I can just hear you, in that lofty tone that makes me want to smack you: "What you don't realize is, I have a very high tolerance. I only snort it, I don't shoot it or smoke it like those fucking tweakers. It hasn't affected me. No one can even tell. *I'm in complete control of my addiction.*"

Damn you. I wish you were dead. I wish you had died on one of your night bike rides, back before you were a filthy drug addict and insane and still had life insurance. We all would have mourned you, the wonderful husband and father you were. Everyone would have told the children how you loved them and sacrificed for them. You would have been a glorified memory; I would have made sure of it.

Damn you, you liar. You don't love us. You're using us. We're nothing but a crutch, a front to make you look normal. As long as we're here, playing our parts, you can pass for a decent human being. But you're not. You're just a fucking tweaker. You're the very thing you hate.

And I hate you too.

Damn you. Damn you to hell.

At some point I talked to Cecelia. I can't remember the conversation, only my rage. This time no amount of venting or wine assuaged my anger. Furious with myself for being deceived, furious with Brian for his constant lies, furious knowing our lives were in the toilet and there was nothing I could do.

"You've been unhappily married for years," Cecelia gently pointed out. I had been so swallowed up in it, I didn't realize. Or I wouldn't acknowledge it. There were many things I refused to look at. I couldn't. It was up to me to hold everything together.

As I dressed one morning, I caught a glimpse of myself in the full-length mirror in our bedroom. Except for putting on make-up, I had actively avoided looking at myself for months, opting to dress in the dark. I knew I had lost weight; sometimes the very thought of food made me ill. I was always slender but now clothes hung on me. I had a photo from that spring, from a birthday party, and I was shocked at my deer-in-the-headlights expression. Was it that obvious to everyone? Now naked and alone, I turned on the light and forced myself to look. If I had been capable of crying then I would have. I resembled a prison camp survivor. Stark white, ribs visible, baby-fine hair even thinner, face gaunt, and that damn haunted expression. I looked like a drug addict as much as Brian did, but I could see it and he couldn't. I looked away.

When word got out that we were losing the house, Brian's mother called. She had been crying, but I was drained of emotion. She said, "You need it to be over, don't you?" I didn't know what she meant. Later I understood she meant my marriage. Like she eventually needed her marriage to Brian's father to be over so she could go on living, I needed my marriage to be over. Even Brian, if he was going to have any chance at all, needed a rude awakening.

Dad got a card in the mail that put him in a foul mood. No return address and rather stilted handwriting in a card that said, *"Where's Walt? Have a heart, Walt. Help Noelle and the girls keep their house."* I had my suspicions who sent it but said nothing. Dad fumed.

"What about Dennis?" he said, sharply. "Why not, 'Where's Dennis?' They're his grandkids too!" Everyone thought my dad had an endless supply of money, when in fact he kept his capital securely tied up in various certificates of deposit. He was very careful with his earnings, which was why he had as much as he did after a lifelong career as a "grease monkey."

But the truth was Dad wasn't going to help save a sinking ship. He said nothing and I said nothing but I knew that's how he felt.

Then Brian lost his "guaranteed" job. I think they came to realize how high maintenance he was, for all this brilliance. Determined to keep the utilities turned on and food on the table, I went back to work, but in sales. The younger kids were too small for me to be away full-time and it would have been safer to ask the cat to watch the kids than Brian, so I worked odd hours and had Lillie and Chloe hold down the fort. Except, whenever Brian was home, it all fell apart. I'd come home to find a huge mess, the kids asleep on our bed or the couch, and dinner spoiling on the stove. All because Brian wouldn't let Lillie and Chloe do as I asked.

I started hiding the money, keeping only enough in the checking account to cover automatic payments for things like the car insurance, making the deposit the day before. The rest I kept as cash in three separate envelopes, in three separate hiding places that I constantly moved.

Aunt Betty and Uncle Raymond stopped by, which they had never done in all the years we lived there, bringing a week's worth of groceries. They didn't say much, just that they wanted me to have it. I'm sure Betty couldn't stand the idea of her sister's child scrounging for food. As it was I was so sick of chicken (the cheapest meat available) I nearly gagged at the sight of it. I was stunned by their generosity but even more by Uncle Raymond's hug before they left. No one from that side of the family had ever hugged me before, ever. I knew then everyone knew how bad things were.

Brian, meanwhile, made everything harder. He'd call me at work, demanding I come home because it was raining. Or to make sure I got there okay (meaning he didn't believe I was at work). Or crying over some movie.

I endured reality. I knew what I had to do.

I went to Dad's alone. Once again, home was the only place I could go. With voice shaking I asked if the kids and I could move in with him for awhile.

"And Brian?"

"We're…separating."

"I'd help you more if you'd just go ahead and divorce him."

Divorce. I could barely say the word "separate" and my quietly conservative father, happily married twice, just gave me his blessing to divorce. "You've been unhappily married for years," Cecelia pointed out. "Your marriage isn't important to him," the counselor interrupted. "You need it to be over, don't you," sympathized my mother-in-law. The weight lifted. It was okay to stop trying. It was okay to stop fighting the inevitable. I caught my breath.

"Walt, don't pressure her," admonished Carol, not knowing what a gift I had just been given.

"I like Brian," Dad said, "but it's been over for a long time." Amazing how everyone else saw it before I did. Even my father, when I tried so hard to keep up a brave front. They made arrangements for the kids and me to move in New Years Day.

When Brian was calm one day, I quietly explained I didn't want to be married anymore, to him or anyone. That he would need to find a place to stay on his own. He got that lost little boy look, and I felt a single pang of pity.

"You don't mean that," he said.

"I do."

"Your feelings are just buried. You still love me and don't know it."

Don't tell me how I feel.

"I didn't bury my feelings for you. You killed them off, *bit by bit*," I said through gritted teeth.

Stunned but undefeated, he asked to talk privately in the bedroom. I knew that meant he wanted sex, thinking it would make everything better. He refused to see his paranoia had driven me away; accusing me of "using" him sexually, of having a relationship with Craig despite all evidence to the contrary, of me putting work before family when I was desperately trying to provide for us. My feelings for him were gone; only vague memories remained along with ever-present anger.

He would wake me during the night for a tryst and I tolerated it, wanting to get it over with. It was like being in an arranged marriage with a twelve-year-old boy. If I thought about it I felt nauseated, so instead focused on everything that needed to be done: packing, keeping the kids busy, hiding the money.

But now he wanted sex in the middle of the day when there was no hiding. He didn't say anything, just gently pushed me onto the bed. It was surreal; I felt nothing, as if this was happening to someone else. He saw my expression.

"What is it?"

"I feel like a whore," I said, with a touch of wonder in my voice. "I don't feel anything at all." He slowly climbed off me and cried. That was the last time we had sex.

I had a dream:

Cold black water, churning slowly in a spiral. And in the middle was Brian, drowning, stretching out his arms to me. I reached down to rescue him, but he grabbed me by the wrists to pull me in. With a euphoric smile and glassy eyes he murmured, "Die with me. Die with me." I screamed and fought with all my might, trying to get a foothold in the black slime, recoiling from the horror.

I woke up screaming. I was alone. I was alive.

As a young girl, I idolized actress Vivien Leigh. I knew she was "manic depressive" but couldn't understand how Laurence Olivier could leave her over that. Now I knew. When you are living with insanity, it doesn't matter how attractive or intelligent or otherwise wonderful the other person is. You have to get out to survive.

I kept up the kids' routine as much as possible, trying to give some stability to their lives. It was also therapeutic for me, having places to go and things to do, not to mention an escape from Brian for a few hours.

Unlike with Cecelia or my online friends, I did not mention to the other ballet moms how my life was imploding. I saw them several times a week and had known them for years, but it was easier to listen to them chat and say nothing. After opening up there is no going back.

But one evening in December, while they discussed plans for Christmas break and the merits of going to Disneyland in winter versus the summer, or if it would be too much to do both in one year, one of them said, "What about you, Noelle? What's going on with you?" They all turned to me, as if noticing me for the first time, and politely waited. I savored one final moment of perceived normalcy, took a slow breath and said:

"Brian's unemployed, mentally ill, and a drug addict. We're bankrupt and losing our house. The kids and I are moving in with my parents. And I'm getting a divorce."

There was stunned silence, which was finally broken by one friend's quiet weeping. She said, "I'm sorry. I'm sorry I mentioned Disneyland." I said it was okay, that someday I'd take my kids to Disneyland too.

They started giving me things. One stopped by on Christmas Eve with bags of groceries and art supplies for the kids. Another gave us nice clothes that (she said) she had planned to get rid of. Others supported my commission sales job, giving me more cash flow, or any cash flow.

People talk about "Mommy Wars" and how women compete and sabotage one another when their children have something to vie for, but that was never evident at ballet. They, along with church members and co-workers, held me up, kept my head above water when I could no longer swim.

Brian switched tactics again. Now he was a drug addict. He told everyone how he was clean, going to narc-anon meetings, and how he was going to win me back. I let him say whatever he wanted. One day he was mentally ill, the next he was a druggie. He made daily proclamations to that effect, as if it mattered.

The first person I told that I was leaving Brian was his brother Eric. Instead of "How could you?" or "What about the kids?" he said,

"We were all wondering what you were waiting for."

So the Reids knew and understood, but Brian didn't realize that.

One day he put his hands on my shoulders and solemnly informed me that he would be taking the kids, because there was no way a judge would give me custody since I couldn't support them. It seemed to escape him that *he* was the one who was unemployed, not to mention unfit. I laughed in his face, first bitterly, then almost hysterically. I couldn't help myself – the whole thing was insane. His expression turned to shock. I stepped back and said with dead seriousness:

"Let me tell you how it's going to be. I will raise the children and you will see them when I think it's okay. If you fight me on this, my entire family *and yours* will back me up."

He stood, stunned, as if unable to believe what he just heard. I did not break eye contact. Finally he drooped and walked away, no doubt to plot his next move. I was barely holding on. It was now mid-December.

I had a dream:

I lay sprawled on a bed in a room I did not recognize but knew was mine. Sunlight streamed in. The white sheer curtain fluttered in the breeze. Wrapped in nothing but a linen sheet I was completely spent but had never felt more alive.

Craig laid next to me and, seeing I was awake, turned onto his side and put his strong, warm arm across me, pulled me to him, and murmured that I was wonderful. He kissed me on the mouth and I melted in the embrace.

"I had a dream about you," I hesitantly emailed Craig. It was such a powerful vision I couldn't stop thinking about it. I never emailed Craig anymore for fear of Brian's paranoia. But I never before experienced a dream more real than reality, where I could actually feel another's touch. I was surprised when he responded:

"I had a dream about you, too." And that was all. Usually I did not have to prod Craig for details on any subject, but this I had to coax out of him. Only after I promised to tell my dream did he reluctantly divulge his:

"I dreamed I was making love to you. You were smooth and wet. I said you felt wonderful and that you tasted wonderful as well."

I sat and stared at the monitor, burning this into my memory, knowing I'd have to wipe it off the computer completely before getting up. Some time must have gone by because he messaged again:

"Too much?"

"No," I wrote. "It's just that I had the same dream."

We said nothing more about it and I deleted the entire exchange from the computer as if it never happened, but everything changed in that moment. I was standing on the edge of a cliff and any little breeze or shifting of the ground could make me fall. And I knew I could fly.

As I packed I sorted, so as not to take things we didn't need. But I was also in a hurry, so finding an old steno notebook I flipped it open randomly. There was my childish, nine-year-old cursive:

Faith, Hope, Grace, Joy.

I stopped. Four daughters. These words, these names. It had been decided even before they were conceived. These children were promised to me when I was still a child. Even when I insisted I wanted three: two girls and a boy – *these* were my children.

Just the year before, I met other moms at a summer camp where Lillie and Chloe took classes. One day we discussed names and realized everyone there had a daughter with the middle name Joy. Except me. But Sophie *was* Joy – she was Joy incarnate. In fact all four personified their pre-birth names. In the distraction of everyday life, I just hadn't seen it.

I thought of my miscarriage, of the surety I felt that it was a boy. I remembered my grief, my anger at God, demanding *Why? Why?*

I think this was the "why," because it would have been infinitely harder to take a son from Brian, since he lost his family when he was a little boy. And it would have been infinitely harder to raise a son without an example of what a man should be. Thinking about this made it slightly more bearable.

Slightly.

It was my birthday and I treated myself to a short reprieve by saying I was running errands. I found Craig at his usual haunt and asked him to drive me through the park. In the darkness I found his right hand with my left, as he had with mine two months before. We didn't talk, or if we did I have no memory of what we said. I felt safe – that is what I remember – that we drove and I held his hand. Back at the otherwise empty parking lot we stood awkwardly.

"Well, happy birthday…" he began as I said, "Well, thank you for the drive…" or some inanity when we both simply stopped and looked at each other in silence.

I fell into his arms at the very moment he pulled me to him. Warmth spread over me like being wrapped in a blanket, like being carried to bed by my parents, a feeling of complete security I had not known in thirty-five years. My mouth instinctively searched out his and I was totally enveloped.

Lightning shot through my body. His arms flexed against my back while his kiss drew me in even closer. Our bodies perfectly matched, every curve and limb found its place. My legs gave out under the sheer power of his embrace – if he had not been holding me I would have collapsed.

His mouth finally released mine and his lips lightly brushed over my hair. I could feel his warm breath as he slowly exhaled. I laid my head on his chest, felt the beating of his heart, and wanted to stay there like that forever.

If Craig had touched me like this before – or touched me at all – there would have been no more relationship between Brian and me. There would have been no marriage. There would have been no children. I loved Brian. I loved him and was faithful to him for twenty years. And I love our children. I will never regret that part of our union. But I regret – deeply and painfully regret – missing the life I might have had with Craig.

When I quietly told Brian I couldn't agree to him "courting" me as he had vowed he would do, he wildly vacillated between anger and despair. He wrote love notes. He wrote hate notes. And pornographic emails I couldn't even read. He cried. He screamed. On Christmas Day he collapsed in the driveway, sobbing. With gritted teeth I reminded him he promised not to do this in front of the children. But they were his audience, his way of making sure I couldn't escape the drama. And as much as I pitied him before, I despised him now.

With simmering fury I packed our lives into boxes. Load after load went to Goodwill. Brian's I stacked against a wall. What was mine or the kids' I took to Dad's. Little by little the house emptied. When I found Brian crying over our wedding photos it only steeled my resolve. I worked with grim determination.

The last room was the kitchen. As I stood up after taping a box, my eye caught the stencil in the archway to the breakfast nook. The one of ivy that I never finished. I felt empty. And angry. And defeated. And now I knew why.

Unemployment, mental illness, drug addiction, repossession, bankruptcy, foreclosure and the complete breakdown of our marriage. It took only nine months to lose everything.

With the kids safely ensconced at their grandparents', I collected the last of the boxes. Dad, Uncle Raymond and his two sons-in-law had already moved the heavy furniture. Most of it was mine: the cabinet and desk our old Swedish neighbor made when I was a child, my grandparents' dining room set, my mother's piano. In fifteen years of marriage we had purchased only our bed, a dinette set, and a cheap entertainment center. Anything else was a cast-off from family or something we found at a yard sale.

One piece was the whimsical end table we brought from Aunt Cora's. I liked it, but since Cora was Brian's relative it made sense for him to have it. He also got the bed and entertainment center.

Other things we had to leave behind. They were either too heavy to move or there was nowhere to store them. Also, I didn't have the mental or emotional energy to deal with anything beyond basic survival. So the kitchen dinette set stayed, as did all the appliances, even the smooth-top range I loved. Someone else would get to enjoy them.

It was January and bitterly cold as well as wet. The power had been cut so we only went to the house during daylight hours. Brian and I agreed to be there on different days to avoid seeing each other. But he always left a calling card. One day it was his journal left open on the bed, describing his despair at my unwillingness to reconcile. Another time, it was a "Divorce Busters" workbook. Once it was a love poem about letting me go (although he had no intension of doing so). I clenched my teeth and focused on my mission to get out alive.

But even with all his destructive drama, I was unprepared for what greeted me on one of the final days: The unity candle from our wedding and Aunt Cora's end table, smashed to bits with a baseball bat.

I checked the rest of the house, expecting to find holes in the walls. But there was just one last statement. The photo of me on the altar steps on our wedding day, the only really good shot of me ever, the one he kept on display above his workbench – no copy, no negative, irreplaceable…Ripped into a hundred angry little pieces.

Chapter 22
~You Can't Go Home Again~

Now I was a five-year-old mother of four. At least that's how Carol saw it. She and Dad were incredibly generous letting us move in, not knowing how long it would be. They even switched to a smaller bedroom so we could have theirs, plus gave us the third bedroom that had been a den.

But everything I did, or tried to do, was subtly undermined or dismissed. Carol "helped" to the point of complete frustration. The kids loved how she would drop everything to play with them or cook for them. She was the "fun grandma" and now they had her at their constant beck and call. She loved and resented it at the same time; loved the favoritism, resented the excess groceries and trash. I told her not to buy the expensive Costco-sized juice, yet she continued. I told her the jugs could be recycled curbside but she didn't believe me. When I finally got her to call and arrange for it, she would throw it all in together: glass with cardboard, aluminum with newspaper.

"You can recycle it, can't you?" she'd say. She was sure she was right about this and everything else. She had to be – she was the mother. End of discussion.

I took to quietly packing up all the glass and plastic and taking it to a recycling center in the valley once a week. The kids came along with promises of lollypops and a trip to the park afterwards. I took them for outings or their usual activities as often as possible. They needed a break from their grandparents and their grandparents needed a break from them.

Dad was no better. Quietly stressed and worried for us, he started criticizing everything we did or didn't do. He wanted me to enroll the kids in school, even though Dagne and Sophie were too young for school, and we had no idea where we would live in just a few months. From what he could tell, the kids got to do anything they wanted anytime they wanted and never learned anything. A few months earlier his grandchildren were brilliant and creative. Now they were just out of control.

"You need to *sit down* with them and teach them out of *books*," he said firmly one day while the two of us were in the kitchen. At that moment, my youngest happened to skip through the room.

"Here Sophie, write your name," I said casually, handing the three year old a notepad and pencil kept by the phone. She paused just long enough to write SOPHIE in perfect block letters before skipping away.

"Well I'll be..." began Dad in wonderment before I also took my leave, although without the skipping.

We were all stressed to the limit. Dad and Carol by trying to provide for us, the kids by having their entire lives upended, and me in the middle and also still dealing with Brian, who refused to believe our marriage was over.

Anything I did that could be perceived as "nice" was taken by him to mean I really didn't want the divorce. Even offering to handle our bills meant I was softening towards him, when I just wanted it settled because my name was also on the accounts. He sent over mutual friends "to talk" to me, after convincing them I was miserable. Their expressions went from concern to shock when I smiled and said I was fine.

Bombarding me with every trick in his repertoire and getting no rise from me irritated him. In an email exchange, he gave it everything he had, dragging the welfare of the kids into it. I wrote they needed stability and calm. He shot back:

"What they need – *and deserve* – is an intact, Christ-centered family!"

"Is that what we had before? I didn't notice."

Whenever he'd pull the God card, I automatically reacted with disdain. It wasn't important to him until he could use it as a weapon. Then suddenly he was the one wronged, the one who God spoke to personally, promising him he would be "restored to his family."

"Noelle," he shot back, "I always thought no one was colder or more non-emotional than your dad, but I was wrong. You're just like your father!"

I thought of my father, who I saw cry only once, who I heard raise his voice only a handful of times, who never lashed out in anger, pouted, ranted, or used any kind of emotional manipulation. Who meant what he said, and showed us he loved us every day, even if he never said it even once.

"Thank you," I replied.

Then Brian landed a great job, the best he ever had as far as pay and benefits were concerned. He figured this would bring me around. I told him the kids and I were cheering him on, but there would be no reconciliation. He took this as a challenge. He told everyone he was going to buy me a house, even though he couldn't even secure an apartment. He dangled the excellent health coverage, regretfully informing me I couldn't share it as long as we were separated. I shrugged and while signing up the kids, added myself with no trouble. Brian never noticed. He asked out one of my best friends, also going through a divorce, knowing how vulnerable she was but not knowing how loyal. She turned him down and immediately informed me. He switched tactics again.

Flowers were mysteriously delivered. I was the only one home at the time. In the mere seconds it took me to answer the door, only the bouquet was there to greet me. No delivery person. No delivery van. About to go outside to investigate, I instead looked at the attached note. It was addressed to Brian, from a woman I did not know. The card read: "Thank you. I had a wonderful time."

I emailed him. He claimed he had lunch with a co-worker, sheepishly calling her a "very forward young lady." I hoped that meant she put out, but only asked why the flowers were delivered here. He blithely replied he used my parents' place as his address for work because he didn't know where he'd be living permanently. In other words, because I lived there.

None of it made sense of course, and I didn't believe any of it, but it really wasn't important.

I personally delivered the bouquet along with divorce papers.

I worked almost daily, adding a part-time position with my church's preschool. Dagne and Sophie could stay with me there, which was an added bonus. The kids' constant noise and mess were wearing out our welcome with Dad and Carol. I tried to clean up after them and take them out of the house often, but it was impossible to stay on top of things, much less ahead of them. And of course the kids were dealing with losing the only home they had ever known, "losing" their father just as effectively, and having the rug pulled out from under them in nearly every way.

They all had colds upon moving in, but soon after came down with a something far worse. Dagne was first. I was about to leave for work when she said her tummy hurt. Dagne was tough – the healthiest of the four. For her to say something hurt got my attention.

Carol said, "If you give her Pepto-Bismol she won't throw up." This came out of nowhere and if I wasn't so distracted I would have put more thought into it, but she sounded so sure of herself that I had Dagne reluctantly take a spoonful of "the yucky pink stuff." She promptly vomited all over Carol's perfectly clean kitchen floor.

I was conflicted, I needed to go to work but didn't want to leave a sick little girl. Carol insisted I go – she would take care of her. I hoped it was a 24-hour thing, or even less, and no one else would catch it. Instead, by the time I got home two more had it. And it was worse. Uncontrollable diarrhea to go with the uncontrollable vomiting. And it went on for days.

Since I didn't know of anything going around, I was afraid it was food poisoning. Our area was the scene of a large-scale E. coli outbreak in the early 1990s, which killed three children and sickened scores more, leaving some permanently damaged. With that in the back of my mind, I anxiously watched for traces of blood.

Lillie and I eventually succumbed as well, but for us it was the 24 hour-variety. Brief but brutal. It felt like I was heaving up my lungs.

Then the three youngest got it *again*, so I had all of them sleep in my queen-size bed to keep an eye on them. But nothing could have prepared me for what happened that night.

Chloe, Dagne, and Sophie had just gone to sleep. Chloe, the favorite, in the middle with a little sister on either side. I quietly typed at the computer, informing their father the kids were very sick and I was concerned. He was concerned also: about himself. A side-effect of drug addiction is being unable to see beyond your own needs. While I understood that intellectually, it made me angry. His daughters were sick. He should care.

After the non-conversation with Brian, I got online with Craig. This was often the only way we could talk – instant messaging after the kids went to bed. He didn't want Brian or the kids to know about him yet and I agreed, so phone calls were rare. We had only gotten as far as saying hello when I heard an ungodly noise behind me. Turning, I saw vomit erupting from Dagne like lava.

I typed *sick kid* and leapt toward the bed, pulling half-asleep Dagne up to sitting. She was as limp as a rag doll while she proceeded to vomit all over the bed, all over me, and overflowing the bowl I had at the ready.

When the heaving finally stopped, she sat sobbing and gasping for breath. "I went potty," she cried pitifully, and I knew she meant diarrhea. But before I could even think of what to do, Sophie turned her head on her pillow and vomited into Chloe's hair. At this, Chloe awoke, sat up and vomited as well. Sophie was still actually asleep, but the others were aware enough to be upset.

I lifted Dagne from the now reeking bed and headed toward the bath, coaxing Chloe to follow. Just steps behind me, she stopped. Hot diarrhea ran down her legs. Her sister's vomit ran down her hair. On the verge of well-deserved hysteria, she started shaking and burst into tears.

"It's okay, honey. It's okay. We'll get you cleaned up," I promised.

"But the rug! Gramma will be mad."

"No she won't. She *won't*. We'll get it clean. Don't worry."

The next five hours were a surrealistic nightmare. I washed the kids one at a time, trying to keep them calm while they tried not to lose more bodily fluids. I thought I would never get all the vomit out of Chloe's long, thick hair. She sat in the tub with her pulled up and head down while I endlessly shampooed and rinsed. It took a supreme effort on my part not to gag at the feel and smell as the tub was filled and emptied, over and over. Though it was the dead of winter I opened the bedroom window to air out the suffocating stench.

We all needed clean pajamas and the bed needed clean everything. I pulled new blankets and sheets and even found an extra mattress pad in the well-stocked linen closet. I was too preoccupied to notice Carol slept through it all.

When the kids and bed were finally clean and dry, I tucked them in and started the first of six loads of laundry, after first rinsing each in the kitchen sink.

Then I remembered Craig. Going back to the computer, I saw he was offline, but had left a message after my cryptic sign-off:

"Boxes of jello on your front porch. Give to your little girls *warm*. It will make them feel better."

Their own father couldn't be bothered, but a man who had never met them – couldn't even keep their names straight – bought jello for them in the middle of the night and delivered it.

After warming some, I put it in cups and cajoled the sick, sleepy kids into taking a few sips. I had some as well, with shaking hands and upset stomach. I had forgotten this home remedy. Carol made it for me when I had my tonsils out – it was one of the few things I could keep down. And it soothes a throat raw from vomiting. Since Craig never gets sick and never had children, I was amazed he even thought of it.

I went back to rinsing, rotating the laundry, sponging the bedroom carpet with water and baking soda in the dark, and scrubbed the entire bathroom, making sure to use bleach so it would be up to Carol's standards. I was so paranoid about spreading the virus I then went around the house with disinfecting wipes, going over anything we may have touched that I hadn't already cleaned.

At 4:00 AM I finally fell, exhausted, on a crib mattress on the floor next to the kids and slept.

That seemed to be the last hurrah and everyone finally recovered. I bought acidophilus tablets to stave off any more diarrhea and we all ate (or drank) a lot of jello.

Then Dad got it and I was guilt-stricken. I didn't know where we picked it up and I had tried so hard to keep it from spreading, but now my father – who never caught so much as a cold – was now sick as a dog. Carol looked after him like a proper nurse, catering to his every need.

"I just hope Gramma doesn't get it, too," I said to Lillie that afternoon.

"Oh she won't. She already had it."

"What?"

Lillie slept in the room next to theirs while the rest of us were in the master bedroom. The younger kids felt better together but Lillie needed her space.

Anyone in her presence was in direct line of fire of her adolescent rage. She was already at a difficult age, had seen and heard too much in the months prior, and now her life was endless uncertainty. I was more than willing to give up the room, over Carol's protests that it should be mine.

"You're rewarding her," she and others said.

"No, I'm rewarding myself," I replied. This day she repaid me with information, though she didn't know she was giving it.

"Gramma had it *first*," Lillie said now. "I heard her get up lots of times one night going to the bathroom and the next day she was really quiet."

When I would go to bed, I was often out before my head hit the pillow. I never heard Carol or anyone in the bathroom. When I came down with it during the night I wretched so loudly over the toilet that Lillie came running. But Carol did not. This was completely out of character.

Now I understood. Just like years ago when she'd go to work sick and contagious, unconcerned because "I don't have a fever," she caught this virus somewhere and instead of making an attempt to quarantine herself or even admit to having it so I was forewarned, she pretended it never happened. She continued to prep food for the kids and allowed us to share the same bathroom. And when we all got it she never said a word except to claim Pepto-Bismol would keep us from vomiting.

And apparently she was okay with me feeling guilty over making Dad ill, because even then she said nothing. Denial had worked for her for her entire life. Ignore it and it isn't real.

We had been there only two months at this point. We had to get out before my feelings for my parents (and theirs for me) were irreparably damaged.

God promised Brian he would be "restored to his family." He was always getting these heavenly messages. I told him unless God himself appeared before me and ordered me to do so, there would be no reconciliation.

His hysterical drama, which included loud wailing when he came to hand over the completed divorce papers, just steeled my resolve to end it. I reminded him again – through gritted teeth – that he promised not to carry on in front of the kids. But he was out of his mind.

He insisted, with wild glassy eyes and a patina of sweat, that he was clean. I reiterated that he would not take the kids anywhere unless I thought it was okay, and that I would see to it his rights were severed if he tried anything. He must have known even in his meth-addled brain that I would make good on my threat because he settled for seeing them with my stipulations.

The kids didn't know about the drugs. They didn't ask "why" and I did not enlighten them. I'm sure Lillie had some idea but she already carried too heavy a burden of knowledge, so I let her think it was just the alcohol and marijuana. Meth was the lowest of the low. It was dirty. Only someone open to self-destruction, someone who didn't care about anyone, including their own family, would even consider using it.

I didn't want them to think of their father that way, so covered for him. And demanded that others cover for him as well. I wanted them to feel normal.

It continued. I was so exhausted by the end of each day that I would invariably fall asleep while reading to the kids. I remember only the first chapter of *The Hobbit*. Lillie finally took over while I slept.

As before, my only real escape was Craig.

The only one who knew about Craig – really knew about him, not just knew *of* him – was Cecelia. I confided in her my long-held desire, my conflicted emotions. She asked the September prior, before I left Brian, if I would consider an affair.

"You only ask because it's all I think about," I answered. She smiled and poured more wine. But she knew as well as I did that thinking about it was as far as it would go. With my endless responsibilities there was no chance I could ever get away, even for an afternoon. And being a middle-aged woman who drove a minivan full of kids, I could not picture myself as an object of desire. But most of all, I was boringly faithful. An affair just wasn't going to happen.

Beyond that, Craig was carrying on three relationships already. All of them shallow and convenient, just the way he liked them. I didn't fit his lifestyle. The sexual tension between us was undeniable, yet we never spoke of it, not directly. Only once did Craig make a remark that if he could do it over again he wouldn't make the same mistake.

"What mistake?" We sat in a corner of his beloved coffee shop.

"Letting you get away," he said, without looking at me.

"You weren't missing anything," I said quietly, after a moment.

"What do you mean?" We looked at each other now, but said nothing more. We went back to discussing movies.

The kiss on my birthday changed everything. It would have been impossible to pretend otherwise. As my life crashed down around me in every other way, this was the one thing I could hold onto.

He didn't say so, but I knew he quietly dismissed his girlfriends. He wanted this to be exclusive. I had no idea where our relationship would go, just told him I would follow his lead. I needed him to think for both of us.

He knew how fragile I was. Carol's endless cooking filled out my figure somewhat. I was now nearly a size 6 and no longer looked starved. But I was still constantly stressed.

In stolen moments we would meet in the park where I finally did what I so desperately wanted to do months before: curl up in his lap. In the privacy of his car, hidden away in the woods with the dark winter rain all around us, I could finally relax. I slept cradled in his arms. It was bliss.

Dad had surprised me yet again when he helped me move the last of the bookshelves from the old house. On the way to his place he suddenly asked, "Do you know any real estate agents?" I said I knew a few. "Well, have one find you a house," he said with no further explanation. I was so stunned I didn't realize my favorite shelf had fallen off the truck and shattered to bits on the freeway.

I started looking for houses right away, in all areas, but kept coming back to Tacoma. I was drawn to it and it was all the kids knew. I wanted to live in the same neighborhood, but the rising prices in the area kept turning me away.

I needed to know my limitations and went to find Dad working in the yard. I started to explain that I needed to know how this was going to work with the mortgage payments, what the maximum was. Dad just shook his head.

"No mortgage payments."

"But you said to find a real estate agent. Do you mean I should rent?"

"No. Cash. I'm not feeding the bankers." Dad hated feeding the bankers. "Call it your inheritance early."

Reeling, I at least had the presence of mind to ask about price limits.

"Keep it under $150,000."

Our old house was purchased for half that, but thanks to refinancing and a second mortgage, we owed $105,000 after living there twelve years. I wasn't going to tell Dad that. I just promised to find a good house for a good price. "Make sure it's big enough," he admonished, like he used to when I was going clothes shopping with his credit card.

I looked through the listings every day, both online, in the newspaper and in the free publications found outside grocery stores. Craig and I drove in favorable areas, looking for signs in the yard. I wanted a three bedroom, one and a half bath house with a bonus room for an office. But thanks to the booming housing market I couldn't find one for the price Dad gave me.

One day while looking at the listings, I had the wild idea of buying back our old house. It wasn't "big enough," as Dad would say, but it was the only place the kids had ever known and I loved the neighborhood. It appraised at $120,000 when we left, so that made it affordable with Dad's limits.

I went through the slick magazine which categorized by price, cheapest first. I started with $110,000. Nothing. $120,000. Nothing. $130,000. I knew the house was up for sale by now – it had to be. I flipped to $150,000 and up. And there it was, for $167,000.

I called Cecelia, furious. "One hundred and sixty-seven thousand! Small wonder they wouldn't negotiate." The mortgage brokers knew they wouldn't lose anything by our bankruptcy. They profited. We were the only ones who didn't.

"You know I really like you guys and hate to do this," said Rachel, chief officer of humiliation, when I had called about making reduced payments the year prior. She promptly cut us off at the knees. I found it supreme irony that her name means "innocent." Innocent like a jackal. After the repossession and foreclosure she had the audacity to tell me she'd love to "work with" us again in the future.

"Thank you, I'd rather work with the mafia," I answered.

I looked and looked but could find nothing decent under $150,000. As weeks turned into months, I was getting desperate. So was Dad, who in a moment of stress accused me of stalling. In reality, I knew we had to get out. That soon became glaringly apparent.

Keith and family arrived for a long visit. They stayed in Dad's travel trailer in the orchard, which was still far too close to the house to suit me. Dad warned me they were coming and that I'd have to put up with it. He was apologetic, barely.

Keith and the little woman mostly sat outside and smoked while toddler Hannah played with Dagne and Sophie. In the rec room, I sat on the couch watching them play. My eye caught the awkwardly-placed calendar on the far wall, the one hung too low near the fireplace. It covered a dent in the wood paneling. The one left when I missed Keith's ugly face with the no. 9 pool ball. It always gave me a small sense of satisfaction to see it, because to dent hardwood over sheetrock, breaking a pool ball in half in the process, took a powerful throw. But at the same time it was a reminder of my failure, because I missed.

My nerves dissected one by one. Besides the constant stress of living under my parents' roof I was now forced once again to sit at the dinner table with the one who took my childhood. My stomach churned. The food was bitter, but only for me. The atmosphere was tense, but only for me. Everyone else was oblivious. Keith didn't act any better or worse; he didn't need to. To me, everything he did was obscene. The way he mumbled instead of talked, the way he sat there like a huge hairy lump, the way he teased his little girl. That was the worst – the way he treated his helpless daughter. I couldn't stand it.

One day that spring while I made lunch for the kids, Hannah played outside with Sophie. I was only half-watching them since there was very little danger in the back yard. Then I heard crying and looked out to see Hannah sprawled on the grass. She had taken a header from the tiny slide, probably trying to copy Sophie's gymnastic antics. I looked around, but neither Keith nor his girlfriend were visible. Dad and Carol weren't anywhere to be seen, either. Not even Lillie.

Only little Sophie, looking at me through the window in consternation. Hannah continued to lie on the grass, wailing.

I went to her and said, "Are you okay?" hoping she would say yes, forget all about it, and go back to playing. Instead, she lifted her tear-stained face and reached out her chubby arms to me.

If it had been any of my other nieces or nephews, related by blood or convention, I would have scooped them up before even asking the question. If it had been a child at daycare I would not have hesitated. Even if it had been a child I had never laid eyes on before who fell at the park, I would have instinctively stepped in, wiping away tears, checking for injuries. But this was the child of the enemy. The only thing I felt for her was a faint sort of pity.

But she was a little girl, crying.

Picking her up nearly put my back out, she was so heavy, but I carried her inside and wiped her face with a wet washcloth. One popsicle later and she was back to playing.

Only then did Keith appear at the bottom of the kitchen stairs. He had seen what happened.

"Thanks for being sociable," he mumbled. And I knew he meant it.

"That's all you're going to get," I replied evenly. And I meant it too.

Without Craig I would have gone mad. My nerves were constantly at the breaking point.

Craig wanted to keep our relationship secret from the kids for now and I agreed. Even without any experience with children and not even able to remember which kid went with which name, he knew this would be a burden for them. "I don't want them to think badly of their mother," he said.

We met whenever possible, wherever possible – stolen moments at the coffee shop, in the park. He seduced me over a series of months: slowly, tenderly, beautifully. I was surprised at the tenderness. Craig always appeared cool and ruthless, at least when it came to women. But not so with me.

He said he had waited for me twenty years. He said I was "the one," that he knew it when he first saw me. He knew it again at my wedding. Even Vicki saw it and told him as such, though he denied it at the time. When our paths crossed yet again, exactly when it needed to happen, we both knew.

I scarcely dared to believe it, because he was so important to me. As emotion drained from me in every other aspect, my new feelings for Craig replaced the emptiness. The night he held me and whispered, "I love you," for the first time, I knew I was finally where I was meant to be.

When we made love, I sometimes didn't know where I was, or where I ended and he began. It transcended everything. We were perfectly matched, perfectly in tune. It was the mutual dream become real, and reality was meaningless in comparison.

Chapter 23

~Emancipation~

Looking at house listings again, I noticed one I had passed over at least twice before. A tiny black and white photo in the paper with this vague description: "Grandma and Grandpa got a condo! Check out this beauty before it's gone! $132,000." And that was it except for the address. I nearly skipped it again, figuring it was going to be a remodeling nightmare or have *some*thing horribly wrong with it for that price.

But I kept coming back to it. With the ad circled, I went to Craig, asking him to find this place and check it out for me. I didn't want to get my hopes up again only to have them crushed. Besides, I had no idea where it was located. It was in some far-flung area of Tacoma I had never heard of.

He called soon after. "It's your house," he said.

"Are you kidding?"

"No," he said firmly. "It's yours. I already told the owners." Craig had insights like I did and this was one of them. He said just upon seeing it from the street, he knew it was the one.

"Can I at least see it before making an offer?"

"No. You're wasting time."

But Craig collected me from an agreed upon location and drove me to "my" house. Seeing the outside I was dubious. It was a simple 1950s contemporary. The neighborhood was an island of middle-class prosperity surrounded by rundown, edgy rentals and questionable businesses. No wonder I never ventured here before. I had only skirted the edges, on the highways that crisscrossed the city. And I didn't get any vibes seeing this house now.

But upon entering, everything changed. It was exactly the right size, had a good traffic flow, natural lighting, a nice layout in the kitchen, *and* – a smooth-top range. Craig had not mentioned that. It wasn't a craftsman of course, but I had had my bungalow. It was time to move on. This felt right.

Standing in the middle of the living room, I remarked I could sit there, watch TV, and still see the kids play in both the front and back yards.

"That's exactly what I did with my four children," remarked the woman. They were the original owners and raised their children here.

"Oh, that's how many I have: four," I said.

She looked at her husband and back at me.

"This really is your house," she admitted, nodding to Craig in acknowledgment. Craig smiled with quiet satisfaction, as he always did when proved correct. It was a charming trait as long as I was not the one being proved wrong.

We set a move-in date of July 1st. The kids and I had lived with Dad and Carol for exactly six months, which was about seven months too long as far as he was concerned. Lillie noted, "Papa loves us, but in small doses."

Beyond informing me this would be a cash transaction and to make sure the house was "big enough," Dad extracted only two promises from me:

~I was never to take out a mortgage.

~Brian was never to live there.

The first promise never entered my mind and the second was even more unimaginable.

My father had saved me once again. He was the ultimate provider but so matter-of-fact about it, never calling it a loan, never lording it over me or mentioning it to others. He only asked that I keep up the place. I promised with the best of intentions.

That same summer, I dropped off Dagne and Sophie with my cousin Laurie to stay for a few days while I went to a business conference, my first. I already left Lillie and Chloe with their uncle Eric. This way everyone had cousins their age to play with.

Brian called my cell phone.

"Chris is dead."

I was standing with Laurie on her front porch, going over last-minute details. I struggled to take in what Brian was saying.

"What do you mean?"

He sounded far away, like he was in a dream. I hoped he was just stoned and talking out of his head. But he continued in the same far-away voice:

"They found him on the floor. They think he didn't mean to…he didn't know how much he took."

In a rare, calm moment much later, I asked Brian why he started meth, knowing what would happen. "I had to keep up with Chris," he smiled and shrugged, almost apologetically.

Chris. Even then, I couldn't hate him. He was Brian's best friend and brother. To Eric, he was another brother. To Joan, a son. Our children called him Uncle Chris. Even his ex-wife, who finally fled the insanity like I did, still loved him. There for every birthday, every special event, Brian's best man, an expected component of family gatherings. He brought me flowers for no reason, wrote hilarious letters from his adventures in Europe, gave me pearl earrings for my birthday because I once mentioned I'd always wanted some.

Christopher. My friend.

No good-bye.

A week later I held Brian's hand at the memorial service while he quietly sobbed. I felt like I was holding the hand of a little boy who was lost and couldn't find his way home.

We had a mandatory sales meeting with a visiting vice-president of the company. There she stood, tall and self-assured. She said to us – the unbelievers – that she wasn't always this way. Years of relentless work made it happen. And honesty. And integrity. It was what you'd expect from a business diva, but she caught me off-guard with her next remark:

"People will lie to you. People will leave you. Don't let that change who you are."

She was referring to co-workers and clients, and did not speak with bitterness or even sadness, but from experience. I had a gut-feeling I needed to remember this, but couldn't imagine why.

Amber was my teenage niece, my brother Paul Mathias' daughter. She was part of a package deal – when he married her mother, Amber had just turned three. Because we tend to seek out the same type of people in our relationships, Amber resembled Paul, even though there was no genetic connection.

Like his father adopted Sharon as his own, Paul adopted Amber. The Mathias family is that way – they want things legal and permanent. I always felt a bond with this niece and attributed that to adoption. When his wife later fell into the drug lifestyle, Paul divorced her and got sole custody of the children, including Amber, because she was legally his. When he remarried and had more children she remained the eldest daughter.

Once we had a professional portrait done of all the grandchildren as a gift to Pamela and Jim, and I drove my kids and Amber to the studio. Looking at the completed product, I noticed how well she blended in.

"You just fit in, Amber. You were meant to be here," I said. She smiled. I wish someone had said that to me once while growing up. All I heard was, "You're so *white*, Noelle!"

I had been warned by Pamela that while Amber's mother's family was "okay," her birth father's family was downright bad. And that we were to protect Amber from them, even hiding her if necessary. So one day when I had a strong premonition about her, I called Paul's house. His new wife – Amber's step-mother – answered, sounding anxious.

"I just had a bad feeling about Amber. Is she okay?"

"She's gone."

"What do you mean 'gone'?"

"She ran away. Left in the middle of the night. And we think she's gone to her father's." If my sister-in-law found it suspicious that I knew something had happened, she didn't say and I couldn't explain it anyway.

Immediately upon hanging up, I went to my online moms' group, asking them to pray for my niece's protection. She was not quite seventeen, and had fled the security of her legal and spiritual father's home for God-knows-what. I knew there was friction between her and her new step-mom, but didn't know if that was enough to make Amber bolt or if it was something else. But that she was running to her birth father's family and not even her mother's was disquieting.

I thought of her often, but she was "gone," as my sister-in-law said.

I heard later, through Pamela, that she was still in Tacoma and did indeed connect with her birth father's family. A few years after that, Pamela said Amber called at Christmastime, wanting to say how much she and Jim meant to her as grandparents and how sorry she was for taking off. Pamela took some solace in that, but the wounds were deep, because they had tried so hard to protect her and she chose her other family over them.

I always hoped to run into her somewhere, but our paths never crossed. Paul was silent on that and any other subject and I didn't want to bring it up, so just prayed she was okay. Still, I wondered what she found. A sense of belonging? A genetic history? I thought of my own birth father, how we never met, how I couldn't find much reason to like him, and yet felt a connection. I hoped at least that much for her: A sense of belonging, a connection.

My sister Heather Havner came to the door that summer. I saw her every so often, whenever she was in town for an extended stay. Her employer had given her an apartment but the project was over, so she was moving on. She stood on my front porch clutching a shopping bag stuffed with clothes. She wanted me to have them. I was touched, said thank you.

"Do you want to see my house?" I said, brightly. She had never been over before and I was excited to show her.

But she glanced around, almost furtively. "No, no I – don't have time. I only wanted to drop these off."

"Oh. Okay," I said, a little disappointed, but asked her to let me know her new address when settled.

I think she agreed to that. I couldn't imagine her doing anything else. We said good-bye, a casual "Bye."

I didn't think anything of it.

The timing belt on my old minivan was starting to shred. Fortunately it did not break altogether, because it started to come apart while the kids and I were on the freeway, halfway to my sister-in-law Stephanie's place. A kind passer-by helped then, cautioning me to get it replaced as soon as possible.

So of course I took it to Dad. But after an hour in his shop, he returned to the house, shaking.

"I can't do it," he said simply. "I can't get it out."

"What do you mean?" I asked, perplexed. My father could fix anything. I swore he could repair a car by osmosis, by just sweeping his hands over the engine. But he said:

"Ask your brother."

Who, John? Carol's son Tom? My brother-in-law Eric? None of them were mechanically inclined, at least not in practical things like cars.

"Your brother, the mechanic."

I realized he meant Paul Mathias.

I called Paul, apologizing, knowing everyone asked him for help anytime something was broken. He already helped me by moving some of the heavier furniture in and had slipped me $100 cash the Christmas prior, knowing I was flat broke. When I tried to protest then he put his hand on mine, the way Craig had done, and quietly said, "Let me help you." Now he said he'd come over and take a look at my minivan. I cautioned him that it would be a tough job, since my father the car god wasn't able to handle it.

Fifteen minutes after Paul arrived, the new belt was on.

"How did you do that?" I asked, incredulously. "Dad tried for an hour."

He gave me a sympathetic look.

"Just tell him I had a hard time with it."

My father, master at his trade, *the* mechanic of the area, the one people trusted and admired, willing to do business with no one else...could no longer work on cars. I was quietly devastated. Dad was the one who took care of people, especially those who were alone in some way: bachelors, widows and the like. He stood in the gap, looked out for them as a son would. But now all those people were gone and Dad was their age. I hadn't noticed the passing of time. Or, to be honest, I couldn't think of Dad as old.

Brian lost his job – the best and highest-paying job he ever had. He was, as our pastor said, high maintenance. It didn't take long until he also lost his car and apartment. For awhile he slept in a rundown van. Then it got too cold. In supreme irony, the only one who would take him in was my brother John, the one my mother-in-law had called a shit, blaming him for Brian's drug addiction. She'd never dream of blaming Chris, the golden child. But I didn't blame Chris, either. I blamed Brian. He was a grown man – he made his own choices.

So he went to live with his former brother-in-law and looked for work between bouts of insanity. I took this to mean I was supposed to work even harder, and put in more hours. Determined to not only support my children but to give them a good life, I strived for a manager position. That way I would earn higher commissions. It wouldn't be easy but I was determined.

I worked like mad to prove myself. The promotion interview was set for March 31ˢᵗ. I felt good about it. Felt good about myself.

That last weekend of March, Brian went off his meds. He had been out of work so long he could no longer afford them. Needless to say, he also had no money for child support.

Craig had a crisis of his own and decided he was too old for me, telling me so in an online chat, completely unaware of what else was going on and the pressure I was under.

The upper-level manager called. "We really like you and all, but…" I couldn't hear the rest. I don't know what else she said.

Early morning April 1ˢᵗ I had my second nervous breakdown. And even in the midst of it I knew I was the April Fool.

For three days all I could do was crouch in the shower and sob. Other than that, I passed off my haggard appearance as suffering from a migraine. I couldn't eat. I couldn't sleep. I had lost everything. I was a failure on all levels, completely shattered.

I knew then why it is called "broken hearted," because it feels like someone is slowly twisting your heart out of your chest, over and over. I pressed my hands to my breastbone but nothing could stop the pain.

I considered suicide. The only thing that stopped me was knowing I couldn't leave my children, that I was responsible for them.

I emailed Cecelia, who was vacationing in Europe. All she could say was, "I'm sorry. I'm so sorry." I told no one else.

The pain was endless, and just like the sunny April sky would suddenly turn black and pour cold rain, the pain returned again and again. Depression is cold like that. Even sunlight is cold. Noises are too loud. Focus too sharp. There is no escape. No dusk, no dawn. Only night and glaring midday. I felt constantly attacked from all sides.

On the third day, Craig called. Repeatedly. I didn't answer. I didn't think I could stand to hear his voice, knowing it was over. But he was persistent. Finally, I picked up.

He said he wanted to talk.

"About what?" thinking he wanted back all the gifts he had given me.

"Come have coffee with me," he said.

I met him in our usual haunt. I was shaking, in part from hunger. He talked, but I barely heard him. And he apparently couldn't see me, really see me as I was at that moment. He was too wrapped up in what he was saying, which translated to, "I was having a moment of doubt. I didn't mean what I said."

So it wasn't over. I was too exhausted to feel anything. But I steeled myself that day. I would never take Craig at his word again. I would always wait, see how it played out. I couldn't stand to be hurt like that even once more. And damn it, if he did ever leave me, it wasn't going to kill me. I loved him, but I wouldn't die for him to prove it.

Since Brian had so much time on his hands, he reignited his campaign to win me back. The fact that we were divorced seemed lost on him. He lost his job, in part, because of an email exchange we had while he was at work. I demanded he finally start a new bank account (one that did not have my name attached) and he balked. Or, I should say, he lied.

First he said he couldn't come in during business hours. Then he said he needed a minimum amount of money before he could start a new account. Then he needed a physical address and not a PO box like he was using. I called the bank to ask about these things. None were true.

"Damn you, Brian. Stop lying," I shot off at my computer. He then wrote back that he just broke down sobbing at his desk, that he was only trying to hold onto things that were "ours" and that I was cruel. *I* was cruel? I thought him bringing ruin to our lives and making me drag him kicking and screaming through divorce proceedings was cruel.

On his next payday I went to our old bank alone. There were already overdrafts though it wasn't even noon. I told the teller I was there to close the account. She said I would need to cover these overdrafts first. Jaw clenched I said if I paid for all that it would be literally taking food out of my children's mouths, because I was paying with the child support money.

She visibly softened. She took the overdraft fees off and let me pay for just the actual debits. She asked if there were any automatic withdrawals coming soon? I replied if so, my ex would have to deal with it. I then closed the account. With very little cash but a very clear conscience, I walked out.

This would happen again and again, where I had to pick up the pieces of Brian's latest disaster. He must have subconsciously been relying on me to do it, but resented me for it as well.

Now that he was "free" from employment, he could devote himself to waging psychological warfare. I stupidly allowed him to come to the house, since there was really nowhere else he could go, to spend time with the kids. I figured it was the safest place. Whenever he was there I would make myself scarce, with work, with errands, with Craig.

While with the kids, Brian repeatedly tried to corral them into a plot to "win me back." The breaking point came when I found a long, graphic love letter left on my bed. I emailed him:

"Let me make this perfectly clear: I nearly vomited reading your letter. Our marriage is over. OVER. Any more letters will go through the children for approval. I will not be reading them."

Brian still didn't know about Craig. Few did. We preferred to keep our relationship secret. It was easier than explaining. And I didn't feel I should have to explain.

Lillie, however, knew. I asked Craig if I could tell her. She needed to know there were men in the world she could count on, having become so disillusioned at a young age. He hesitantly agreed. When the three of us met in a coffee shop, we all relaxed.

Craig was as mysterious to Lillie as all my children were to him. She had never met anyone like him and he never really knew any children or teens, except when he was one himself. He pretended not to care, but would occasionally drive past my house while I was at work, just to check on them. Once he saw Sophie climbing a tree and called me, alarmed. I asked what was wrong.

"She was *hanging* there!"

"Yes…?"

"Like a flag!"

If he expected *Little Women* he had the wrong family. Even Jo March's feistiness paled in comparison. My daughters were warriors, not princesses. They were messy, loud and fearless, but also caring and polite when called for. The neighbors were rather in awe of them, but then so was I.

The kids always enjoyed rough and tumble fun with their dad, but one day when Brian was here all they wanted to do was watch TV. Brian needed to withdraw cash for the child support and asked them to walk with him to the ATM but inexplicably, none of them wanted to go. Instead he drove the short distance alone.

Meanwhile, the Cosmos was setting me up once again. Craig and I had gone out for breakfast and afterwards I developed a crushing headache. Instead of continuing our day I said I needed to go home. He drove me to my car, which I had left in a nearby parking lot. The same one with an ATM, where Brian was now withdrawing cash.

As Craig and I embraced and kissed our good-byes, I felt rather than saw Brian looking at us. I turned to see his car slowly pulling out of the parking lot.

"That's Brian. He saw us."

"Are you sure he saw us?"

Yes, I was sure. I felt it in the pit of my stomach. Brian and I arrived at my house simultaneously. Crying, hardly able to speak, he counted out the child support money.

"I would have done anything. Anything," he choked out.

"Brian, I didn't want to hurt you, but it's over." Alarmed at his appearance I added cautiously, "The kids need you."

"I would never do that to them."

Really? Because I would, I thought. If I believed my children were better off with me dead, I would kill myself.

It didn't take long for him to twist the revelation of "Noelle and Craig" into something he could use against me. I took all the kids to a park one day. As the younger ones played, Lillie confided, "Dad told me the reason you broke up was because of Craig."

I felt myself go cold.

"He said what?"

"He said the reason you got divorced was so you could be with Craig."

"How did he know *you* knew about Craig?"

"He didn't. He thought he was telling us."

"*Us* who?"

"Me and Chloe."

Furious but trying not to show it, I called Chloe over. We sat on a park bench far away from the play area.

I explained how it all came to be. The drugs, the bi-polar condition, losing everything.

"I want you to know there was never anyone else, for either of us. I was faithful to your dad and as far as I know he was faithful to me. Craig and I did not get involved until it was over. I never want you to worry about that."

I wanted to tell them that their father had a mistress named Meth but saved my venom for Brian. The opportunity presented itself soon after. He asked to meet at an outdoor café so he could make certain confessions, as part of his narc-anon therapy. I found it ironic that he was going through the motions when he had no intention of getting off the drugs. Still, I sat and listened while he read his self-serving list. When finished he started to get up, very nobly.

"I have a few things to say," I snapped. Startled, he sat down again.

"Using Craig as the reason I left you is a filthy lie and you know it."

He started to stammer a protest.

"Don't you *ever* talk about me to the kids like that again. I don't allow anyone to speak badly about you to them and I expect the same in return."

He could only stare at me with that deer-in-the-headlights look. But behind the blank expression, he was no doubt plotting. He wouldn't give up that easily.

Kim-chi, our faithful, bedraggled Siamese, would no longer use the litter box. She did not appear sick, but it's always a bad sign when cats won't go where they're supposed to. I couldn't afford a vet, so asked about it online.

Friends sadly suggested kidney failure but said a special (expensive) diet would lessen the pain and prolong her life. I couldn't afford a special cat diet. I couldn't even afford to have her put down. I hated my life.

Kim-chi was a constant component for the kids. She had always been there, being the same age as Lillie. She moved along with us to Dad's and then to the new house. She greeted me every morning when I came downstairs and curled up in my lap as I drank my coffee at the computer. "Meh," she would say as I stroked her silky fur.

The morning I had the money to pay for the deed, I told the kids it was time to say good-bye. They all cried and petted Kim-chi, who howled when I put her in the cat carrier. She continued to howl all the way to the Humane Society.

With tears running down my face I signed the death warrant. She cried piteously as they took her to the back. I could almost hear screaming, "You promised! You promised it was forever!" like I thought I could understand my cats when I was a child. Now instead I was disposing of her like inconvenient trash. She went silent.

Outside, I clutched the empty cat carrier to my chest and sobbed. I had failed her. She saved Lillie's life and now in thanks I snuffed hers out, when I should have made sure she lived out her days in comfort.

The next morning there was no cat to greet me at the foot of the stairs. No cat on my lap at the computer. I hated myself. I prayed for Kim-chi to forgive me, but why would she? I was a liar.

My brother John was also unemployed, and had been for quite some time. In construction it's feast or famine. He moved from his rundown rental into something barely better with his current insane girlfriend, Robin. We barely heard from him during this time. But he always remembered my birthday. He was one of the few who did. That year I received an unexpected greeting:

"Robin kicked me out. I need to move in with you."

That was all. No preamble, no request. Just letting me know.

He never did say, "Happy birthday," by the way.

Our just-big-enough house was suddenly crowded. John took the bonus room in the basement and for the most part kept to that part of the house. He was depressed from his long unemployment but since he's so quiet by nature it was difficult to tell. I liked having him around. It felt safer knowing he was there at night. And I was used to his idiosyncrasies. So I didn't see a problem.

But while I was accustomed to living with John, the kids were not. He had always been their "Silly Uncle John" who loved watching cartoons and always gave them money for their birthdays and Christmas. But now he was living with them, and even though he was quiet, he definitely cramped their style.

Over that winter a severe influenza was going around. I caught it, then Craig and also his mother. When I was barely recovered I went between work, Craig's apartment, and his mother's house, trying to care for everyone and everything. I felt responsible because they got it from me.

What I couldn't see, was that in relying on the kids to look after themselves, I had isolated them with John, who was clinically depressed. One day he snapped at Chloe – something about her not having any friends because she was weird. Chloe, an instant friend to anyone she met. Her sisters immediately came to her defense but the damage was done. They never looked at their uncle John the same way again. And they resented him living with us.

When Lillie told me, I reminded her that John was unemployed and depressed but that I would talk to him about it. I told him he was out of line and not to talk to any of the kids like that again. He apologized, but just to me, not to the kids. I thought it was over. When I looked at John or thought of him, he was my brother – the little blonde boy with the shy smile, my faithful playmate. Not a cranky uncle I had to live with.

I failed Chloe that day. I should have made John apologize to her personally, but I didn't. I should have kicked him out, but I didn't. He and the kids settled into a cold war truce. It was never the same after that and it was my fault.

Brian eventually found a job, in Kansas. He had high hopes, as always, and promised the kids the moon for Christmas. First, they were each getting an expensive gift. Then, something less so. Then, just something practical. Finally, he told me he was sending one gift for all of them to share and would I wrap it for him? I rolled my eyes.

When the box came I found a cheap DVD player. ("I got a deal on it!" Brian exclaimed, as if I'd be proud of him for pulling the rug out from under the kids, again.) He seemed to forget we had no DVD's, only VHS tapes. Or he knew full well and just wanted to make things harder for me, knowing I couldn't afford to replace them. I went to find Craig so I wouldn't blow up in front of the kids.

"What are they supposed to do? Gather around and *look* at that thing Christmas morning? He knows they think he's sending something great. What am I supposed to say to them? How was I so *stupid* to have this man as the father of my children?!" I raged.

Craig said, "Let me take care of it," and gently took the box from me. I had no idea what he could do other than return it for something even cheaper, not having a receipt. I tried to concoct a story, so the kids would not think even less of their dad when they got nothing from him, instead of the elaborate gifts they had been promised.

Christmas morning, I woke to the kids indeed staring at a package mysteriously left under the tree. Beautifully wrapped in gold foil, the tag read: "To the cubs. From your father." I swore it looked exactly like Brian's printing. Another gift was next to it, which said, "To Mom. From Santa."

The kids gleefully opened the package and found an expensive combination DVD/VHS player, along with the latest Pixar blockbuster that had just been released.

"Look what Daddy got us! What did you get, Mommy?" I opened my box to find a beautiful new robe.

"You know what I think?" said Dagne in conspiratorial tones. "I think Santa is *Daddy*." I could only nod, then quietly slipped into the bathroom so they wouldn't see me cry.

When I asked Craig later, he said he could only get store credit for the return, so gave the voucher to his mother and bought the rest of it himself. When I asked how he knew about the movie, he said he saw it displayed and figured the kids would like it. (They watched it three times that day.) Of course he had a house key for emergencies and was as stealthy as a ninja so I knew how he got in. Finally I asked how he made his printing look like Brian's but he only shrugged. Magicians do not divulge their secrets.

I don't know if Craig realized that he not only saved Christmas for the kids but also saved face for Brian. He never brought it up, never mentioned it again. He was my hero.

Brian soon sent another letter. A permission slip, giving me carte blanche to have a relationship with Craig for the time being. I didn't know if I should laugh or scream. Craig just shrugged.

"Sooner or later he'll realize you're divorced. Don't worry about it."

I hoped he would find someone, but first he needed to get clean. He was more and more unyielding in personality – still grappling for control – yet the wild bi-polar effects were in full swing. I was grateful he was so far away that there was little opportunity for interaction between him and the kids. He was a stranger to them at that point.

While in church confirmation class, Lillie was asked to write a one word description of her parents. She didn't need time to think about it.

"Dad: Fragile. Mom: Hard-working." This devastated me. No one should have to think of their father as "fragile". Even "crazy" would have been better.

I confided in my online moms' group. I would often vent about Brian, just to get it out. I didn't want the kids to know, so this was a safe place.

But one day, a newer member (a rather strange one) wrote that she prayed for the restoration of my marriage and forgiveness of my sin of adultery. *Excuse me?* I replied I'd sooner put a bullet through my head than reconcile with my ex. Others came to my defense, asking her what her problem was. She said she had been talking to another member privately, this is what they believed, and she felt compelled to tell me for the sake of my immortal soul.

Again, the others were outraged. I tried to reason with her, saying while I hope she gets her heart's desire (reconciliation with her own husband) that I had absolutely no interest, that the very idea made me ill, and that the kids were better off in a "broken" home where their mother was happy, than living a lie.

Brian came home for a visit – something he couldn't afford, but when had that ever stopped him? In a private moment he asked how I was getting along. I said I was fine. He said sarcastically:

"I guess it's better you're happy than living a lie."

We locked eyes. I stepped back. We both knew, but said nothing. I contacted the moderator of the online group, asking if I could look at the membership rolls. Scrolling through the hundreds of ID's, I came across just one that made me suspicious: "CherishNow". This individual had never posted to the list, never made an introduction, and had joined only a month before. I asked the moderator to edit the membership to "no mail," thus keeping their identification while stopping the flow of messages.

The next time we spoke, Brian assured me how happy *he* was, that he was starting a new life and the kids would be able to stay with him months at a time.

"Cherish now, that's my motto," I said.

"What?" his expression changing from smug to startled.

"Cherish now," I said again. "Don't you agree?"

This time he stepped back while I stared at him evenly, never breaking eye contact. *Don't threaten me with our children,* I thought, in an attempt to telepathically bore the message into his addled brain. *Do not underestimate what I would do.*

Chapter 24
~Mangled Time~

I figured it was time to bring Craig into the open. When I told Dagne and Sophie, Sophie was unfazed but Dagne dramatically begged, "Promise you'll never get married!" She just couldn't handle any more change. But after getting to know him, she revised her stance:

"If you love Craig so much, why doesn't he live here?"

"Where would he stay?"

"Right *there*," she said, pointing to the only open space in the entire living room.

"I think he needs more room than that."

"No. All you need is love. Love…and pizza."

Regardless, he didn't move in. He had no desire to give up what at least looked like the single life, or his aesthetically perfect apartment. And I had no desire to marry again. We had very different ways of doing things. Living together would have been the end of our relationship. The only downside was, I think Brian took our lack of official commitment to mean it was temporary.

I told Dad and Carol I was seeing someone. They visibly tensed. I said, "He's nothing like Brian." They relaxed.

I brought Craig over. After five minutes of conversation over coffee, Craig said to Dad, "Enough chit-chat. Where are those cars?" and they were immediate friends. Craig wasn't a mechanic, but had an incredible store of knowledge about cars. He even knew factoids about the Chrysler that Dad didn't. He could tell at a glance what make, model, and year nearly any vehicle was.

"How can you possibly know it's a '54 and not a '55, or anything else?" I asked once, after a car I could only recognize as "a car" whizzed by.

"Can't you see the grill is different? I thought your father was a mechanic," he chided.

As for his part, Dad could scarcely believe Craig was not only an artist, but earned a living as one. They were very different, Dad and Craig, but they shared a calm demeanor, liked watching the same sports, and agreed on most things. Dad and Carol did not know about his wild youth and I did not enlighten them. They really relaxed when I mentioned we were not interested in marriage. Funny how in just one generation's time society became so ambivalent on that subject.

After the bout of flu, I had lingering symptoms, mainly a cough I couldn't shake and a pain in my side. Craig figured out later that I had thrown a rib out from the violent coughing episodes. All I knew was I was exhausted. Talking to Carol on the phone one day, I mentioned this and she said brightly, "Maybe you're pregnant!" Unable to even form a response I ended the call.

Livid, I told Craig.

"That's the same thing my mom said," he responded.

Now I was angry at both our mothers. I had been pregnant *five times*, I was pretty sure I knew the symptoms, none of which include coughing. To have these post-menopausal women (one of whom never experienced pregnancy) suggest I could be expecting and not have the mental capacity to figure it out infuriated me.

I left Craig's mother to him, but I emailed Carol:

"Never again suggest I might be pregnant. I know I married the wrong man, and I wish I could have a child with Craig but that is never going to happen. It hurts to hear you say that, so *don't*."

She quickly apologized and never brought it up again. One of my insights told me if I did not have a child with Craig by the time I was forty-five it would never happen. The day I turned forty-six was bitter-sweet.

I had many dreams during this bout of depression. This was by far the most disturbing:

I entered Craig's apartment. I was in my early twenties, he in his late thirties. He pulled me into his arms but I did not respond. He stepped back, took me by the shoulders and smiled.

"I thought you said you would only have an abortion if you hated the father."

"I do hate you," I replied, my voice cold, my heart dead.

This is why I could never have a child with Craig, why I could not let that happen. In others dreams we had a son. A brilliant, artistic, wonderful son. But he had to stay there in my dreamscape to be safe. He was from another reality, one that could not happen, one I could not allow to happen.

After the second breakdown, I did not bounce back like after the first. Any little thing would shove me back into depression. Not an overwhelming depression like at the beginning, but one that co-existed with the life everyone could see. I was always tired and edgy and had an unusually short fuse. It felt like swimming with heavy weights on my legs. Above the surface I was swimming – that's what people saw. Below the surface I was at risk of drowning if I ever stopped kicking, even for an instant. This went on for years.

In the Age of Disorders, where every quirk or trait had to be named, I gamely decided to call what I had Chronic High-Functioning Depression. I couldn't completely get rid of it, but for the most part it did not overtly affect my life. Or so I thought.

September is usually one of my favorite months. The weather is perfect and while others go back to their fall routines, the kids and I reap the benefits of not being tied to a school schedule. But this particular September was different. I tried to explain to Cecelia that it was almost like an out-of-body experience, like everything was happening to someone else. And time was moving differently but only for me.

I started having exhausting dreams but couldn't remember them. They haunted me, becoming so powerful I couldn't get out of bed upon waking. Instead I would lie there, staring at the ceiling with tears running down my face, overwhelmed. With what, I did not know.

For the first several hours each morning, all I could do was contemplate death. Not suicide, not that I thought I was dying, but the reality of death. And I couldn't stop. I could barely function until nearly one in the afternoon. Before that I was dragging, unable to shake off the heavy spiritual weight.

By mid-September the dreams were so strong I dreaded going to sleep. All I could remember later were the emotions: Anger, despair, and regret. Mainly regret. What was I regretting? Why couldn't I work this out? I had flashes of visions: Talking with someone important to me, but not recognizing who they were once I was awake. In the dream I knew them, but in "real" life I saw only shadows.

I am usually a morning person while the kids are all night-owls. Before the dreams started, it was a perfect arrangement because I could have my quiet time and get a lot accomplished before they even had breakfast. Now I rose later and later, drained by the nocturnal "sessions".

"Mommy?" said an unfamiliar voice. I was in the midst of conversation. It was important. I couldn't see who interrupted.

"Mommy," the small voice said again. How could someone so small be next to my ear, and why couldn't I see her?

I opened my eyes, although I thought I already had them open. Everything was sideways. I was falling. No, when I closed my eyes now, I was standing. When I opened them in this new place I was lying in bed.

I looked at a little girl I didn't recognize, in a room I didn't recognize.

Don't panic. Don't react. She thinks I'm her mother. Maybe if I answer I can go back.

"What?" I said, as casually as possible, my own voice strange to me.

"I *said*, Can I play on the computer?"

What is a computer?

"Alright," I answered, and she trotted off into a hallway. I stared after her, then closed my eyes again and straddled the two realities, afraid to move.

Is this insanity? Think! Who are you? Where are you? When is this happening? Was I thrown forward in time? Or back?

Suddenly I was released and felt myself fall onto the bed, only I was already on it. I knew then where I was and who I was and that I had been speaking with my own daughter Sophie.

But who was I before? Who was I talking to and what was I so desperately trying to resolve? Was I losing my mind or was I channeling someone, and if the latter, *why?*

I told no one.

I do not believe in channeling, by the way. Living this close to JZ Knight's compound has provided enough exposure of her "gift" for me to disbelieve everything about it. But I do not know another term for what I experienced. I was someone else in my sleep. Someone I didn't know. And it was so overpowering that upon being "interrupted" (awakened) I didn't recognize my own "real" existence.

The dreams tapered off after that, but did not completely leave me until after New Years. I could never remember them.

Now time was completely mangled. To this day, I cannot recall the chain of events, only bits and pieces, like a puzzle taken apart and strewn across the floor. Although I carried on in my day-to-day life, anything "extra" would overwhelm me. I held myself together for work, smiling and pretending everything was fine, when all I wanted to do was crawl into a dark room and sleep. I was invariably exhausted after being forced to socialize at work, at church, even holiday get-togethers. I had nothing left for Craig or the kids.

I was someone else, someone I didn't recognize or like. A simmering anger was always with me, just under the surface. I would force it down knowing the delay was temporary, that the rage would have to come out. Fatigue made it worse because I didn't have the strength to fight it. Some little thing would set me off and I'd completely lose control.

I do not remember specifics, but once I screamed at Lillie to never have children. She made me angry about something and that was my response: *Don't have children, Lillie. Never have children!* I'm still shocked when I think of it.

My linear memory shredded, I tried again and again to recall certain moments, to make sense of them, but it was a mess I couldn't put back together. I missed so much during this time. And in doing so I failed those closest to me, most importantly my children. There was a disconnect I was not aware of as it happened, and when I finally re-emerged, they were older and changed. I'll never get that time back. It is my greatest regret.

There was also despair. Dad always like my cousin Britt, who no doubt reminded him of Lillian. At Britt's wedding, I sucked in my breath at the sight of her – she never resembled her aunt more than on that day: tall, elegant, confident. But it wasn't just that. She did everything Dad thought a woman should do. She had a career, bought land in her own name, married late, had just two children and when they were school age, went back to work full-time while still managing her properties. She settled in Cedarlake so she saw Dad and Carol often. More often than I could.

Dad would talk about Britt's farm, how she handled everything with aplomb, how her boys were so well-behaved, even after Britt and her husband divorced. I acknowledged this, because it was true, but still dug my nails into my palms. Carol looked to her for advice on various subjects, including computers, when Britt knew precious little about them. When I had tried to offer help on the same subject, I was flat-out ignored but whatever Britt said was gold. They relied on her. *Like a daughter.*

I tried not to let it bother me. It was only natural, I told myself. Clarence and Evelyn were both gone so Britt turned to this uncle and aunt as surrogate parents and also as grandparents for her sons. And that was fine, until I found out she also vacationed with them.

Dad never said as much, but I knew he thought of Britt as the daughter he and Lillian might have had. Just like it hurt when Mom used to hold up Linda and Laurie as examples of *"What you should have been but aren't"*, Dad now unwittingly did with Britta.

I sat in the car outside the post office, tears running down my face as I wrote in his birthday card, "I'm sorry I'm not what you wanted." He never mentioned the card. Maybe he had no idea what I was referring to. Maybe it made him too uncomfortable to think about.

More often, I did not send cards or letters to anyone, or I would think I had then find them later, unfinished. In my previous life, I was the one who always remembered birthdays, the first to send a congratulatory note or gift. Now I would find the perfect card then tuck it away, forgotten.

Because it took all my strength and resolve to get through the day, I let go of relationships without even realizing it. Time had become the enemy; I was trying to walk through hip-deep mud while others ran on dry ground. I stopped calling people; I didn't want to talk with anyone, unable to deal with the angry exhaustion that overtook me.

Of course the one friend I could always count on was Cecelia. No matter how angry I was or how long it had been, she would always be there. But when the clouds finally lifted, I looked around and realized she was gone.

I emailed. I sent a gift. I sent another email. And a letter. I was worried. Finally I wrote a sappy letter saying I was praying for her. I had to know what was wrong.

But there was no explanation. There was no good-bye. Merely an email after the sappy card saying, "I'm fine. Everything's fine, thanks." Then silence.

I was closer to Cecelia than any other person in my life. As close as I imagined a sister would have been. She was a perfect friend. But then she was gone, without so much as a parting shot or backwards glance, leaving me to think it was all some mistake. That if I just reached out *enough* she would explain.

She had dumped friends before. I played witness to the fact. They had done something, said something she couldn't tolerate. But they knew when it happened. And if they came back, thinking it could be the way it was before, they were met with cool dismissal. But I never got a pink slip. As far as I knew I never violated any terms of friendship. If I did while lost in depression, I was unaware and not informed.

I had to make sense of it. I thought back to the last time I remember seeing her, speaking with her. I asked her and Craig to co-sign my will and other legal papers. She drove out of her way to meet us in the office of a notary public. She seemed uneasy, smiling wanly, as if she was there to do her duty then escape. I thought there must be something on her mind concerning work. I was always good at making excuses for people.

Now my mind went to where I didn't want it to go. I knew Cecelia had self-imposed, Kennedy-esque rules of behavior, the first and foremost being "Never tell." I had lamented to Craig more than once how he thought the worst of everyone, including Cecelia, but I was guilty of the opposite: I steadfastly believed in people.

"People will lie to you. People will leave you…" But when we were told this, we were not told *why*. It was the "why" I couldn't live with, but there was nothing to do about it.

I was never going to see Cecelia again. I wrote an addendum to my will, releasing her from all responsibility. It struck me that she had been my friend for twenty years, as long a relationship as I had with Brian. It ended very differently, but if possible this split was even more final.

My sister Sharon called about plans for a party. Then, as an afterthought or (more likely) a casual aside so not to alarm me:

"By the way, Mom had a stroke."

My heart stopped. *No,* I thought. *No. No, no, no.*

I managed to ask what happened.

Pamela and Jim went out for dinner. He noticed she was acting strangely. She went to the restroom where another woman found her on the floor, sobbing. She was taken to the hospital, where Jim called Sharon to tell her.

"Pray for your mother," he said in conclusion. She didn't realize the seriousness of the situation until he said that. He had never asked her to pray about anything or anyone before.

Tentatively, I asked how she was. "Oh, much better now. You should visit her and see."

"Where is she?"

"Saint Joe's."

No. Not there. I can't.

And like a coward, I didn't visit. My siblings did, daily. But all I could do was muster up the courage to call. I relaxed upon hearing her voice, sounding strong and sure. I told her I would visit as soon as she was home. I didn't say why. Perhaps she guessed, perhaps that's why Sharon told me the way she did.

Upon seeing her I was even more relieved. Her natural expression had not changed. There was no difference in personality. If anything she was just more serene. I prayed, "Please God, leave her this way." I was afraid of her becoming like her own mother after a series of mini-strokes, confined to a wheelchair and chronically dissatisfied. But even more, I was afraid of her being forever changed like Lillian.

I can't lose her the same way. I can't.

It was a prayer of defiance, a "Don't cross this line" sort of threat. I'm sure God could discern my panic and forgive me, but I still meant it.

Then she had another stroke. And then she had another.

I saw the last one happen. We all did. It was Thanksgiving. We spread out the holiday gatherings so we could visit with nearly everyone on "the circuit." We would see Dad and Carol next. And Brian's family (sans Brian) later that weekend. Everyone was there that day at the Mathias house.

We were having dessert. Conversation and laughter abounded. Suddenly Paul's wife said, "Pam, are you okay?" and we all turned to see her listing to one side, expression completely blank, eyes staring into nothingness. My stomach dropped. I knew that look. Sharon was already on the phone with 911 and, since we lived in the city, the paramedics were there in mere minutes. She started to feel better after having oxygen and wanted to stay home, but no one was willing to risk it. She went back to the hospital. And this time I forced myself to go.

I stood on the sidewalk outside St. Joseph Hospital, steeling myself. Told myself sternly this wasn't the same situation and there was nothing to feel tense about. It helped that the place had been remodeled since those endless days when Dad and I would visit Lillian. Although the outside looked the same, the interior was unrecognizable. I even got lost finding my way to her room.

When I finally arrived, I informed her that the other kids and I had discussed it and decided she was never allowed to be overly happy about anything ever again. From here on out, it was nothing but peace and tranquility.

"Okay," she said, and she smiled. Not a lopsided smile, but her own. *Thank God.*

Brian was fired yet again and moved yet again for another job. This time to Colorado. And within a month he was living with someone. I was always glad when he was dating because it meant he was less interested in me and what I was doing. During his last serious relationship he finally seemed to give up on me, only four years after our divorce. But still, he left that girlfriend without so much as a shrug.

This one was different. It was immediate and permanent. Only a few months later he brought her home for a visit. On Mother's Day weekend. I thought, "She must be really young and not have children," but that wasn't the case. She was older than I was and had a son older than Lillie. Then I thought, "Her mother must not be alive," but that was not true either. Finally I settled for the obvious: Brian wanted to make Mother's Day weekend all about him.

If he expected it or not, I liked Gwen. She had that Midwestern aura I admired and Brian needed: self-sufficient and family-oriented. It was obvious when I saw her why Brian was instantly drawn to her. She was a blonde version of his mother. It was downright uncanny. But the deciding factor was that she liked the kids, practically loved them on sight. And they liked her.

That Mother's Day we all went to church, with me on one end of the pew and Brian and Gwen on the other, the kids between us. It was rare now for all the girls to be there, the older ones being teens who thrived on sleep.

After the service, while Brian showed off Gwen, I shook hands with Pastor in the customary receiving line.

"It's nice to see all your children with you," he said.

"Yes, all five," I answered.

Being Norwegian, he almost smiled.

Sharon was hosting a Mother's Day afternoon barbeque. I went solo. Brian commandeered the kids, as I figured he would.

"You're here alone?" asked Paul, turning steaks on the grill.

"The kids are with Brian."

"That's…odd."

"Yes. Isn't it."

What was really "odd" was that Gwen didn't seem to find the timing of the visit unusual. She blithely went along with whatever Brian wanted to do. More evidence of his charm at work. He could make nearly anything sound like the best idea ever. Even ditching your mother and child on Mother's Day weekend.

By the end of summer they were engaged, and came out for a big family reunion. Since I was still included in all the Reid activities and someone needed to drive the kids, I was there as well. I took it upon myself to take Gwen around and introduce her to various family members, since Brian was busy socializing without her. We came upon one of Brian's nephews:

"This is your new aunt, Gwen."

"So you won't be my aunt anymore?" he asked with more hope than I would have liked.

I said, "No, now you'll have us both, so watch yourself." Gwen laughed.

The kids flew out for the wedding. I had them bring a photo album we put together. Brian had entrusted to me (or simply abandoned) all of our photos and personal papers, including those of his parents and grandparents. Now I was able to finally return those, and share copies of the best shots of the kids over the years. It was our wedding gift to them.

I truly wanted him to be happy and settled, because that meant he would be healthy, and *that* in turn meant he would be a better father to the kids.

I asked Gwen if I could call her my sister-in-law for the sake of simplicity. She said that would be fine. Once a Reid, always a Reid. I also asked if Brian was off drugs. She said yes. I had no idea when/how he beat it and was concerned he would replace one addiction with another. But I couldn't let that be my problem.

Lillie wanted to take some college classes and needed her birth certificate to enroll. I went to the buffet – part of the dining set I inherited from Pamela's parents – and reached into the drawer where I kept all our important papers. When we divorced I gave Brian his birth certificate, but I had to replace it from Vital Records twice since then. Every time he moved he needed a new one because he lost the previous copy. I had not needed any of the documents myself for a number of years.

So now I pulled the drawer open just a few inches and reached for the familiar folder in the back. It wasn't there. Pulling the drawer open completely I stared, then pawed through the empty space in disbelief. The folder was gone. Instead I found Glenn's birth certificate, Lillian's death certificate, and some old letters loose in the drawer. The kids' birth certificates, our marriage license, the divorce papers, and both of my birth certificates were gone.

My birth certificates. The official, magic, amended document with the gold seal declaring I am Noelle Ardahl. And the original, secret paper that whispers I am in fact Infant Girl Linden. The only evidence that I am two people, with claims to two sets of parents. Both impossible to replace. The original sealed, the amended now computerized, so even if I ordered another it would look nothing like the first.

I tore through the house. Every drawer, every box, every hiding place I could think of. Disbelieving the obvious, not willing to accept they could really be *gone*, I searched until there was no other possibility.

There was only one person capable of something so cruel. Someone so self-centered, desperate, and insane as to take irreplaceable documents that mattered only to me. I thought of the photo of me at our wedding, the one ripped to shreds. He considered that his, also. Anything to hurt me, to show me how much *he* hurt, was fair game.

The times I allowed him in my house while I was gone so he could see the kids – I must have been out of my mind. I know he invaded my personal space while here, leaving love letters on my bed. But I never imagined him *taking* anything. There was nothing to steal. Or so I stupidly thought.

He had moved so many times since then. He lost his own birth certificate again and again. Or at least he said he did, so I would have to replace it. Was even that a lie, so I would realize mine were gone? Was he holding them hostage? Were they a bargaining chip? So much time had gone by. Even if they weren't lost before they would be now – lost or destroyed. Gwen would have mentioned it if she had found them.

Years later, Brian had Gwen ask me for a copy of our divorce decree, because they needed it for some legal matter. Brian used Gwen as the go-between whenever possible so he wouldn't have to talk to me directly. I said the divorce decree and a lot of other important documents went missing years ago. I waited to hear some improbable story, but they never mentioned it again, never asked what exactly was gone, never asked if I found them.

People will lie to you. People will leave you... They will use you, hurt you, betray you, and they will call it "love". They will say it was for your own good, they will say it was better than the truth, they will say anything as long as it serves their purpose.

Don't let that change who you are… Why not? Why the hell not? Everyone else gets to become jaded and bitter, why not me? I hated myself, hated my belief in people.

It never stops hurting. And I fall into the trap of believing in people no matter how many times I'm burned. It's in my nature, so no one need worry about me changing. I can't.

I want to, but I can't.

I heard through the grapevine that one of the distant cousins on Lillian's side of the family was turning seventy-five. Milestone birthdays are a big deal in Scandinavian culture and this particular cousin was also a genealogist, so he relished an excuse for a family get-together. He previously connected the dots for me in an hour-long phone call, explaining his lineage and Lillian's, tying together the names I remembered so well from my early childhood – the cousins who I knew belonged, but not how.

He wanted a birthday celebration with the remaining cousins. It would be like the parties at Gramma's from decades past. I was keen to go for that reason. I stopped by Dad's to make sure they knew about the invitation.

"Did you hear about Dale Renstrom's birthday party?" I asked them.

"Who?" Carol said.

"You know, Dale. Lillian's cousin. The one who lives in Seattle."

Blank stares.

"Come on. *Dale Renstrom.* Hattie's son. You remember him."

Nothing.

"We went to his daughter's wedding together. Diane. Remember?"

"Oh sure," Carol said suddenly. Dad looked uncertain.

"Good. So you'll go?"

"Well, we don't really know him, do we?" Carol continued.

"Of course you know him. You know Christie, right?"

"Sure."

"He's her first cousin. Every time you see Christie, you see Dale. He's at every event on Gramma's side of the family. Now he's turning seventy-five and he wants us all there for his birthday."

"But...do we *know* him?"

Desperate, I turned to Dad. "Dad, Dale is Lillian's cousin. You've known him for *fifty years*." I could see him tossing it about in his mind.

"Dale?" he said.

"Yes. *Dale,*" I said, completely exasperated.

"Maybe we could send a card," Carol offered.

I gave up. I thought later I should have said, "Britt will be there," which would have guaranteed their attendance. At the party, everyone asked about Dad and Carol. I felt like saying, "They don't remember you," but just sighed.

I was used to them being capable and cognizant. I *needed* them to be capable and cognizant. But whenever one was ill or stressed or overwhelmed in any way, it spread to the other and they both acted senile. I had frustrating conversations with them, met with blank stares from Dad and nervous giggling from Carol, because they couldn't follow what I was saying but wouldn't admit it.

Britt handled it gracefully, as always. I was dragged into my parents' old age kicking and screaming while she smoothly adjusted. Small wonder they adored her. And even though John lived with them (after Dad stole him away from me, saying he needed help on the place), it was Britt who understood them. John and I had quiet conversations expressing our frustration over the latest fiasco. Britt had no such difficulty.

Dad couldn't help himself. He told me Keith's girlfriend had a son, a little brother to the unfortunate Hannah. He felt compelled to tell me because they named him Sam Ardahl, after Dad's father. Even with all the sons, grandsons and great-grandsons, no Ardahl had chosen the name Samuel in all those years.

Dad was pleased the legacy would continue. My stomach turned. To me, it tainted the name. I wondered what kind of miscreant this new Sam Ardahl would turn out to be, if his talent would lie in certain crimes, such as robbery or fraud, if he would use people the way his father did, how many prisons he would serve time in. I thought all this before the child was even out of diapers.

I didn't lay eyes on him until he was old enough for preschool. Then I was shocked to find a very intelligent and well-mannered child who adored his "Papa Walt." I pitied him then, and his sister, who Dad told me was "smart as a whip." What kind of life could they have, considering their parents? Could they possibly fight their genetics *and* upbringing and win? I was glad I wasn't responsible for them. I never, ever wanted that.

Chapter 25
~Reality Shifted, Part II~

A distant family member died. I did a casual search online for the obituary, to add to my highly disorganized genealogy file. I kept every piece of paper I had ever scribbled on if it contained any facts or musings concerning my family tree, going all the way back to when I searched for Pamela. Even though I had a deep, ongoing relationship with my birth family I still kept the notes. I don't know why.

The deceased's last name started with an H, which reminded me of my birth father. I knew he wasn't dead but put his name in the search bar of the genealogy site anyway, to see if other Havner relatives might come up.

"Glenn P. Havner of Boise, Idaho, died December 30…"

Like in a movie when cold water is splashed in the face of someone sound asleep, I now sat frozen in shock, completely awake.

Died. Died December 30th. Three and a half years ago.

My biological father died three and a half years ago.

Three and a half years ago.

What the *hell* had I been doing for three and a half years? In a waking coma, unaware of the passage of time. When was the last time I talked with Heather or Kelli? It couldn't have been that long.

They would have told me. Of course they would have told me.

"…died December 30th surrounded by his family…"

"Your father died and they didn't have the courtesy to tell you?!"

When was the last time? How long ago was Heather on my front porch, nervously glancing around, as if afraid of being caught there? Not willing to come in, to see my new house, but wanting to gift me some of her clothes because she was moving again? She never sent a forwarding address. Of course (I rationalized) she was busy. Her job kept her so very busy. Always traveling. And Kelli, with a baby. Babies take up so much time! Feedings and diapers. The baby would be how old now? Five. Starting kindergarten.

It had been more than four years since I had heard from either of them but couldn't admit it to myself until that moment.

I immediately wrote Jenny a raw, gut-wrenching email, because I knew she alone would understand. I didn't call because I knew if I heard her voice I would break down.

She never responded. I found out much later she had a psychotic roommate who intercepted all her messages.

I called Craig.

"Those people are nothing to you!" He wanted me to himself, with no other entanglements. That I could be distraught over some "stranger" (he said) cutting ties with me made him angry. He didn't want me to care.

"They're not strangers. They're my sisters," I choked out.

"Then confront them. Force the issue," he demanded, wanting to end the matter one way or another.

"I can't," I said, but couldn't explain why. Even I didn't know why. But the door had been slammed shut and I couldn't bear to knock again now.

I spoke with my birth father once but never had a conversation with him.

I saw my birth father once but never met him.

I was nothing to him in life, except proof incarnate he broke his vows.

But why didn't my sisters tell me? My gracious, intelligent, generous, relentlessly upbeat sisters. How long did it last, this gift? Three years? Four years? From one month before giving birth to Sophie until that summer day on the front porch with Heather. She wanted to tell me something but had a greater need to run. *You could have left a goddamn note in the bag, Heather.*

Something happened. Something so important that she and Kelli made a pact never to contact me again. Despite my own increasingly haphazard letters and gifts, there was never a response. Never a hint. Did their mother find out they knew me? Did she make them promise to cut off contact?

But, after our father died – Why couldn't they even tell me that? Cruelty seemed completely out of character for them. They were so accepting when I first dropped into their lives. How could they cut me off with no explanation?

Maybe it wasn't Shirley. Maybe it was Glenn.

A scenario played out in my mind: He knew he was dying. Even with dementia, he knew. He was very brave, trying to ease the pain for his wife, children and grandchildren. Toward the end, they were willing to agree to anything – any promise, any vow, a deal with the devil – to alleviate the suffering. So Heather and Kelli promised one another, or perhaps their parents, to cut me off completely. It would be as if I didn't exist. Again.

I had no way of knowing if this was even close to the truth, but needed a plausible explanation in order to move on. So I settled for this.

I was used to settling.

I emailed one of my most spiritual and literary friends, who wrote eloquently on visions and dreams and how deceased loved ones send us messages, if we would only allow ourselves to see them.

"Why would God let me continue to pray for my father years after he died?" I demanded. "I mean, what's the *point*? To make me feel stupid?"

Why didn't anyone tell me?

I was fourteen again, waking to find my mother gone. And everyone knew – my cousins, the neighbors – everyone but me. I was a child, allowed to sleep through it like it didn't matter. Like *I* didn't matter.

This was worse. This time I wasn't told after the fact, I wasn't told at all. I was having a conversation with Heather and Kelli, looked away for a moment while I happily prattled on about nothing and turned back to find them gone. I was left standing there talking to no one and feeling like a fool.

Why was there no goodbye? Why is there never a goodbye?

I remembered them on their birthdays. I specifically prayed for Glenn every Sunday morning at church, even before I connected with my sisters and had very little feeling for him or any of them; I had prayed for over twenty years, during the Prayers and Intercessions:

"You may now pray aloud or in your hearts."

God, be with my birth father and his family. Keep them healthy and safe.

God bless Glenn and Shirley Havner and their entire family.

Bless and keep Glenn Havner, his wife and all my brothers and sisters.

So (I now assailed my friend) where do prayers go when the person you're praying for is dead? Is it like undeliverable mail at the post office? Is there a "dead prayer" center where prayers just sit around, useless?

She insisted prayers are never useless, even if we don't understand why things are the way they are.

God is too big for us to understand.

My Baptist mother admonished that we do not pray *to* or *for* the dead, because once we die we are either with God in glory or we are suffering eternally in hell, based on the choice we made in life. We were either "saved" or "unsaved," with God or forever separated from Him. To pray for someone already dead would be to mock God. Of course I didn't know, so if I was sinning I was doing so innocently, which could be forgiven.

But it was still pointless.

Sometime after this cruel epiphany, I went to the cabinet where I keep wrapping paper and decorations. While searching through the messy supplies, a box fell out. I stood looking at the baby gift and card I thought I sent to Kelli five years earlier. I could only recall the emotion connected to it, that nothing I found was good enough. I returned my purchases twice. This was the third.

In the back of my mind, I must have noticed the silence, but it was too painful to examine. I couldn't be sure about exact dates. Dates were numbers, cold and logical. Depression meant I measured time by moments and events: The Christmas the kids had chickenpox, the summer I was in a car wreck. There is no linear time in depression, no chronological order. There are memories piled in a heap, tossed into an overflowing box, not dealt with.

"I'll sort it later," I said.

So I sorted this over the summer, pondering and re-pondering. I studied with renewed interest the differences in belief between Catholics and Protestants, focusing on the afterlife. I had to make sense of it.

From everlasting to everlasting, You are God. (Psalm 90) Eternity does not "pass," it simply "is," with no past or future, no time as we know it. God exists in eternity. He is time itself because He created time. But He does not exist in what we think of as time. God is not linear. "God's time" is not linear. If I were to believe this, my prayers were not wasted. But still, what was the point of them? Did they just make me feel better, like I was a good person because I prayed? Were they merely self-serving?

Before the Great Schism, it was considered a duty for the entire Christian Church to pray for the dead. Even after the Reformation it continued. Martin Luther believed it was "useless" because it was not commanded by God, yet late in life he gave in slightly, allowing for it if done privately:

I regard it as no sin to pray with free devotion in this or some similar fashion: "Dear God, if this soul is in a condition accessible to mercy, be thou gracious to it." And when this has been done once or twice, let it suffice.
(Luther's Works, Vol. 37, p. 369)

So while the Lutheran church's definitive Book of Concord contains no special rites to pray for the dead and has no mention of anything like Purgatory, it does not expressly forbid the belief or practice either.

Glenn was Catholic, even if he never stepped foot in a church for anything other than weddings, baptisms and funerals. On some level he probably believed in Purgatory. Devout Catholics will tell you it's real if you believe in it or not. Described as a process, not a place, prayers are urged for souls there to hasten the necessary cleansing, for *years* after someone has died, followed by the Prayer of Eternal Rest:

Eternal rest grant unto them, O Lord, and let perpetual light shine upon them. May the souls of the faithful departed, through the mercy of God, rest in peace. Amen.

I didn't say this prayer. I didn't even know this prayer. Instead I made supplications as if Glenn was still alive. Did his family pray for his soul? Did anyone? Shirley was not raised Catholic and beyond the most basic requirements the kids did not seem to observe any rituals. Was I the only one who prayed after he was gone and that's why God let me continue, because the dead *need* to be prayed for? Was this was the one and only gift I could give him?

I didn't know, and it haunted me.

I had a dream:

Someone was speaking to me. Deep in sleep, I was aware and comprehending. He was young and healthy and earnestly telling me something as he stood before me. It came to me it was my birth father, and when that conscious thought invaded, the dream began less real. The more I fought to concentrate the less I understood.

"What?" I said. "What?" My voice was loud and sharp. He said it again, but I couldn't hear him and the dream dissolved. He went from a vision stronger than reality to color film to the old black and white photographs in the high school annual. As he disappeared completely I could only see him mouthing the words silently, earnestly, over and over.

Pamela called. I am not like her other children in that she speaks to them on a weekly, if not daily, basis. We call or visit every month or so, sometimes going even longer. I never feel disconnected from her and I know she will call if there is something important to tell me – a new baby in the family or they are going on vacation. But this time she took me by surprise.

"Is Glenn still alive?"

She had asked me that only once before, a few years prior, and since I didn't know any better I said he must be, because I was sure his daughters – my half-sisters – would tell me otherwise. After my gut-wrenching discovery to the contrary I tried to get Pamela in a private moment to let her know, but her husband had become so attentive since her last stroke we never had a moment alone. The entire summer had passed and it was now mid-autumn. She waited for Jim to run an errand before calling me.

"No, he died nearly four years ago."

"Four *years*—"

"I didn't know until last May," I said, hurriedly. "I've wanted to tell you but there was never a good time."

"Four years..." she said again as if pondering something.

"Why do you ask?" then, lightly: "Is he haunting your dreamscape too?"

"Yes!" she exclaimed, emphatically, as if relieved to finally say it.

We decided to meet at a restaurant where the staff didn't mind their patrons lingering over pie and coffee. After decades of keeping her hair short and curled, Pamela now let her champagne-colored tresses fall naturally to her shoulders, contrasting against her Bain de Soleil complexion. She looked years younger than her actual age.

I told her how I found out about Glenn. We reasoned why my sisters didn't tell me and further, why they cut contact, but it was all speculation. I then told her of my dream, vague and frustrating as it was. I asked about hers.

"Well, I feel like he's trying to make me remember."

"Why?"

"So I accept responsibility for my part in it. I'm culpable also," she said, gently putting her hand up in the "stop" gesture when I was about to protest. "I didn't want what happened but I was an adult; I should have known better. Besides," she added, "now I understand something."

I waited.

"When we went to that roadside diner to drink and dance, I remember the bartender gave me the dirtiest look. I thought he was disgusted – like he knew I was there with a married man. But now I think he was looking at *Glenn*. I think he knew Glenn had done something to my drink. That's why it hit me so hard."

It made sense.

"So you think he was trying to make you feel guilty? By invading your dreams like that?"

"No," she said thoughtfully. Pamela was always thoughtful in what she said, carefully measuring her words. "I think he was saying he's sorry. He was showing me what really happened."

I let this sink in.

"What do you think he was trying to say to me, then?" I asked.

"I don't know." And after a pause, "Why do you think it's taken nearly four years for him to do it?"

"It took him that long to get sober?" I quipped, very unlike Pamela but very, very much like Glenn.

She laughed, though shocked. And I had the feeling Glenn Havner would have laughed, too.

It was early morning, the day after Christmas. My most coveted times are just after a celebration, knowing the pressure is off, that it went well, and all that is left is to bask in the afterglow. My best time of day is early morning, just before dawn if possible. With the kids still asleep I felt the quiet and savored it.

I turned on the Christmas tree lights but not the TV. The room was otherwise dark and silent. Still in the process of waking, straddling dreams and complete awareness, I settled in to check my email. I had only gotten as far as turning on the computer when the voice said:

"Johannes Peter Havner."

I sat frozen, my hands poised over the keyboard. Johannes Peter Havner? Johnny Havner, my grandfather? The one my sister Heather wouldn't discuss? The one so far removed from his two eldest children they were not even mentioned in his obituary, who died more than ten years ago having no knowledge of my existence? What could possibly be the point?

But the voice said nothing more. The google home page waited. I typed *Johannes Peter Havner* into the search bar, expecting nothing.

Suddenly I was looking at a sixty page document – a family history – complete with names, dates, stories, and photographs going back to the 1800s. Suddenly, here was my grandfather, my great-grandfather, my great-great-grandfather. Suddenly, my grandfather's brothers and sisters and their spouses and children had names and faces and histories. Stunned, I watched as page after page spread out before me: names, maps, documents, and photos.

"Well, happy birthday and merry Christmas to me," I whispered. And on that day between the anniversary of my birth and his death, I finally knew what my birth father had been trying to tell me.

"Thanks Dad."

From the web address, I saw it came from ancestry.com. This meant of course that someone put the information there, and recently. I checked the source and found an email address for someone in Phoenix. Cautiously, I sent a message with the following subject line:

Just found your link and I think we're cousins.

As it turns out, we were second cousins. Her name was Donna and she had been working on genealogy for years, compiling her vast wealth of knowledge on ancestry.com. The Havner family history was a recent offering; adding it page by tedious page. The original was created decades prior by Donna's uncle as a tribute to his grandparents, our great-grandparents.

I did not discover this for a few days, though. At the moment I ran between the printer and bathroom, getting ready to leave and forcing myself not to read the contents. I wanted to savor this. When it was late enough I called Craig and asked him to meet me at Starbucks.

Barely touching my americano, I scanned the papers, looking for any mention of my grandfather. It was easy enough because the author did a separate section for every "child." Johnny was last, being the youngest.

I tried to make out detail in the grainy black and white photocopies and excitedly showed Craig all the pictures containing my grandfather.

"He doesn't look like you at all," he said matter-of-factly.

"I know. I look like my grandmother." I knew that from the one snapshot I had of her via Kelli – same small frame, small face. My grandfather, by contrast, was a strapping man in middle-age.

The mystery of how he could make a living as a musician in small town in Idaho during the Depression was finally answered. He played in his brother's band in a tavern, owned by another of his brothers. Entertainment was one of the few industries that did not suffer in the Depression, along with "soft" vices such as smoking and drinking. Put them all together and you couldn't lose.

Apparently all of the Havners were musical, both in singing and playing instruments. This vocation was not noted in his obituary; I suspect because it was before his second wife knew him so she didn't find it important. I also realized the obituary listed his mother with the wrong name, while this family history had my grandmother's name misspelled. But at least this made mention of his first wife and their children instead of pretending they never happened.

Then, a word I never expected caught my attention: Tacoma. Johnny Havner moved to Tacoma when WWII broke out to work in the shipyards. I looked out the window of Starbucks towards the very tideflats where so many ships were built and could scarcely take it in.

"He lived here! He lived in Tacoma!" I exclaimed to Craig. Then, following a hunch, started checking the siblings' pages. And here it was again and again: Tacoma. One would follow the other and soon at least five of them were on this side of the mountains.

"They came for the war effort," I said. "Then back to Idaho when—" I stopped.

"What? What now?"

"They're *still here*," I said in wonder, then reading further, words tumbled out: "A few brothers were here just for the war, but two sisters – the youngest, the ones closest in age to Johnny – they stayed. Let me see your computer." In just seconds I found my grandfather's sisters' children. My father's first cousins. My second cousins and their children. Some had lived just blocks from my old house.

"Oh God, more family? Do you really need *more*?" groaned Craig.

"I just hope you haven't slept with any of them," I grumbled.

As much as Craig appreciated Chinese culture, he had no love for the numerous Red Threads that ran through my life. For me they made a beautiful tapestry. For him they were trip wires, attached to explosives. After researching all the names I could find, he was relieved to find he didn't know any of them.

I was not supposed to be born in Tacoma. A footnote to my adoption story is that Pamela's mother took her and Sharon to San Diego "and then just left us there!" She was supposed to quietly wait out her pregnancy, relinquish the baby, and go back to Spokane like it never happened. But feeling too far from home, Pamela traveled north. Portland or Olympia would have made more sense, getting there first, or Seattle since it was directly across the state from Spokane, making for an easier trip home later. But she said it felt right in Tacoma, and that is where she took refuge for those few weeks.

She was not supposed to stay, though. Didn't plan to stay. But something made her come back after spending Christmas with her parents. She got a job, fell in love, married, bought a house and raised her family here, never moving from the house she and her husband agreed was "temporary." If she had remained in Spokane or had "gone back to Idaho" like my adopted family expected, I would not be enjoying the close relationship I have with her and my siblings. And my children would not know their cousins.

My mother Lillian was born in Tacoma. Her mother never expected to live in America, much less in a city in America, but that is where they were when the children were born. Even after moving to the country, they remained members of the church from their old neighborhood, so drove into town several times a week.

Shirley Havner's sister lived in Tacoma, not Coeur d'Alene or anywhere else in Idaho, or any other city in Washington. Somehow she came to Tacoma and that is why I was able to see my birth father – just once – because the death of Shirley's nephew brought them here.

Craig's newly married parents visited Tacoma on a whim and stayed the rest of their lives. And although Craig traveled the world and lived in many places, he was always in Tacoma exactly when I needed him.

Even Brian and I did not plan to live here. We were going to buy Aunt Cora's place and put a new house on it. Brian always wanted to live in the country. When that fell through it was our friend Chris who pointed out how Tacoma was central to everyone we knew and affordable compared to other areas. The very day we fired our realtor, we stumbled across the house we would buy, and the seller had put out the for-sale sign just that morning. When I saw it I remembered how I loved craftsman-style houses and the idea of living in town, a dream I had suppressed for years.

These Havner great-aunts of mine probably didn't think they would stay when they moved to Tacoma along with their brothers during the war, but they did, and their families stayed as well.

For all of Tacoma's assets – the parks, the bay, the rich history, architecture, industry and arts – it is usually thought of (if thought of at all) as merely a lesser version of Seattle. But time after time, it was Tacoma where people somehow connected to me were when I stumbled across them. Not only that, as an adult I found myself there again and again – drawn to it in a way no other place has ever drawn me, as if by a dream.

Chapter 26
~Revelations~

Since I had a good Christmas financially, I gave myself a one year subscription to ancestry.com. New cousin Donna and I started a long, online conversation.

I explained my circumstances. She did not seem shocked, probably because she didn't know Glenn; it was all at a safe distance for her, so there were no loyalty issues. Surprisingly, she knew some of the local cousins well (from a one-year college stint in the area) so was able to tell me something about them. This made them less intimidating. I started forming a plan to make contact.

I dove into ancestry.com like there was no tomorrow. Donna had done an excellent job of cataloging all the family members she knew or could find. Now with my info on the forgotten Havners (Glenn et al) she was able to fill the gaps of that branch while I built the massive Krenn-Havner tree on my own site. When one of us would find something the other was close behind, and we used our combined hints to track down even the most obscure records.

The most mysterious of all was, as always, my grandmother Anita Krenn Havner. All I knew was she was either widowed or divorced from her second husband (name not mentioned); that while in Coeur d'Alene on one occasion she could be heard screaming at her adult son; that she moved to Los Angeles to live with her daughter many years ago; forbade her daughter from marrying; enjoyed spending Christmas with her sister in Arizona, and was, in words of my sister Heather, "really sharp." That's it.

Before I knew Heather and Kelli, I wasn't even sure of her name, birthplace or birthday. Glenn's birth certificate was handwritten in such messy cursive I could only guess her first name was Anita, Anete, Amita, or some other variation. The birthplace was "Something-ton" in Washington. And since the certificate gave only the parents' ages at the time I could merely guess on the year she was born.

I tried a records search many years prior, sending my check to Olympia with a letter containing the above hints, saying this was my grandmother. A few weeks later I was excited to see the return envelope, only to find a birth certificate for a Baby Boy Krenn, born Sept 1911 in Porton, WA, son of E. Krenn and F. Martin. At least that's what I could make out.

I wrote again to Vital Records:

"I admit I don't know much about my grandmother, but I'm fairly certain she was not born male."

This garnered me an actual phone call. The clerk must have just opened my letter because she was laughing. She told me this was the closest record she could find.

This was all I would know until the receptionist at the church in Coeur d'Alene told me about the Krenn family. The record was for my grandmother's younger brother. So I knew by deduction that she was born in 1910. I wouldn't know her actual birthday or her correct name until I asked Kelli. And neither she nor Heather knew (or would give up) her middle name. Or mention her second married surname. Certain information they were protective of and I never knew what those things would be. I also knew she must have died prior to Glenn, because she wasn't mentioned in his obituary.

Donna and I continued searching.

My next step was to contact my birth father's cousins. I chose Kenneth and Marjorie Madsen, in part because they lived only blocks from my old house, and Ken was the son of my grandfather's sister nearest to him in age. At least that was my logic. I hoped these youngest two had been close as well, despite her staying in Washington while he returned to Idaho. They were all gone now, these Havner siblings. The only spouse left was my grandfather's much younger second wife, and she was now in her eighties.

I wrote a short letter, introducing myself as Johnny Havner's previously unknown granddaughter, who found them via genealogy research. I hoped my instinct was right, that this cousin would be receptive being "far-enough" removed from Glenn's immediate family.

Days later the phone rang. Caller ID said *Ken Madsen*. Heart pounding, I answered.

And Marjorie Madsen immediately became one of my closest allies and sources of knowledge of the Havner family.

They had been married so long they "shared a brain," as the saying goes. And she was much more communicative by nature. And so it was Marjorie who gave me info over the phone that day, rapid-fire, while I did my best to keep up, scribbling on the back of the nearest envelope.

She was both pleasant and matter-of-fact, never holding back on information. She kept telling me I should talk with Dan Vogel, part of the vast Vogel clan, offspring of the third from youngest Havner who also made her home here.

"Dan and Joyce. They're great people. You should call them."

I promised I would, but asked if I could meet her in person first. Maybe she could bring some old photos?

We sat in the same booth at the restaurant where Pamela and I discussed our dreams just months before. And Ken, my birth father's first cousin, came along. Marjorie told me later she didn't think he would, but he was intrigued by my sudden appearance. He shyly showed me a photo of his mother as a teen. Long curls framed a delicate, angelic face, reminding me of Mary Pickford.

"Beautiful. Just beautiful," I said. He smiled.

They gave me the correct pronunciation for all the unusual family names. I wrote them in my notebook phonetically. They knew everyone: all the Havner siblings and their children, Ken and Glenn's first cousins. There was a multitude of their generation created by the twelve siblings, and they could be found all over the western half of the country.

They also kept making reference to my step-grandmother Barb and her family, as if they knew them well.

"Were they from Tacoma? Is this where Johnny met her?" That would make sense since they married after the war. Ken and Marjorie looked at me rather incredulously.

"Barb is Ken's step-sister," Marjorie said, speaking for her husband out of habit.

"What?"

"His dad married Barb's mother way back. I thought you knew."

No, I certainly didn't know that choice bit of information. So Ken's aunt by one marriage was also his sister by another marriage. What magic made me look up these two first? They were the closest to my grandfather out of anyone from that generation, because they were connected by family ties, twice.

Then *I* had to clear up a misunderstanding I didn't know I had created. Marjorie made reference to my mother, Jean. "No, no. I'm sorry," I interrupted. "I should have made that clear in the letter. Jean is my aunt. Glenn is my father. Since he was married to Shirley...You can see the problem."

They took the news nonchalantly. When you're in your seventies you've pretty much heard it all.

"Did you know Glenn? Spend any time with him?"

"Not really. We saw him on a few occasions but that's about it."

I guess Glenn and Jean really were cut off from the Havners for the most part, being close instead to the Krenns, their mother's family.

"Have you called Dan and Joyce yet?" Marjorie asked in a phone call soon after.

"No..." I sheepishly admitted.

"Well you should," she said simply but firmly. Marjorie is the type one does not argue with, since her logic is inescapable. I called.

Marjorie had already told them about me, so that was out of the way. Dan was very cordial on the phone and we agreed on a day I would visit. I brought a small recorder so I could get some of what he said on tape, not having to rely on hurriedly scribbled notes. Of course I didn't know I would stay three hours, much longer than the tape lasted.

He met me as I got out of the car, "Well, you look like a Havner," he said jovially. Although I think I look more like a Krenn, I felt complimented. He was a big man, with a build you'd expect for a very physical career. His wife was tiny in comparison.

He took my coat, introduced me to his wife, invited me to sit, offered me a drink. Simple manners sadly rare for my own generation.

He and Joyce showed me around their home, which Dan himself had built. They also lived just a few blocks from my old house and we wondered if we had ever passed each other on the street.

"There's a lot of us, so it's possible." Dan said.

He told me about their kids and grandkids, and like Heather had been in the beginning, he was frank and didn't white-wash anything. I heard the good, bad and ugly, but I was glad to hear it was mostly good. He proudly showed me copies of news articles about various family members, winning awards and such.

I asked about my grandfather, Dan's uncle. He knew him well. Johnny had stayed with the Vogels in Tacoma in the 1940s, along with other Havner brothers who had come for the war effort.

"That house was open 24 hours," he laughed. "And your grandfather, he liked the Rose Tavern. I suppose it isn't there anymore."

"The one on Pacific Avenue? I pass it every time I go to the bank."

It amazed me to think my grandfather had hung out at a place I recognized. A tidy little building, not rundown even after decades of use. I tried to imagine him there in his thirties, younger than I was now.

Like the other Havners, Johnny was handy, able to tinker in many trades as a hobby if not as a career. Musician, mechanic, carpenter. And wine maker.

"Wine? I thought all they liked was beer."

"No," he said emphatically. "Sure, they drank beer but Uncle Johnny loved to make his own red wine. And brandy." I looked over at Craig, who had joined us after about an hour. He never approved of my fondness for merlot.

"What kind of brandy?" I asked, half-knowing the answer.

"Apricot."

The only time I ever had brandy I was twenty and on a trip to Victoria, B.C. with Dad and Carol. Since the drinking age is lower in Canada, I could have alcohol, although my parents didn't approve. After looking over the vast beverage menu, I ordered apricot brandy. Maybe it wasn't the Havners who loved beer. Maybe it was the Krenns.

"I think you look like him," Dan insisted.

"I think we might have the same coloring," I conceded. "But mostly I think I look like my grandmother, Anita. Did you know her?"

"I met her once when I was eight, if that counts," he said, laughing.

"Any idea why they divorced?"

"No, but I was awfully young when they did, so even if it was discussed I wouldn't have known."

"Did you know Glenn at all?"

"He was a pall bearer at Grandpa Havner's funeral. I don't remember him much except for that."

At least I was finally being filled in on the extended family. They seemed overall to be stand-up people. Smart, industrious, and honest, with just a few tragic exceptions you'd expect to find in any clan. They reminded me of the Ardahls in how they helped each other – working together, building houses together, having younger adult members stay with extended family to give them a good start in life.

They also knew my step-grandmother and those mysterious aunts Heather wouldn't talk about. There were many close friendships, mainly between people the same age, regardless of bloodlines.

Not long after this, during my morning routine of catching up on email while listening to the local news, I found myself drawn to a breaking story. A fatal car wreck on a mountain pass.

"Pay attention," the voice nudged. I did, but the victim's description didn't seem familiar. Still, I emailed my moms' group:

Bad wreck in the news. Have the feeling we need to pray about this. They immediately prayed, as they always do when asked. Later that day I discovered why I felt drawn to the story: The victim was my second cousin, one of the Vogels.

Marjorie Madsen called. "You need to come to the funeral. You're family now." Since it is pointless to argue with Marjorie because she is right, I attended the Mass, finding a place near the back. I looked around and wondered how many there were my relatives.

Afterwards, Marjorie found me and asked why I did not sit with them.

"I figured the front was reserved for immediate family," I began.

"I didn't see a sign that said 'immediate family'," she gently admonished, but took me around and introduced me to several other cousins. Every family needs a Marjorie.

Donna and I were determined to find a lead on my grandmother, who would have been in her late nineties if she was still alive. Once I figured out her exact name via census records, we followed the crumbs. Turns out, that branch of the family *was* Irish, at least that was the ethnicity they claimed. Like I ignored the German side in favor of the Scandinavian, they ignored the Krenn side in favor of the Martins. Although they had a German surname, they only seemed to celebrate all things Irish.

Almost simultaneously, Donna and I found Anita's obituary. It was vague and contained several errors, including her place of birth, but it did give me her second married surname, and overall was glowing with praise. One line caught my eye: "Moved to Los Angeles to be near her daughter, who lovingly cared for her these past forty years."

Cared for her? For four decades she was being "cared for"? Due to what condition? In the one snapshot I possess, taken about ten years after moving to California, she appeared well and healthy, standing in the sun with her adult children. Heather always described her as "really sharp" and made no mention of an illness or handicap.

They told me frankly that our father had dementia stemming from a stroke, was an alcoholic, later a diabetic, and was afflicted with SAD. If they could tell me all that, why couldn't they tell me anything about our grandmother?

She once screamed at Glenn so ferociously that all the neighbors could hear. And a few years later she was in California, being "cared for."

Was she nuts? Was that the big secret? Is that why she and my grandfather divorced, not because of his wandering eye, but because he simply could no longer live with her unstable behavior?

Of my Havner grandfather's many siblings, the only other who divorced was his sister closest in age. She was diagnosed with "manic depression" and committed to a sanitarium when she was very young. But as far as I know, Anita was never hospitalized and she not only worked, but went on to marry again. Still, there was no mention in the obituary of a career or employment of any kind once she moved to be close to her daughter. Forty years of...what?

She died just four months before Glenn. She in California, he in Idaho. She in September, he in December.

Then it hit me.

The exhausting dreams when I felt I was someone else, talking with someone I didn't know, the horrible feeling of regret I carried for months after – this was when it happened. The zenith being mid-September, when I was interrupted mid-dream and didn't recognize my own daughter. This was when Anita died. I was somehow connected to her via dreams as she was dying. But what was it I experienced and why?

Then I remembered a co-worker's phone call from some years before. Ellen was completely rattled – traumatized – and needed to talk it out. Just before her alarm was set to go off that morning, she dreamed she was in a house not far from her own. A small house she had passed many times but had never been in. She was in that house, sitting in a corner of the sparse living room. Only she wasn't herself – she was someone else. A young woman, college age. Two male friends were also in the room, one at the computer. Two other men burst in the front door and opened fire. Just before her spirit rose up, she saw one of the shooters re-enter, look around, and walk out. Ellen (through the eyes of the victim) saw the roof of the house and businesses across the street as she rose into the air. She only shook herself free from the other woman's psyche with the thought that she needed to get her daughter to school.

After returning home, she called her husband who had been at work this entire time, and told him of the dream.

"You'd better turn on the news," he said.

"Why?"

"You'd just better turn on the news," he repeated.

Everything she saw happened as she dreamt it. A young woman and two friends were murdered by two "friends" of the male victims. She was in a corner of the living room and had time only to stand before she was shot. Ellen saw the interior of the house, the other people in the room, the street view from above the house, as it was happening.

Ellen never listened to TV or radio news. There was no way for her to know about this. But she saw it.

"You intercepted her last thoughts," I heard myself say.

"I didn't even know her."

"But you were a perfect receiver at that moment – you were nearly awake but not quite. She knew she was about to die, so her spirit sent out one last strong 'signal' to the universe and you got it. Maybe others did, too."

"But what for?"

"I don't know. Maybe just so someone, somewhere would know what happened?"

The killers were soon apprehended and convicted. They looked just like Ellen described in her dream.

I had been intercepting my grandmother's last days. But I couldn't see anything except in shadow. Was she conscious? Was she dreaming? Who was she speaking with – her living daughter, her dying son, her deceased parents? And what was I doing there? Was I just a third party, a witness, a human "range extender" she needed to connect with the others? Did she even know I existed or did that matter?

All I could remember were strong feelings, trying to resolve something important, perhaps restore a relationship. I don't know why I was included. I don't know if others were as well. It was like reading the dust jacket of a book, never knowing the contents or final page, and trying to make an epilogue out of it.

Chapter 27

~Finding My Father~

I was telling Dad about ancestry.com and asked him a few questions so I could start building a tree for the Ardahl side of the family. Genealogy experts tell you it's easy, just start by asking your older family members simple questions. I assure you, the experts do not have Norwegian elders.

"What do you remember about your grandparents?"

"She was a good cook. He was really old," he said after careful consideration.

"What did he do?"

"He was a farmer." (Why do I even bother…?)

"Anything else?" (Long silence.)

"No."

"Alright. Your dad was what, nine years old, when he came to America. Did he ever tell you anything about Norway?"

"No," Dad replied, shocked I would even entertain such a question. *Talk, for no reason? Do you think we're Swedes?*

"You do at least know the names of your dad's brothers and sisters?"

"Yes," he said and listed them. I wrote the names phonetically, having no clue as to the actual spellings.

"What was your grandfather's name?"

"I don't remember. He died in Norway."

"Wait. Then who was your grandmother married to in Minnesota?"

"Erickson, Tomas Erickson."

"Did they have children together?"

"No," he said, then leaned forward slightly as if confiding a shameful secret:

"She adopted some out," shaking his head in disgust.

"You mean there were *more*?"

"No…" his voice wandered off as he tried to sort it himself. Finally he said, "You should talk to my cousin Karin. She knows."

"Was it the youngest, or the oldest? Was it because she couldn't afford to keep them? Didn't she have family here?"

"You should talk to Karin," he repeated.

I called Dad's cousin Karin. She was just a little younger than Dad and very spry. She suggested I come over. I arrived with a notebook. She had spread out a huge box of family history papers on the kitchen table. We sat. She talked. I wrote in my notebook at a furious pace.

It turned out Karin was *the* person to ask, because she alone was witness to much that went on in her grandmother's house – the grandmother who supposedly discarded some of her children, my dad's aunts and uncles.

"No, no. It wasn't like that," Karin assured me. "When Bestemor[7] came over she was a young widow and mother of six. Some of them went to cousins. It was more like a foster relationship. My mother and Uncle Samuel (your grandfather) stayed with her. They were the only two that stayed together – that's why they were always so close. Bestemor married her employer, an old bachelor – she had been his housekeeper."

"So the others lived with older cousins. They still saw their mother?"

"Oh yes," she said and found a formal family photo of my adopted great-grandmother, her husband, and "their" children. They looked well-off, not at all like a woman in a desperate situation. I noticed a small boy, obviously the youngest. Carl Ardahl.

"Why was Carl fostered out? You'd think he would have stayed with his mother." He would have barely been school-age. He had huge, sad eyes. At least they looked sad to me.

"I don't know," Karin answered. "But they all went to well-to-do people. Carl went to a family that had no children of their own. They didn't officially adopt him but they left him everything – a small fortune." All these Norwegian farmers seemed to be prosperous, at least eventually.

"So Tomas Erickson was fairly rich as well? And your mother and my

---

7 Bestemor = Grandmother in Norwegian.

grandfather inherited his farm?"

Now her expression changed.

"I was eight when he died. I was there. I took care of him like a little personal assistant – shaving him, helping him with his shoes. My mother had been taking care of the house for years after Bestemor died. And your grandfather, he worked *hard*."

I could see her remembering it.

"The day Grandfather died, his lawyer came to see him. He changed his will there on his deathbed. I wasn't in the room, but I know that is when it happened. He changed his will and left everything to a couple of bachelor nephews of his who already had a place of their own. They never did a thing for him. Your grandfather did. He ran everything, worked on the place like it was his own. It *should have been his*."

The other brothers and sisters were fostered by cousins and inherited as if legally adopted. The only two who belonged to the family they lived with were cut off, discarded as if nothing more than hired hands. Dad never mentioned this. I wonder if his father even told him. Apparently the only time my grandfather spoke of it was with his sister, in their thick dialect. Although Karin was fluent in Norwegian, she could barely understand them.

There was no legal adoption at the turn of the century, not as we know it. It was left to the whim of the individual as to who inherited their worldly goods if they were "without issue." But there were societal norms. In giving his farm to his nephews, Tomas Erickson effectively abandoned his step-children and the memory of his wife, all of whom had worked tirelessly for him. I wondered what the community thought. I wondered if it was discussed in whispers or aloud in righteous anger. They had been married nearly forty years.

"*Ten percent! Ten percent! That's all she meant to them!*"

It amazes me what others find justifiable.

I asked about the Depression, since this was when it happened. "Did anyone you know lose their farm?"

"No. Well, no one except Uncle Samuel."

"You mean, losing the Erickson place?"

"No, his place in South Dakota," she said, surprised I didn't know.

My mind went blank for a minute. The thousand-acre farm, biggest in the county. Dozens of hired hands at harvest time. The big white house. My grandmother cooking for thirty or more. The draft horses that wore silver in their bridles when going to town.

"There was no money, but we never went hungry. Men would come around looking for work – you know they lost their jobs in the Depression. Pa didn't have any work for them, but Ma would always give them a good meal before sending them on. That's all we could do for them."

I always felt glad they had their farm even if "there was no money."

"Pa was an excellent provider. He could lay up twice as much feed as any two other men."

They worked for everything they had. They helped their neighbors, helped their relatives. They took in each others' children when necessary. Nieces and nephews worked for the ones with businesses "in town." But there was no money for the farmers. Not enough to pay the taxes. The biggest wheat farm in the county. Lost to foreclosure.

"I'm not feeding the bankers."

Now I knew why. I finally understood why Dad hated debt, would not take out a loan for any reason. Why he paid cash for everything, even my house. Why he insisted I promise to never take out a mortgage. "The bankers" weren't getting any more from him.

Dad always looked out for his family, neighbors, and friends, and at the same time refused to give to charity. He gave to those he knew. Instead of throwing money at an organization to care for the needy, he gave directly in the form of hospitality, car repair, advice, or anything he had to share. His family, like so many others, made it through the Depression by helping each other, not by giving or taking hand-outs.

My grandfather, Samuel Ardahl, is just a vague recollection to me. I created a memory of him through stories and photographs. It was easy because my father is the son who most resembled him. As Dad aged, I could envision my grandfather more and more. In the black and white photos I saw a dignified man, never smiling or frowning. His posture and manner of dress made him look almost elegant, in a Cary Grant sort of way. His arm casually stretched out on the back of the couch, one knee crossed over the other, dressed in a suit and tie as if it was everyday wear.

It must have crushed him to lose his property, again and again. They left Norway because there was nothing for them there. Due to ancient inheritance laws, the fact that only five percent of Norway is farmable, and the population explosion that occurred in the 1800s, they literally ran out of room. America was the answer. Here they could finally own land, the noblest of quests.

His first homestead attempt was thwarted by bad soil. The successful farm where all of his children were born was taken by the bank. Then what should have been his and his sister's inheritance – the thing that would redeem his previous losses – was given to others. In his fifties now, he rented a farm and worked it. But eventually he followed cousins to Washington State. With our snow-topped mountains, rivers, lakes, and green forests, I think it reminded him of the Norway of his childhood.

None of his children were farmers. Instead they found more relevant employment in business. But they all revered farming. It was honorable work.

When one of Dad's brothers died, I received more insight into my grandfather, which in turn helped me understand my father. A cousin I had never heard of sat across from me at the memorial reception. She was in her seventies and like most of the Ardahl family (by blood or marriage) she was fit and well-groomed. But unlike the Ardahls I knew, she had no love of farming.

"First it was eggs. Then strawberries. I even hated the strawberries," she said across the table, heavy-laden with the type of food you'd expect to be served at harvest time. "It was Sam Ardahl who talked some sense into my husband."

"My grandfather?"

"Sam was your grandfather?" People were always surprised by this.

"He was past eighty when I was born. What did he say?"

"Well I don't know exactly, but I know what he did. I had a toddler and a baby then and here I was trying to keep house and tend *strawberries*," she said "strawberries" as if she had been sorting a landfill. "Sam stopped by. He was a lot older than my husband even though they were cousins. When he saw me and all I was trying to do, he took the kids – even the baby – and told me to go inside and rest. And I did. I took a *nap*. When I woke up, Sam was gone, my husband was there, and I knew he had gotten a stern talking-to. I never had to do any of the farm work after that."

I remembered how Dad would quietly seethe at the amount of yard work I did with little kids running around, even carrying a baby in a sling while mowing the grass, while Brian would be watching TV or gone somewhere. As sexist as it sounds, he felt certain activities were meant for men while others were meant for women, especially mothers. Not because we were not capable, but because we were overextended.

I had to cajole him into holding the babies when they were newborns. Once they could sit well, you couldn't get him to put them down, but before then he felt they should be held only by the mother, or grandmother, or just anyone who was a mother.

The one thing he had against me not sending the kids to school was that I would "never get a break." It took only sixteen years for him to see I was actually more relaxed with the kids at home.

Even luxuries were carefully considered. When I was really small, he thought about having a pool put in. But first he bought a large above-ground pool to try out the idea. When the neighborhood found out we had a pool, my mother had no rest. Women would show up with their kids clad in swimsuits, clutching towels, saying, "You don't have to watch them – they know how to swim," then gleefully depart. The kids would then upend any plans Mom had because she indeed did have to watch them for fear of someone drowning. Not only that, but they would traipse through the house soaking wet, asking for snacks, needing to use the bathroom. The day Walt came home to find Lillian in tears over the fact she could get nothing done was the day the pool came down. We would go to the lake every summer instead.

Dad was old-fashioned, but in a good way. While he lauded women who worked, he found it offensive when they had no relief as mothers of small children. He expected men to give their wives the support needed so the mothers could give their children the necessary care and attention. Not daycare. Not strapping the baby onto the mother's back so she could continue to work in the fields (as he often saw with migrant farm workers). But cherish them and that brief time when it is so important for mother and child.

Every major decision Dad made was with Lillian or Carol in mind. Anything he bought – from paint to clothes to furniture and appliances – all needed their approval. And in the interim, I filled the gap. Although he put his foot down about Mom and me going to Sweden, he also absolutely refused to put Lillian into a nursing home after her stroke. Instead he practically signed over his paycheck to have a live-in nurse care for her. Had Mom lived, I'm certain we would have made the trip and I'm nearly as certain he regretted not letting us go at the time.

I remember Mom sighing when, on her birthday, Dad gave her a kiss on the cheek before going to work and slipped her a $100 bill, saying, "Go buy yourself something nice." That was back in the 1970s when $100 could buy a lot of nice things. But she would sigh because he never considered choosing something himself. I think he just had no idea and wanted *her* to figure it out. Besides, he needed to get to work. It's what he did best.

Dad's prime directive was to provide and cherish. And he did it well.

Chapter 28
~Loose Ends~

"I have a small world story."

"Your life is a small world story."

I finally succumbed to Facebook and soon wondered why I had resisted so long. It was the perfect vehicle for finding long-lost relatives. While ancestry.com starts with now and goes backward, Facebook starts with now and moves forward. While most use it for social networking, I added it to my arsenal of search tools. And one day I stumbled onto an incredible find.

While adding one of Sharon's sons to my contacts, I noticed my niece Amber on his friends list – the one who ran away at seventeen to join her birth father's family. She would now be in her mid-twenties. It made sense for her to be "friends" with this cousin because they were playmates when they were little. Her profile was wide open so I perused her wall and realized with a start why I always felt connected to her, and it wasn't because we were both adopted.

She was a Vogel, though she never carried the name. At birth, she was given her mother's maiden name. After adoption, she was a Mathias. But here on her wall was a conversation between Amber and her father, Jesse Vogel. Jesse, my second cousin. The "bad one." I didn't know his name before so there was no way for me to put two-and-two together until this moment.

I immediately emailed Marjorie, asking how these could be the horrible people I had been warned about when I had met Jesse's uncle Dan who was a wonderful person?

"That part of the Vogel family tells us what they want to tell us," she replied. Marjorie was completely straightforward. If she was implying her husband's cousins had less-than-sterling members in branches of their family tree, she said it in the most matter-of-fact of terms.

I let some time go by, not sure how to casually bring this up. Then, as if on cue, Amber posted something on Facebook about family being more than bloodlines. I sent a personal message:

"Remember how I once said you seemed to fit in everywhere...?"

Amber replied with happy surprise. She was just thinking of sending her father (my brother) Paul an apology for taking off all those years ago and to thank him for being an actual father to her, unlike the birth father she found.

"It's funny how U said that I fit in because that's why I left. I wanted to feel like I belonged somewhere," she wrote. Instead she found out why Paul and others tried to shield her, because her birth father was, in her words, "a loser" who only cared about his "constant temporary happiness." His extended family tried to make up the difference; they were really there for her, unlike either of her biological parents.

Only after severing ties did she realize what she had given up, mainly a relationship with her younger siblings, Paul's other children. I knew something about forging relationships late in life and encouraged her to go forward, to write the letter to Paul. She did, and posted it on Facebook for all to see. Paul commented, thanking her.

I was proud of her. Writing that message took guts.

"I figured out what's wrong with me," I said recently to my therapist. "I'm boring." She snickered appreciatively. I should mention this is my massage therapist.

On a whim I did the DNA test provided by ancestry.com. That way if any lost relatives also did the test we would be connected. It would be undeniable proof that I was "real".

I figured I would find German, some form of Celtic or British, and Nordic. Weeks went by, then a notice appeared online. Excited, I clicked View Your DNA Results:

97% Scandinavian

3% Uncertain

Are you kidding me? Okay, I know the Vikings invaded the British Isles and parts of Germany and Russia and possibly even beyond, but I thought they "intermingled" with the conquered population, didn't obliterate them altogether.

I now had visions of little Viking DNA bits, driving out the poor Celtic and German DNA bits at spear-point.

Upon reading the explanation at the website, I learned DNA is shuffled from one generation to the next, so the percentages expected would not necessarily be what was passed down. Like certain genes and disorders are inherited by luck of the draw, the same is true for DNA.

So, at least with this preliminary test, I was almost completely Nordic. 97% Scandinavian: from Sweden, Norway, or Denmark. Exactly what my adoptive parents had asked for. I always wanted to be Swedish.

Then I realized the date. It was Lillian's birthday. I looked skyward.

"Happy birthday, Mom. I got you what you wanted."

I knew though, that my heredity was more varied. My adoptive parents were told I was "mostly Swedish, with some English, Irish and maybe German." After meeting Pamela, I realized that was really a description of her, not me. But all she knew about Glenn was that he had a German surname. I looked like him and he took after his mother, who also had a German surname. But they did not look German. I finally discovered through genealogy research that the Krenns came from Bavaria, and the Martins were from Ireland.

But even then, my looks didn't "fit." Extremely pale skin, light brown silky hair, and dark brown eyes. That's not typical Irish.

The DNA test on ancestry.com expanded. Now the results said:

Scandinavia 37%

Ireland 26%

Great Britain 22%

East Europe 15%

East Europe? The map circled the areas my ancestors could have hailed from. Germany resembled an island, surrounded on the east, west and north. How could I not be German, *at all?* How could the Havners not be German? And if not German, then what?

I couldn't afford another test, so instead I plugged this DNA data into GEDmatch.com. Once there I was instantly overwhelmed with the myriad of ways the data could be interpreted. A genealogist friend suggested I try the Jtest in the Eurogenes list. And I was thus enlightened:

North-Central European 26%

Atlantic 25%

South Baltic 18%

East European 13%

West Mediterranean 10%

Ashkenazi 5%

Once again, I found myself staring at a computer screen, stunned.

I finally knew where my dark eyes came from. My Bavarian ancestors were apparently first from the Mediterranean. And besides being part of the Irish diaspora, I could also claim heritage with the dispersed European Jews. *Y'hudey Ashkenaz:* Jews of Germania.

It was incredible, knowing this. Just *knowing,* on a gut-level, that it was right; that final piece of a life-long puzzle. Nothing had changed, but everything had changed. A paradigm shift.

Memorial Day we stood in the familiar cemetery. I could walk directly to the graves where we lay bunches of rhododendrons; I had it memorized. Dad prefers using something from the yard, something with meaning. All those we remember had seen the very bushes the flowers came from. It was the same every year. Same graves. Same flowers. No standing around, just put the bouquets down then go out for breakfast. Late May is often cool and wet in the Pacific Northwest and this year was no exception. Mist hung from the trees and clung to the gravestones.

But this time Dad fussed over the flowers, not happy with the in-ground vases. He was now in his late eighties, older than any of the deceased lived to be. He crouched there at the shared headstone of his parents, this son with white hair and arthritic hands that trembled with palsy, arranging and rearranging the flowers. I broke the stems to make a better fit. Satisfied, we stood up, him stiffly and me slightly less so.

As he headed to the car, I realized Carol wasn't with us. I turned to see her standing off by herself with tears running down her face. I went to her.

She had stumbled across the headstone of her favorite uncle. He'd been there all along of course, but Carol has a way of avoiding things. She must have known his grave was nearby but never searched for it, just accompanied us as we put flowers down for Lillian and George, Dad's parents and other uncles and cousins I barely knew and she never knew.

This uncle and aunt were the only relatives who were really kind to Carol growing up. She would mention them fondly. I wondered why she had never sought out this grave before, so we could lay flowers there as well.

"I buried them both that day. It was the only way I could stand it." She said quietly, still staring at the decades-old marker. Not understanding, I looked at the headstone, at the date, and in one moment many questions were answered.

Susan. The baby taken from her. This is when it happened, a month after the one surviving photo was made, of Susan crawling toward the camera under the Christmas tree. This is why Carol couldn't bear the thought of Susan finding her, because in order to go on she had to think of her as dead. It was like a self-imposed version of exile usually forced upon birth mothers: *That child is dead and gone; go on like you never had a baby.*

She nearly died herself, reduced to a mere eighty pounds in her anguish. Only the knowledge that Shelley and Tom needed her pulled her back from the brink. So when she stood in this same spot all those years ago, mourning her uncle, she buried her loss of Susan in the same grave.

It was suddenly clear why I mattered so much, why I was never allowed to grow up in her eyes, why she was determined to be not only a step-mother to me but a mother: I was only a few months younger, also adopted, also a daughter. I was a replacement, if Carol meant to think of me that way or not, I was a replacement for the one who was stolen.

For the first time I put my arm around her – something I should have done thirty years earlier, even if it does go against my nature. She did not react, simply accepted the gesture. And we stood there like that, in the cold, wet grass. Stood looking at an old man's grave, grieving for a little girl who did not die, but who was gone.

"Do you remember this?" I said, handing Lillie a photo of her dad playing with her and her sisters back at the old house. Every once in awhile we pulled out a box of photos and looked through them. I expected a smile and a "yes." She did smile but said, "I really only remember the drama."

I stopped. "Seriously?" I asked. She shrugged.

If Lillie didn't remember the good times, the *normal* times, then what could her little sisters possibly remember? I knew Sophie could only recall that the old house had stairs, but she was just a toddler when we left. Remembering the house wasn't important. Remembering their father before he got into drugs, before he changed forever, was.

It grieved me that their entire perspective was based on the post-Brian, not the pre-Brian, the one I fell in love with and married. I know I can't rebuild memories, but I can remember on their behalf. And so children, this was your real father:

He read *Farmer Giles of Ham* aloud to you, with appropriate voices and accents.

He took you on bike rides, and bus rides, and hikes – just for fun.

He wrote poems and rhymes for you.

He was sad when you outgrew infant drawstring gowns, because he could no longer pretend you were a "baby ghostie."

He made wonderful bacon and egg breakfasts on Saturdays.

He moved the couches together to watch Star Wars with you.

He would make the car "mysteriously" die when passing a Dairy Queen, insisting the only way to make it start again was to eat ice cream.

He was amused to discover his shoes had been turned into Barbie cars.

He gave you his oversized t-shirts to sleep in during heat waves.

He pretended to be Tigger, or Ratigan, or Captain Hook. Whatever you wanted to play at that moment.

And up until the end, no matter how bad the morning or how late for work, he would quietly climb the stairs to give you a good-bye kiss as you slept.

That was your real father.

Dad called. "I need to discuss something with you. A couple of things." My stomach dropped. Dad never calls just to talk. He doesn't *talk* just to talk. Usually he makes Carol call on his behalf, but this was apparently between the two of us. I figured it had to be something financial.

In his living room that November, he was at his best. No faulty memory, no hesitation. We first discussed various relatives in decline. He was now the last living male on his side of the family and the only one fully aware, even factoring in his younger sister. He was losing family and friends at a rapid rate. He accepted this quietly, as he did with everything.

"Do you have any Alzheimers in your family?" he asked after getting an accounting on everyone's health. He could say "your family" casually, knowing he was secure in his role. He would often say, "How's your mother?" meaning Pamela, not hesitating at all, not needing to use a politically correct term, knowing this was not a slight against Lillian or Carol.

"Only...just about everyone," I said in answer to his question.

He shook his head: "That's a tough break."

I agreed.

Then he got down to business.

"You know my estate is separate from Carol's. Her kids will inherit from her and you kids will inherit from me." I did know this. They had agreed to it when they married over thirty years earlier and made no secret of it.

"And," he continued, "Carol is to live here as long as she wants." I nodded. More old news. If anyone deserved this house it was Carol – she had knocked herself out caring for it all these years.

"And John can live here as long as Carol does, to help out." This is what I figured was behind Dad insisting John move in with them, after living with me for four years. Dad was always planning ahead, always thinking of Carol. But I still didn't know why I needed to be told this.

"I gave both Keith and John money years ago," he continued "and they blew it. Both of them. With Keith, it's never enough. He thinks the world owes him. But John...I don't know what he spends it on. He has no one to pay for except himself but he's always just scraping by." He shook his head.

I had only theories so said nothing. He came to the point.

"I've changed my will again. All the grandkids will get something. Not a lot, just something to help them with college or whatever. I cashed out all the rest of the CD's. That's it. There's nothing left." I tried not to look stunned. It was a brilliant move on his part. Whenever any of us had a financial crisis (usually of our own making), we could always count on Dad. He had been quietly selling his extra vehicles and plots of land he had accumulated over the years, converting the proceeds into certificates of deposit. Now there was nothing left to ask for. The "Dad Bank" was closed.

Finally I said, "Why do I need to know this?"

He gave me the "I can't believe you need to ask" look.

"You're the executor."

Time stopped. I always figured his lawyer would be the executor. In depressed nightmares he assigned the duty to Linda and Laurie while leaving everything to Britt. But I never considered this scenario.

"Why?" I said.

"The lawyer said it was too complicated the other way." *What other way?* I thought, but he was already speaking again.

"You'll need to come down and sign papers. But," now getting to the root of the matter, "you have to promise me. If I leave you everything, you have to take care of Carol, and when she's gone, sell the place and divide it up between the three of you."

"A third and a third and a third. That's fair." I could hear my Swedish grandmother's voice on her eighty-ninth birthday. She wanted to remember Lillian equally with her other children. But my uncle had other plans and my aunt gamely went along. Now all of them were gone – Clarence and Evelyn, Betty and Raymond – leaving their own children to fight over the remains. I was surprised how much I missed them.

I never told my cousins about Gramma's will and what their parents had done. I didn't want bad blood.

"Do you know how this *feels?*" my youngest cousin Lisa cried, turning to me in a rare moment when feeling abandoned.

"Yes. I know how it feels," I replied.

"What did you do?"

"Nothing. Time has a way of working everything out."

Dad never forgot how Lillian was slighted; never forgot that this land was Lillian's wedding gift from her mother; never forgot how his mother-in-law turned to *him* for advice on her will, trusting him to make it right, only to have her wishes swept away when she was made to feel a "burden."

And in the back of his mind must also have been how his own father was cheated out of his inheritance and no one protested the injustice.

We now came full circle. Now Dad was nearly ninety as Gramma had been. And it was left to me to make sure *this* will – half Lillian's in spirit – was carried out the way it was intended. That's why Dad wanted me as executor – he knew I would do as he asked because I understood how it felt to have it taken away. He was a born provider, like his father – it was how he showed love. To make sure his last bestowment was settled before he also slipped away, he gave me my orders now.

"You'll have to be tough," he warned. "Keith will try to bully his way into getting more, like it's his to begin with. Just the other day he was here, wanting $5000. I said no and he stormed out, slammed the door."

"I worry about the kids," he continued, meaning Keith's. "I'm afraid there will be nothing left for them because Keith will spend it all. I wanted them named as heirs, but the lawyer said it would be too complicated. Then the girlfriend took them and left so I thought I could make her a trustee. But then she went *back* to him. I'm just disgusted," he said, shaking his head.

"I don't worry about you, and John doesn't have anyone but himself, but those kids may not even get an inheritance if Keith is around."

Inheritance. When Keith is no longer around. An idea began to form in my mind. I had the answer.

"I can do it," I said slowly, knowing I was committing to staying for an untold number of years, effectively kissing my emergency escape plan good-bye.

"I don't know what happened to Keith," Dad said out of nowhere, shaking me from my reverie. I knew what he was alluding to and why. He needed to make sure I did not punish Keith's children because of their father.

"You'll have to be tough," he said again, uncertain.

"Don't worry, Dad. I'll take care of the kids. And Carol."

"Do you promise?" he asked as we sat in the fading light of autumn. We were sitting over the very spot where Keith stole my childhood. I thought of him briefly and all he had taken. But overriding that, all that Dad had given. The vow came easily:

"I promise."

"Life doesn't stop," she often said. My mother (and her mother) meant there was never a moment to slow down, to take it all in. I take that sentiment a step further. My life began generations before I was born and it will continue on long after I am gone. There really is no death, just a time when our souls inhabit these temporary bodies and we call it "living". Life does not stop, it only continues elsewhere. I am connected to the souls who came before me and those who will come after. I can't explain it and won't even make the attempt. I only feel compelled to tell it so my daughters know.

"Life doesn't stop" also means the end of my story here – with me promising I will do right by my father's wishes – is not actually an ending. I just figured fifty years was enough, and that this conversation with Dad really did bring us full circle in regards to birthrights, which is obviously a theme.

There are still revelations and epiphanies to be had. Reality will no doubt shift again and again. The Red Thread will continue to weave its tapestry. And I know some of my questions will not be answered in this life.

I also know that people will leave me and people will lie to me and there's absolutely nothing I can do about it.

I continue on with the belief that life is worth living.

Elle Cuardaigh

Made in the USA
Lexington, KY
31 January 2018